# Corporate Governance and Enlightened Fiduciaries

# Corporate Governance and Enlightened Fiduciaries

CHRISTOPHER C. NICHOLLS
*W. Geoff Beattie Chair in Corporate Law*
*Western University, Canada*

OXFORD
UNIVERSITY PRESS

OXFORD
UNIVERSITY PRESS

Great Clarendon Street, Oxford, OX2 6DP,
United Kingdom

Oxford University Press is a department of the University of Oxford.
It furthers the University's objective of excellence in research, scholarship,
and education by publishing worldwide. Oxford is a registered trade mark of
Oxford University Press in the UK and in certain other countries.



Published in the United States of America by Oxford University Press
198 Madison Avenue, New York, NY 10016, United States of America.

British Library Cataloguing in Publication Data

Data available

Library of Congress Control Number: 2025950214

ISBN 9780198904168

DOI: 10.1093/9780198904199.001.0001

Printed and bound by
CPI Group (UK) Ltd., Croydon, CR0 4YY

The manufacturer's authorised representative in the EU for product safety is
Oxford University Press España S.A. of Parque Empresarial San Fernando de Henares,
Avenida de Castilla, 2 – 28830 Madrid (www.oup.es/en or product.safety@oup.com).
OUP España S.A. also acts as importer into Spain of products made by the manufacturer.

FSC www.fsc.org MIX Paper | Supporting responsible forestry FSC® C013604

# Preface

The business corporation was an ingenious invention, and perhaps an older one than has usually been imagined.[1] But it has not always been much beloved. Almost a century ago, American law professor Maurice Wormser invoked the grotesque image of Mary Shelley's Frankenstein's monster as a sinister metaphor for the American corporation. His 1931 book, *Frankenstein Incorporated*, contained strong words of condemnation for certain corporate practices, and stern censure of those corporate lawyers who played a role in allowing corporate excesses. His call for reform was bold. 'The entire concept of the corporation,' he concluded, 'must be modified in the interest of public service.' 'The theory of social interest and public trust must supplant the doric simplicity of the old *laissez faire*. . . . Modern and enlightened ideas of social and economic responsibility must supplant the individualistic philosophy of the early common law and of the business man of the [18]80s and [18]90s.'[2]

Professor Wormser's frustration with the corporation is one that many modern commentators share. But while genuine corporate chicanery certainly deserves rebuke, it would be unwise and unfair to vilify all corporations, or to suggest that there is something inherently nefarious about pursuing—even maximizing—profits. When shareholders invest in business corporations they entrust their capital, and in many ways their future, to the decisions of human beings, not to clockwork machines. Those human beings are understood to be bound by specific laws, and subject to mysterious and at times punctilious fiduciary duties. But they are also human beings who are guided by the same social norms, the same moral sense, and the same basic human civility and decency as every other member of the community.

There have been many recent calls for the need to imbue business corporations with an expressly pro-social 'purpose', or to facilitate or even perhaps mandate the pursuit of non-financial goals, whether in the name of CSR, ESG, or otherwise. The proponents of such ideas not infrequently suggest that they express modern, enlightened views that should rightly replace the rather stale

[1] David Le Bris, William N Goetzmann, and Sébastien Pouget, 'Creative Contracting for Corporate Recapitalization in 17th Century Toulouse' (2025). <online: ssrn.com>.
[2] Maurice Wormser, *Frankenstein Incorporated* (McGraw-Hill 1931) 240.

antediluvian notion of 'shareholder primacy'. But old ideas are not quite like old technology. A modern smartphone is far superior to a first generation dial telephone (or, for those of us old enough to remember such things, the hand 'crank' telephones that preceded dial technology). But an 'old fashioned idea' may be more like an 'old fashioned play' by William Shakespeare. There are no new plays that are really as good. There never likely will be. For that matter, some people are prone to insist that 'old ideas' are out of date only if they personally happen to disagree with them. When old ideas please them, they are likely to be revered as 'timeless wisdom'. So it is that for some committed advocates of 'corporate purpose', Milton Friedman's dogged insistence on shareholder primacy in the 1960s and 70s is hopelessly out of date and dishearteningly unenlightened. However, still older historic views of the corporation that conceived it as a vehicle for public works are trumpeted as key sources for a proper understanding of the modern business firm. This sort of special pleading suggests that ideology is interfering with clear thinking.

This book is an attempt to blend the very old with the very new and, most important of all, to focus upon the invariably human element in all corporate decision-making.

The corporation is an economic institution and economists have greatly enriched our understanding of it. Over a number of years while refining my thoughts about the corporation, and more recently during the writing of this book, I have had the extraordinary opportunity to host some of the world's leading economists at Western Law, including Henry Hansmann, Gary Gorton and Nobel laureates Bengt Holmström, Sir Oliver Hart, Myron Scholes, Robert Shiller, George Akerlof, and (via Zoom during the pandemic) Jean Tirole. Being in the company of these extraordinarily insightful and brilliant individuals is, needless to say, profoundly humbling. But it is also inspiring and thought-provoking, and I am grateful to all of them, as well as to the dozens of other pre-eminent business law scholars from around the world who have visited Western Law over the past decade or so. I have enjoyed rare and invaluable opportunities to hear, learn from, and exchange ideas with all of these remarkable thought leaders .

While completing the manuscript, I was a visiting scholar at the Stanford Law School and a senior visiting academic at Oxford University's Faculty of Law Commercial Law Centre. I am very grateful to Michael Klausner at Stanford Law School who hosted my wonderful visit there, and to Kristin van Zwieten, the director of the Commercial Law Centre at Harris Manchester College, Oxford as well as John Armour, Dean of the Oxford Faculty of Law for their help and support during my time at Oxford.

I reserve my greatest thanks, as always, for my wife Andrea who has not only provided me invaluable support and boundless patience, but has also graciously and generously shared her wisdom, insight, and experience as we discussed and debated many of the ideas in this book. Her help has been immeasurable, and I am deeply grateful.

*CCN*

# Contents


1. The Purpose of Corporate Purpose or the End of the Business Corporation 1

2. Fiat or Accord? 27

3. The 'Berle-and-Means Spirited' Corporation 63

4. The Prophets and Profits of Shareholder Primacy Part I: In Search of the Right Side of History (and the Left Side of the Balance Sheet) 83

5. The Prophets and Profits of Shareholder Primacy Part II 109

6. The Corporation as a Nexus of Conflicts: Anomie of the People 143

7. How Does a Corporation Do? CSR and ESG: Doing Well by Doing Good? Doing Good by Doing Well? 165

8. Whose Corporation Is it Anyway? Myopic Gadflies and Institutional Share Ownership: Is Shareholder Activism a Short-sighted Solution? 203

9. The Deconstructed Corporation: Financial Innovation and the Clouding of Corporate Duties 221

*Index* 245

# 1

# The Purpose of Corporate Purpose or the End of the Business Corporation

'The proper study of mankind is man.'

Alexander Pope

## Introduction

Any book about business corporations is really about human beings: those who act on behalf of corporations and those whose lives, health, and financial resources are affected by them.

As a matter of law, the corporation is a 'person';[1] not a natural person like the readers of this book, but, as William Blackstone declared in his *Commentaries on the Laws of England*, 'an artificial person.'[2] What should be the guiding purpose of an artificial person? At one time, this would have seemed a fanciful question; an entertaining subject for speculative fiction, perhaps, but hardly a serious question of law.

Has something changed? Is it possible that, once conceived by the human imagination, even fictional persons today are expected to have a transcendent purpose? Readers may be familiar with Nobel-prize winning playwright Luigi Pirandello's absurdist 'experimental metaplay',[3] *Six Characters in Search of an Author* (*Sei personaggi in cerca d'autore*).[4] Often considered Pirandello's greatest work, this ingenious drama, according to Pirandello himself, is about the 'mystery of artistic creativity'.[5] But it also depicts the animating power of

[1] See eg (USA) 1 US Code § 1; (UK) Paul L Davies, Sarah Worthington, and Christopher Hare, *Gower's Principles of Modern Company Law* (11th edn, Sweet & Maxwell 2021) 33; (Australia) Acts Interpretation Act 1901 s 2C(1); (Canada) Interpretation Act RSC 1985 c I-21 s 35(1).

[2] William Blackstone, *Commentaries on the Laws of England*, vol 1 (University of Chicago Press 1979, originally published 1765) 455.

[3] See Nobel Prize Outreach, 'Nobel Prize in Literature 1934, Luigi Pirandello: Facts' https://www.nobelprize.org/prizes/literature/1934/pirandello/facts/.

[4] Luigi Pirandello, *Six Characters in Search of an Author* (Edward Storer tr, EP Dutton 1922).

[5] See Luigi Pirandello, 'Pirandello Confesses' (1925) 1 The Virginia Quarterly Review 36, 37.

*Corporate Governance and Enlightened Fiduciaries*. Christopher C. Nicholls, Oxford University Press.
 DOI: 10.1093/9780198904199.003.0001

individual purpose or meaning. Six not-yet-fully-realized fictional characters arrive on stage as living beings, to the great surprise, and considerable annoyance, of a company of provincial actors labouring to rehearse yet another impenetrable Pirandello play. These six characters have emerged from their fictional realm, compelled, it appears, like Coleridge's ancient mariner, continually to retell the irrepressible and immutable stories that define them. Memorializing these perpetual narratives requires an author. Any author, it seems, will do. Their search is existential. Their overarching purpose is unwavering. As one character explains: 'Every true man, sir, who is a little above the level of the beasts and plants does not live for the sake of living, without knowing how to live; but he lives so as to give a meaning and a value of his own to life. For me this is everything.'[6]

Who, though, in Pirandello's play is truly in search of a life with value and meaning? We recognize at once that these six inchoate dramatic characters can have no needs at all, beyond those invented for them by their very human creator. Their 'search' is literally play-acting. It is nothing more than the projection of Pirandello's own human consciousness onto these half dozen imaginary creatures. Fictional persons can neither have, desire, or fulfil, any purpose of their own. It is only our peculiar human inclination to anthropomorphize (or to 'reify') that could ever make it seem otherwise. To understand a fictional person's purpose we must always search for the human being behind the curtain.

Consider again the sort of fictional person that is the subject of this book: the corporation. Can a corporation—like a Pirandello play character—be said to have a purpose? Apparently it can. That, at any rate, seems to be the consensus view of many recent corporate governance reports,[7] studies, codes,[8] commentaries,[9] and initiatives.[10] Modern corporations, it is said, not only can but

[6] Pirandello (n 4) Act III.

[7] See eg National Association of Corporate Directors, *The Future of the American Board: A Framework for Governing into the Future* (NACD 2022) 16 https://www.nacdonline.org/all-governance/governance-resources/governance-research/future-of-the-american-board---reports/fab-report/.

[8] See eg UK Corporate Governance Code s 1.

[9] See eg *The Davos Manifesto 2020: The Universal Purpose of a Company in the Fourth Industrial Revolution* https://www.weforum.org/agenda/2019/12/davos-manifesto-2020-the-universal-purpose-of-a-company-in-the-fourth-industrial-revolution/?DAG=3&gclid=EAIaIQobChMIq8CN8LCvgAMVK-_jBx1uegWGEAAYASAAEgJkuvD_BwE; Martin Lipton and others 'It's Time to Adopt the New Paradigm' (11 February 2019) https://www.wlrk.com/webdocs/wlrknew/ClientMemos/WLRK/WLRK.26357.19.pdf; Big Innovation Centre, *The Purposeful Company: FRC's Review of the UK Corporate Governance Code* (April 2017) https://thepurposefulcompany.org/wp-content/uploads/2025/06/2017-jul_interim-submission-on-frc-review-of-corporate-governance-code.pdf.

[10] See 'Enacting Purpose Initiative' online at https://enactingpurpose.org/. It is worth noting that many of these apparently disparate calls for corporations to commit to the pursuit of a social purpose actually involve the same individual proponents or are based on the work of the same individual

indeed most certainly should have a clearly defined—and explicitly socially beneficial—'purpose'. The World Economic Forum's *Davos Manifesto* goes so far as to purport to define the pro-social purpose common to *all* business corporations:[11]

> The purpose of a company is to engage all its stakeholders in shared and sustained value creation. In creating such value, a company serves not only its shareholders, but all its stakeholders – employees, customers, suppliers, local communities and society at large. The best way to understand and harmonize the divergent interests of all stakeholders is through a shared commitment to policies and decisions that strengthen the long-term prosperity of a company.

This modern view of corporate purpose is frequently offered as a supposed enlightened antidote to the crude antediluvian corporate formula proffered more than a half-century ago by that notorious champion of free markets, Nobel-prize winning economist Milton Friedman. As the title of his famous 1970 *New York Times Magazine* essay put it, for Friedman, 'The Social Responsibility of Business is to Increase its Profits'.[12]

Friedman's essay is controversial today. But it was equally controversial at the time of its original publication. What's more, as Brian Cheffins has recently argued, despite its notoriety, it is improbable that Friedman's article had much if any impact on the years-later embrace by American corporations of the doctrine of shareholder primacy: the notion that business corporations should be operated so as to maximize the wealth of their shareholders exclusively or, at least, primarily.[13] Nevertheless, in the decades since it was first published, Friedman's essay has become a kind of textual battleground for champions and opponents of shareholder primacy. As progressive voices have risen to ascendancy in many academic and political circles, particularly in the past decade or so, Friedman's views have been particularly savaged. As Alex

proponents. Thus, what may at first seem to be a rising confluence of independent voices may actually be more like a repetitive series of familiar echoes.

[11] *Davos Manifesto* (n 9): 'The purpose of a company is to engage all its stakeholders in shared and sustained value creation. In creating such value, a company serves not only its shareholders, but all its stakeholders – employees, customers, suppliers, local communities and society at large.'

[12] Milton Friedman, 'The Social Responsibility of Business is to Increase its Profits' *The New York Times Magazine* (13 September 1970) 32. An earlier version of Friedman's argument appeared in his book, *Capitalism and Freedom,* originally published in 1962. See Milton Friedman, *Capitalism and Freedom,* forward by Binyamin Applebaum (University of Chicago Press 2020) 160–63.

[13] Brian Cheffins, 'Stop Blaming Milton Friedman!' (2021) 98 Washington University Law Review 1607.

Edmans has wryly observed: 'To declare that you reject the Friedman doctrine has become almost a requirement for acceptance into polite society.'[14] Opponents of the once-dominant shareholder primacy philosophy insist that corporations must, instead, set for themselves a purposeful course that will include selfless service to a wide array of corporate stakeholders and broader social interests. The ubiquity of the corporate purpose movement is undeniable. Corporate purpose, as Spamann and Fisher have put it, has become 'the talk of the town.'[15]

Yet dissenting voices persist. To some, recent talk of corporate purpose is the product of muddled thinking or motivated ignorance. It is often psychologically comforting, politically savvy, and even financially rewarding to behave as though one believed that corporations have some real existence and will of their own, distinct from the living, breathing people that perform all of their business activities, gain financially from their success, or suffer financially from their failure. Populist politicians, for example, have often found it convenient to pretend that the burden of taxes paid by corporations is somehow—rather magically—not actually borne by any human beings. This is an undeniably clever political ruse. And it has proved surprisingly effective. Yet, to say that corporations pay taxes is rather like saying my credit card company pays my electricity bill. In a mechanical sense, it is quite true. But it is entirely misleading in terms of locating the real economic consequences of the transaction. The credit card company is simply the means by which funds are transferred from my bank account to my creditor's. Corporate taxes, too, are simply a means by which dollars are transferred from the pockets of ordinary working people and investors to the government, but with rather ingenious political cover that largely obscures or eliminates the transparency and accountability that would otherwise accompany the collection of more forthright (and thus unpopular) taxes on individuals.[16]

[14] Alex Edmans, 'What Stakeholder Capitalism Can Learn from Milton Friedman' *Oxford Business Law Blog* (13 November 2020) https://blogs.law.ox.ac.uk/business-law-blog/blog/2020/11/what-stakeholder-capitalism-can-learn-milton-friedman.

[15] Holger Spamann and Jacob Fisher, 'Corporate Purpose: Theoretical and Empirical Foundations/Confusions' (2022) ECGI Law Working Paper No 664/2022 http://ssrn.com/abstract_id=4269517.

[16] There are, of course, many legitimate reasons to support the imposition of taxes on business corporations. Among other things, if corporations were treated as non-taxable entities, with income tax levied entirely at the shareholder level when corporate profits were distributed as dividends (or perhaps as capital gains realized on share buybacks), the possibilities for deferral and avoidance of taxation could lead to significant losses in government revenue and genuinely inequitable incidence of taxation. It is not suggested, therefore, that business corporations ought not to be subject to tax, only that it must be recognized that such a tax is ultimately borne by individual taxpayers at rates that are undeniably less transparent than if the taxes were imposed directly on those individuals.

## Corporate Purpose vs Corporate Objects

The call for corporations to commit to a purpose may at first seem a distorted echo of the distant past. When the business corporation emerged as an innovative legal vehicle to solve problems of collective and fluid ownership of property, perpetual succession, and convenient transferability of economic interests, among other things, legislators considered it prudent to circumscribe this novel legal creature's sphere of operations narrowly. Each corporation was confined to the pursuit of specific objects set down in the corporation's charter or special act of incorporation.[17] Indeed, it was sometimes argued that a firm did not legitimately exist as a corporation at all whenever its activities strayed beyond those objects for which it had been expressly created or chartered.

This once common legal requirement for corporations to state, and strictly to limit their operations to, specific charter objects was the basis for the historically significant corporate law doctrine of ultra vires. Any deviation from the corporation's stated objects was 'beyond the powers' of the corporation, and thus forbidden.[18] Any purported corporate action or contract that fell outside the objects' perimeter could be declared void by the court. So significant was ultra vires to the conception of the nineteenth-century British corporation, for example, that the author of a weighty 1877 legal tome on the subject of ultra vires declared that: 'Perhaps indeed the Law of Corporations may be considered for most practical purposes as in reality only the application and development of the Doctrine of Ultra Vires.'[19]

Our understanding of corporations and the law that governs them has, happily and fruitfully, moved on. Ultra vires is no longer a concept of much corporate law significance in most large, industrial countries.[20] Corporate objects clauses are still required by corporate statutes in some parts of the world,[21]

[17] The term 'charter' here is intended to refer to the corporation's constitutional or constating documents such as its incorporating statute in the case of an English corporation incorporated by special act of Parliament, or the memorandum and articles of association in the case of a corporation incorporated under a general incorporation statute such as the early UK Companies Act of 1862. For earlier companies incorporated under Royal Charter, it is generally understood that the doctrine of ultra vires did not apply in any event.

[18] An early articulation of this principle may be found in Blackstone, *Commentaries* (n 2) bk I: 'The general *duties* of all bodies politic, considered in their corporate capacity, may, like those of natural persons, be reduced to a single one; that of acting up to the end or design, whatever it may be, for which they were created by their founder' (original emphasis).

[19] Seward Brice, *A Treatise on the Doctrine of Ultra Vires* (2d edn, Stevens & Haynes 1877) x.

[20] See eg (US) Robert Clark, *Corporate Law* (Aspen Publishers Inc 1986) 675; (UK) Davies, Worthington, and Hare (n 1) 184–85; (Australia) Rosemary Teele Langford, 'Purpose Based Governance a New Paradigm' (2020) 43(3) UNSW Law Journal 954, 966; (Canada) Christopher C Nicholls, *Corporate Law* (Emond-Montgomery 2005) 182.

[21] See eg Companies Act 2017 (Pakistan) s 26(1), requiring the memorandum of association of a company to include a 'principal line of business'.

and are permitted by corporate legislation in some others. But in most larger commercial centres today such clauses are drafted so broadly that they constitute no meaningful constraint on a corporation's operations.[22] And where they are no longer legally required, objects clauses are rarely adopted voluntarily by corporations.[23]

There were many good reasons to abandon both the legal requirement for corporations to adopt meaningfully restrictive objects clauses and the related rigidities of the judicially crafted ultra vires doctrine.[24] As a Canadian Supreme Court Justice once explained, ultra vires had over time become 'a protection to no one and a trap for the unwary'.[25] But recent calls for statements of corporate *purpose* should not be mistaken for retrograde pleas to restore the ossified relic of corporate *objects*.[26] Modern proponents of corporate purpose have grander ambitions. Purpose is intended to be more than an operational boundary description or a quotidian menu of specific lines of permitted money-making activities. Corporate purpose in the current context is less about imposing restraints than on framing broad *pro-social* goals and lofty aspirations.[27] Purpose is not a mission statement or a vision statement and it is certainly not a mere charter objects clause. It is the corporation's *raison d'être*;[28] its *ikigai*; or its overarching *plan de vida*.

Broad bromidic purpose clauses may strike cynics as ineffective or even disingenuous. Some may well be. But others, it is claimed, offer important, tangible benefits. Colin Mayer, for example, has suggested that corporate purpose

[22] See eg Delaware General Corporation Law § 102(a)(3): '[The certificate of corporation shall set forth: . . . ] The nature of the business or purposes to be conducted or promoted. It shall be sufficient to state, either alone or with other businesses or purposes, that the purpose of the corporation is to engage in any lawful act or activity for which corporations may be organized under the General Corporation Law of Delaware, and by such statement all lawful acts and activities shall be within the purposes of the corporation, except for express limitations, if any.'

[23] See eg Davies, Worthington, and Hare (n 1) 183.

[24] See eg Robert WV Dickerson and others, *Proposals for a New Business Corporations Law for Canada* (Information Canada 1971) para 81.

[25] *Communities Economic Development Fund v Canadian Pickles Corp* 1991 CanLII 48 (SCC) (1991) 3 SCR 388, 406 (Iacobucci J).

[26] See eg Edward B Rock, 'Business Purpose and the Objective of the Corporation' in Elizabeth Pollman and Robert B Thompson (eds), *Research Handbook on Corporate Purpose and Personhood* (Edward Elgar Publishing 2021) 27, 45.

[27] See eg British Academy, *Policy and Practice for Purposeful Business: Final Report of the Future of the Corporation Programme* (2021) 6: 'We use the term "purposeful business" to summarise a system in which the purpose of business is creating profitable solutions for problems of people and planet, and not profiting from creating problems.' See also David Kershaw and Edmund Schuster, 'The Purposive Transformation of Corporate Law' (2021) 69 The American Journal of Comparative Law 478, in which they refer to a corporation's 'mission-purpose' which they define as 'an animated idea of why a company exists similar to the understanding of purpose found in the management and policy literature . . . ' ibid 481.

[28] Indeed, Article 1835 of the French Civil Code, as amended by the 2019 'PACTE' Act (no 2019-486) specifically refers to the ability of corporations to include a '*raison d'être*' in their by-laws.

is about producing '"profitable solutions to the problems of people and planet, and not to profit from producing problems for people or planet". It is about producing solutions, doing so profitably not just philanthropically, and measuring fair—not fake—profits'.[29] As Professor Mayer has suggested elsewhere, a corporation's stated purpose and values can become benchmarks for the corporation's commitments to stakeholders other than the corporation's shareholders. If a corporation can credibly commit to such purpose and values, the need for external regulation is reduced, making possible 'a richer set of commercial arrangements that in turn promotes economic efficiency and well-being'.[30]

Other bold claims have been made for the salutary effect of a deftly-crafted and faithfully pursued corporate purpose. Asset manager Blackrock's chief executive officer (CEO) Larry Fink, for example, once said that a company's purpose 'is its north star in this tumultuous environment'.[31] The Enacting Purpose Initiative has described corporate purpose as a 'key driver informing strategic choices, helping directors make the critical trade-offs and decisions that are required to fulfil their board responsibilities'.[32] Chief Executives for Corporate Purpose, an organization founded somewhat improbably by the late film actor Paul Newman, sees its goal as 'creating a better world through business', and asserts that '[corporate] purpose is the solution to many challenges'.[33] The British Academy's Future of the Corporation programme issued three self-described 'landmark' reports from 2018 to 2021[34] proclaiming, among other things, that:

> A corporation must have a set of clearly defined and aligned purposes—the goals it actively pursues and its contributions to societal goals or public interests. These should be complemented by an inherent commitment to trustworthiness and supported by an enabling organisational culture . . . The

[29] Colin Mayer, 'It's Time to Define the Purpose of Business. Here's a Roadmap' https://www.weforum.org/agenda/2020/01/its-time-for-a-radical-rethink-of-corporate-purpose/#:~:text=So%2C%20let%20me%20be%20clear,problems%20for%20people%20or%20planet%E2%80%9D.

[30] Colin Mayer, 'Conceiving Corporate Commitment: Creation and Confirmation' in Jennifer G Hill and Randall S Thomas (eds), *Research Handbook on Shareholder Power* (Edward Elgar Publishing 2015) 211, 228 (hereafter Mayer, 'Corporate Commitment').

[31] Since one assumes Mr Fink was not suggesting that corporate purpose was inapplicable to companies operating in the Southern Hemisphere—where the north star cannot be seen—perhaps he might have used an alternative metaphor such as 'the guiding light' or 'lodestar'.

[32] Enacting Purpose Initiative, *Enacting Purpose Within the Modern Corporation: A Framework for Boards of Directors* (2020) 4 https://enactingpurpose.org/assets/enacting-purpose-initiative---eu-report-august-2020.pdf.

[33] See *The Value of Chief Executives for Corporate Purpose* (2023) https://cecp.co/wp-content/uploads/2023/05/CECP-valuebrochure-final-52342.pdf.

[34] See British Academy 'What is the Future of the Corporation?' https://www.thebritishacademy.ac.uk/programmes/future-of-the-corporation/about/.

> importance of corporate purpose derives from the fact that it is the basis on which relations of trust are created in business.[35]

The US National Association of Corporate Directors' *Report on the Future of the American Board* included this sweeping claim about corporate 'purpose':

> Purpose is the force that attracts and motivates employees and drives innovation while focusing corporate activities. It guides boards and management in setting priorities and making strategic decisions, and it provides discipline in resource allocation.[36]

Proponents of corporate purpose are not naïve. They recognize that sanctimonious public statements of corporate purpose could often be little more than self-serving, greenwashing puffery.[37] But the value of an idea cannot fairly be judged by pathological examples of misuse. For at least some corporations (and perhaps for many) statements of corporate purpose may genuinely reflect commitment on the part of a corporation's directing minds to employ corporate resources in pursuit of social benefit rather than merely financial gain. Could there be any harm in that? Corporations are a human invention, after all. Should they not reasonably be expected to operate for the benefit of humanity?

On the ends, all surely agree; but on the means, many differ. There is universal agreement that business corporations are rightly expected, ultimately, to produce a net benefit to society. So much is clear. But is it enough to trust that the generation of this net social benefit will occur merely as the fortuitous by-product of profit-seeking activities?[38] Is profit-seeking (or shareholder wealth maximization) the appropriate narrow 'sub goal'[39] for corporations to pursue to ensure gains to the economic system overall that outweigh any social costs imposed by corporate operations and so ultimately benefit society to the greatest extent possible? Or is there a better way? To ensure that corporations

[35] British Academy, *Reforming Business for the 21st Century* (2018) 16–17 (footnotes omitted) https://www.thebritishacademy.ac.uk/documents/76/Reforming-Business-for-21st-Century-British-Academy.pdf.

[36] NACD, *Future of the American Board: A Framework for Governing into the Future* (2022) 16.

[37] See eg Mayer (n 30) 213: '[w]e would be happy if we had one iota of confidence in these statements. Our scepticism derives from the fact that we know full well that "from the CEO down" what they are really committed to is their own and their owners' interests, and ours and our societies only feature to the extent they are consistent with theirs.'

[38] See eg Henry Hansmann and Reinier Kraakman, 'The End of History for Corporate Law' (2001) 89 Georgetown Law Journal 439, 441.

[39] Spamann and Fisher (n 15).

provide maximum net social benefit, should corporations, instead, directly and explicitly commit to serve the common good, sacrificing maximum financial gains to do so if need be? That is the more pressing and interesting question.

It is widely acknowledged that some statements of pro-social corporate purpose are likely insincere and that insincere statements of corporate purpose are at best worthless and at worst positively harmful. But there is considerable disagreement about the social value of those statements of corporate purpose that are genuine, heartfelt, and result in corporate actions that differ materially from the actions taken by those corporations that are committed exclusively to shareholder primacy. Are these sincere corporate purpose statements the hallmarks of socially useful business? Or are they, instead, a well-intentioned but misguided idea, one paradoxically bound to lead—as Adam Smith once famously suggested—to less social benefit than would be achieved through the single-minded pursuit of self-interest?[40]

## Corporate Purpose, Synthetic Conscience, and the Common Good

If sincere statements of corporate purpose could, indeed, be expected to lead to socially beneficial results, what is the mechanism by which this pleasant outcome would most likely be achieved? Corporations can act only through human agents.[41] Only those human agents can articulate interests, set goals, show compassion, make, and honour commitments. Advocates of the purposeful corporation thus must seek in effect to imbue fictional corporate persons with a sort of synthetic conscience. They hope, perhaps, that the human beings charged with managing the purposeful enterprise will regularly be reminded by edifying statements of corporate purpose not to ignore the dictates of their own genuine human consciences in a relentless amoral pursuit of financial or career gain.

[40] Adam Smith, *Wealth of Nations* (Prometheus Books 1991) bk IV 351–52: '[h]e intends only his own gain, and he is in this, as in many other cases, led by an invisible hand to promote an end which was no part of his intention. Nor is it always the worse for the society that it was no part of it. By pursuing his own interest he frequently promotes that of the society more effectually than when he really intends to promote it. I have never known much good done by those who affected to trade for the public good. It is an affectation, indeed, not very common among merchants, and very few words need be employed in dissuading them from it.'

[41] I do not use the word 'agent' here in its technical legal sense, recognizing, for example, that some key corporate actors have, for example, been identified by courts in the UK and other commonwealth jurisdictions as the very directing minds of the corporation and not merely agents.

Two important considerations complicate the practical translation of aspirational statements of corporate purpose into effective corporate contributions to the common good: the extent to which broad pro-social corporate purpose statements reflect a particular view about the respective roles of the state and private for-profit firms; and the inevitably non-binding nature of broad declarations of corporate purpose.

With respect to the first issue, disagreement over the role and significance of corporate purpose often centres around conflicting premises about the extent to which it is appropriate for business corporations to undertake tasks that are conventionally considered to fall within the mandate of modern governments. In short, why should private business be relied upon to perform public duties? Adolf Berle, in a 1969 preface to a revised edition of his seminal book with co-author Gardiner C. Means, *The Modern Corporation and Private Property* (discussed further in chapter 3), made this bold assertion about the role of the large corporation in America:

> Few American enterprises, and no large corporations, can take the view that their plants, tools and organizations are their own, and that they can do what they please with their own. There is increasing recognition of the fact that collective operations, and those predominantly conducted by large corporations, are like operations carried on by the state itself. Corporations are essentially political constructs.[42]

A very different response to the same public/private question lies at the heart of Milton Friedman's famous denunciation of those business leaders who spoke of the 'social responsibilities of business in a free-enterprise system'. For Friedman, such business leaders were 'preaching pure and unadulterated socialism'.[43] Corporations that diverted resources away from generating higher profits and toward (profit lowering) social purposes, in his view, were imposing a tax on their shareholders. Such a tax, Friedman contended, was

[42] Adolf A Berle, 'Property, Production and Revolution: A Preface to the Revised Edition [of *The Modern Corporation and Private Property*'] in Adolf A Berle and Gardiner C Means, *The Modern Corporation and Private Property* (Transaction Publishers 2005) xxxviii. Contemporary readers may recognize echoes of Berle's statement in former US President Barack Obama's widely-quoted 2012 campaign speech in which he declared: 'Somebody helped to create this unbelievable American system that we have that allowed you to thrive. Somebody invested in roads and bridges. If you've got a business—you didn't build that.' 'Remarks by the President at a Campaign Event in Roanoke, Virginia, July 12, 2012' National Archives, The White House, President Barack Obama https://obamawhitehouse.archives.gov/the-press-office/2012/07/13/remarks-president-campaign-event-roanoke-virginia.

[43] Friedman (n 12).

illegitimate because 'the imposition of taxes and the expenditure of tax proceeds are governmental functions'.[44]

But what are governmental functions? Proponents of corporate purpose frequently appeal to the historic origins of the corporation in support of the proposition that the corporation was originally designed to fulfil public purposes alongside private gain.[45] Economies of the past were well served, they argue, by this broader corporate ethos that prevailed before the emergence of general incorporation statutes in the mid nineteenth century. Thus, if overtly public-spirited aims strike some commentators today as out of place for a private sector institution, perhaps, as Elizabeth Pollman has suggested, we should reconsider our current conception of the public/private divide and conceive the corporate purpose statement as an appropriate reflection of the fact 'that corporations are a collaboration between public and private spheres'.[46]

Should we conclude then, that, for corporations, history is, or should be, destiny? If the corporate form was at one time conceived as a valuable privilege, concession, or franchise granted to entrepreneurs by the state in exchange for the assumption of certain public responsibilities, should modern corporations not likewise see themselves as recipients of uniquely state-granted benefits? And should those corporations therefore be duty-bound to recompense the state by sacrificing some money-making ambitions in the interests of serving the common good? Perhaps. However, the suggestion that incorporation represents a valuable state concession (for which some reciprocal public duties might be expected in return) is by no means universally accepted. As early as 1928, Adolf Berle had hotly disputed the notion that the corporation could properly be regarded as such a 'franchise'.[47] This position was reiterated by Berle and his co-author Gardiner Means in an often-overlooked footnote in *The Modern Corporation & Private Property*[48]in which the authors contended that even the benefits of limited liability should not be considered a state-granted privilege. Many modern scholars have similarly rejected the 'franchise'(or 'concession') argument.[49]

[44] ibid.

[45] See eg Leonardo Davoudi, Christopher McKenna, and Rowena Olegario, 'The Historical Role of the Corporation in Society' (2018) 6 Journal of the British Academy 17.

[46] Elizabeth Pollman, 'The History and Revival of the Corporate Purpose Clause' (2021) 99(7) Texas Law Review 1423, 1425.

[47] Adolf A Berle Jr, *Studies in the Law of Corporation Finance* (Callaghan and Company 1928) 11: '[a]s a matter of history, corporations existed first, and if they wished to exercise governmental power, then asked for a franchise; but they could exist without the franchise and a considerable number had existed thus for several centuries.'

[48] See Berle and Means (n 42) 120 n 2.

[49] See eg Paul G Mahoney, 'Contract or Concession: An Essay on the History of Corporate Law' (2000) 34(2) Georgia Law Review 873.

Yet, resolving the matter of whether incorporation should or should not be regarded as a valuable state-granted concession or franchise does not entirely settle the issue of how corporate managers ought to understand the ambit of a corporation's putative social responsibilities. The question of what are and have been properly regarded as matters of 'public' and 'private' responsibility is somewhat more fluid than some commentators suggest. It might also be observed that, in most contexts, historical norms are not invariably, or even usually, regarded as exemplars on which it is wise to model modern best practices. For example, the historical link between organized religion and the founding of many of the world's most prominent universities is not usually cited as compelling proof that, as wholly secular universities today, these same venerable institutions have hopelessly lost their way.

Some forty years ago, Robert Clark thoughtfully unpacked the link between corporate purpose and varying views of the corporation's appropriate relationship to government including the proper scope of what should be considered government services.[50] The five major 'clusters of views'[51] he identified ('dualism', 'monism', 'modest idealism', 'high idealism', and 'pragmatism'[52]) appear to capture nicely the range of opinions found to this day in academic and industry literature dealing with the propriety and efficacy of corporate purpose.

Dualism was the term Clark used to refer to the Friedman-like notion that the private and public spheres are properly separate and distinct. Corporations should focus on maximizing shareholder value, subject to all legal and ethical boundaries, strictly honoring their legal obligations to the corporation's various stakeholders, while pursuing shareholder benefit as their residual goal.

Monism, on the other hand, was Clark's label for the competing view that there is, in fact, a range of public-oriented activities that a business corporation is right to pursue, precisely because the pursuit of such activities will, in the long run, benefit the wealth-generating capacity of the corporation. This would seem to describe what Milton Friedman had rather harshly dubbed 'hypocritical window dressing'.[53]

Clark's 'modest idealism' refers to the generally uncontentious view[54] that corporations should invariably comply with all applicable laws, even if a

[50] Clark (n 27) 677.
[51] ibid.
[52] ibid 677.
[53] Friedman (n 12).
[54] However, one notes that Stephen Bainbridge has contended that it may in fact be quite appropriate for corporations to engage in a cost-benefit analysis with respect to compliance with at least some laws, such as those that relate to minor infractions (such as parking violations) that may be classified as

careful evaluation of the expected cost of any violation, taking into account the probability of detection, would support a conclusion that the firm's shareholders would gain from a failure to comply.

'High idealism' is Clark's term for a stakeholder constituency view in which the corporation has as its residual goal the service not only of shareholders but also of multiple stakeholders or of the public interest generally. The principal reason for corporations to be operated on the basis of high idealism, Clark suggests, is a perception that government has failed to discharge its functions adequately.[55] (This latter observation features regularly in recent discussions of the perceived need for corporate purpose and related issues.[56])

Finally, 'pragmatism' is Clark's label for a view held by some that business corporations should be more significantly relied upon by government, contractually, to deliver goods and services to the public on a for-profit basis. Pragmatism is premised on the belief that private industry can in general be expected to operate more efficiently than government.

In each case, one's view of the propriety and relative efficacy of corporate commitment to an explicitly pro-social purpose will largely depend on one's view of the proper role of government and its ability to fulfil that role.

Although more recent academic analyses of the role, impact, and validity of non-shareholder centred 'corporate purpose', as discussed later in this book, offer important nuances, the core elements of the purpose vs profit debate remain those identified in Clark's taxonomy.

## The Non-binding Nature of Statements of Corporate Purpose

Theoretical debates about the value of statements of corporate purpose and the optimal public/private divide would be of little or no practical significance if statements of corporate purpose—no matter how publicly they have been

*malum prohibitum* rather than *malum in se*. See Stephen Bainbridge, 'Don't Confound the *Caremark* Mistake by Extending it to ESG Oversight' (2021) 77 Business Lawyer 751.

[55] Clark (n 27) 691.

[56] See eg Jonathan R Macey, 'ESG Investing: Why Here? Why Now?' (2022) 19 Berkeley Business Law Journal 258: 'People are turning to corporations for solutions to problems that are typically in the government's domain because government has failed.' See also Marcel Kahan and Edward Rock, 'Corporate Governance Welfarism' (2023) 15 Journal of Legal Analysis 108, 110: 'Welfarism rejects the faith that market forces will promote general welfare and lacks confidence in the government's ability to set proper boundary constraints.' See also Oliver Hart and Luigi Zingales, 'The New Corporate Governance' (2022) 1 University of Chicago Business Law Review 195, 197: 'In a more populous and interdependent world, the importance of externalities has also greatly increased, and many feel that governments are not dealing with them.'

declared—could be ignored with impunity by corporations that have adopted them. It is trite to observe that inspiring statements of corporate purpose on their own neither prevent misconduct nor compel compliance. Consider, for example, the prominent declaration of 'Our Values' featured in the last Annual Report released by Enron Corporation in May 2001, just months before it imploded into scandal and bankruptcy.[57] In addition to trumpeting the corporation's commitment to 'Communication', 'Respect, and 'Excellence', Enron also assured the world of the high value it placed on integrity:

> Integrity
> We work with customers and prospects openly, honestly and sincerely. When we say we will do something, we will do it; when we say we cannot or will not do something, then we won't do it.[58]

More recently, the former CEO of disgraced cryptocurrency exchange FTX Trading Ltd had, before the collapse of the firm, regularly trumpeted his commitment to 'effective altruism', assuring FTX investors and anyone else who would listen that 'in the end my goal is to do as much good as I can for the world'.[59] The explosion of these hollow assurances prompted cynical assessments of the effective altruism movement generally,[60] and even led some to speculate that, as Ralph Waldo Emerson once warned,[61] perhaps it is those very individuals and firms that speak most often about their virtue that are most apt to engage in disreputable conduct.[62]

[57] Enron Annual Report (2000) 53.

[58] ibid.

[59] Sam Bankman-Fried, quoted in John Hyatt, 'This Climate Change Non-Profit Didn't Ask for FTX's Money, but Got $200,000 Anyway' *Forbes* (22 November 2022) https://www.forbes.com/sites/johnhyatt/2022/11/22/this-climate-change-nonprofit-didnt-ask-for-ftxs-moneybut-got-200000-anyways/?sh=3ed2ba0e5e9c.

[60] See eg Michael Hiltzik, 'How Sam Bankman-Fried Exploited the "Effective Altruism" Fad to Get Rich and Con the World' *Los Angeles Times* (21 November 2022).

[61] See Ralph Waldo Emerson, 'Worship' in *The Conduct of Life* (Ticknor & Fields 1863) 184: 'We were not deceived by the professions of the private adventurer—the louder he talked of his honor, the faster we counted our spoons.'

[62] There is evidence, for example, of the phenomenon of 'moral self-licensing'. That is, people who believe they have performed good deeds in the past, view that past behaviour as a justification or licence to engage in subsequent unethical acts. See eg Anna C Merritt, Daniel A Effron, and Benoît Monin, 'Moral Self-Licensing: When Being Good Frees Us to Be Bad' (2010) 4 Sociology and Personality Psychology Compass 344; Irene Blanken, Niels van de Ven, and Marcel Zeelenberg, 'A Meta-Analytic Review of Moral Licensing' (2015) 41(4) Personality and Social Psychology Bulletin 540; C Daniel Batson and Elizabeth R Thompson, 'Why Don't Moral People Act Morally? Motivational Considerations' (2001) 10(2) Current Directions in Psychological Science 54, 55, reporting on results from one moral licensing experiment: 'Ironically, this [moral] hypocrisy pattern was especially strong among persons scoring high on a self-report measure of moral responsibility.'

The inefficacy of corporate purpose statements is hardly surprising, in any event. Even if there were universal or near universal agreement on precisely where to draw the boundary between the public and private functions of the modern business corporation, the wholly voluntary nature of aspirational corporate purpose statements would make it untenable for society to place any real reliance upon corporations to fulfil lofty public-spirited goals to which they may claim to be committed. The directors and officers of conventional business corporations,[63] when first enunciating these statements, might well genuinely intend to try in good faith to conduct corporate operations in accordance with an underlying purpose that transcends the mere maximizing of shareholder wealth or enterprise value and reflects the importance of service to a broad range of corporate stakeholders or the public interest generally. But things change. Faced with altered circumstances (or a change in management personnel) any such explicit public-oriented purpose could be amended or resiled from at any time. Corporate purpose may thus represent at best a heartfelt but inconsequential moral hope on the part of corporate managers at a particular moment, rather than anything like a permanent or enforceable legal obligation. Statements of corporate purpose are perhaps better treated as sanguine New Year's resolutions than solemn sworn oaths or commitments.

Recognizing this critical shortcoming, some commentators have urged the adoption of specific governance structures that would empower stakeholders to enforce pro-social corporate commitments or that, in at least some cases, would make corporate directors subject to a fiduciary duty to uphold their corporation's stated purpose.[64] Would it really be possible to make pro-social corporate statements of purpose legally enforceable, at least in common law jurisdictions such as the UK, the US, and Canada? Even if possible, would such an approach be desirable? For individuals, failure to fulfil self-imposed ethical commitments (where that failure does not involve actual breaches of law) neither could, nor should, be subject to penalties or other forms of enforcement by the coercive power of the state. (No one, after all, should fear jail time for failing to fulfil their New Year's resolutions.) Should corporate directors not likewise be free to exercise their discretion, as circumstances demand from

[63] The performance of some public benefit could be mandatory for non-conventional corporations such as the relatively new benefit or public benefit corporations. The implications of these alternative corporate forms are discussed further in Chapter 7.

[64] See eg British Academy (n 35) 22: 'However, alignment of corporate with public purposes needs to be made explicit in the case of corporations that perform social and public functions, such as utilities and corporations with significant market power. In these cases, regulation should require companies to incorporate their licences to operate in their charters and articles of association, thereby imposing fiduciary responsibilities on directors to uphold their public as well as private purposes.'

time to time, unfettered by the dictates of any extra-legal statement of corporate purpose, adopted at some point in the past when the circumstances facing the corporation may have been vastly different?[65] In most leading commercial centres, any attempt to mandate pursuit of a broad pro-social corporate purpose would appear doomed to be frustrated by the business judgment rule or equivalent principles of wise judicial deference to managers' unconflicted, good faith business decisions.

Critics might then understandably conclude that a corporate purpose that can impose no real legal obligation is a toothless tiger. In fact, it could be rather worse than a toothless tiger at preventing corporate wrongdoing or promoting social welfare for at least two reasons. First, the unintended consequence of the adoption of a sufficiently broad corporate purpose statement may be to insulate directors and managers from whatever practical shareholder accountability might otherwise have served to discipline their behavior. Secondly, the adoption of such statements might dull the impulse for governments or regulators to act to regulate in respect of the matters covered by statements of corporate purpose.[66] Cynics may even argue that some corporate purpose statements may appear carefully crafted precisely to ensure they remain too vague or obtuse ever to become legally or even morally constraining.[67]

Of course, such a simple bifurcation between enforceable and unenforceable statements of purpose may be criticized as misleadingly reductionist. The expressive value of unenforceable or unenforced (and unenforceable) laws has

[65] At common law, directors were not permitted to fetter their discretion, since they were obliged to exercise their independent judgment at all times, taking into account the circumstances under which their decisions are made. The parameters and implications of this common law doctrine, and the extent to which it may be modified by specific statutory provisions, has long been the subject of discussion. See eg Davies, Worthington, and Hare (n 1) 290 ff.

[66] See eg Lucian A Bebchuk and Roberto Tallarita, 'The Illusory Promise of Stakeholder Governance' (2020) 106(1) Cornell Law Review 91, 171: 'Such unrealistic expectations and hopes might lead defenders of stakeholders to push for acceptance of stakeholderism, might make them less motivated to seek the adoption of external laws, regulations and policies that would constraint [*sic*] and incentivize corporations to protect stakeholders, and might reduce their sense of urgency to obtain such reforms'; Leo E Strine Jr, 'Corporate Power is Corporate Purpose 1: Evidence from My Hometown' (2017) 33 Oxford Review of Economic Policy 176, 177: 'Pretending that corporate boards—an odd recourse for ordinary people anyway—are to be looked at as a source of protection and solace for workers, the environment, and consumers dilutes the focus that is actually needed, which is on the protections from externalities that other constituencies deserve.' But cf Elizabeth Pollman, 'Corporate Acceptance of Stakeholderism: Will It Hinder or Boost Government Regulation of Corporate Externalities' in *ECGI Blog Review* (August 2024) 60, 61: 'On the other hand, corporate acceptance of at least a measure of stakeholderism might create an environment in which government regulation of corporate externalities is more likely.'

[67] See eg Jill E Fisch and Steven Davidoff Solomon, 'Should Corporations Have a Purpose?'(2021) 99 Texas Law Review 1309: 'At most, these charters commit corporations to aspire or strive to act in a sustainable manner, but not actually to so act.'

long been recognized in a variety of contexts,[68] such as in cases alleging breach by directors of their duties in the case of Delaware corporations that have included in their certificate of incorporation a provision eliminating the liability of their directors and officers for such breaches of fiduciary duty, as permitted by § 102(b)(7) of Delaware's General Corporation Law. And enforcement of corporate purpose need not be confined to formal judicial proceedings in any case. Fisch and Davidoff Solomon have argued, for example, that: 'Corporate purpose . . . can be used to direct and manage the expectancy interests of the corporation's stakeholders.'[69] They acknowledge that corporate purpose statements are not, and should not be, legally enforceable, but suggest that they may nonetheless be enforceable in the market:

> Concrete and transparent purpose statements are increasingly enforceable, however, through market-based mechanisms. Customers who are attracted by a corporation's commitment to the welfare of its workers can sanction the corporation's lack of attention to working conditions in its supply chain by refusing to buy its products. Employees can sanction corporations that do not adhere to their environmental or social policies by working elsewhere. Purpose thus extends the potential for discipline beyond the capital markets to the product and labor markets.[70]

Legal unenforceability, from this perspective, could be both inevitable and irrelevant. Reliance on market forces alone, however, depends not only on the willingness of market players to act in accordance with their (often non-financial) values, but also on an assumption of corporate transparency that may be unrealistic.

## *Esse Quam Videri* (To Be Rather than to Seem)

Should market pressures to adopt and conform to pro social corporate purposes be expected to create incentives as powerful as legal enforceability? It seems entirely plausible that the decisions of a corporation's current or prospective employees, customers, investors, or other stakeholders might well

[68] See eg Cass R Sunstein, 'On the Expressive Function of Law' (1996) 144:5 University of Pennsylvania Law Review 2021; Richard H McAdams, *The Expressive Powers of Law: Theories and Limits* (Harvard University Press 2015).
[69] Fisch and Davidoff Solomon (n 67) 1339.
[70] ibid 1344.

be influenced by that corporation's genuinely pro social *actions*. Is it equally clear, however, that a mere *statement* of corporate purpose, on its own, should be expected to have a material effect on the actions or decisions of corporate stakeholders? Customers who are genuinely concerned about the working conditions of a corporation's employees, for example, would surely be expected to scrutinize the actual treatment of such employees, regardless of whether their corporate employer has, or has not, previously issued a magnanimous purpose statement claiming its deep commitment to its workers' welfare. Likewise, employees who object to the environmentally or socially harmful actions of their own corporate employers should be neither more nor less inclined to seek alternative employment simply based on reassuring (but non-binding) words of commitment to sustainability contained in their employer's corporate purpose statement. Either a corporation's *actions* offend (or please) interested constituents or they do not. That such actions may also deviate from (or adhere to) a corporate purpose statement seems to be an irrelevant consideration, except, perhaps, to the extent that a protesting constituent wishes to add a charge of 'hypocrisy' to the litany of a vilified corporation's wrongdoings.

Yet, recent research has suggested something curious. Investors (at least in the United States) may be prepared to allocate their funds on the basis of claims of social responsibility even if those claims do not correspond to the actual practices of the firm receiving those funds.[71] Specifically, institutional investors in the United States that sign the Principles for Responsible Investment[72] are likely to receive increased fund flows regardless of whether or not they implement the responsible investment principles. While this research relates to institutional investors, not to direct investment by retail investors in business corporations, it seems plausible that US business corporations that adopt pro social statements of corporate purpose might expect to attract similar positive attention from retail investors regardless of whether they take any actual steps to adhere to such statements. There are several possible reasons such a flow

[71] Rajna Gibson Brandon and others, 'Do Responsible Investors Invest Responsibly?' (2022) 26 Review of Finance 1389, 1417.

[72] The Principles for Responsible Investment (PRI) refer to six 'voluntary and aspirational' principles for investment to which more than 5000 'signatories,' including asset owners, investment managers, and service providers, have subscribed. See https://www.unpri.org/. The term is also used to refer to the non-profit organization, the PRI Association, that was established in 2010 to coordinate, operationalize and advance these principles of responsible investment among the more than 5000 PRI signatories. The PRI trace their origins to an initiative of the United Nations Environment Programme (UNEP) Finance Initiative that began in 2002 and ultimately culminated in the launch of the PRI at the New York Stock Exchange by UN Secretary General Kofi Annan in 2006. See Cornis Van der Lugt and Klaus Dingwerth, 'Governing Where Focality is Low: UNEP and the Principles for Responsible Investment' in Kenneth W. Abbott, Philipp Genschel, Duncan Snidal, and Berhard Zangl (eds), *International Organizations as Orchestrators* (Cambridge University Press 2015) 237.

of investor funds might occur. Perhaps a significant number of investors are simply indifferent as to the veracity of claims of social responsibility, at least where effective monitoring of corporate compliance with such statements might require them to incur material time or expense. Perhaps investors know, or at least suspect, that broad pro-social statements are not meaningful or enforceable. However, they may also believe (or hope) that, all else equal, a firm that noisily commits itself to social responsibility may be more likely, or at least not less likely, than its less overtly sanctimonious competitors to be attentive to important social concerns. In either case, investors may rationally prefer to remain wilfully blind. Provided self-declared 'purposeful' firms also deliver reliably strong financial performance, even non-binding pro-social declarations may offer investors a costless virtue signal.

There is, however, an obvious downside to rewarding firms that make disingenuous commitments to social 'values' rather than financial 'value'. To the extent that other sincere firms may incur material costs in honouring moral obligations, prevaricating firms would enjoy a competitive advantage in capital markets. If investors do not, or cannot, distinguish between sincere and insincere corporations, then, in competitive markets, there would appear to be some incentive for firms to dissemble, at least if the probability of detection and the ultimate social sanction for being exposed is considered sufficiently low.

## Corporate Purpose and the Spirit of the Times

There are few convincing reasons to believe that the current generation of corporate managers, investors, and customers is any more socially conscious (or, for that matter, more hypocritical) than at any earlier era in history. Some thirty years ago, in 1994, for example, Edward Freeman was prepared to declare that: 'I believe we can safely say that the stockholder theory is or at least should be intellectually dead.'[73] Decades earlier, in 1959, Edward S. Mason wrote that, although corporate managers 'have traditionally been considered to have as their single-minded objective . . . maximization of business profits',[74] times had changed. Voices now asserted, he said, 'that corporate managements are really concerned with equitable sharing of gains among owners, workers, suppliers, and customers'.[75] Indeed, it is regularly argued that in the decades

[73] R Edward Freeman, 'The Politics of Stakeholder Theory: Some Future Directions' (1994) 4(4) Business Ethics Quarterly 409, 413.
[74] Edward S Mason, 'Introduction' in ES Mason (ed), *The Corporation in Modern Society* (Harvard University Press 1959) 11.
[75] ibid

following the Second World War, there was within the largest American corporations a widely held view of 'managerialism'. Managerialism, as Harwell Wells has put it, 'saw the corporation as having developed into a "social institution", run by managers who had taken on responsibility to (at a minimum) employees, consumers and shareholders, or (at maximum) all of society'.[76] And as early as 1928, as Adolf Berle pointed out, Owen Young of the General Electric Company was 'able to say . . . that The General Electric Company owed its first duty to its labor, its next to the public it served, and its third obligation in rank to its stockholders'.[77]

But, at least in the Anglo-American corporate world,[78] it does seem that there is something distinctly new about the recent proliferation of interest in corporate purpose—often conjoined (some might say confused) with explorations of 'ESG'[79] (environmental, social, and governance issues), sustainability, social responsibility, stakeholder democracy, and, at times, grave warnings of the supposed dangers of corporate 'short-termism'.[80] Heightened interest in corporate purpose is often linked to significant twenty-first century environmental, economic, and social phenomena. On this view, the central premise of the shareholder primacy doctrine associated with Milton Friedman[81] and

[76] Harwell Wells, 'Corporation Law is Dead: Heroic Managerialism, Legal Change and the Puzzle of Corporation Law at the Height of the American Century' (2013) 15 University of Pennsylvania Law Review 305, 331.

[77] Berle (n 47) 1.

[78] Dan Puchniak has recently argued that many years before the recent 'discovery' of corporate purpose in the Anglo-American world, major Asian economies had already adopted conceptions of corporate governance centred on corporate purpose and stakeholderism. See Dan W Puchniak, 'No Need for Asia to be Woke: Contextualizing Anglo-American "Discovery" of Corporate Purpose' ECGI Law Working Paper No 646/2022 (2022) http://ssrn.com/abstract_id=4122483.

[79] ESG was originally framed as a term that would not be seen as interchangeable with concepts such as 'sustainability' or 'corporate social responsibility', but rather as a framework that could be part of a mainstream analysis of corporate performance, integrated into the investment process as a useful method for identifying and assessing relevant and 'decision-useful' business risks and opportunities. See The Global Compact, *Who Cares Wins* (2004) 1–2 https://www.unepfi.org/fileadmin/events/2004/stocks/who_cares_wins_global_compact_2004.pdf. For a more detailed discussion of ESG see Chapter 7.

[80] Warnings of the ubiquity and perils of corporate 'short-termism' are multitudinous. This topic will be explored in greater detail in Chapter 6. At this point, one need only mention a few examples of the many criticisms that have been made of short-termism. See eg Dominic Barton, Jonathan Bailey, and Joshua Zoffer, 'Rise to the Challenge of Short-Termism', https://www.fcltglobal.org/docs/default-source/default-document-library/fclt-global-rising-to-the-challenge.pdf; Rebecca Carr and Tim Koller, 'How to Build an Alliance Against Corporate Short-Termism' https://www.fcltglobal.org/docs/default-source/default-document-library/fclt-global-rising-to-the-challenge.pdf; Wachtell, Lipton, Rosen & Katz, 'The Threat to the American Economy and Society from Activism and Short-Termism', https://corpgovlaw.harvard.edu/2015/01/27/the-threat-to-the-economy-and-society-from-activism-and-short-termism-updated/; The Aspen Institute, *Overcoming Short-Termism: A Call for a More Responsible Approach to Investment and Business Management* (15 December 2009) https://assets.aspeninstitute.org/content/uploads/files/content/images/BSPonlineBroch.pdf; Lynne L Dallas, 'Short-Termism, the Financial Crisis and Corporate Governance' (2012) 37 Journal of Corporate Law 265; Kent Greenfield, 'The Puzzle of Short-Termism' (2011) 46 Wake Forest Law Review 62.

[81] Friedman (n 12).

other like-minded thinkers—that society is best served when corporations pursue financial gain alone—has broken down. The Western social order, some insist, is failing.[82] Capitalism is broken.[83] The world is on fire.[84] Climate change, income and wealth inequality, and systemic racism are thought, in particular, to signal the need for a fundamental reordering of corporate values and investment priorities.

This is not simply a case of mass production of old wine to fill a burgeoning oversupply of (environmentally-friendly) new bottles. A discernible shift in social perspective and priorities appears to have occurred within the past twenty years. The shift has been rapid, though certainly not without warning. Significant events in the first decade of the twenty-first century directly impugned the integrity and social value of business corporations. First, market-rattling accounting scandals destroyed reckless corporate titans such as Enron and WorldCom. Several years later, the global financial crisis of 2007 to 2009 brought the global financial system perilously close to the brink of collapse.

These salient acute conditions added a sense of urgency to more slowly-evolving chronic economic and political issues. The corporation, as the central institution of modern capitalism, was increasingly being called to account for its ubiquitous role in these developments. General perceptions of widening income inequality were buttressed by statistical evidence of the growing gap between rates of return on capital and labour explored meticulously by French economist Thomas Piketty.[85] The practical implications of this gap were manifested in the frustrating and at times painful lived experience of millions of workers thwarted by the stagnation of real wages in the United States and other industrial countries. Shattered dreams fomented unrest, anger, and resentment, culminating in political action and popular attacks targeting the wealth and power of the top echelon of income earners and property owners—the vilified '1%'. Declining wages and eroding industrial working conditions, particularly among less educated workers, were linked to the growing power of shareholder-focused corporations and corporate lobbying efforts that had weakened the influence of unions and skewed the public agenda away from the concerns of lower wage earners. Nobel Prize winning author Angus Deaton and co-author Anne Case have even tied these developments in the United

[82] See eg Rachel Nuwer, 'How Western Civilization Could Collapse' *BBC* (18 April 2017) (bbc.com).
[83] See eg Ferris Eanfar, *Broken Capitalism: This is How we Fix It* (Gini Foundation 2017); 'Fixing the Flaws in Today's Capitalism' *Economist* (9 May 2018); David Leonhardt, 'American Capitalism Isn't Working' *New York Times* (2 December 2018); Joseph Stiglitz, *People, Power and Profits: Progressive Capitalism for an Age of Discontent* (Norton & Company Inc 2019).
[84] See eg Rebecca M Henderson, *Reimagining Capitalism in a World on Fire* (Public Affairs 2020).
[85] Thomas Piketty, *Capital in the Twenty-First Century* (Belknap Press 2014).

States to what they have documented as an 'epidemic' of 'deaths of despair', including suicide.[86]

Shocking incidents of social and racial injustice spurred specific calls for immediate reform of many of society's institutions, and fostered demands for longer term multi-dimensional solutions expressly aimed at enhancing equality, diversity, inclusion, and decolonization. These often painful and dramatic social and economic events unfolded against the ominous backdrop of the global threat of climate change, as broad scientific consensus surrounding evidence of 'global warming' evolved into widespread global fears of an imminent and potentially cataclysmic 'climate crisis'[87] or 'climate emergency'.[88]

Urgent demands to address this litany of concerns arose, particularly in the United States, even as the electorate's faith in government's ability to solve complex social issues was waning. Fading confidence in government efficacy was connected, at least in part, to a growing cynicism about the extent to which government processes were themselves significantly influenced by self-interested lobbying on the part of the nation's largest corporations.[89] The system, as US President Donald Trump once famously declared, was 'rigged'.[90] Legislative inertia and dysfunction created a gap for urgently-needed reform. This gap, some argued, could, paradoxically, only be filled by the very corporate actors whose thumbs had for so long seemed firmly pressed on the scales of economic and social justice.

Champions of corporate purpose asserted that public demands required that corporations recommit themselves to the fulfillment of social goals beyond enhancing the wealth of their shareholders. Corporations must accommodate such demands, it was argued, as a condition of their 'social license' to operate. Thus, for example, a survey commissioned by B Lab UK in May 2020 indicated that 72 per cent of the public in the UK believe that business 'should have a legal responsibility to people and the planet' and more than three-quarters of

[86] Anne Case and Angus Deaton, *Deaths of Despair and the Future of Capitalism* (Princeton University Press 2020) ch 15.

[87] See eg United Nations, 'The Climate Crisis: A Race We Can Win' https://www.un.org/en/un75/climate-crisis-race-we-can-win.

[88] See eg United Nations Environment Programme, 'The Climate Emergency', https://www.unep.org/climate-emergency.

[89] See eg Christopher D Stone, *Where the Law Ends* (Harper & Row Publishers 1975) 94: 'To claim society's desires will be realized so long as the corporations "follow the edict of the populus" fails to take into account *the role of corporations in making the very law that we trust to bind them*' (original emphasis).

[90] See Donald Trump, 'Speech to the Republican National Convention' (21 July 2016): 'A number of these reforms that I will outline tonight will be opposed by some of our nation's most powerful special interests. That is because these interests have rigged our political and economic system for their exclusive benefit.' https://abcnews.go.com/Politics/full-text-donald-trumps-2016-republican-national-convention/story?id=40786529.

the public believe that capitalism is not working and that business should have a legal responsibility to protect the natural environment.[91]

Debates over corporate purpose filled television, internet, and print news sources. There was also a cascade of academic writing on the topic. Indeed, interest in broad pro-social corporate purpose within the past half decade may be said to have reached levels of 'obsession'[92] similar to (or even, perhaps, surpassing) ruminations about the abstract concept of corporate personhood that had cloyed academic journals a century ago.[93] That earlier wave of academic theorizing is usually said to have been mercifully scotched in 1926 following the publication of John Dewey's article, 'The Historic Background of Corporate Personality'.[94] Dewey aptly observed that corporate personhood, as a legal matter, must be understood entirely from a functional, consequential perspective. In short, corporate personhood meant whatever the law intended it to mean, in any given context, to enable corporations to discharge the functions for which they had been conceived. No grander metaphysical or philosophical exploration of the 'personhood' concept served any useful purpose except to confuse. A similar debate-ending resolution may await the current spate of ESG/corporate purpose cerebrations. In the meantime, Brian Cheffins has argued that any apparent recent shift in corporate priorities from maximizing shareholder value to serving instead broader stakeholder interests should not, in any event, be expected to herald any significant, long-term shift.[95] The shareholder value norm, he contends, has simply became too

[91] See Better Business Act, 'What the Public Think', https://betterbusinessact.org/what-the-public-thinks/.

[92] The number of recent academic articles dealing with the subject of corporate purpose is enormous. A very partial and incomplete list of representative examples would include Lisa M Fairfax, 'Stakeholderism, Corporate Purpose and Credible Commitment' (2022) 108 Virginia Law Review 1163; Mark Roe, 'Corporate Purpose and Corporate Competition' (2021) 99(1) Washington University Law Review 223; Edward B Rock, 'For Whom is the Corporation Managed in 2020?'(2021) 76 Business Lawyer 363; Elizabeth Pollman, 'The History and Revival of the Corporate Purpose Clause' (2021) 99 Texas Law Review 1423; Hillary A Sale, 'The Corporate Purpose of Social License' (2021) 94 Southern California Law Review 785; Stephen M Bainbridge, 'Making Sense of the Business Roundtable's Reversal on Corporate Purpose' (2021) 46 Journal of Corporation Law 295; Brian Cheffins, 'The Past, Present and Future of Corporate Governance' (2023) ECGI Working Paper No 713/2023; Rosemary Teele Langford, 'Corporate Purpose: Meaningful Change or Marketing Tool?' (2024) 55 Victoria University of Wellington Law Review 527; Grant M. Hayden and Matthew T. Bodie, 'The Problem of Corporate Purpose in Corporate Law' (2025) 62 Houston Law Review 611; Andrew Keay (n 93); Robert Bood, Hans van Ees, and Theo Postma, *The Role of the Board in Corporate Purpose and Strategy* (Cambridge University Press 2022); see also Elizabeth Pollman and Robert B. Thompson (eds), *Research Handbook on Corporate Purpose and Corporate Personhood* (Edward Elgar 2021).

[93] Andrew Keay, citing a number of scholars, asserts that 'the issue of the corporate objective is the most important in corporate finance and corporate law' and 'that the need to resolve this issue has become increasingly important'. See Andrew Keay, *The Corporate Objective* (Edward Elgar Publishing 2011) 19.

[94] John Dewey, 'The Historic Background of Corporate Legal Personality' (1926) 35 Yale Law Journal 655.

[95] Cheffins (n 90).

strongly entrenched following the 'critical juncture' of the wave of hostile takeover bids in the 1980s.

## Corporate Purpose and the Human Factor

The implications and the likely legacy of these complex and intersecting issues on the law and governance chiefly of the Anglo-American form of business corporation will be explored in this book. The prevailing focus, however, will be upon the human beings who define, interpret, and operationalize the interests of the corporation, rather than upon the reified corporation itself. The central organizational premise of the corporation requires that it be managed by directors and officers. Those directors and officers perform their respective roles subject to a fiduciary duty, a duty anchored in trust and defined by loyalty: loyalty in the service of an interest other than one's own. Such a duty, which requires directors and officers generally to forego their own personal interests and act with outgoing concern toward the corporations they serve, ought to be seen *ex hypothesi* as antithetical to notions of managerial greed, self-interest, and short-termism that are frequently condemned as the source of modern corporate dysfunction. The corporation's dealings with third parties may be transactional and self-interested; but the corporation's internal governance structure is relational and premised on the corporate fiduciaries' duty of denial of self-interest. Admittedly, these duties have been significantly qualified in some jurisdictions, particularly in the key American state of Delaware.[96] The historical success of the corporation as an engine of economic growth, nevertheless, cannot be fully understood except in the context of the central role traditionally played by concepts of fiduciary duty and trust. The regulatory environment within which many corporations operate may not be sufficiently robust. Critical improvements may be necessary. But those improvements must be incremental, not foundational. To try to compensate for political failings by undermining or redefining core corporate principles is almost certain to do more harm than good.

In short, the corporate form, the central institution of the acquisitive capitalist system, has been premised on an expectation (and legal requirement) that its managers must act in accordance with the best aspects of human

[96] See eg Marc I Steinberg, *Corporate Director and Officer Liability: "Discretionaries" Not Fiduciaries* (Oxford University Press 2025), arguing that, under the broadly permissive Delaware corporate law, directors are more appropriately viewed as "discretionaries" than as fiduciaries.

nature.[97] When they fail—as of course they all too often do—it is a distinctly human failing, not a corporate failing. Indeed, the corporation is typically the first, if not the principal, victim of managerial breaches of duty. But flagrant breach of fiduciary duty is not the only source of corporate controversy. Even the most loyal and incorruptible corporate managers face unique challenges in the twenty-first century. Before they may serve 'the interests of the corporation' managers must first discern what those interests are. That task of discernment has been hampered by problems of definitional indeterminacy arising from evolving patterns of share ownership, financial innovation, and the constructive (or perhaps deconstructive) ambiguity of legislative, judicial, and popular directives.

A corporation's purpose is a product of human imagination and must be understood within the context of human incentives operating within a corporate governance structure centred on the concept of fiduciary duty. The chapters that follow will develop the background for analysing corporate governance within the modern political and financial context, focusing upon the formation and achievement of goals by enlightened fiduciaries. To begin, we must first review traditional approaches to analysing the firm and the relation of the firm to its officers and directors as well as to its shareholders and other financial and non-financial stakeholders or constituents. We will then turn to consider how those traditional concepts can be usefully reevaluated in light of the changes to the financial, political, and economic forces that have led to recent calls for repurposing and reform of the corporation and the law that governs it. Throughout this broad study of the workings and influence of the great and powerful corporation, we will keep a constant eye upon the fallible human beings behind the screen and beneath the corporate curtain.

[97] One notes the following comment by Nobel-prize winning economist, the late Elinor Ostrom: 'Extensive empirical evidence leads me to argue that . . . a core goal of public policy should be to facilitate the development of institutions that bring out the best in humans.' See also Elinor Ostrom, 'Beyond Markets and States: Polycentric Governance of Complex Economic Systems' (2010) 100 American Economic Review 641, 665.

# 2

# Fiat or Accord?

## Introduction: Who Needs Business Corporations?

Business may well be concomitant with human society. Adam Smith apparently thought so. There is a 'propensity in human nature', he declared, to 'truck, barter, and exchange':[1] a human propensity, in short, to carry on business. That may be so, although the proposition is not empirically verifiable and is by no means beyond dispute.[2] What is beyond dispute is that business thrived for many centuries without the business corporation. Whatever propensity they may have to 'truck, barter, and exchange', human beings certainly have no correlative propensity to create artificial legal persons—of ever-increasing size, scope, and complexity—to engage on their behalf in all that trucking, bartering, and exchanging. Smith himself was famously skeptical about the doubtful usefulness of corporations in most business ventures,[3] a skepticism formalized by modern economists centuries later into agency theory.

The business corporation in its modern form was neither an inevitable development in human trading relationships nor an obvious one. Although historical antecedents to the business corporation may be traced to classical antiquity,[4] the unique features of the modern business corporation represent a

[1] Adam Smith, *An Inquiry into the Nature and Causes of the Wealth of Nations* Edward Cannan (ed) (Methuen & Co 1904), vol 1, Bk 1 ch 2.

[2] See eg Karl Polyani, *The Great Transformation* (Farrar & Rinehart 1944) 43, 44, who maintained that Smith's claimed human propensity 'to barter, truck and exchange' 'had hardly shown up on a considerable scale in the life of any observed community . . . and the alleged propensity of man to barter, truck, and exchange is almost entirely apocryphal'. See also Peter Drucker, *Concept of the Corporation* (The John Day Company 1946) 237: 'We know today that there is no such thing as a natural instinct to "truck and bargain".'

[3] Smith (n 1), vol 2, ibid, bk V, ch 1, pt III, art I: 'The only trades which it seems possible for a joint stock company to carry on successfully, without an exclusive privilege, are those, of which all the operations are capable of being reduced to what is called a routine, or to such a uniformity of method as admits of little or no variation.'

[4] Blackstone credited the Romans with the invention of the corporation. William Blackstone, *Commentaries on the Laws of England*, vol 1 (1775) (University of Chicago Press 1979) 456. Gower chronicles the development of the English joint stock company seeing it as the product of the 'invasion' of partnership principles of trading on joint account into the operation of 'regulated companies', incorporated enterprises created chiefly to serve as a vessel to which state monopoly trading rights could be conferred for the benefit of company members each of whom originally traded on their own behalf. LCB Gower, *The Principles of Modern Company Law* (Stevens & Sons 1954) 23 ff. He also notes that, by

*Corporate Governance and Enlightened Fiduciaries*. Christopher C. Nicholls, Oxford University Press.
 DOI: 10.1093/9780198904199.003.0002

discontinuous creative jump. It was a jump that made economic history. Robin Marris observed that 'the social architects of the nineteenth century invented the public, joint-stock, limited liability company, and thus invented modern capitalism.'[5]

The business corporation has proved to be a financial innovation of unparallelled economic significance,[6]as instrumental to the rise of modern Western capitalism as any other single institution or technological advance.[7]

It is the very transformational contribution of the corporation to the modern capitalist system that presents a long-recognized and intriguing paradox. The corporation is a vehicle for pooling and coordinating human, physical, and financial resources. It is a distinct sort of collective or group enterprise. And it is, most importantly for this book, an organization that operates under a hierarchical central 'command and control' structure. As Adolf Berle and Gardiner Means observed in their influential work, *The Modern Corporation and Private Property*:

the end of the seventeenth century, 'some idea had been gleaned of one of the primary functions of the company concept—the possibility of enabling the capitalist to combine with the entrepreneur.' ibid 26.

[5] Marris, *The Economic Theory of 'Managerial' Capitalism* (Palgrave Macmillan 1964) 4.

[6] Christopher C Nicholls, 'Piercing the Corporate Veil and the "Pure Form" of the Corporation as Financial Innovation' (2008) 46 Canadian Business Law Journal 233.

[7] In fact, as Max Weber once argued, it is only in Western capitalist economies that the business corporation has achieved such a prominent position, and one important aspect of the unique rise of capitalism was the 'legal separation of corporate from personal property'. See Max Weber, *Protestant Ethic and the Spirit of Capitalism* (Talcott Parsons (tr), Charles Scribner's Sons 1930) 22. Other commentators have noted that the corporation has become the quintessential institution of capitalism. Colin Mayer, for example, has described the corporation as 'the central instrument of economics'. See Colin Mayer, *Firm Commitment* (Oxford University Press 2013) 1. Robert Clark has observed that: 'Corporations are overwhelmingly predominant . . . in manufacturing, transportation, public utilities, and wholesale trade' and 'overall, the business corporation is the principal form for carrying on business in [the United States]'. See Robert Clark, *Corporate Law* (Aspen Publishers Inc 1986) 1, 2. Nicholas Murray Butler, then President of Columbia University, famously remarked in a speech to the New York State Chamber of Commerce in 1911: 'I weigh my words, when I say that in my judgment the limited liability corporation is the greatest single discovery of modern times . . . Even steam and electricity are far less important than the limited liability corporation, and they would be reduced to comparative impotence without it.' Nicholas Murray Butler, 'Politics and Business', Address to New York State Chamber of Commerce (16 November 1911) CLXIII Annual Banquet of the Chamber of Commerce of the State of New York (Chamber of Commerce Press 1911) 43, 47. *The Economist* magazine, in 1926, similarly declared: 'The economic historian of the future, viewing in perspective the enormous expansion of the world's trade and industry during the nineteenth and twentieth centuries, may be inclined to assign to the nameless inventor of the principle of limited liability, as applied to trading corporations, a place of honour with Watt, Stephenson, and other pioneers of the Industrial Revolution.' See 'The Ownership of British Industrial Capital-I' *Economist* (18 December 1926) 1053. Although the business corporation has been important in the development of modern economies, it has also been contended that the development of the business corporation itself depended on the rise of the modern state. See Taisu Zhang and John D Morley, 'The Modern State and the Rise of the Business Corporation' (2023) 132 Yale Law Journal 1970.

> The idea that an army operates on the basis of 'rugged individualism' would be ludicrous. Equally so is the same idea with respect to the modern corporation . . . Group activity, the coordination of the different steps in production, the extreme division of labor in large scale enterprise necessarily imply not individualism but cooperation and the acceptance of authority almost to the point of autocracy.[8]

Yet, it is this centrally planned collective vehicle that has emerged as the most important profit-making institution within most (perhaps all) free enterprise economies. Within the corporation, all decisions about the allocation of resources are deliberately placed under the conscious control of identifiable human actors who have been appointed with a mandate to serve the ends of others and not their own. Resource allocations within the metaphorical walls of the corporation avoid the anonymous and somewhat mysterious give and take processes of the market in which there is neither central plan nor central planner, that bustling 'catallaxy'[9] where all participants are assumed to be acting exclusively in pursuit of their own interests alone.

We shall have more to say about what these 'interests' might comprise in a later chapter. For now we return to the foundational question of why the corporation assumed such prominence in the pro-market countries of the western world. Market economies, after all, are thought to depend for their success on the competitive initiative of individuals, not the cooperative interaction of groups. And for advocates of such economies, the price mechanism, operating through free market exchanges, is prized as a far more efficient means of allocating resources than the dubious dictates of any centrally controlled hierarchy.[10]

The apparent anomaly presented by the hierarchical corporation's dominant role within disaggregated market economies was recognized decades ago. It

[8] Adolf A Berle Jr and Gardiner C Means, *The Modern Corporation and Private Property* (The Macmillan Company 1933) 349.

[9] The term 'catallaxy' was coined by Friedrich Hayek to refer to 'the order brought about by the mutual adjustment of many individual economies in a market'. See Friedrich A Hayek, *Law, Legislation and Liberty*, vol 2 (The University of Chicago Press 1976) 109.

[10] As Milgrom and Roberts have put it: '[e]conomic historians have repeatedly argued . . . the emergence, expansion, and eventual dominance of the market system in western economies since the Middle Ages crucially contributed to economic growth and the resulting accumulation of wealth and rising standards of living for much of the population'. Paul Milgrom and John Roberts, 'Economic Theories of the Firm: Past, Present, and Future' (1988) 21(3) The Canadian Journal of Economics 444. The authors note, however, an alternative view to the effect that markets might be regarded as a more primitive way of allocating resources that is no longer well suited to many modern transactions of considerably more production complexity than the simple commodity markets of a bygone era. ibid 445.

has kindled many interesting[11] and several amusing meditations. Writing in 1937, for example, Yale Law School professor Thurman Arnold offered a simple but provocative thesis about corporate law linked to this corporate/market dichotomy. He suggested, with a wry hint of conspiratorial suspicion, that it was the need to address this very disquieting paradox that accounted for the law's dogged insistence on treating the corporation as a single distinct legal person rather than, say, as an association of individuals akin to partnerships or trade unions.

This corporate 'legal person' conceit, for Arnold, was a myth-preserving attempt to assuage any uncomfortable doubts about the indispensable role of 'rugged individualism' that might otherwise unsettle the minds of devoted champions of capitalism struggling to reconcile the undeniable dominance of a group enterprise—the corporation—with the mythos of the individualistic free-market system.[12] This shrewd act of jurisprudential legerdemain, he asserted, offered the comfortable assurance that the corporation was itself really just another individual market actor: a single competing 'person', rather than a collective.[13]

Arnold's ironic observation is clever and amusing. It evokes the terms of an old theoretical debate familiar to students of corporate law: the aggregate vs

[11] Karl Marx, for example, albeit for different reasons than the corporate attributes referred to here, recognized that corporations (or 'joint-stock companies') were essential to the massive expansion of the scale of production in capitalist economies, but also regarded the rise of large, increasingly monopolistic corporations as representing 'the abolition of the capitalist mode of production within the capitalist mode of production itself, and hence a self- dissolving contradiction, which *prima facie* represents a mere phase of transition to a new form of production'. See Karl Marx, *Capital: A Critique of Political Economy*, vol III (F Engels (ed), Progress Publishers, 1959 (originally published 1894)) ch XXVII 436, 438. John Maynard Keynes in 1926 similarly observed what he saw as 'the tendency of big enterprise to socialise itself', as corporations grew to such a size that management became entirely detached from shareholders and 'the general stability and reputation of the institution are the more considered by the management than the maximum of profit for the shareholders'. See John Maynard Keynes, 'The End of Laissez-Faire' in E Johnson and D Moggridge (eds), *The Collected Writings of John Maynard Keynes* (Royal Economic Society 1978) Vol 9, 272, 289.

[12] It is, perhaps, worth noting here that Alfred Marshall suggested in *Principles of Economics* (Macmillan and Co 1890) 84 that 'the earlier English economists paid too exclusive attention to the motives of individual action, to the neglect of those which lead to collective action'.

[13] Thurman Arnold, *The Folklore of Capitalism* (Yale University Press 1937) 187–88. In a later preface to his book written in 1962, Arnold dismissed the chapter in his book dealing with 'The Personification of Corporation' as 'largely obsolete' (ibid ix). But by this he appeared to mean only that one of the key consequences of treating the corporation as an individual—namely, that it should be as free of government interference as an individual trader—could no longer be seen as sacrosanct, given the 'amount of regulatory interference with business' that had become commonplace by 1962 (ibid ix). See also Morton J Horwitz, 'Santa Clara Revisited: The Development of Corporate Theory' (1986) 88 West Virginia Law Review 173, 221: '[i]n their emphasis on corporate "personality," early natural entity adherents attempted to simply capitalize on the language of natural rights individualism by portraying the corporation as just another right bearing person.' Harry Glasbeek has made the same point in a more colourful way: '[I]f the corporation can be made to appear as a market actor, just as if it were an individual flesh and blood human being, all will be hunky-dory in market-capitalism land.' Harry J Glasbeek, *Wealth by Stealth* (Between the Lines 2002) 80.

entity distinction.[14] Yet it glances over the many nuances of that dichotomy which, as Morton Horwitz has put it, had risen at one point in the early twentieth century to become something of a scholarly 'obsession'.[15] It also ignores distinct jurisdictional differences in the historical evolution of the business corporation.[16] Finally, it hints at, but does not really appear to engage with, a particular notion of 'corporatism',[17] a concept of collective interest formation which, intriguingly, seems to share certain similarities with what one medieval scholar has described as the 'medieval ideas of the organic nature of society'.[18] As Bratton and Wachter explain, corporatism was a concept that had become influential in Europe by the early 1930s.[19] In the US, too, at least by the time of Franklin Delano Roosevelt's election in 1932, a version of corporatism had been expected by the new president's contemporaries to influence the incoming administration's Depression-era reforms.

But to name is not to explain. Apart from identifying the collective/individualist tension, Arnold offered no suggestions as to why or how corporations had come to achieve such economic prominence particularly in the United States. Nor did he consider what distinct questions this institutional pre-eminence might raise for market-focused models of the economy. This is hardly surprising. Arnold was a lawyer, not an economist. Although law is crucial both to

[14] For a fascinating and insightful exploration of the early history of the aggregate vs entity characterization of corporations and partnerships see Naomi R Lamoreaux, 'Partnerships, Corporations, and the Limits on Contractual Freedom in US History: An Essay in Economics, Law and Culture' in Kenneith Lipartito and David B Sicilia (eds), *Constructing Corporate America: History, Politics, Culture* (Oxford University Press 2004) 29.

[15] Morton J Horwitz, *The Transformation of American Law 1870-1960: The Crisis of Legal Orthodoxy* (Oxford University Press 1992) 101, cited in Brian R Cheffins, 'The Trajectory of (Corporate) Law Scholarship' (2004) 63 Cambridge Law Journal 456, 478.

[16] In particular, in the United Kingdom, the general business incorporation legislation introduced in the nineteenth century consisted originally of a mechanism for formally registering unincorporated joint-stock companies, rather ingenious combinations of partnership, trust, and contract law that had carried on business effectively for many years in the wake of the disruption and uncertainty caused by the restrictive and opaque Bubble Act of 1720. Thus, as the English company law scholar LCB Gower once noted: '[t]he modern English business corporation has evolved from the unincorporated partnership, based on mutual agreement, rather than from the corporation, based on a grant from the state, and owes more to partnership principles than to rules based on corporate personality'. See LCB Gower, 'Some Contrasts between British and American Corporation Law' (1956) 69 Harvard Law Review 1369, 1371–72. See also David Kershaw, *The Foundations of Anglo-American Corporate Fiduciary Law* (Cambridge University Press 2018) 288 ff.

[17] Corporatism, Bratton and Wachter explain, offered an alternative to traditional political pluralism in which only the preferences of individuals were relevant to the determination of government policy: 'Corporatism privileges cooperation over competition and emphasizes group over individual interests.' William W Bratton and Michael L Wachter, 'Shareholder Primacy's Corporatist Origins: Adolf Berle and the Modern Corporation' (2008) 34 Journal of Corporate Law 99, 102. See also Oscar Molina and Martin Rhodes, 'Corporatism: The Past, Present, and Future of a Concept' (2002) 5 Annual Review of Political Science 305.

[18] Christopher Dawson, *Religion and the Rise of Western Culture* (Image Books 1958) 175.

[19] Bratton and Wachter (n 17).

the creation of corporations and to establishing enforceable boundaries within which all commercial operations take place, it provides few tools to explain why or how commercial institutions evolve in one way rather than another. For that, we might expect economists to offer additional insights. And so they have, at least in recent decades.

But the relative recency of economic interest in the phenomenon of the business firm is itself more than a little curious. Firms (such as business corporations) were for many years routinely left unexplored by 'classical' (and neoclassical) economists. As Oliver Hart once observed, neoclassical economics had very little to say about the firm. It was simply treated as a 'production function', assumed to be operated by a (somewhat inexplicably) 'selfless manager . . . who chooses input and output levels to maximize profit'.[20]

The apparent early indifference of economists to the firm (as opposed to the market) was not an inconsequential matter. As Ronald Coase noted, the fact that neoclassical economists showed such a conspicuous lack of interest in the existence and nature of firms was 'quite extraordinary, given that most people in the United States, the United Kingdom, and other western countries are employed by firms, that most production takes place within firms, and that the efficiency of the whole economic system depends to a very considerable extent on what happens within these economic molecules'.[21]

These economic molecules are not clusters of inanimate matter or self-driving clockwork machines churning out goods in mechanical compliance with some deterministic algorithm. They are integrated organizations of human beings operating under the conscious authority of human leaders directing actions with some definite goal or bundle of goals in mind.

The neoclassicists' rudimentary picture of the firm, as Hart described it, therefore highlights at least three gaps in the early economists' assumptions about the role of firms within market economies. First, they made no attempt to explain why firms of any sort emerge as alternatives to uncoordinated market transactions, let alone what may account for the development of a menu of distinctly different legal forms of business enterprise such as corporations, partnerships, limited partnerships, LLCs, and others. Second, as Coase recognized, they offered no rationale for the observed scale or scope of firms; no

[20] Oliver Hart, *Firms, Contracts, and Financial Structures* (Clarendon Press 1995) 15. The reference to 'profits' as the maximand in this familiar formulation was significantly refined in the mid twentieth century, as discussed further in Chapters 4 and 5. It is, therefore, more customary today to refer to the corporate goal as maximizing shareholder wealth (as evidenced by the price of the corporation's shares) or, occasionally, corporate enterprise value (that is, the value of all outstanding corporate financial claims, both debt and equity).

[21] RH Coase, *The Firm, the Market, and the Law* (University of Chicago Press 1988) 6.

explanation as to what, if anything, might limit the size (ie the 'boundaries') to which firms ultimately might, or optimally should, be expected to grow as they envelop more and more transactions within the corporate tent. Finally, and most important of all for our purposes, they ignored an apparent contradiction between two central assumptions (or axioms) of neoclassical economic theory: namely, that firms consistently maximize profits, while individuals consistently act in their own self-interest.

In the operation of corporations, these two assumptions seem to collide. The success of the corporation, as an artificial legal entity, depends on the reliably firm-directed efforts of its individual managers. Yet if we must reasonably assume that those very managers are subject to the same personal predispositions as other individual market actors, one might expect them to seek first to maximize their own personal utility, not to willingly subordinate their individual interests in the dutiful pursuit of maximizing profits or otherwise ensuring the success of the firm instead. Of course, some corporate managers might well be shareholders, themselves. But what of that? Even equity-owning managers would still appear to be irrefutably better off (provided their ownership interest constitutes anything less than 100% of the corporation's equity) by diverting directly to themselves value generated by the business rather than faithfully working to ensure that profits are maximized exclusively for the benefit of their corporate principal[22]and so necessarily shared with their fellow shareholders. Thus, if the corporation is genuinely the profit-maximizing institution neoclassical economics assumed it to be, how are we to understand the actions and incentives of the corporation's individual human managers?

Economists have not been unaware of the apparent contradiction between the Janusian assumptions of individual self-interest and firm profit-maximization. In 1972, for example, a finance text co-authored by two future Nobel-prize winning economists characterized the challenge of reconciling the assumptions of individual self-interest and firm profit maximization as a 'good question and one for which economists have not yet been able to supply a completely satisfactory answer'.[23] The search for an answer, whether satisfactory or otherwise, seemed to be a very low priority for early neoclassicists. Nothing useful seemed to turn on explaining why corporate managers might

[22] Value, in this case, of course need not be confined to cash rewards or even financial value. Lavishly appointed offices, opulent private jets, and gallery-quality corporate art collections all enrich the daily life of the corporate executive at the expense of the corporation and the corporation's shareholders. And since leisure is also of considerable value to most human beings, diversion of value could consist not only of 'looting' the corporate coffers, but also of 'lounging' at the expense of the corporation.

[23] Eugene F Fama and Merton H Miller, *The Theory of Finance* (Dryden Press 1972) 75.

be counted on to behave so dutifully in service of the financial interests of others. No answer seemed necessary or especially illuminating. It was the operation of the market price mechanism that mattered, and that mechanism really involved aggregate rather than individual behaviour. Although this simplistic 'black box' or 'production function' picture was criticized as a 'caricature of the modern firm',[24] it nevertheless served a passably useful role in formal models and in considering certain issues relating to the interaction of firms with each other and with external forces.[25] It seems that neoclassical economists were early adopters of Herbert Simon's 'satisficing' behaviour when it came to their own economic model building.[26]

But as the significance of the large corporation within modern economic systems became undeniable, the need for a richer theory of the corporation became apparent. To understand the corporation as both a product and a tool of human motivations arcing, if not exactly towards justice,[27] at least towards contributing to the social cohesion upon which commercial transactions and all human progress ultimately depend, then at least one of the two apparently contradictory premises of neoclassical economics must yield. Or, perhaps some more nuanced novel economic theory might still be proposed that would preserve the two fundamental axioms yet satisfactorily reconcile or resolve any apparent contradiction.

What might this solution look like? One may quickly reject some improbable possibilities. For example, one might posit, for sake of argument, that those exceptional individuals who have won the corporate executive 'tournament'[28] and bested their peers in successfully scaling the proverbial corporate ladder are simply cut from rather nobler cloth than the rest of humanity. Perhaps, for them, achieving financial goals on behalf of another—the

[24] See eg Oliver Hart, 'An Economist's Perspective on the Theory of the Firm' (1989) 89(7) Columbia Law Review 1757, 1758.

[25] ibid.

[26] Herbert A Simon, 'Rational Choice and the Structure of the Environment' (1956) 63(2) Psychological Review 129: '[i]t appears probable that, however adaptive the behavior of organisms ... this adaptiveness falls far short of the ideal of "maximizing" postulated in economic theory. Evidently, organisms adapt well enough to "satisfice"; they do not, in general, "optimize".'

[27] See Theodore Parker, 'Of Justice and the Conscience' in Theodore Parker, *Ten Sermons of Religion* (Crosby, Nichols & Company 1853) 66, 84–85: 'Look at the facts of the world. You see a continual and progressive triumph of the right. I do not pretend to understand the moral universe, the arc is a long one ... But from what I see I am sure it bends towards justice.' A version of this quotation is often attributed to Martin Luther King, Jr who, in a sermon delivered at the National Cathedral on March 31, 1968, said, 'We shall overcome because the arc of the moral universe is long but it bends toward justice.' Martin Luther King, Jr, 'Remaining Awake Through a Great Revolution', included in Congressional Record-House, Vol. 114, Part 7, 9 April 1968, 9395, 9397, online:https://www.congress.gov/bound-congressional-record/1968/04/09house-section.

[28] See eg Sherwin Rosen, 'The Economics of Superstars' (1981) 71(5) American Economic Review 845.

corporation—somehow trumps the narrow pursuit of their own individual self-interest. But would this explanation seem to reflect, as Frank Knight put it, 'human nature as we know it'?[29] Could corporate managers really be content (unlike the rest of us, evidently) to subordinate their personal goals in favour of devoting themselves, instead, to the purpose of enriching others, inexplicably motivated, perhaps, by what one early twentieth century commentator dubbed a philosophy of 'vicarious acquisitiveness'?[30] This proposition, to say the least, seems highly dubious. Yet, if we must concede that corporate managers are, at least, no less venal than the general population, why should we then expect any business corporation they manage to function as a 'perfectly efficient "black box", inside which everything operates perfectly smoothly and everybody does what they are told'?[31]

Let us consider a second possibility. Perhaps it is our assumption that individuals in general persistently act in their own interest that is flawed or at least importantly incomplete. Are we quite wrong to assume that individuals are such avaricious creatures, after all? Perhaps, as Nobel-prize winning economist Ronald Coase suggested, 'the rational utility maximizer of economic theory bears no resemblance to the man on the Clapham bus or, indeed, to any man (or woman) on any bus.'[32] Is it simply mistaken or misleadingly reductionist to suggest that individuals—whether corporate managers, corporate shareholders, or anyone else—consistently act in pursuit of their own self-interest, ever seeking to maximize their own utility?[33] Or, somewhat more

[29] Frank Knight, *Risk, Uncertainty, and Profit* (Houghton Mifflin Company 1921) 270.

[30] E Merrick Dodd, 'Is the Effective Enforcement of the Fiduciary Duties of Corporate Managers Practicable?' (1935) 2 University of Chicago Law Review 194, 195. For an exploration of the question of whether there is, indeed, an acquisitive instinct see Chester Rohrlich and Edith Rohrlich, 'Psychologicial Foundations for the Fiduciary Concept in Corporation Law' (1938) 38(3) Columbia Law Review 432.

[31] Hart (n 20) 17.

[32] Coase (n 21) 4. Alfred Marshall, often regarded as one of the founders of neoclassical economics, was himself dismissive of the notion that individuals acted solely in their self-interest. See eg Alfred Marshall (n 12) Introduction 6: 'And again sympathy with those who are strangers to us is a growing source of a kind of deliberate unselfishness that never existed before the modern age'; Book I ch 6 § 1: 'It is sometimes said that economists regard it as "natural" or "normal," and in some sense even right, that man should be governed only by selfish motives; this opinion may however be dismissed at once as a popular error, which finds no support in the teaching or practice of the best economics. But again it is said that the scope of economics is limited to the consideration of those actions which are governed by self-regarding, if not by selfish motives. This view also seems to be mistaken.' Marshall then goes on to examine the proposition more closely, recognizing that such an examination is necessary given that there is 'so much authority' for this mistaken proposition. For example, he argues that: 'When the motive to a man's action is spoken of as supplied by the money which he will earn, it is not meant that his mind is closed to all other considerations save those of gain. Even the most purely business relations of life assume honesty and good faith; while many of them take for granted, if not generosity, yet at least the absence of meanness.'

[33] As Ronald Coase once wryly observed: 'There is no reason to suppose that most human beings are engaged in maximizing anything unless it be unhappiness, and even this with incomplete success.' See Coase (n 21) 4.

subtly, is it only that the personal 'utility,' for example, that managers seek to maximize includes elements far more varied than merely amassing material wealth, a 'utility' that involves seeking some significant measure of psychic benefits such as pride, self-respect, and honor? These coveted values money cannot buy; they may only be attained through dutiful service to one's corporate employers.

Yet, the pursuit of a certain set of conventionally 'selfish' interests may also well prove incidentally to serve the common good while diverting actors from indulging other more nefarious individual interests that offer no such collateral social benefits. Seeking material gain, then, at least within carefully sanctioned boundaries, may well be not only the lesser of two, or the least of a bad many, evils, but may also produce genuine social benefit: the unexpected social bounty reaped by a sort of lamb in wolf's clothing. In Chapter 6, we will return to consider the intriguing idea, explored at length by Albert O. Hirschman,[34] of how building strong social foundations may be modelled as an engineering problem of balancing competing forces of self-interest. We will canvass, too, many of the complex incentive problems facing corporate managers which were eventually addressed by agency theory.[35]

Still, when it comes to deciding upon what constitute the most realistic assumptions about human nature and human behaviour, not everyone agrees that unbridled selfishness and a relentless competitive drive are inevitable and dominant human impulses. We know that there is something more to the story of human interaction. People also have an apparently natural proclivity, in many contexts, to cooperate with others rather than compete. And we have all gratefully witnessed the capacity of many human beings to perform acts of extraordinary self-sacrifice and altruism,[36] not only within the community of their own families and close friends, where altruism is very often the norm rather than the exception, but also in circumstances where the beneficiaries of altruistic acts are complete strangers to the altruist.

[34] Albert O Hirschman, *The Passions and the Interests: Political Arguments for Capitalism Before Its Triumph* (Princeton University Press 1977).

[35] The identification of the role of corporate managers as economic 'agents' for the corporation's shareholders seems to have first been made by Stephen Ross, 'The Economic Theory of Agency: the Principal's Problem' (1973) 63(2) American Economic Review 134, 138: 'To mention one more path of interest—in a world of true uncertainty where adequate contingent markets do not exist, the manager of the firm is essentially an agent of the shareholders.'

[36] There have occasionally been attempts to dismiss apparent examples of altruism and self-sacrifice by employing the tautological device of defining self-interest in terms of maximizing 'utility', then proposing that, for some people, helping others increases their own utility. The circularity of this reasoning is clear. Human beings are said to maximize their own utility, and utility is then simply defined as whatever an individual human being chooses to maximize.

Cooperation and competition,[37] then, both appear to be natural for human beings. Both represent common modes of human interaction. Altruism and selfishness are, likewise, both common strands of human nature's 'mingled yarn',[38] although not always, perhaps, of equal length or weight. Although human beings are undoubtedly capable of great acts of genuine altruism, however, they do not seem particularly addicted to them. It betrays no excessive cynicism to suggest that, if asked to wager on whether a stranger in any isolated set of circumstances is more likely to choose an act of selfishness over one of pure altruism, few of us would gamble our lives or our fortunes on the prospect of the stranger making the altruistic choice.

But even if our selfish, competitive inclinations seem all too often to dominate our cooperative and altruistic impulses, is it possible that this outcome is not due entirely to some innate human quality after all? Although Smith may have accurately perceived a correlation between human acquisitiveness and the mechanisms of our economic system, could he have mistaken the direction of the causal arrow? Is it possible that robust competitive markets are not merely marshalling the inevitable human desire for more, but are, instead, aggravating that very desire? Could capitalism, as I have mused elsewhere, function more as a spur than a harness?[39]

## Through a Glass Darwinianally

Determining what is truly 'natural' to human beings is better left to evolutionary biologists or perhaps cognitive neuroscientists than to lawyers. In the absence of rigorous scientific evidence, it is tempting for non-experts to invoke simplistic hypothetical models of human evolution in support of deeply

[37] It might be noted that Nicholas Murray Butler's famous tribute to the corporation, quoted in note 7 above, came in the context of a speech in which President Butler argued the age of individual competition had ended and had been superseded by 'a new and larger principle of cooperation' (46) and that that principle of cooperation had 'manifested itself in the last sixty or seventy years chiefly in the limited liability corporation' (47).

[38] William Shakespeare, *All's Well that Ends Well*, Act IV, sc. 3.

[39] Christopher C Nicholls, 'The Corporation and Modern Capitalism: Folk, Broke and Woke' in Oonagh E Fitzgerald (ed), *Corporate Citizen: New Perspectives on the Globalized Rule of Law* (Centre for International Governance Innovation 2020) 39, 56. One notes in this context research suggesting that the study of economics may increase a person's selfishness. See eg J Ifcher and H Zarghamee 'The Rapid Evolution of *homo economicus*: Brief Exposure to Neoclassical Assumptions Increases Self-interested Behavior' (2018) 75 Journal of Behavioral and Experimental Economics 55. However, while such reported results often receive significant media attention, the basis for these conclusions has been challenged. See Daniele Girardi and others, 'Does Studying Economics Make You Selfish?' (2024) 90 Southern Economic Journal 792.

held (but sparsely proven) intuitive beliefs. Might we not expect, for example, that the pursuit of brazen self-interest would enhance survival and so, over time, emerge as a dominant human trait? Conversely, on the one hand, if a capacity for altruism has a genetic source at all, perhaps, as more nuanced theories of evolution evidently suggest, we might at most expect a somewhat circumscribed role for altruism to have manifested chiefly as a mechanism for propagating familial, rather than individual, genes.[40] On the other hand, could our evaluation of the most probable evolutionary vectors itself be biased by our prior beliefs about the relative social importance of individual and group endeavour?

It was a central contention of Darwin's, and more recently expounded upon by Wilson and Wilson,[41] that, while selfish behaviour is the best strategy for an individual to pursue *within* any group, groups characterized by altruistic behaviour will dominate other groups characterized by selfish behaviour. Some sociobiologists have evidently challenged atomistic models of evolution altogether, arguing that there may be reason to embrace the once-rejected evolutionary notion of 'group selection' rather than individual selection.[42] Although controversial, group selection theory is consistent with the proposition that a genetic predisposition towards a broad sense of altruism (not limited merely to the proliferation of one's own familial genes) could indeed have human survival advantages. Or, again, are our apparent vices and virtues best understood entirely in clockwork mechanical terms? Are empathetic thoughts and actions, for example, merely the result of blood flow activity in the brain's ventromedial prefrontal cortex?[43]

Yet, whether the product of natural selection or of social forces, or of some combination of the two, might we even be mistaken about the relative moral value of selfishness and competitiveness, on the one hand, versus altruism and cooperation on the other? It is understandably tempting to characterize our cooperative impulses as more virtuous than our competitive tendencies; but on closer scrutiny this characterization seems overly simplistic and even misleading. Competition and cooperation may be complementary, at times ineluctably so. We cooperate in competing. Almost a century ago, R.G. Collingwood aptly pointed out: 'The parties to an economic action co-operate

[40] See eg Richard Dawkins, *The Selfish Gene* (Oxford University Press 1989).
[41] David Sloan Wilson & Edward O. Wilson, 'Rethinking the Sociological Foundation of Sociobiology' (2007) 82 The Quarterly Review of Biology 327.
[42] ibid.
[43] See eg Steven Pinker, *The Blank Slate: the Modern Denial of Human Nature* (Penguin 2003) 59.

in competing, like two chess players.'[44] In the language of cognitive scientists, human beings are—critically—capable of 'shared intentionality'.[45]

The social utility of altruism might also be somewhat overstated. As philosopher Charles Dyke once observed, '[i]t seems to me that it would be almost impossible to govern a nation of practicing altruists'.[46] And such a world, as suggested by Bernard Mandeville, in his infamous eighteenth-century satire *The Fable of the Bees*,[47] might even prove to be one of considerable poverty and misery. Do we, then, organize ourselves in groups because of our naturally cooperative behaviour or might we dare to suggest that we organize ourselves in particular sorts of groups not to nurture, but in fact, to counteract our naturally cooperative behaviour in the interests of greater material benefit?

How people cooperate is an important consideration in evaluating the institutional forms through which people carry on cooperative activities, whether for profit or otherwise. Without presuming to judge either the inevitability or inherent moral or functional superiority of any particular human characteristics or inclinations, we may nevertheless observe that markets certainly cannot exist without the interaction of self-interested individuals, and firms cannot exist without the interaction of cooperative individuals. It is equally clear that the competitive pursuit of self-interest occurs both within firms and when firms interact with third parties. Further, organized, orderly, and well-functioning competitive markets clearly depend upon the cooperative behaviour of admittedly self-interested parties. Neither firms nor markets, then, should be seen as the necessary or inevitable product of any single particular human proclivity whether for competition, cooperation, selfishness, or altruism.

But before we set to one side the puzzle of reconciling the twin presumptions of individual pursuit of self-interest and firm profit maximization, we must, of course, consider one alternative solution. Perhaps it is not the first economic

[44] RG Collingwood, 'Economics as a Philosophical Science' (1926) 36(2) The International Journal of Ethics 162, 177.

[45] See eg Steven Sloman and Philip Sternbach, *The Knowledge Illusion: Why We Never Think Alone* (Riverhead Books 2017) 14.

[46] C Dyke, 'The Vices of Altruism' (1971) 81 Ethics 241, 247.

[47] Bernard Mandeville, *The Fable of the Bees*, Phillip Harth (ed), (Penguin Books 1970). The earliest version of Mandeville's fable appeared in pamphlet form in 1705 under the title *The Grumbling Hive: or Knaves Turn'd Honest*. A longer version was published in 1714 as *The Fable of the Bees: or Private Vices, Publick Benefits*. He later published expanded versions in 1723 and 1724. Mandeville's shocking suggestion that the deliberate pursuit of virtue could actually be detrimental to society so scandalized some of his contemporaries that Mandeville was condemned as the embodiment of evil and was the subject of a Presentment of the Grand Jury for the County of Middlesex. See Introduction 11. In Mandeville's lines one may see the seeds of Adam Smith's invisible hand: 'And Vertue, who from Politics/Had learn'd a Thousand cunning Tricks,/Was, by their happy Influence,/Made Friends with Vice: And ever since/ The Worst of all the Multitude/Did something for the Common Good', 68 and 'So Vice is beneficial found,/When it's by Justice lopt, and bound', 7.

assumption—that of individual self-interest—that must be modified or qualified, but rather the second. That is, it may be that corporations simply do not in fact, should not in theory, and must not in law, relentlessly maximize profits.[48] The nuances of that eminently plausible possibility we take up in some detail in Chapter 5, along with the overarching questions of what constitutes 'utility', 'interests', and 'profits'.

## Markets vs Corporations

Defer, for the moment, the challenge of reconciling individual wealth-seeking and firm profit-maximizing and the ambiguities arising from the richness, complexity, and opacity of human motivations. Return now to the more basic and stubborn question which underlies economic analysis, organizational theory, and the form and structure of corporate law itself: why, in a market economy, are firms of any sort needed? To be more precise, why is some productive business activity conducted within firms, such as corporations, while other activity is conducted through more or less spontaneous market transactions relying upon individual contracts?

Market or firm. Which business choice is likely to prevail when and why? This question—sometimes framed in the economic literature as the 'make or buy' decision[49]—was famously posed by Ronald Coase in his 1937 article, 'The Nature of the Firm'.[50] Coase's point was simple but fundamental. Why do we observe some (but not all) business activity in market economies carried on through market exchanges, while other business activity is conducted through firms such as corporations in which a hierarchical authority structure seems specifically designed to avoid the market—to insulate intra-firm transactions from competitive market forces altogether? As Coase put it, the very

[48] Alternative views of the corporation's purpose are discussed at length elsewhere in this book. One only notes here that not all economists have agreed with Milton Friedman's position that 'the social responsibility of business is to increase its profits'. Nobel prize winning economist Kenneth Arrow, for example, once observed that: 'Some economists, much taken with the system, have indeed argued that, for example, business corporations are committing a social wrong if they try to engage in socially desirable activities; that their aims should be properly only to maximize their profits, and that is indeed the socially most desirable activity they can engage in. This is a proposition for which there is some warrant in price theory, although it stretches the point rather considerably.' See Kenneth J Arrow, *The Limits of Organization* (WW Norton Company Inc 1974) 21. Nor was Arrow's a lone voice in the economic wilderness. See eg C Addison Hickman, 'Managerial Motivation and the Theory of the Firm' (1955) 45(2) The American Economic Review 544, 545.

[49] See eg Oliver Williamson, 'The Modern Corporation: Origins, Evolution, Attributes' (1981) 19 Journal of Economic Literature 1537.

[50] Ronald Coase, 'Nature of the Firm' (1937) 4 Economica 386.

'distinguishing mark of the firm is the supersession of the price mechanism'.[51] If we are to believe that resources are most efficiently allocated by the markets, then firms ought not to be necessary or desirable. Conversely, if organizing productive activity within firms, and so bypassing the price mechanism, is actually more efficient than undertaking market transactions, why should firms not continue to grow until they become giant global behemoths that eventually supplant markets altogether? Why doesn't all productive activity shift from markets to firms—or, for that matter, to one immense global firm? Why do we observe, to use D.H. Robertson's striking metaphor, as quoted by Coase, 'islands of conscious power in this ocean of unconscious co-operation like lumps of butter coagulating in a pail of Buttermilk'?[52] So was the question asked (and putatively answered) by Coase.

The business landscape has changed since 1923. Today, we might reframe Robertson's question. For Robertson, in 1923, and perhaps for Coase too, in 1937, 'islands of conscious power' were found only 'here and there'.[53] It would seem more accurate, in today's environment of massive corporate enterprises dominating ever more aspects of industrial economies, to speak not of small scattered 'islands', but of imposing continents of conscious power towering above receding seas of unconscious cooperation. What determines the scope of activities that will be carried on within firms and the size to which firms will grow to undertake these activities? What, in other words, determines the ultimate 'boundaries' of the firm?

For Coase, the key to understanding both the origin and the boundaries of the firm was to be found in what he described as 'the cost of carrying out [transactions] by means of an exchange on the open market'.[54] This verbose concept later writers would more pithily dub 'transaction costs'. And to modern firm theorists, Coase's simple proposition is now as familiar as images of intersecting supply and demand curves: 'firms will emerge to organize what would otherwise be market transactions whenever their costs were less than the costs of carrying out the transactions through the market'.[55] Firms will continue to grow, too, 'until the costs of organising an extra transaction within the firm become equal to the costs of carrying out the same transaction by means of an exchange on the open market or the costs of organising in another firm'.[56]

[51] ibid 389.
[52] DH Robertson, *Control of Industry* (Nisbet & Co Ltd 1923) 85, quoted in Coase (n 50) 388.
[53] Robertson (n 52) 85.
[54] Coase (n 50), 395.
[55] Coase (n 21) 7.
[56] Coase (n 50) 395.

Coase's idea was later developed by other economists, including Oliver Williamson.[57] Williamson's work, for which he ultimately received the Nobel Prize in economics, emphasized the notion that firms must be understood as economizing mechanisms—that is, as structures designed and operated to reduce transaction costs. This perspective differed from other approaches to understanding the growth, governance, and operation of firms—particularly larger firms—that viewed the firm chiefly as an anticompetitive tool. This perspective, which Williamson refers to as the 'inhospitality tradition' (borrowing language from a former US Antitrust official)[58] presumed that 'organizational innovations have anticompetitive purposes'.[59] Williamson proposed replacing that presumption with a more sanguine view, namely a 'rebuttable presumption that organizational innovations are designed to economize on transaction costs'.[60] The Williamson approach emphasizes the consideration of the firm as a governance structure, and not merely, as in the neoclassical view, simply a production function.

The transaction cost approach also, importantly, made two key human behavioural assumptions: bounded rationality[61] (human beings are rational and intentional actors, but they do not have unlimited capacity); and opportunism (human beings have a tendency to act opportunistically—not only in an honest if self-interested way, but also with 'guile').[62] Bounded rationality makes complete contracting impossible and so opens the door for the creation of institutions that substitute for markets. And opportunism makes such alternatives necessary: incomplete contracts are a problem when parties cannot be assumed to be wholly trustworthy.

Coase had not used the word 'hierarchy' to denote the key characteristic distinguishing firms from markets. However, it was to Coase and Coase's paradigm that we owe many of the later theoretical developments that focused on the characteristic 'hierarchy' of firms in contrast to the decentralized operation of individual contracting in market exchanges.[63] Coase had certainly emphasized the critical role of intra-firm authority—namely, the authority of the employer in the employer-employee relationship. That relationship he saw as

[57] See in particular Oliver E Williamson, *Markets and Hierarchies: Analysis and Antitrust Implications* (Free Press 1975); Oliver E Williamson, *The Economic Institutions of Capitalism: Firms, Markets, Relational Contracting* (Free Press 1985).

[58] The reference to 'inhospitably' from which he derives the notion of 'inhospitality' is attributed to Donald Turner. See Oliver Williamson (n 49) 1540 n 5.

[59] Williamson (n 49) 1540.

[60] ibid.

[61] This term is attributed to Herbert Simon. See Williamson (n 49) 1545.

[62] Williamson (n 49) 1545.

[63] ibid.

essential to understanding the firm as an alternative to the market price mechanism. That this authority relationship must result in economic benefits for all willing participants was, for him, self-evident since he could discern no inherent psychological preference any person might have for agreeing to become subject to the authority of another. Parenthetically, he may have been mistaken about that. Some years after the publication of Coase's famous paper, Nobel-prize winning economist Kenneth Arrow, acknowledging that authority (subject to appropriate responsibility) was 'among the most widespread characteristics of organizations',[64] allowed at least for the possibility, once suggested by Erich Fromm's work, *Escape from Freedom*,[65] that the desire to be subject to authority might in fact, at times, actually be as instinctive for human beings as the pursuit of freedom.[66] There is at least some evidence that varying appetites or tolerances for risk could well account for differing preferences for working under the direction of others in exchange for a wage or salary that would not be subject to the oscillating fortunes of one's employer. Conversely, as Frank Knight observed, few employers would be willing to guarantee a fixed wage to an employee 'without being given power to direct his work'.[67]

The characterization of the firm as a top-down hierarchy, which places particular importance on the employer–employee relationship, has been resisted by some commentators[68] and reinterpreted by others. Coase's characterization of resource allocation decisions within a firm has at times been opposed by imagining market transactions which the participants themselves would scarcely recognize. Alchian and Demsetz, for example, argued that intra-firm relationships can themselves be characterized as market transactions: that each direction (or apparent 'order') given by a manager to an employee is no more or less obligatory than the demands made upon an independent shopkeeper by one of her customers. Accordingly, in their view, the premise that the corporation replaces market negotiation with top-down direction is simply false; the notion that the corporation has any real power of 'fiat', they argued, was simply a 'delusion'.[69] Perhaps. However, although it is true that an employee might well refuse to follow an employer's reasonable instructions—just as a shopkeeper might choose not to accede to a disagreeable customer's demands—it seems wholly unrealistic to ignore the significance of the very different consequences

[64] Arrow (n 48) 63.

[65] Erich Fromm, *Escape from Freedom* (K Paul, Trench, Trubner & Co Ltd 1941).

[66] Arrow (n 48) 76.

[67] Knight (n 29) 270.

[68] Armen A Alchian and Harold Demsetz, 'Production, Information Costs, and Economic Organization' (1972) 62(5) American Economic Review 777.

[69] ibid n 70.

likely to ensue in each of these two cases. As a practical matter, it is a rare employee whose human capital is so diversified that they are indifferent to the possible reprisals of a thwarted employer. It is, likewise, a rare shopkeeper whose livelihood is effectively dependent on preserving the business and goodwill of each and every individual customer, no matter how disagreeable or unreasonable.

Nor is it only differences in the degree of vulnerability to economic reprisals that differentiate the two scenarios. The relationship between employer and employee, as a matter of law, social convention, and psychological importance[70] is fundamentally different from the relationship between the typical buyer and seller of goods and services transacting in the market. Thus, it seems more useful and practical to recognize that the growth of massive corporations has altered the relative relationship between the automatic, disaggregated workings of anonymous, impersonal markets and the centrally directed allocation of resources within firms.

## Firms vs Corporations: What Law Has to Do with It

Coase's 1937 article has been described as a 'classic',[71] 'pioneering',[72] and 'seminal'[73] contribution to economic literature. But there were some intriguing precursors to Coase's work. And, surprisingly, the immediate impact of Coase's paper on economics, at least according to Coase himself, seemed minimal.[74] In the longer term, however, the paper spawned the field of transaction cost theory or, as Oliver Williamson would later dub it, 'new institutional economics'.[75]

[70] Oliver Williamson, for example, notes the 'oversimplification' of the position that workers with transferable job skills can readily be replaced 'without productive losses to either worker or firm'. See Williamson (n 57) 302 n 5, who cites Knight's observation that: 'Laborers are attached to their homes and even to their work by sentimental ties to which market facts are ruthless.'

[71] Williamson (n 57) *The Economic Institutions of Capitalism* 3.

[72] Hart (n 20) 57.

[73] Michael C Jensen and William H Meckling, 'Theory of the Firm: Managerial Behavior, Agency Costs and Ownership Structure' (1976) 3 Journal of Financial Economics 305, 310; R Hahn, 'Ronald Harry Coase (1910-2013)' (2013) 502 Nature 449.

[74] Coase (n 21) 6.

[75] According to Coase, the term 'new institutional economics' was coined by Oliver Williamson. See Ronald Coase, 'The New Institutional Economics' (1998) 88(2) American Economic Review 72. On his own contribution, Coase amusingly observed: 'It is commonly said, and it may be true, that the new institutional economics started with my article, "The Nature of the Firm" (1937) with its explicit introduction of transaction costs into economic analysis. But it needs to be remembered that the source of a mighty river is a puny little stream and that it derives its strength from the tributaries that contribute to its bulk.' ibid 72.

Notably, for our purposes, Coase's article examined the role of imprecisely defined 'firms', not the specific legal form of business corporations. He conceived of the firm broadly, describing it in functional rather than legal or institutional terms as 'the system of relationships which comes into existence when the direction of resources is dependent on an entrepreneur'.[76] Employment relationships and employment law were central to Coase's analysis of the key features distinguishing the firm's operations from market-based resource allocations.[77] But technical features of corporate law neither illuminate, nor are illuminated by, Coase's theory of the firm.

From a legal perspective, one might reasonably ask why Coase theorized about the supposed nature of the legally ambiguous concept of 'firms' and did not consider, more specifically, corporations.[78] Surely, after all, Coase, and those firm theorists who followed him, generally had corporations in mind, rather than, for example, partnerships, or other alternative business structures, some of which, such as the US LLC, did not yet exist at the time Coase published his famous article.[79] This is not a trivial consideration. Not for lawyers, at any rate. The importance of legal structure is too often overlooked or obscured in economic discussions of the corporation. But economic theories of the firm have rarely found it necessary to distinguish firms on the basis of technical legal forms. This omission apparently arises not from any lack of awareness amongst economists of formal legal distinctions between alternative forms of business enterprise, but from a determination that the latent function of all such forms of enterprise is, or ought to be, the same. Thus, for example, Gérard Debreu once wrote that: 'In the study of production, when one abstracts from legal forms of organizations (corporations, sole proprietorships, partnerships) ... one obtains the concept of a *producer*.'[80]

[76] Coase (n 50) 393.
[77] ibid 403–404.
[78] The ambiguity of the word 'firm' has itself prompted some discussion. In her influential 1959 book *The Theory of the Growth of the Firm*, Edith Penrose suggested that 'the economist's firm in the "theory of the firm" is not at all the economic institution that ordinary people would think of as a firm'. See Edith Penrose, *The Theory of the Growth of the Firm* (4th edn, Oxford University Press 2009, first published 1959) 57, with a new introduction by Christos N Pitelis.
[79] The first US state to enact LLC legislation was Wyoming in 1977. The key ruling by the US Internal Revenue Service, permitting LLCs to be taxed as partnerships and thus making the LLC a valuable alternative to the traditional corporation, was issued on September 2 1988 (IRS Ruling 88-76). This was followed in 1994 by Revenue Procedure 95-10 (Rev Proc 95-10; 1995-1 CB 501) and, ultimately, by the so-called 'check-the-box' regulations in 1996 (Treas Reg ss 301.7701-1-4 (1996)). By that time, all 50 US states had enacted LLC legislation. See Susan P Hamill, 'The Origins Behind the Limited Liability Company'(1998) 59(5) Ohio State Law Journal 1459, 1477.
[80] Gérard Debreu, *Theory of Value: An Axiomatic Analysis of Economic Equilibrium* (Yale University Press 1959) 37.

On the one hand, economists have thus seemed to care rather little for technical distinctions between alternative legal forms of business organizations.[81] Lawyers, on the other hand, have often cared about little else.[82] The challenge has been not merely to determine why transactions ought to occur within 'firms' rather than 'markets', but additionally to discern why 'corporations', specifically, are chosen for carrying on business rather than any one of the many other sorts of firms available to entrepreneurs. Practitioners may approach this choice of form question from the perspective of identifying congruence between the personal financial circumstances and goals of prospective business venturers, on the one hand, and the defining legal attributes of particular legal forms of enterprise on the other. Is limited liability for certain equity investors essential, for example? Is perpetual existence of a proposed enterprise necessary or desirable? Do investors demand the flexibility and liquidity that comes from ready transferability of their proprietary interests? What form of enterprise, under given circumstances, is the most tax efficient?[83] Beneath the layers of all such fact-dependent technical analysis lies the central question: *cui bono?* For whom, specifically, will the proposed business operations be conducted—however those operations happen to be undertaken, whether through, or deliberately directed away from, market exchanges? Does the answer differ in any material way depending upon whether a chosen type of 'firm' is or is not a business corporation?

Distinguishing the genus 'firm' from the particular species, 'corporation', and related studies of entrepreneurial decisions to organize productive activity within one legal form of enterprise rather than another have generated a surprisingly diverse academic literature. That literature, for example, confronts the question of whether the lawyer's 'corporation' invariably corresponds with the economist's 'firm', and vice versa. The importance of the legal distinction, to be sure, was not always a first order consideration even for lawyers

[81] See eg P Temin, 'The Future of the New Economic Theory' (1981) 12(2) Journal of Interdisciplinary History 179, in which the author suggests for economists, 'there is an implicit assumption that the organization form used to accomplish an objective does not matter'.

[82] As early as 1928, William O Douglas described how 'the *form* of business unit' had become the 'focal point' of study in law school courses, while advocating for a different approach that would focus upon the functions performed by business enterprises rather than the technical differences between the particular vehicles employed. See William O Douglas, 'A Functional Approach to the Law of Business Associations' (1928) 23 Illinois Law Review 673. For a modern discussion of the origins and development of alternative forms of business enterprise see the late Larry E Ribstein's book, *The Rise of the Uncorporation* (Oxford University Press 2010).

[83] John Armour, Henry Hansmann and Reinier Kraakman survey the familiar litany of corporate characteristics, common to corporations in jurisdictions throughout the worldin 'What Is Corporate Law?' in Reinier Kraakman and others (eds), *The Anatomy of Corporate Law* (2nd edn, Oxford University Press 2009) 1, 5–16.

or lawmakers. It may be useful to recall, for example, that the earliest English general incorporation statute, the Joint Stock Companies Act of 1844[84], was intended to mandate public registration by existing joint-stock companies—an early modified form of partnership—not to create afresh a wholly new form of business enterprise.[85] But as corporations have grown in size and economic significance, and as legal commentators have increasingly drawn on the insights of economists to illuminate the purposes and refine the interpretation of certain elements of corporate law doctrine, the putative distinction between 'firms' and 'corporations' has been scrutinized alongside questions raised by the 'make-or-buy', /'firms', and 'markets' dichotomy.

Daniel Spulber has argued, for example, that a firm exists when, and only when, the objectives of a business enterprise are distinct from those of its owners.[86] On that definition, corporations would almost always be firms, while basic (general) partnerships would never be. This conclusion may seem incongruous to lawyers in those jurisdictions where partnerships (but not corporations) are defined statutorily as 'firms'.[87] Jean-Philippe Robé, by contrast, explicitly excludes corporations from the definition of 'firm'. On the one hand, a 'firm', he says, is an 'organization performing an economic activity',[88] but it 'is not a legal person; it is an organization of resource providers'. The corporation, on the other hand, is, for Robé, 'a totally different concept', although his definition does seem to allow for the use of the corporation as a 'vehicle' used to structure large firms.[89]

One legal scholar, the late Lynn Stout,[90] argued that a 'firm', as an economic concept, could include any 'organization of economic activity involving more than one person, outside of formal markets'. Those persons need not all

[84] 7 & 8 Vict c 110 (UK).

[85] See eg Bernard J Kilbride, 'The British Heritage of Securities Legislation in the United States', (1963) 17 Southwestern Law Journal 258.

[86] Daniel Spulber, *The Theory of the Firm: Microeconomics with Endogenous Entrepreneurs, Firms, Markets and Organizations* (Cambridge University Press 2009).

[87] See eg UK Partnership Act 1890 s 4(1); UK Public General Acts 1890 c 39; New South Wales (Australia) Partnership Act 1892 s 4; Ontario (Canada) Partnerships Act, s. 5; New Zealand Partnership Law Act 2019, Public Act 2019 No 53 s 10. However, Simon Deakin, David Gindis, and Geoffrey M Hodgson, 'What is a firm? A reply to Jean-Philippe Robé' (2021) 17 Journal of Institutional Economics 861, 862, assert that (evidently, in spite of these sorts of extant statutory references): 'The English practice of calling certain partnerships "firms" has died out.' This claim might come as a surprise to lawyers at most modern law *firms*.

[88] Jean-Phillippe Robé, 'The Shareholder Value Mess (And How to Clean it Up)' (2020) 10(3) Accounting, Economics, and Law 1, 2; See also Jean-Phillippe Robé, 'The Legal Structure of the Firm' (2011) 1(1) Accounting, Economics, and Law 1.

[89] ibid 3.

[90] Lynn Stout, 'The Economic Nature of the Corporation' in Francesco Parisi (ed), *The Oxford Handbook of Law and Economics: Volume 2: Private and Commercial Law* (Oxford University Press 2017) 337.

be entrepreneurs or equity holders; they could include employees. Thus, in Stout's formulation, a sole proprietorship with employees could be considered a firm,[91] while a sole shareholder corporation without employees might not be.

Deakin, Gindis, and Hodgson correctly observe that 'at least as a first approximation, a *firm* is an economic phenomenon and the *corporation* a legal form'.[92] However, they also maintain 'the term *corporation* is not the sole property of lawyers'.[93] They suggest that the fact that the term 'corporation' is the 'principal legal concept used to order the business firm' especially in Anglo-American common law jurisdictions, 'is a sign of the priority which corporate law tends to give to financial interests over productive ones'.[94] As for the term firm, that they define 'to apply to individuals or organizations with legally recognized capacity to produce goods or services for sale'.[95] Significantly, however, they contend (and they are surely correct) that 'a *corporation* is a kind of firm'.[96]

Should it matter whether the legal form of 'corporation' is or is not coextensive with the economist's more generic concept of the firm? It may. The distinction would be unimportant if the law governing the corporation and, critically, the duties of corporate directors (and senior corporate managers) had evolved entirely within its own distinct fundamentalist doctrinal silos. But it has not. The worlds of law and economics are hardly two solitudes. As the law of corporations developed particularly throughout the twentieth century, legal scholars and judges increasingly came under the influence of economic concepts of the role and purpose of 'firms'.[97] Economic theories of the firm, as William Bratton has noted, 'inform and undergird corporate law', although, he argues, until the emergence of the 'nexus of contracts' view of the firm, they were not at the foreground of legal analysis.[98]

Efforts by economists to understand the generic 'firm' at a conceptual level have thus inevitably come to shape an understanding of the contours of the business corporation, the legal obligations of corporate directors and officers, and the rights of shareholders, creditors, and other parties who contribute to a corporation's business or are affected by a corporation's operations. Whether

[91] ibid.
[92] Deakin, Gindis, and Hodgson (n 87) 861.
[93] ibid 862.
[94] ibid.
[95] ibid 865.
[96] ibid.
[97] See eg Roberta Romano, 'After the Revolution in Corporate Law' (2005) 55 Journal of Legal Education 342.
[98] William W Bratton Jr, 'The New Economic Theory of the Firm: Critical Perspectives from History' (1989) 41 Stanford Law Review 1471.

economists in refining their economic theories of the firm have, in turn, shown a comparable sensitivity to the significance of key legal distinctions between various forms of business enterprise is less clear.

The distinct significance of the business corporation, in contradistinction to other for-profit business firms, has been explored by a number of commentators.[99] Most of this literature is not relevant to the role and function of corporate managers, although we will return to consider some of the unique attributes of corporations, and in particular corporations with publicly traded shares, in later chapters. At this point, as a preliminary matter, we offer the trite observation that the corporation is at least one particularly important form of business enterprise that relies upon the allocation of resources through organizational hierarchy rather than market exchange. It is the role of this hierarchy and its implications for the economic functions, interpersonal relationships, and the consequent legal duties of the human beings who serve as its 'hierarchs' that are important here.

## Dogmas and Catallaxies

For lawyers seeking to understand the optimal structure and governance of the corporation, Coase's conception of the firm, oriented around the hierarchical employer-employee relationship, must be viewed in part in contrast, and in part in alignment, with other prominent twentieth century economic—and perhaps sociological—ideas about the firm and firm governance. Embedded in every theory of the proper role and purpose of the business corporation—and the corresponding legal rights and obligations needed for the satisfactory fulfilment of those roles and the achievement of those purposes—are fundamental assumptions about human nature and social organization. Such assumptions also underlie analyses of economic systems.

Economists have sought to understand, predict, and explain how society's resources might best be maximized and allocated based on harnessing presumably immutable human characteristics such as a presumed tendency to pursue one's own interests and so maximize one's own 'utility'.[100] The law is based on

[99] Jensen and Meckling, for example, considered this question explicitly, noting that the positive agency costs associated with the corporate form made the dominance of the corporate form over other forms of business enterprise something of a puzzle. See Jensen and Meckling (n 73) 330. Some years later, Jensen even declared that the publicly-traded corporation had 'outlived its usefulness in many sectors of the economy and is being eclipsed.' Michael C. Jensen, 'Eclipse of the Public Corporation' (September-October 1989) Harvard Business Review 61.

[100] But, as Albert Hirschmann contends, and as discussed further in Chapter 5, the concept of 'interests' has undergone an intriguing evolution in Western legal thought and language.

many of the same assumptions about human motivations.[101] But there is an essential difference. Law does not primarily seek to harness those natural impulses; law's role is more typically to regulate and, where necessary, to restrain them.[102] Indeed, as Sigmund Freud one author once suggested, civilization depends upon repression.[103] The 'incentives' provided by the legal system thus very often take the form of *disincentives*, such as penalties for unwanted conduct, not rewards for desired outcomes. Law is generally a more effective tool of prohibition than of prescription.

Are human inclinations immutable? Are they even discernible? Can one readily distinguish between those behaviours that reflect innate propensities and others that are guided by social norms? The empirical basis for any observer's casual claims about 'human nature as we know it'[104] may be contestable. Anecdote is not science. But no matter. To proponents of any particular theory of human behaviour, the validity of their own premises may appear reassuringly self-evident. Belief in favoured economic (or, for that matter, psychological or sociological) theories can be similarly powerful and unshakeable. Keynes famously declared that 'practical men' often find themselves shackled to the views of some 'defunct economist'.[105] In a less well-known passage, Thurman Arnold asserted to like effect that 'Basic economic beliefs are religious in character'.[106] So it is, for example, following the classical economic model of Adam Smith and the later neoclassical economists, human beings are generally assumed to act in their own self-interest or perhaps in the interests of themselves and members of their own family. Because society's resources are limited,[107] on this view, human beings, in pursuit of their apparently natural

[101] Leading law and economics scholar, and later judge, Richard Posner, for example, argued that 'the purely formal characteristics of a just legal system . . . can also be derived from the wealth-maximization principle.' Richard A Posner, 'Utilitarianism, Economics, and Legal Theory' (1979) 8(1) The Journal of Legal Studies 103, 127.

[102] As Justice Holmes famously put it in his dissenting opinion in *Adkins v Children's Hospital* 261 US 525, 568 (1923): '[p]retty much all law consists in forbidding men to do some things that they want to do.' Holmes made this comment in the context of questioning the 'dogma' of 'Liberty of Contract' since, he argued, 'contract is no more exempt from law than other acts'. The *Adkins* decision dealt with the question of whether or not Congress could enact a minimum wage for adult women and minors in the District of Columbia without infringing upon a constitutional right to freedom of contract within the due process clause of the Fifth Amendment to the US Constitution.

[103] '. . . the existence of civilization pre-supposes the . . . suppression [or] repression . . . of powerful instinctual urgencies.' Sigmund Freud, *Civilization and its Discontents* (Joan Riviere tr, Hogarth Press 1930), 63.

[104] Frank Knight (n 29).

[105] John Maynard Keynes, *The General Theory of Employment, Interest and Money* (Macmillan 1936), 383.

[106] Thurman W Arnold, *The Folklore of Capitalism* (Yale University Press 1937), from a new preface to the work from 1962 at xxiii.

[107] If resources were unlimited, there would be no need for corporations, pricing mechanisms, the burdens of work, or the books of economists.

longing for 'more', find themselves locked in a continuing competition with their fellows, with each competitor determined to obtain for themselves the greatest possible share of those scarce resources.[108] This competition for resources, Adam Smith famously argued, led to productive activity and so to greater satisfaction of human wants—as though self-interested actors were somehow led by Smith's iconic 'invisible hand' to serve interests of others through pursuing their own.

The remarkable 'spontaneous order'[109] made possible by market transactions is frequently contrasted with the central command and control of planned economies. When centrally planned economies are weighed in the balance, they are frequently found wanting not only for their failure to meet the material needs of their citizens, but even for posing a threat to individual liberty.

This familiar free market narrative is compelling. It offers the promise of a kind of socio-economic alchemy. Base human instincts are transformed into golden opportunities. The economic success of participants in a market-based economy need not depend on either the gratuitous and inconstant 'kindness of strangers',[110] or the largesse of a heavy-handed, and potentially coercive, inefficient, or wasteful government. Instead, the bounty of all actually thrives on the prevalence of individual cupidity. *Cupiditas est radix prosperitatum.* If the pursuit of self-interest and a relentlessly competitive spirit are indeed natural human qualities, then a free enterprise, capitalist system may be celebrated as an ingenious way of marshalling those ignoble but inexorable inclinations in service of the creation of societal wealth: of expanding the total size of the economic 'pie'.

The bigger the pie, of course, the more potential 'slices' available for ultimate division and distribution for the common good, through taxation, for example, transfer payments, the construction of roads, bridges, schools, hospitals, parks, and the delivery of a myriad of other services citizens in affluent nations have come to look to government to provide. Contrary to the naysayers, then, who deride capitalism as the engine of a shamelessly undemocratic plutocracy or kleptocracy, it is not only the privileged few who benefit from a robust free enterprise system. It is the many. This is so, Smith contended, because the wealthy

[108] One might equally contend, with Thomas Paine, that man's natural inclination for more than he can produce for himself leads to reciprocal co-operation in the production and exchange of goods, rather than competition. See Thomas Paine, *The Rights of Man, Part the Second* (EP Dutton & Co Inc 1951) 157.

[109] Hayek (n 9) 110.

[110] See Tennessee Williams, *A Streetcar Named Desire* (John Lehmann Ltd 1949) scene XI.

members of society, 'are led by an invisible hand to make nearly the same distribution of the necessaries of life, which would have been made, had the earth been divided into equal portions among all its inhabitants, and thus without intending it, without knowing it, advance the interest of the society, and afford means to the multiplication of the species.'[111]

There are reasons to question whether the bounty created by the forces of free enterprise will be distributed quite as generously as Smith had suggested or as universally. Nor is it apparent that law and regulation are enforced reliably enough to restrain rapacious practices and widespread negative externalities that undermine the basis for trusting the uncoordinated chaos of market transactions to unequivocally advance the common good. At the level of the individual, the free market picture is also unsatisfying. An assumption of universal human selfishness is not only disappointing, but also highly unrealistic. As Oliver Williamson observed: 'The human agents who populate the economic [ie, the economists' models of the] institutions of capitalism are lacking in compassion.'[112] One understands that economic models are not intended to be wholly realistic. The very point of such models—rather like a map—is to simplify in order to help clarify analysis. Just as one does not expect (or want) a road map to display with meticulous photographic accuracy every rock and tree lining the side of each charted street and highway, one does not expect a useful economic model to incorporate all nuances of human behaviour. As Milton Friedman once famously put it:

> [t]he relevant question to ask about the 'assumptions' of a theory is not whether they are descriptively 'realistic,' for they never are, but whether they are sufficiently good approximations for the purpose in hand. And this question can be answered only by seeing whether the theory works, which means whether it yields sufficiently accurate predictions.[113]

Of course, as other prominent economists have noted, we also cannot wholly ignore the extent to which assumptions underlying economic models depart markedly and materially from reality.[114]

[111] Adam Smith, *The Theory of Moral Sentiments* (A Millar 1759) pt IV, ch 1.
[112] Williamson (n 56) 391.
[113] Milton Friedman, 'The Methodology of Positive Economics' in *Essays in Positive Economics* (University of Chicago Press 1966) 15. Friedman went further in this essay, asserting that: 'Truly important and significant hypotheses will be found to have "assumptions" that are wildly inaccurate descriptive representations of reality, and, in general, the more significant the theory, the more unrealistic the assumptions (in this sense).' ibid 14.
[114] See eg Dani Rodrik, *Economics Rules* (Oxford University Press 2015) 26 ff. In particular, Rodrik notes: 'It is perfectly legitimate, and indeed necessary, to question a model's efficacy when its critical

The terms of the putatively inevitable and perpetual competition between individuals in a market economy must be restrained by laws that preserve social order by strictly forbidding the use of physical force and other forms of coercion by non-state actors. Properly prevented from resorting to force, competitors must devise ways to convince others to furnish them with the goods and services they covet through entirely voluntary exchange. For the honest and diligent craftsperson, this means outshining one's competitors by producing goods or services of recognizably superior quality or value. But, regrettably, for many products and many more services, superior quality is not always easily observable. And where market transactions are isolated and do not involve the trust-building and information-enhancing participation of 'repeat players', consumers must frequently rely upon highly imperfect and readily manipulable signals of quality and value. The system can all too easily be gamed. And the most venal players in this unending social game, very much aware of these market imperfections, will, sadly, stoop to trickery, guile, and unscrupulous opportunism.

Law and regulation must work to curb the distorting role of dishonesty, bad faith, and unscrupulous opportunism because deception and exploitation vitiate genuine consent as surely as brute force. They can have no place in transactions that may be considered genuinely voluntary. Malfeasance is not a moral problem only. It is an economic one, too. Dishonesty and chicanery in market transactions not only harm victims directly, but also generally distort the allocation of society's resources. When resources are allocated on the basis of misinformation or deception, the promised social benefits from market transactions are forfeited. The misallocation of economic resources destroys societal wealth, and the destruction of societal wealth contributes, over time, to lower standards of living for everyone. A scoundrel may gain from a dishonest bargain, which is bad enough. But the material loss to society makes matters worse. If, however, force and guile are judiciously restrained, the self-interest of each market participant can be effectively channelled into personal and social prosperity. Or so is the promise of Adam Smith's invisible hand.

When we speak of truly voluntary exchange, then, we refer to transactions that are not only free from coercion but which also are untainted by elements of deception, information asymmetry,[115] and exploitation of monopoly

assumptions are patently counterfactual . . . In such instances, we can rightly say that the modeler has oversimplified and is leading us astray.' ibid 29.

[115] Information asymmetry is not, strictly speaking, a bar to voluntary exchanges because the market price can reflect the uncertainty that arises from asymmetrical information. It was this possibility, and

or monopoly like power. Where these ideal preconditions are satisfied, every market transaction between two or more parties must, necessarily, benefit each of them. Willing buyers must believe themselves better off when they surrender their money and receive in exchange some offered good or service. Willing sellers, similarly, must believe themselves better off accepting an agreed price in return for providing a good or service.

Economists may prefer to formalize the mutual benefits derived by buyers and sellers in market transactions using terms like 'consumer surplus' and 'producer surplus'.[116] But the reasoning is intuitive: every genuinely voluntary contract invariably represents, to invoke a hackneyed popular expression, a 'win-win'. This does not mean that each buyer and seller gains equally in all, or indeed in any, transactions. Nor does it ignore either the transactional impact of differences in relative bargaining strengths or the inevitable possibility for post-transaction buyer (or seller) remorse. A buyer might well have preferred to have paid something less than the price agreed upon in a given transaction, while the seller in the same transaction might have naturally wished to have received a little more. But whatever the price upon which unconstrained and fully informed market actors finally settle between themselves must necessarily be satisfactory to both parties. No consensual deal would ever have been reached otherwise. We may therefore be sure that, although contracting parties are expected to guard and advance no interests but their own, every voluntary market transaction will, nevertheless, reliably benefit every party to that transaction (although the benefits, very possibly, will not be distributed in equal shares).

So long as private market transactions satisfy the additional condition that they do not impose harm on third party strangers to the contract ('negative externalities'[117]), every such transaction must make the world a little better off,

the potential consequences for hypothetical markets, that was explored by Nobel-prize winning economist George Akerlof in his well-known paper, 'The Market for "Lemons": Quality Uncertainty and the Market Mechanism' (1970) 84 The Quarterly Journal of Economics 488.

[116] The terms 'consumer surplus' and 'producer surplus' (or consumer and producer 'rents') are usually said to have originated with the nineteenth-century economist Alfred Marshall.

[117] Coase credits Paul Samuelson with first coining the term 'externalities' to refer to the effect of market transactions on third parties, although the concept predated Samuelson's coinage, being referred to in older economics literature as 'external economies' or diseconomies. See Coase (n 21) 23. The concept had been previously invoked by economists using other terms as well. For example, Milton Friedman referred to the impact of private transactions on non-contracting parties as 'neighbourhood effects'. See eg Milton Friedman, *Capitalism and Freedom* (University of Chicago Press 2020) 35. While the simplest examples of negative externalities are unjust harms to third parties—of which pollution generated in the production of some goods is perhaps the textbook example—economists have also identified a more subtle type of externality: the pecuniary externality, a concept that seems to have been first identified in 1954 by Tibor Scitovsky. See Tibor Scitovsky, 'Two Concepts of External Economies' (1954) 62 Journal of Political Economy 143. A pecuniary externality refers to the impact

by unequivocally benefiting the parties to the transaction itself while causing harm to no one else.[118] In this way, as Adam Smith explained, the pursuit of self-interest, paradoxically, contributes to the common good. So the 'private vice' of selfishness is transformed into the 'public benefit' of industry, as Mandeville had dared to suggest in his provocative *Fable of the Bees*[119] more than half a century before Smith published *Wealth of Nations*.

The benefits of free market exchange do not end there. The voluntary exchange of goods and services allows for specialization and the economic expansion which only specialization can facilitate. As Nobel-prize winning economist Kenneth J. Arrow once put it, 'The blacksmith . . . is not expected to eat horseshoes; he specializes in making horseshoes, the farmer supplies him with grain in exchange, and both . . . can be made better off'.[120] Society as a whole is greatly enriched as it becomes feasible for people to devote their time to developing highly specialized skills. Specialization begets progressively greater specialization. And so the productive capacity of a technologically advanced society may be fully unleashed as people develop increasingly rarefied technical skills not only to become competent blacksmiths and farmers but also adept tinkers, tailors, soldiers, sailors, auto mechanics, computer scientists, immunologists, oncologists, and quantum physicists.

The business corporation and the market system within which it has flourished rely for much of their legitimacy on these promises of Pareto efficiency and the wealth-producing gains from greater and greater degrees of specialization. Of course, this sanguine neoclassical story has not gone unchallenged. For example, early twentieth-century progressive scholars like Robert Lee

on a third party's prices that may result from perfectly legitimate transactions between other parties. See eg Martin Shubik, 'Pecuniary Externalities: A Game Theoretic Analysis' (1971) 61 The American Economic Review 713.

[118] Economists would refer to such a happy result as a Pareto improvement, after the Italian political economist Vilfredo Pareto. Smith eloquently described the societal benefits arising from ostensibly selfish behaviour in his now famous declaration that 'It is not from the benevolence of the butcher, the brewer, or the baker, that we expect our dinner, but from their regard to their own interest. We address ourselves, not to their humanity but to their self-love, and never talk to them of our own necessities but of their advantages.' See Smith (n 1) bk I, ch II. One might argue that market transactions that increase the wealth of a few could be seen as socially harmful even if they leave the wealth of all others unchanged, if one believes that changes in relative wealth inequality are themselves harmful. However, the very point of Smith's argument is that the production of material wealth depends upon the incentives created by the market, and those incentives could not exist in a society in which inequality of wealth and income were made impossible. If all decisions that create or increase inequalities of wealth or income are to be disparaged, then even every act of charity would need to be condemned since if I donate money to one needy person and not to another I have potentially created an inequality of wealth that did not exist before I made my donation.

[119] Mandeville (n 47).

[120] Arrow (n 48) 19.

Hale[121] and more contemporary proponents of 'law and political economy'[122] have challenged the notion that ostensibly free bargains between parties of unequal economic power should be genuinely considered free of coercion. One might, with R. G. Collingwood, offer the sobering if cynical rejoinder to such criticisms that: 'If people who cannot get as high a price as they want for their goods or labor complain that only a ruthless competitive system prevents them from getting more, they are merely throwing a cloak of hypocritical moralizing over their own disappointed greed.'[123]

But perhaps this is both misdescriptive and unfairly harsh. In any event for our purposes the question is not whether the market reliably functions as a positive social utility machine. It is whether the diversion of productive activity from markets in favour of hierarchical firms (and more specifically, to corporations) is more likely to amplify or vitiate whatever contribution to net social benefit that activity might otherwise offer. It is also important to recognize, as Hansmann did, that costs need not be pecuniary only, and that subjective senses of 'alienation', for example, or 'exploitation' can also be a consequence, and so a very real cost, of market activity. Some people, as Hansmann notes, simply do not like engaging in market transactions and may suffer a sense of exploitation that is hard to measure but is surely real.[124]

## Methodological Individualism

If markets are regarded as one manifestation of collective or aggregate human interaction and firms as another, how are we to understand the inferred 'will' or 'purpose' of these differing institutions that reflects the underlying will or interests of individuals? This sort of question has sometimes been framed by sociologists in terms of 'methodological individualism'.

For an admittedly simplistic notion of methodological individualism, it is useful to recall a famous (and frequently criticized) comment of former

[121] See eg Robert L Hale, 'Coercion and Distribution in a Supposedly Non-Coercive State' (1923) 38 Political Science Quarterly 470.

[122] See eg Jedidiah Britton-Purdy and others, 'Building a Law-and-Political-Economy Framework: Beyond the Twentieth Century Synthesis' (2020) 129 Yale Law Journal 1784.

[123] Collingwood (n 44) 177–78.

[124] A number of years ago, General Motors, in response to the distaste for price negotiation voiced by many automobile purchasers, introduced a firm 'no haggling' price policy for its Saturn line of vehicles. See Peter Valdes-Dapena, 'Saturn: Secrets of the "No-Haggle" Price' (24 September 2006) https://money.cnn.com/2006/09/19/autos/debating_no-haggle/index.htm?section=money_latestexpressed. The no-haggling policy ended with GM's 2009 decision to discontinue the Saturn brand. See 'Saturn: A Wealth of Lessons from Failure' (28 October 2009) https://knowledge.wharton.upenn.edu/article/saturn-a-wealth-of-lessons-from-failure/.

UK Prime Minister Margaret Thatcher. In September 1987, Prime Minister Thatcher was interviewed by Douglas Keay for the magazine *Woman's Own*.[125] In that interview, Thatcher said: 'Who is society? There's no such thing! There are individual men and women and there are families and no government can do anything except through people and people look to themselves first . . . There is no such thing as society.'[126]

An abstract collective—such as society—in other words amounts to no more or less than the particular human beings of which it is composed. The actions or responsibilities of 'society', then, cannot be understood as something apart from the actions and responsibilities of those same individual human beings. On a more formal and sophisticated level, the concept of methodological individualism was explored by German sociologist Max Weber, who noted of certain social collectives (including business corporations):

> For other cognitive purposes, such as legal knowledge, or for purely practical ends, it might be useful (and indeed unavoidable) to treat social constructs (eg the 'state,' 'association,' 'companies,' 'charitable foundations') as if they were individual persons with rights and duties, or as the performers of legally relevant actions. By contrast, for sociological construal and understanding of action these entities remain merely processes and specific contexts for the action of individual people, since for us these are the sole understandable agents of meaningfully oriented action. But of course even for its own ends, sociology cannot simply ignore the collective conceptual apparatus of other intellectual perspectives.[127]

Is a business corporation this sort of 'abstract collective'? Or is it, as Dicey[128] and Gierke[129] supposed, a real and distinct person? Corporations themselves certainly participate in markets. They regularly enter into contracts with other corporations and with individuals, too. This was the point of Arnold's observation: the corporation is itself a market player. But in the conduct of day-to-day

[125] The transcript of this interview is reproduced on the Margaret Thatcher Foundation website. See https://www.margaretthatcher.org/document/106689.

[126] ibid.

[127] Max Weber, *Economy and Society A New Translation* (Keith Tribe ed and tr, Harvard University Press 2019) 89–90.

[128] In a passage quoted by Adolf Berle, in turn quoting a 1905 article by Jethro Brown, Dicey asserts that: 'It is a fact which has received far too little notice from English lawyers that, whenever men act in concert for a common purpose, they tend to create a body which, from no fiction of law, but from the very nature of things, differs from the individuals of whom it is constituted.' Quoted in Adolf A Berle, *Studies in the Law of Corporation Finance* (Callaghan and Company 1928) 4.

[129] Otto Gierke, *Political Theories of the Middle Age* (Frederic William Maitland (tr), Cambridge University Press 1900).

operations within the walls or boundaries of the firm, matters are different. Decisions must be made about how to use the firm's physical resources and about when, where, and how the firm's employees should perform their tasks. These allocations are not the result of the interplay of market forces. All of these decisions are subject to central authority and direction, rather than the result of separately negotiated agreements.[130]

The allocation of resources and the assignment of duties within the corporation are thus the result of conscious decision-making directed towards the achievement of some deliberate purpose or goal. The corporation is thus, to use the terminology of philosopher Michael Oakeshott, an example of a purposeful 'enterprise association'.[131] Resource allocations through markets are different. The adjustments of markets certainly reflect individual decisions, but these decisions are neither coordinated nor deliberately directed towards some overall consciously framed goal. And, significantly, in market transactions, there is no expectation of fiduciary obligations. Each participant's actions are generally directed, and understood by other participants to be directed, towards a purely economic end, not a moral one. As Collingwood suggests:

> As opposed to moral action, economic action is not affected by the idea of duty or moral obligation. That there are actions into which this idea does not enter is generally admitted. To invest money in a stock chosen for its promise of good dividends, or to obey a law or other command for fear of punishment may be right or wrong when judged by moral standards; but such actions can be done, and frequently are done, without the agent's raising any moral issue whatever. It may be argued by a rigid moralist that no one ought to invest money in a concern without asking whether he ought to do so; which would involve inquiring into its aims and methods of doing business, and satisfying himself that they are morally praiseworthy; but no one will suggest that this inquiry is one which investors always, or as such, undertake.[132]

That corporate allocation decisions, unlike the uncoordinated allocation of resources effected through market transactions, are the product of deliberative

[130] I am referring here to private actors only rather than governments. Of course, as discussed in Chapter 6, one may characterize the firm as a hub or nexus of contracts. The employment relationship need not be seen as one involving orders and obedience but rather as a contractual relationship in which an employee contractually agrees, during the term of the contract, to carry out the employer's reasonable directions. But this characterization simply shifts the form of the question. One must still ask why is some productive activity organized in which these longer-term service contracts are used rather than individual agreements for services.

[131] Michael Oakeshott, *On Human Conduct* (Clarendon Press 1975) 114.

[132] Collingwood (n 44) 164.

human action becomes especially significant as the size and impact of corporations grow. As Adolf Berle had observed more than seventy years ago, a key change represented by the emergence of the largest mega corporations of the twentieth century was that the resource allocation decisions of such enterprises could have profound consequences on the entire industries of which they were a part and the communities in which they operated. So significant was this power, in Berle's view, that 'Mid twentieth-century capitalism has been given the power and the means of more or less planned economy, in which decisions are or at least can be taken in the light of their probable effect on the whole community'.[133] Berle's view echoes earlier suggestions by Keynes and Marx that emergence of the modern large corporation may, paradoxically, represent a tendency of modern capitalist systems to socialize themselves.[134]

Within collective enterprises such as corporations, conflicts among participants will be inevitable, and rules to resolve those conflicts essential. In the case of business corporations, those rules include imposing fiduciary obligations on directors and managers and providing voting rights to shareholders. We will have more to say in later chapters about the accommodation of disparate interests within the typical corporate structure that formally accords voting rights to shareholders alone. Here we only suggest that the firms would not have proliferated in the absence of sufficient confidence in the leaders of those firms—typically the directors and officers[135]—to serve the interests of those firms faithfully. And as Gorton and Zentefis have recently argued,[136] the culture of the firm (a 'system of shared norms and values formed inside the firm'[137] in no small part through the actions and decisions of managers together with interactions between managers and employees) becomes 'the glue that binds employees together and directs their collective behaviour at work'.[138] The enduring success of the corporation may thus be seen as a tacit endorsement of faith in human loyalty: of faith in faithfulness itself. Without such faith, business would be impossible and life, largely unbearable.

Yet embedded within the corporate strength that comes from the institutional loyalty of directors and officers there may be a latent weakness as well.

[133] Adolf A Berle, *The 20th Century Capitalist Revolution* (Harcourt, Brace & World Inc 1954) 35.
[134] See Marx (n 11) and Keynes (n 11).
[135] Throughout this book I distinguish between directors (members of the board) and officers (senior managers including, for example, the CEO and CFO), although corporate statutes in some jurisdictions may, as a technical matter, define the term 'officer' to include a director. See eg UK Companies Act 2006, s. 1173(1).
[136] Gary B Gorton and Alexander K Zentefis, 'Corporate Culture as a Theory of the Firm' (2024) 91 Economica 1391.
[137] ibid.
[138] ibid.

As Holmström and Kaplan have argued, it may be that while corporations are highly effective at allocating capital in the case of ongoing business activities, such firms may be less effective when circumstances demand that capital must be shifted from declining (sunset) industries to emerging (sunrise) industries. That fact may, for reasons they explain, account in a significant way for the 'break up' merger wave that occurred in the United States in the 1980s.[139] Thus the very loyalty essential to the success of the corporation as an institution may, paradoxically, create the conditions for the proliferation of disruptive market transactions.

## Conclusion

Alfred Chandler, in his famous study of the modern business corporation, makes the case that with improving technology and growing markets, the administrative coordination under a managerial hierarchy proved a more profitable means of allocating resources than the market.[140] Then, once such hierarchies became established, 'the hierarchy itself became a source of permanence, power and continued growth.'[141] Significantly, he argues that professional managers chose policies that 'favored the long-term stability and growth of their enterprises to those that maximized current profits'.[142]

The allocation of resources through the market may reflect the aggregate impact of uncurated self-interested human interaction. Within the corporation, however, outcomes reflect concerted human action. Yet, it is not the action, or the will, of the 'members' of the corporation (or of any other corporate stakeholders) that defines the corporate mandate. Rather, it is the directors and officers whose duty it is to discern, define, and then serve that collective will. As we will explore in later chapters, this institutional structure could lead to a kind of separation of ownership and conscience, such that the corporation could well serve as a device for insulating corporate decision-making from the compassionate instincts of its shareholders and so leading it to function as a 'vice amplifier,' shamelessly acting as a structurally-delegated instrument

[139] Bengt Holmström and Steven N Kaplan, 'Corporate Governance and Merger Activity in the United States: Making Sense of the 1980s and 1990s' (2001) 15 The Journal of Economic Perspectives 121.

[140] This reference to the relative costs of firms and markets has obvious similarities to Coase. One curious minor error in Chandler's book is that he misidentifies the earlier author as 'Richard' (rather than 'Ronald') Coase. See Alfred D Chandler Jr, *The Visible Hand: The Managerial Revolution in American Business* (Belknap Press 1977) 515 n 3.

[141] ibid 8.

[142] ibid 10.

to absolve shareholders of moral accountability while performing their lucrative 'dirty work'[143] with impunity. But there is a more sanguine alternative. If, instead, the effect of conscious human deliberation in the form of managerial decision-making actually refines and rehabilitates baser animating interests of shareholders, then the corporation may not only be the great producer of societal wealth but could also emerge as one of the most powerful civilizing forces in the modern world.

The corporate profit motive and its implications for the relationship between the corporation, its directors and its shareholders has evolved in the economic, management, and legal literature. There are both definitional and conceptual ambiguities about the concept of profit and the economic function of the corporation that are rarely explored or even referred to in judicial decisions. These ambiguities have led, at times, to lack of clarity. The relationship between corporate law and corporate management practices is dynamic, iterative, and reflexive. Although there have long been important debates about the extent to which corporate law should be regarded as mandatory or merely enabling,[144] even those who regard corporate law as largely devoid of any significant mandatory rules or restrictions would acknowledge that the goal of corporate law is to enhance the net socially beneficial effects of business operations. It is for corporate managers to conduct those business operations in accordance with internalized principles and expertise that are part of the craft of business management, a craft which precedes legislative and judicial intervention. Economists who theorize about the role and function of the business corporation rarely advert to the fact that corporations are created, and must operate, within a specific legal framework that may or may not adhere to the supposed economic theory of the firm. For this reason, among others, the seminal conjoining of legal and economic perspectives in Adolf Berle and Gardiner Means's[145] analysis of the large American publicly-traded corporation and the resulting enriched understanding of the role and duties of corporate managers represented an important milestone in the study of the corporate phenomenon. We turn to consider key implications of their landmark contribution in chapter 3.

[143] Roland Bénabou and Jean Tirole, 'Individual and Corporate Social Responsibility' (2010) 77 Economica 1, 4. See also Barry M Mitnick, *Fiduciary Rationality and Public Policy: The Theory of Agency and Some Consequences* (American Political Science Association 1973) https://doi.org/10.2139/ssrn.1020859.

[144] See eg Bernard Black, 'Is Corporate Law Trivial?' (1990) 84(2) Northwestern University Law Review 542.

[145] Adolf A Berle and Gardiner Means, *The Modern Corporation and Private Property* (Macmillan 1933).

# 3

# The 'Berle-and-Means Spirited' Corporation

## Introduction

It was a remarkable book, produced through an unusual writing partnership. The lead author was a brilliant young lawyer; his co-author, an even (slightly) younger economist. Their collaboration over roughly a four-year period from 1927 to 1931 culminated in the 1932 publication of what would become the most famous book on corporate law ever written in the English language: *The Modern Corporation and Private Property*.[1] And its authors, Adolf Berle and Gardiner Means, would become household names among corporate law scholars and economists for generations.

## Ripley (Believe It or Not)

*The Modern Corporation and Private Property* had been funded by a 1927 Social Science Research Council and Laura Spelman Rockefeller Foundation grant to study US corporations. This grant had been obtained with the assistance of Harvard economics professor William Z. Ripley.[2] Ripley had, in important ways, already laid the foundation for Berle and Means's work with his own 1927 book *Main Street and Wall Street*.[3] Ripley had expressed significant misgivings about the rise of the corporate form—not simply the growth of large corporations, but also the extraordinary proliferation of the corporate institution itself as a preferred form of American business enterprise. He traced historical American wariness of the corporate form back more than a century,

[1] Adolf A Berle and Gardiner Means, *The Modern Corporation and Private Property* (Transaction Publishers 1991, originally published in 1932).

[2] Andrew Smith, Kevin D Tennent, and Jason Russell, 'Berle and Means's *The Modern Corporation and Private Property*: The Military Roots of a Stakeholder Model of Corporate Governance'(2019) 42 Seattle Law Review 535, 550.

[3] William Z Ripley, *Main Street and Wall Street* (Little, Brown, and Co 1927).

*Corporate Governance and Enlightened Fiduciaries*. Christopher C. Nicholls, Oxford University Press.
 DOI: 10.1093/9780198904199.003.0003

quoting the following passage from the 1820 work of early American economist Daniel Raymond:

> Every moneyed corporation is prima facie injurious to the national wealth, and ought to be looked upon by those who have no money with jealousy and suspicion. They are, and ought to be, considered as artificial engines of power, contrived by the rich for the purpose of increasing their already too great ascendancy and calculated to destroy that natural equality among men which no government ought to lend its power in destroying. The tendency of such institutions is to cause a more unequal division of property and a greater inequality among men than would otherwise take place.[4]

Ripley chronicled the unprecedented proliferation of American corporations. He particularly lamented what he saw as the insidious effect of reckless state competition for corporate charters.[5] Such charter-mongering, in his view, had led to a disturbing statutory laxity that had facilitated the increasing power of corporate managers 'to function in practical independence of the shareholding body'[6] by, among other things, issuing shares without extending 'traditional' pre-emptive rights to existing shareholders.[7] Ripley's *Main Street and Wall Street* thus provided a sort of prologue to *The Modern Corporation and Private Property*'s probe into the legal and economic implications of the evolution of the American publicly traded corporation.

## The Authors

The lawyer member of *The Modern Corporation and Private Property* writing team was Adolf Berle, for whom an academic appointment (which he obtained at the Columbia Law School in 1927) had been prescribed as a necessary precondition to receipt of the grant that was to fund the project.[8] Gardiner Means

[4] Daniel Raymond, *Thoughts on Political Economy* (Fielding Lucas Jr (ed), 1820) 427. The link drawn by Raymond between trading corporations (or, as he called them, 'money corporations') and increasing economic inequality seems especially prescient. In the passage immediately before the paragraph quoted by Ripley, Raymond had written: 'The very object of a money corporation, is to give to the members an artificial power, which they would not otherwise possess, or to exempt them from some liability, to which they would be subject, but for the act of incorporation. The very object then of the act of incorporation is to produce inequality, either in rights, or in the division of property.'

[5] Ripley (n 3) 28–37.

[6] ibid 43.

[7] ibid 38 ff.

[8] Fenner Stewart Jr, 'Berle's Conception of Shareholder Primacy: A Forgotten Perspective for Reconsideration during the Rise of Finance' (2011) 34 Seattle University Law Review 1457, 1467.

was an economist and a friend of Berle. The two had met during military training shortly after enlisting following the entry of the United States into the First World War in 1917.[9] A graduate of the Harvard Business School, Means had only recently begun a PhD programme at Harvard when his collaboration with Berle began. Berle, something of a prodigy, had matriculated at Harvard College at the age of 14, and had graduated from Harvard Law School at the age of 21—becoming the second youngest graduate in the law school's history.[10] Thus, although Means was only about a year younger than Berle, Berle was at the time of the project very much the senior academic 'partner'. Indeed, Means has sometimes been described as little more than Berle's research assistant on this project, although Berle himself did not appear to minimize his co-author's role. Berle would, of course, gain national prominence shortly after the publication of *The Modern Corporation and Private Property* as a member of US presidential candidate Franklin Delano Roosevelt's 'Brain Trust'.[11] And his long and much-storied academic career has since made him an iconic figure.

## 'Almost Worth Suppressing'

*The Modern Corporation and Private Property* was considered controversial at the time of its initial release. As Berle explained some years later, the work was originally considered 'so dangerous as to almost be worth suppressing'.[12] But once in print under the imprint of its permanent publisher,[13] its impact became apparent in very short order. Writing in 1935, Ben W. Lewis said that 'few books in this century have occasioned a stir in economic and legal circles comparable to that produced by *The Modern Corporation and Private Property*'.[14] Benjamin Graham and David Dodd's classic 1934 value investing treatise,

[9] Smith, Tennent, and Russell (n 2) 548.

[10] 'Young Prodigy Graduates' *New York Times* (7 June 1916) 11. This story also states that the youngest graduate in Harvard Law School's history was Louis Brandeis, a feat made somewhat easier for Brandeis as the Harvard Law School degree in Brandeis' day could be completed in two years rather than three.

[11] See eg Robert B Thompson, 'Adolf Berle During the New Deal: The Brain Truster as an Intellectual Jobber' (2019) 42 Seattle University Law Review 663. Despite the role played by Berle in Roosevelt's election campaign, he did not have a formal role in Roosevelt's administration.

[12] Adolf Berle, 'Modern Functions of the Corporate System' (1962) 62 Columbia Law Review 433, 434.

[13] The book was originally published by Commerce Clearing House, an affiliate of the Corporation Trust Company. According to Berle, when the original publisher discovered 'the viper they had nourished in their corporate bosom', it suspended publication. The book was subsequently published by The Macmillan Company. See Berle (n 12) 434.

[14] Ben W Lewis, 'Berle and Means on the Modern Corporation' (1935) 43 Journal of Political Economy 548.

*Security Analysis*,[15] refers to Berle and Means's then recent book as a 'significant work',[16] although ultimately Graham and Dodd's view of the role and importance of the corporate shareholder was rather more robust than Berle and Means's (or perhaps, judged from Berle and Means's world perspective, merely more old-fashioned).

The book has continued to be a source of spirited debate. Both the methodology and certain key conclusions of its authors have been challenged, in particular by some law and economics scholars.[17] Yet none of these criticisms appears to have diminished the continuing influence of what may very well be the most widely read book ever written on the American corporation. Certainly, few works of corporate law scholarship have enjoyed a more enduring and influential legacy.

## Berle and Means's Fundamental Propositions

*The Modern Corporation and Private Property* is principally remembered today for two fundamental propositions: first, that the unprecedented size of America's largest publicly traded corporations had implications for our understanding of their role within the economic system, and perhaps of the functioning of the economic system itself;[18] and, secondly, that because the shareholders of the publicly traded shares of these large corporations were so widely dispersed, such corporations had come to be characterized by a

[15] Benjamin Graham and David Dodd, *Security Analysis* (McGraw-Hill Company Inc 1934).

[16] ibid 509.

[17] George Stigler, for example, quipped that: '[Berle and Means] planted once and for all the idea that the two hundred largest corporations in America are bigger than the other biggest corporations.' Quoted in Edmund W Kitch, 'The Fire of Truth: A Remembrance of Law and Economics at Chicago, 1932-1970' (1983) 26(1) The Journal of Law and Economics 163, 174. Stigler, however, was in no doubt about the significant influence of the book, noting that: 'It has entered into the culture in a way that could probably never be fully eradicated.' Brian Cheffins and Steven Bank have challenged the notion that American corporations really did undergo a separation of ownership and control in the way and in the time period documented by Berle and Means. See Brian Cheffins and Steven Bank, 'Is Berle and Means Really a Myth?' (2009) 83 Business History Review 444. This latter conclusion is also echoed by Lipartito and Morri: see Kenneth Lipartito and Yukomiko Morri, 'Rethinking the Separation of Ownership from Management in American History' (2010) 33 Seattle University Law Review 1025; and Eric Hilt, 'The "Berle and Means Corporation" in Historical Perspective' (2019) 42 Seattle University Law Review 417.

[18] Yet, although Adolf Berle was acutely aware of the potential dangers of the concentration of economic power within large American corporations, he never wavered in his recognition that the American economic system had resulted in the greatest prosperity gains ever achieved in human history. See eg Adolf A Berle, *The 20th Century Capitalist Revolution* (Harcourt Brace & World Inc 1954) 10–11: '[American capitalism's] economic achievement is unsurpassed. Taking all elements (including human freedom) into account, its system of distributing benefits, though anything but perfect, has nevertheless left every other system in recorded history immeasurably far behind.'

'separation of ownership and control', which effectively freed corporate managers from any effective oversight and called for a conceptual re-evaluation of certain traditional concepts of property and corporate law. The latter observation has become so closely identified with the authors that the publicly traded corporation with widely dispersed shareholders is sometimes referred to today as 'the Berle-Means corporation'.[19]

Berle and Means were not the first commentators to recognize the emerging phenomenon of the 'separation of ownership and control' in the large, publicly traded business corporation where numerous and widely dispersed shareholders had become rationally apathetic *rentiers*,[20] with neither the knowledge nor the practical means to challenge decisions taken by a corporation's directors and senior managers. A decade before the publication of *The Modern Corporation and Private Property*, for example, Frank Knight had identified as the 'most important characteristic' of the corporation, 'the combination of diffused ownership with concentrated control'.[21] Thorstein Veblen, too, as early as 1904, asserted that 'the nucleus of the modern corporate capitalization is the immaterial goods covered by the common stock. This method of capitalization, therefore effects a somewhat thoroughgoing separation between the management and the ownership of the industrial equipment'.[22] And, a generation before Berle and Means, Alfred Marshall's 1890 *Principles of Economics* noted the rising significance of publicly traded corporations[23] and recognized the separation of residual risk bearing and control within those corporations.[24]

Conversely, some commentators have argued that, as an empirical matter, the extent to which ownership and control had separated in large American corporations by the time of Berle and Means's work is debatable, depending on

[19] Brian Cheffins credits Harvard law professor Mark Roe with coining this term in his 1991 article, 'A Political Theory of American Corporate Finance' (1991) 91 Columbia Law Review 10, 11. See Brian R Cheffins, 'The Rise and Fall (?) of the Berle-Means Corporation' (2018) 42 Seattle University Law Review 445, 446 n 3.

[20] Edward Mason in 1959 had characterized the shareholder of the modern corporation as a passive '*rentier*'. See Edward Mason, 'Introduction' in Edward Mason (ed), *The Corporation in Modern Society* (Harvard University Press 1960) 1, 2. See also Paddy Ireland, 'Defending the *Rentier*: Corporate Theory and the Re-Privatization of the Public Company' in John Parkinson and others (eds), *The Political Economy of the Company* (Hart Publishing 2001).

[21] Frank H Knight, *Risk, Uncertainty, and Profit* (Houghton Mifflin 1921) pt III, ch X.

[22] Thorstein Veblen, *Theory of Business Enterprise* (Charles Scribner's Sons 1904) 158.

[23] See Alfred Marshall, *Principles of Economics*, (MacMillan and Co 1890) Book IV, ch XII, 363–64: '[f]rom the end of the Middle Ages to the present time there has been a movement of constantly increasing force toward the substitution of public joint stock companies, the shares of which can be sold to anybody in the open market, for private companies, the shares in which are not transferable without the leave of all concerned.'

[24] ibid 364: 'The ultimate undertakers of the risks incurred by a joint stock company are the shareholders; but as a rule they do not take much active part in engineering the business and controlling its general policy; and they take no part in superintending its details.'

what percentage of ownership interest might realistically be thought to represent effective control.[25]

Some technical matters in Berle and Means's work may be subject to criticism, too, but, as Cheffins and Bank have argued,[26] the central insight of their book remains useful and important. Berle and Means made an influential contribution to twentieth-century corporate governance literature by compiling a statistical picture illustrating the size of American corporations, the dispersion of share ownership, and the concentration of economic power. They also provided both an extended analysis of the phenomenon of the separation of corporate ownership and control and a thoughtful and provocative consideration of the implications of this separation for law and public policy.

For our purposes, there are three particularly noteworthy aspects of *The Modern Corporation and Private Property*. First, by documenting the basis on which one might reasonably infer that the diverging interests of managers and shareholders could be a defining feature of the large, public corporation, the book laid the foundation for what economists decades later would articulate as agency theory.[27] Secondly, the book provided a novel analysis of the concept and role of profit in a corporate-dominated economic system of divided ownership and control, an analysis that is relevant to a proper understanding of the pecuniary objects of the corporation, as explored later in Chapters 4 and 5. Finally, Berle and Means explored a potentially transformative idea, namely that one implication of the separation of ownership and control in the large corporation is that it has 'placed the community in a position to demand that the modern corporation served not alone the owners or the control [ie the groups that have practical control over the corporation] but all society'.[28] This latter idea, that by severing the traditional link between the corporation and the owners of its equity shares, a corporation might be imbued with a purpose that transcends the enhancement of shareholder value, is particularly intriguing. It offers a provocative counterpoint to the narrower shareholder-oriented view of corporate directors' responsibilities that had been advanced

[25] Hilt (n 17) 433.
[26] Cheffins and Bank (n 17).
[27] The application of agency theory to the corporate law context is usually associated with the publication of Michael Jensen and William Meckling's 1976 article. See Michael Jensen and William Meckling, 'Theory of the Firm: Managerial Behavior, Agency Costs and Ownership Structure' (1976) 3 Journal of Financial Economics 305. However, prior to Jensen and Meckling's work, Stephen Ross's seminal paper on agency theory also adverted to the characterization of the relationship between corporate managers and shareholders in agency terms: '[w]here adequate contingent markets do not exist, the manager of the firm is essentially an agent of the shareholders.' See Stephen A Ross, 'The Economic Theory of Agency: The Principal's Problem' (1973) 63 The American Economic Review 134, 138.
[28] Berle and Means (n 1) 312.

by Berle himself in his famous *Harvard Law Review* exchange with Harvard law professor E. Merrick Dodd, as discussed further in Chapter 4.

## Corporate Powers as Powers in Trust

Berle and Means's book did include a version of this traditional argument about the proper shareholder-oriented object of corporate power similar to the position defended by Berle in his contemporaneous debate with Dodd. Corporate powers, according to this argument, were to be understood as 'powers in trust', 'necessarily and at all times exercisable only for the ratable benefit of all the shareholders as their interest appears'.[29] Yet Berle and Means recognized that leading corporate lawyers of their day had come to a rather different view of the matter. This opposing view held that 'corporate development has created a new set of relationships, giving to the groups in control powers which are absolute and not limited by any implied obligation with respect to their use'.[30] Although Berle and Means did not endorse such unrestricted power, they did suggest that, by surrendering both control and responsibility over the corporation, passive shareholders of large, widely held corporations could be said to have also simultaneously surrendered the right to demand that the corporation be operated in their interests alone.

In his law review exchange with Dodd, Berle had initially argued in support of a narrow version of shareholder primacy premised on the notion that it would be unwise and impractical to relax directors' presumed duty to serve shareholders' interests alone, absent some reliable method of ensuring the enforceability of any purported duty to serve the interests of some larger body of corporate constituents. He thus rejected Dodd's contention that corporate managers ought rightly to balance the interests of multiple corporate stakeholders. Berle's emphasis in his interchange with Dodd on the rights of shareholders may be seen as an interstitial or temporary position[31]—the only feasible approach until a redefinition of legal structures that would allow for achievement of the ultimate goal, as envisioned by Berle and Means: that is, of a corporation that serves neither managers' nor shareholders' interests

[29] ibid 220.

[30] ibid 311.

[31] ibid 312: 'Rigid enforcement of property rights as a temporary protection against plundering by control would not stand in the way of the modification of these rights in the interests of other groups. When a convincing system of community obligations is worked out and is generally accepted, in that moment the passive property right of today must yield before the larger interests of society.'

exclusively but one which is rather an important social institution. In effect, managers committed to shareholder primacy would function as a kind of 'vanguard of the *proprietariat*'.

Berle and Means's work offered an important and nuanced qualification to the narrow position Berle had advanced in his exchange with Dodd in which he had emphasized the trustee-like responsibilities of corporate directors. Their modified approach became an important forerunner not only of economic agency theory but also of modern calls for 'stakeholder capitalism' and corporate social responsibility, a topic to which we will return in Chapter 7.

## Implications of the Separation of Ownership and Control

The separation of ownership and control in the modern, large, publicly traded corporation held the promise for Berle and Means of a new potential era for the corporation. Once both the traditional 'logic of property' and the 'logic of profits' had been discarded as no longer fit for purpose in the modern corporate age, the path had been cleared for an eventual conceptual reconfiguring of the business corporation. T Corporate controllers could one day be freed from the legal obligation and investor expectation to operate in the interests of shareholders alone. They would become, instead, a 'purely neutral technocracy, balancing a variety of claims by various groups in the community and assigning to each a position of the income stream on the basis of public policy rather than private cupidity'.[32]

## The Uniqueness of the Shareholder's Position

Berle and Means's analysis represented an important stage in the evolution of thought about the corporation as an engine of prosperity and a forum for the resolution of competing economic and social interests. Severing the bond of constitutive identity between shareholders and the corporations in which they held shares had gradually been recognized as a practical reality, an economic necessity, and a legal inevitability. The original concept of the English business corporation was that the shareholders were not merely passive providers of capital: they were the very members of the corporation. It was they who became incorporated and thus constituted the corporate entity. 'Company'

[32] ibid 312–13.

was a collective noun that referred to the company of shareholders, in general meeting. However, by the time of the modern Berle–Means corporation, such a concept was not only legally misdescriptive, it was also fanciful. In fact, as Oliver Williamson would later note, it was certainly not the shareholders of the large corporation that identified themselves with the firm. Rather, it was 'management [that] is often encouraged, for good reason, to think of itself and the firm as one'.[33]

Yet, there is a very real risk in cultivating a sense of firm identification among a corporation's controllers. It is the risk that arises when the human virtues of cooperation and loyalty are misapplied or misdirected to an inappropriate end. Loyalty is a powerful norm. It is also potentially a dangerous one. While we want directors to be 'loyal' to the corporations they serve, there is an inherent danger that their loyalty may come to be directed, instead, to their fellow directors or the corporation's senior managers, even in circumstances when that loyalty does not serve the interests of the corporation, the shareholders, or any other socially beneficial goal. We are all too sadly familiar with some unscrupulous chief executive officers' apparent definition of 'integrity': a person who will never lie *to* me, but will always lie *for* me. Similarly, an employee who is unreservedly honest may find that their genuine loyalty to the corporation and its success as an entity is derided by corporate colleagues. Such an employee, paradoxically, may even come to be regarded as lacking in integrity if she cannot be 'trusted' to follow without question dishonourable orders and to conceal without reservation the nefarious secrets of senior managers who demand and value personal loyalty from their subordinates above all else.

The Berle-Means identification of the separation of ownership and control therefore became the foundation for two important and distinct perspectives on corporate governance. First, by recognizing the possibility that self-serving corporate officers and directors may behave opportunistically in the absence of any effective oversight by the corporation's 'owners', this framework prompted the exploration of intra-firm incentives. Intra-firm incentives underlie economic agency costs theory and the characterization of corporate officers and directors as economic agents who are tempted to pursue their own interests in enjoying perquisites and leisure at the expense of the corporation's shareholders, albeit subject to significant but ultimately imperfect market constraints.

But that is not the whole story. By characterizing the reorientation of the shareholders' relationship with the corporation as a voluntary relinquishing

[33] Oliver E Williamson, *The Economic Institutions of Capitalism* (The Free Press 1985) 313.

by shareholders of any claim to conventional proprietary rights or privileges in exchange for the liquidity offered by tradable shares, together with immunity from the corporation's debts, the Berle and Means framework also bolstered arguments of later progressive scholars that the interests of corporate shareholders—financial or otherwise—were undeserving of the singular focus of the corporation's directors. The corporation was not an incorporated collective of its shareholders, and shareholders were neither legally nor economically the 'owners' of the corporation. They were merely providers of one corporate input—equity capital—an input no more essential to the corporation's operations than labour, credit, raw materials, or, for that matter, the convenience and benefit of public roads, hospitals, schools, and other elements of government-funded infrastructure upon which all modern businesses had come to depend. Corporate directors could certainly not ignore shareholders who should reasonably expect a 'reasonable' or 'just' return on their capital.[34] But no additional obligation to maximize shareholder wealth or value was either owed or should be expected.

As we will discuss further in Chapter 6, neoclassical economists would later seek to distinguish the unique nature of the shareholders' interests from those of other corporate stakeholders and so to justify the fact that shareholders enjoyed the exclusive right to elect the corporation's directors and should indeed rightfully expect to be the principal beneficiaries of the directors' fiduciary duties.[35] Shareholders, it was argued, were stakeholders like no others. Their position was more precarious than that of other corporate constituents. Unlike

[34] 'Reasonable' profits, as Adolf Berle wryly noted some sixty years ago, are the 'twentieth-century lawyer's parallel to canon-law thinking of the Middle Ages, when ethical considerations—notably that of a "just price"—were the imperatives.' See Adolf Berle, 'Foreword' in Edward S Mason, *The Corporation in Modern Society* (Harvard University Press 1959) ix, xii. See also Raymond de Roover, 'The Concept of the Just Price: Theory and Economic Policy' (1958) 18 Journal of Economic History 41;and Hayek's related discussion of 'reasonable wages', a concept which he also links to the 'futile medieval search for the just price and the just wage': Friederich A Hayek, *Law Legislation and Liberty*, Vol 2 *The Mirage of Social Justice* (University of Chicago Press 1976) 75.

[35] The fact that shareholders alone elect the corporation's directors has been recognized as the most practical constraint on any expectation that directors would sincerely and concertedly pursue the interests of any other stakeholders or a broader social interest in the absence of express mandates to do so such as those contained in the articles of benefit corporations. See eg Leo E Strine Jr, 'The Dangers of Denial: The Need for a Clear-Eyed Understanding of the Power and Accountability Structure Established by the Delaware General Corporation Law' (2015) 50 Wake Forest Law Review 76. The Berle–Means approach must, however, be revisited in light of the important changes that have recently occurred in institutional share ownership and shareholder activism: the phenomenon former Delaware Supreme Court Chief Justice Leo Strine has cleverly described as 'the separation of ownership and ownership'. See Leo E Strine Jr, 'Toward Common Sense and Common Ground? Reflections on the Shared Interests of Managers and Labor in a More Rational System of Corporate Governance' (2007) 33 Journal of Corporation Law 1; Leo E Strine Jr, 'Can We Do Better by Ordinary Investors? A Pragmatic Reaction to the Dueling Ideological Mythologists of Corporate Law' (2014) 114 Columbia Law Review 449. We will return to these topics in Chapter 8.

creditors, employees, suppliers, and customers, shareholders had no enforceable contract with the corporation; their commitment of funds to the business was permanent and irreversible. They had no way to withdraw or credibly threaten to withdraw their financial stake in order to extract benefits or even to ensure equitable treatment. In fact, it was the very fact that their capital was 'locked-in' that was said to account in a major way for the importance and success of the corporation as a business form.[36]

Not only were shareholders 'locked-in' and so uniquely subject to the possible vagaries of managerial opportunism, but they also stood at the very end of the line of corporate financial claimants. They were the 'residual risk bearers'. They could expect to receive no return on their investment unless all those corporate stakeholders with enforceable and prior-ranking contractual claims had first been paid or otherwise provided for. By focusing upon the goal of maximizing the value of the shareholders' interests, it was argued, directors of the corporation would necessarily also protect and enhance the claims of all those prior ranking, contractually protected stakeholders, *ex hypothesi*.

But did shareholders genuinely face materially greater risk than other corporate stakeholders? That claim was disputed by opponents of shareholder primacy. Characterizing the shareholders of the corporation as the sole 'residual risk bearers' and the interest holders most closely identified with the corporate entity itself seemed to some commentators to strain credulity. Surely, some argued, in most corporations it is the rank and file employees who must bear the residual risk of the firm's failure in at least as significant a way as the shareholders. And the identification of employees with the company that employed them was certainly no less proximate than that of the company's shareholders. As Gower had once noted, 'the employees are members of the company for which they work to a far greater extent than are the shareholders whom the

[36] Henry Hansmann referred to the issue of 'lock-in' in his 1996 book, *The Ownership of Enterprise* (Belknap Press of Harvard University Press 1996) 55. The phrase 'capital lock-in' was used by Margaret Blair in her article 'Locking in Capital: What Corporate Law Achieved for Business Organizers in the Nineteenth Century' (2003) UCLA Law Review 387. The concept is functionally similar to the notion of 'affirmative asset partitioning', a concept coined by Henry Hansmann and Reinier Kraakman in Henry Hansmann and Reinier Kraakman, 'The Essential Role of Organizational Law' (2000) 110 Yale Law Journal 387. See also Lynn Stout, 'On the Nature of Corporations' [2005] University of Illinois Law Review 253. Indeed, it has been suggested that this sort of asset partitioning or capital lock-in is more fundamental to corporate law than limited liability. Limited liability, at least with respect to voluntary creditors, could be achieved contractually, albeit at significant cost. Locking-in shareholder capital and insulating corporate capital from the claims of shareholders' creditors requires organizational law. Although Hansmann and Kraakman have provided a detailed explication of this point, it is noteworthy that the English corporate law scholar LCB Gower made a similar general observation several years earlier. See LCB Gower, *Gower's Principles of Modern Company Law* (5th edn, Sweet & Maxwell 1992) 23. The concept and significance of capital 'lock-in' is discussed further in Chapter 6.

law insists in regarding as its proprietors.'[37] Nor did the fact that employees enjoyed contractual rights not available to shareholders dissuade the critics of shareholder primacy. Information asymmetries, power imbalances, lack of employee mobility because of family and other personal circumstances, and the cultivation of firm-specific, non-transferable job skills were all said to tilt the employee/employer contracting process profoundly in favour of the corporate employer.

Alternative justifications or rationalizations were offered for the exclusive rights of shareholders' in Delaware and in many other jurisdictions worldwide to elect directors and thus, incidentally, to expect their interests to be exclusively or primarily championed at the boardroom table. Shareholders, as Hansmann noted, were alone among corporate stakeholders in having homogeneity of interests: namely, the shared desire to maximize wealth.[38] Traditionally, it has been contended that allowing other constituents, for example employees, to elect directors would create irresolvable conflicts of interest. As we will discuss in Chapter 7, the premise of homogeneity of shareholder interests has been challenged by those who argue that it should not be assumed that shareholders' preferences are limited to maximizing their financial interests alone.[39] Shareholders may well have diverse preferences as to the way corporations in which they invest are managed. And progressive scholars have maintained that the relative permanence of employees and their significant personal identification with their corporate employers also belie the claim that giving employees a right to elect directors would lead to an irreconcilable conflict of interest. It is commonly noted by critics of the notion that shareholders alone should enjoy the right to elect directors that certain jurisdictions, such as Germany, adopt a co-determination model of governance that requires employee representatives to be members of the supervisory boards of certain of the largest corporations. But the German co-determination model has not been immune from criticism,[40]and it seems unlikely that it offers a governance model that merits universal adoption.

[37] Quoted by Williamson (n 33) 300.

[38] 'Investor-owned firms have the important advantage that their owners generally share a single well-defined objective: to maximize the net present value of the firm's earnings. The costs of collective decision making are thus relatively low for investor-owned firms.' See Hansmann (n 36) 62. Hansmann also notes that this feature of homogeneity 'is neither is neither a necessity nor an accident, but instead the product of design': ibid 63.

[39] See eg Oliver Hart and Luigi Zingales, 'The New Corporate Governance' (2022) 1 University of Chicago Business Law Review 195.

[40] See eg Charles M Elson, Craig K Ferrere, and Nicholas J Gossen, 'The Bug at Volkswagen: Lessons in Co-Determination, Ownership, and Board Structure' (2015) 27(4) Journal of Applied Corporate Finance 36.

Homogeneity of interests was not the only basis upon which economists argued that shareholders merited special board representation and protection. It was also claimed that the firm-specificity of the shareholders' investment justified this preferred status.[41]

Oliver Williamson's analysis of board representation, for example, turns mainly on the extent to which a corporate constituency may be said to have made a firm-specific investment. That is, the greater the degree to which those assets contributed to a corporation by a stakeholder (whether represented by human or financial capital) are not redeployable, the stronger the case for that stakeholder to be given board representation. It might seem, on a superficial analysis, that shareholders in a publicly traded corporation do not have a significant enough connection to the firm to justify the privileged position they enjoy as the exclusive electors of the board of directors and, perhaps most importantly, that such shareholders enjoy easy avenues of exit. One of the most important attributes of a shareholder's interest in a public corporation is, after all, the liquidity of tradable shares? However, Williamson argues that the apparently limited stake that shareholders have in corporations (given, among other things, the relative ease with which they can sell their shares on public markets and so exit the firm) arises from the 'fallacy of composition'.[42] Although individual shareholders may enjoy avenues of exit, shareholders *as a group* do not, and it is only as a group that one may properly analyse the true relationship of shareholders to the firm. That relationship is unique in that: 'They are the only voluntary constituency whose relation to the corporation does not come up for periodic renewal.'[43]

So it is, at least in Williamson's view, that the board of directors of a corporation 'arises endogenously' to safeguard transaction-specific investments from expropriation and, for that reason, 'the board of directors should be seen as a governance instrument of the stockholders'.[44] Needless to say, there are many

[41] As Williamson points out, it may at first seem that the tradability of shares makes the argument that share interests are firm specific seem implausible. But this objection, he argues, is owing to the fallacy of composition. See Williamson (n 33) 304, and text following n 42 below.

[42] ibid 304.

[43] Ibid 304.

[44] ibid 306. One sometimes overlooked aspect of Williamson's approach is that its premises are in direct conflict with the premises underlying one of the most foundational building blocks of modern financial theory to be discussed in Chapter 9: the Modigliani-Miller capital irrelevance theorem. As Williamson points out, his approach emphasizes the significance of asset-specific investment. A firm will be relatively more reliant upon equity financing the more its assets are less redeployable, since lenders would be comparatively unwilling to secure loans on assets that could not be readily deployable in the event of default. Thus, as he says, 'Theories of finance that do not make the asset specificity distinction predict, by contrast, that there will be no such association. The Modigliani-Miller theorem (1958), which maintains that the cost of capital is independent of the capital structure of the firm, is thus at variance with the asset specificity/governance structure approach': ibid 307. Modigliani-Miller's famous 'no arbitrage' proof of their theory (and, indeed, no arbitrage proofs in finance generally) also

competing views on the appropriate beneficiaries of corporate directors' fiduciary duties. To this important matter we will return in Chapter 6.

## Managerial Discretion and the Corporate Objective

For the moment, however, we return to search for clues to understanding the link between Berle's defence of corporate powers as powers in trust for the shareholders alone, and the more radical possibility offered in the latter pages of *The Modern Corporation and Private Property* of the corporation as a device for explicitly serving the broader public interest.

Berle may have foreseen in 1932 the complicated paradox of the modern socially responsible corporation. In 1954, decades after publication of *The Modern Corporation and Private Property*, he argued the 'corporation, almost against its will, has been compelled to assume in appreciable part the role of conscience-carrier of twentieth-century American society'.[45] Nor was Berle entirely enthusiastic about this prospect. As he put it: 'Our ancestors feared that corporations had no conscience. We are treated to the colder, more modern fear that, perhaps, they do.'[46]

Enjoying the near 'absolute power' that the business judgment rule offers honest directors of at least reasonable diligence in the modern American corporation, it is very possible that at least some and perhaps many directors of post-war corporations may have been inclined simultaneously to seek public approbation and private reward by making disingenuous claims of magnanimous corporate public service, while stealthily focusing primarily upon shareholder value instead. Years later, shielded by the same legal protections afforded by the business judgment rule but now more vulnerable, perhaps, to the potentially career-ending junk bond-fuelled 'market for corporate control', canny and compassionate directors of post-1980 corporations may well have disingenuously claimed to be unabashedly pursuing shareholder value while discreetly attending to a broader array of stakeholder and social interests. In either case, directors may very well have been seeking to do no more than what they adjudged best, for their own reputations as well as for the well-being and

depend on the proposition that financial instruments of comparable risk-adjusted return may be regarded as fungible, a proposition that does not obtain to the extent that investments are regarded as firm or asset specific.

[45] Berle (n 18) 182.
[46] ibid 184.

success of their corporations, secure in the knowledge that they would face no adverse legal consequences in any event.[47]

Could they ever be compelled to do otherwise? Can corporate law place effective boundaries on the exercise of managerial discretion? Does the duty of loyalty to which corporate directors are subject prescribe or merely proscribe? Does it merely censure the most egregious displays of conflict and self-interest or positively mandate some specific service duty that transcends the duty of care, and includes some obligation to 'maximize' (something), or, perhaps, in the view of some, to serve financial interests of some non-shareholders and non-financial interests of others.

## Mitnick's Fiduciary Paradox

The concentration of managerial power and discretion in the hands of a body electable exclusively by shareholders may lead to another rather unorthodox outcome, an outcome that reflects dangers very different from the conventional concern that managers might not be relied upon to pursue the financial interests of shareholders quite as vigorously in Berle-Means firms as in firms where managers are also proprietors. Berle and Means, and the later framers of agency theory, flagged the familiar temptation for managers to operate the corporation in their own selfish interests or perhaps in a misguided attempt to balance the competing but immeasurable interests of a number of diverse corporate stakeholders resulting in harm to shareholders' interests, a potential loss of efficiency, and a wasteful sacrifice of societal wealth. But consider an alternative possibility: perhaps the separation of ownership and control may not dampen or mitigate the shareholder-value focus of the corporation but instead actually amplify the extent to which the corporation is operated in the financial interests of shareholders, totally without regard to competing non-financial considerations to which shareholders themselves might well yield if they were able to exercise direct operational control.

This possibility was alluded to in a colourful way decades ago by Barry Mitnick, one of the original (if somewhat less celebrated) originators of agency

[47] I emphasize here that I do not speak of the reprehensible corporate officers and directors whose defalcations led to scandals such as the turn-of-the-century accounting debacles at Enron, WorldCom, Tyco, Adelphia, etc. Nor do I refer to cases in which directors may have failed in their oversight duty under circumstances where egregious risk to human life and health may also lead to financial harms to the corporation. See eg *Marchand v Barnhill*, 212 A 3d 805 (Del 2019).

theory.[48] Mitnick had settled on the use of the term 'agency' in his own economic work, at least in part because of his study of the law of agency in the course of preparing a paper he wrote in 1973.[49] Accordingly, agency may be seen as a legal term that came to have 'a role in the naming of [economic] agency theory'[50] and then, as an established economic concept, re-entered legal theory.

Mitnick's early work identified the possibility of what he termed the 'fiduciary paradox'[51] of 'fiduciary maximization', the notion that 'the maximization [by a fiduciary such as a corporate director] of the principal's [ie the shareholders'] interest will typically go beyond that point at which the principal would stop were [the principal]... acting [directly] for [the principal's]... own interest, and beyond that point at which the fiduciary agent would stop were that interest [the agent's]... own'.[52] This surprising result, he argued, may occur for a number of reasons which he illustrates with the following example drawn from the cartoonish excesses of silent screen film era villains:

> [c]onsider the archetypal situation of the villain, his henchman, and the heroine to be tied to the railroad tracks. The villain instructs his henchman to do the dirty work, and settles back with a fat cigar to wait news that the deed is done. The villain could have performed the deed himself. The henchman, being in a fiduciary relation to the villain carries out his discharge with dispatch ... By the nature of his 'contract' and the nature of the fiduciary norm, he can ignore the pleadings and possible bribery offers of the victim. Had the villain acting for himself done the job, he might have succumbed to the pleadings, the bribery, or the charms of the heroine ... It is thus clear that the fiduciary norm may play a major role in ensuring the 'efficient' consummation of many necessary acts in our society.[53]

[48] See Barry M Mitnick, 'The Theory of Agency Redux' (2021) 7(2) Academy of Management Discoveries 171, 178.

[49] Barry M Mitnick, 'Origin of the Thoery of Agency: An Account by One of the Theory's Originators' (2006) <https://sites.pitt.edu/~mitnick/agencytheory/agencytheoryoriginrev11806r.htm>..

[50] ibid.

[51] Barry M Mitnick, 'Fiduciary Rationality and Public Policy: The Theory of Agency and Some Consequences' Paper presented at the Annual Meeting of the American Political Science Association (1973), New Orleans, LA, in Proceedings of the American Political Science Association, 1973, available at SSRN: https;//ssrn.com/abstract=1020859.

[52] ibid 38.

[53] ibid 9. It goes without saying that no such acts of violence would ever be considered 'necessary' or permissible in this or any other society. But the common responses to seeming acts of business callousness or indifference—'It's business, not personal'; 'I'm just doing my job'; 'I wish I could help, but there's nothing I can do'—may be seen as milder less pathological versions of the scenario envisioned by Mitnick. An idea similar to Mitnick's in the corporate context had, indeed, been recognized many years earlier. William M Gouge, in 1835, had observed that 'As directors of a company, men will sanction actions of which they would scorn to be guilty in their private capacity.' William M Gouge, *Paper Money*

The plausibility of Mitnick's theoretical 'fiduciary paradox' has been buttressed by the behavioural research of Dana and others[54] and Hamman and others.[55] Their experiments suggest, among other things, that, although people are not invariably as selfish as the most simplistic version of the classical *homo economicus* might suggest, they frequently behave opportunistically in order that they may preserve a self-image of selflessness, while actually enjoying the benefits of purely selfish endeavours. Thus, when given the opportunity to choose to avoid acquiring knowledge about whether or not their actions are harmful to others, many people will choose to remain uninformed in order to reap the material rewards of wholly selfish actions without endangering their self-esteem. Summarizing the impact of Dana and others and the work of Hamman and others in the context of an analysis of corporate social responsibility, Nobel prize winning economist Jean Tirole and his co-author Roland Bénabou explain: 'Put differently, economic agents are eager to delegate the "dirty work" that they would not want to do themselves; somehow, not directly choosing the selfish action seems to exonerate them from what would be the logical damage to self-esteem.'[56]

Economists are familiar with certain 'separation theorems,' associated with the work of economists such as Irving Fisher[57] and James Tobin.[58] The central insight of Fisher's separation theorem, for example, is that investment decisions are, properly, independent of financing choices. Accordingly, a corporation's investments should not be affected by the individual preferences of the corporation's shareholders. As developed in the economics and finance literature, Fisher's separation theorem provides a tractable solution to the otherwise impossible task of trying to aggregate the preferences of individual shareholders.[59] That solution, at least under perfect market conditions, is for

*and Banking* (B & S Collins 1835), 17, quoted by Joel Seligman, 'A Brief History of Delaware's General Corporation Law of 1899' (1976) 1(2) Delaware Journal of Corporate Law 249, 259.

[54] J Dana, J Kuang, and R Weber, 'Exploiting moral wiggle room: experiments demonstrating an illusory preference for fairness' (2007) 33 Economic Theory 67.

[55] JR Hamman, G Loewenstein, and R Weber, 'Self-interest Through Delegation: An Additional Rationale for the Principal-Agent Relationship' (2010) 100 American Economic Review 1826.

[56] Roland Bénabou and Jean Tirole, 'Individual and Corporate Social Responsibility' (2010) 77 Economica 1, 4. See also Christine L Exley and Judd B Kessler, 'Information Avoidance and Image Concerns' (2023) 133(656) The Economic Journal 3153.

[57] Irving Fisher, *The Theory of Interest* (MacMillan 1930), 125 ff esp 136.

[58] James Tobin, 'Liquidity Preference as Behavior Towards Risk' (1958) 25 The Review of Economic Studies 65.

[59] See Eugene F Fama and Merton H Miller, *The Theory of Finance* (Dryden Press 1972) 68, citing Kenneth J Arrow, *Social Choice and Individual Values* (John Wiley & Sons Inc 1951) as the original source of this proposition and that it is otherwise impossible to combine or aggregate shareholder preferences so as to determine a valid criterion for making decisions 'in the best interests of the owners.'

corporate managers to abandon the fruitless goal of trying to discern shareholders' individual interests, and focus instead simply on seeking to maximize the market value of the corporation's shares.

Tobin's separation theorem, similarly, illustrates why investors selecting their personally optimal portfolio allocation of risk-free debt and risky securities may select the basket of securities to be included in the risky portion of their investment portfolio without regard to their individual appetite or tolerance for risk or their specific willingness to trade increased risk for greater expected return. That does not mean, of course, that all investors will be expected to hold identical investment portfolios. More risk-averse investors may choose to hold a relatively greater proportion of their total portfolio in risk-free assets and a relatively smaller proportion in a bundle of of risky securities. Conversely, investors with a greater appetite for risk will prefer to hold a relatively smaller proportion of their portfolio in risk-free securities. But the central insight of Tobin's separation theorem is that, while the relative portion of each investor's portfolio that is invested in risky securities will vary, every investor should, counterintuitively, hold the same optimal combination of risky securities (albeit in different total amounts)—at least under ideal market conditions.

The important lesson embodied in these well-known separation theorems is that investment decisions can be most efficiently made wholly independent of the individual preferences of investors (or shareholders).

The notion that a corporation's investment decisions both can and should be wholly independent of the subjective preferences of its shareholders suggests a further, albeit controversial, possibility. Shareholders of large publicly traded corporations are largely insulated from operational, financial, and ethical decisions undertaken on behalf of those corporations by directors on whom substantial, practically unlimited, discretion has been conferred. It is for this reason that a non-controlling, passive investment in the shares of a corporation could result on the part of shareholders in what might somewhat uneasily be described as a separation of ownership from conscience.[60]

That separation, however discomfiting and potentially problematic in many respects, could actually offer at least one possible advantage: the mitigation

[60] During the final editing stages of this book, I became aware of an article by James D. Nelson which also uses the term 'separation of ownership of conscience' in a similar way to what is described here. Nelson argues that such a separation in the corporate context effectively addresses the necessary conflicts in a pluralist society to allow for cooperative production within the corporation. See James D Nelson, 'The Separation of Ownership and Conscience' (2023) 48(3) The Journal of Corporation Law 577.

of a particular human cognitive bias once suggested by Hayek. Certain pro-social human instincts, he argued, that are ideally adapted to life within the small, close-knit communities of our distant ancestors—and which are still rightly valued today within the family and other small, non-anonymous social groups—can actually have unexpected and adverse outcomes in the context of larger modern societies characterized by more casual and frequently anonymous transactional interactions.[61] Investment through a corporate structure insulates corporations from such individual shareholders' preferences. These preferences in many cases reflect goodwill and genuine generosity of spirit. It is also possible, however, that in at least some cases, shareholders may be motivated by a desire to signal pro-social concern that they might otherwise happily forego in the interests of financial gain, provided their choice to do so could be concealed. In either case, corporate actions taken to accommodate shareholders' genuine or affected social concerns may, inadvertently, lead to destruction of value. Such value destruction, paradoxically, could ultimately result in harm to the very social interests individual shareholders would wish to protect.

## Conclusion

Berle and Means highlighted and focused attention upon a key defining characteristic of the large American corporation of their day. Their work would provoke debate for the decades that followed. Free from the effective oversight or discipline of widely dispersed shareholders with neither the incentive nor the means to act collectively, the directors and officers in control of large publicly traded corporations enjoyed almost unlimited discretion to direct the company's resources however they saw fit. Although directors were formally subject to the uncertainties of periodic election or re-election by shareholders, even this modest and infrequent theoretical source of accountability was rendered largely ineffective owing to the practical control incumbent managers were able to wield over the proxy voting process.

This separation of ownership and control might well be expected to lead at times to managerial nest-feathering and underperformance. That wasthe worrying prospect that featured most prominently in the later ruminations of agency theorists. But this institutional separation implied something else as

[61] Friedrich A Hayek, *Law, Legislation and Liberty*, vol 2: 'The Mirage of Social Justice' (University of Chicago Press 1976) 88 ff.

well. The modern corporation had evolved beyond its origins as a mechanism for serving the narrowest financial interests of shareholders. The door was thus opened not only to the disappointing prospect of kleptocratic managerial opportunism, but also to the more intriguing possibility of the emergence of the modern director-statesman, the sort of paternalistic managerialist said to be commonly encountered in the boardrooms and C-suites of post Second World War firms. Of course, at the time Berle and Means completed their seminal study, they did not anticipate the development of alternative methods of managerial discipline such as a potentially robust market for corporate control or the concentration of share ownership in the hands of titanic asset managers who could, at least under ideal conditions, act as effective corporate overseers. These modern market realities, as Ronald Gilson and Jeffrey Gordon have suggested, mean that the Berle-Means framework in which the shares of large public corporations are widely held by small, dispersed shareholders is 'factually obsolete and now provides a misleading framework for contemporary corporate governance theorizing'.[62]

The implications of these changing circumstances will be discussed in later chapters. In the meantime, we have raised another provocative alternative implied by the Berle and Means framework that Berle and Means did not consider: the possibility that the separation of ownership and control might paradoxically facilitate an increased emphasis on the relentless and unmitigated pursuit of shareholder financial goals after all, even in circumstances where the conduct of most investors would usually be regulated by moderating considerations of conscience. Under the management of directors and officers faithfully fulfilling their duties as fiduciaries, the corporate form may thus amplify the presumed profit-seeking goal of the shareholders and minimize the possibility of tempering the profit maximization motive with countervailing considerations of conscience or empathy.

This provocative possibility involves, among other things, an exploration ofthe concept of the corporate financial goal, a concept that appears to have evolved along with the emergence of financial economics in the mid-twentieth century. It is to this subject that we turn in the following chapters.

[62] Ronald J Gilson and Jeffrey N Gordon, 'The Agency Costs of Agency Capitalism: Activist Investors and the Revaluation of Governance Rights' (2013) 113 Columbia Law Review 863, 864.

# 4

# The Prophets and Profits of Shareholder Primacy Part I: In Search of the Right Side of History (and the Left Side of the Balance Sheet)

## Introduction

It has become a central question for the law of corporations and the delineation of corporate directors' duties. Should the corporation (and therefore its directors) seek to serve the interests of its shareholders exclusively, or at least primarily, with those shareholders' interests understood to mean desire for financial gain alone? Or is this too narrow a view? Should the corporation, instead, in one or more ways, take account of a broader array of non-financial interests and of non-shareholder constituents (or 'stakeholders') including employees, creditors, suppliers, customers, the natural environment, the community, and so on?

The first proposition, that it is the (financial) interests[1] of the shareholders alone or primarily that the corporation should serve, has frequently been identified as the 'shareholder primacy' view of the corporation or, at least, as the central element of the 'shareholder

[1] The possibility has been mooted that the notion of shareholder primacy might envision the corporation serving a wider range of both financial and non-financial shareholder interests. For example, economist Robin Marris in 1967 asserted that: 'Business-school texts increasingly emphasise profit *and shareholder-welfare maximization* as normative axioms.' Robin Marris, *The Economic Theory of 'Managerial' Capitalism* (Macmillan 1967) 72–73 (emphasis added). The notion that governing corporations solely in the interests of shareholders could involve sacrificing shareholders' financial gains in order to pursue non-financial interests favoured by shareholders themselves is essentially the proposition underlying the approach to corporate governance recently urged by Hart and Zingales. See Oliver Hart and Luigi Zingales, 'The New Corporate Governance' (2022) 1 University of Chicago Business Law Review 195, 197: '[W]e think the [shareholder value maximization (SVM)] paradigm needs to change. This is true even if one accepts, as we do, the idea of shareholder primacy, that is that companies should act on behalf of shareholders. When externalities are important and at least when some investors are prosocial, we argue that shareholders will want companies to pursue *shareholder welfare maximization* (SWM) not SVM.' We will revisit this idea in chapter 7.

*Corporate Governance and Enlightened Fiduciaries*. Christopher C. Nicholls, Oxford University Press.
 DOI: 10.1093/9780198904199.003.0004

primacy'[2] view. Shareholder primacy (at least in the United States) is usually thought to have become and to have remained the dominant view among corporate managers themselves since at least the 1980s, if not somewhat earlier. Whether the dominance of this management philosophy may be said to have lost ground in the last several years will be examined later in this chapter. But the notion of 'shareholder primacy' has become such a critical rallying point for legal, economic, ethical, and political debates about the role of the corporation in modern society that it is important to consider the nuances of the concept more closely.

The sometimes simplistic, often dogmatic invocation (or, for that matter, rejection) of the concept of 'shareholder primacy' obscures the complex and ambiguous history of the idea as a mooted business norm, a technical economic observation, and a putative legal standard. Some contrarians, in fact, have altogether rejected the practical significance of the shareholder primacy norm.[3] Others, while somewhat begrudgingly recognizing the irrefutably dominant role assumed by the shareholder primacy norm within the business and legal communities since the 1970s or at least the 1980s, nevertheless contest its legitimacy and desirability on several grounds. They argue that shareholder primacy's purported status as a descriptively accurate and normatively superior principle for the management of business corporations is misleading and harmful. Shareholder primacy, they insist, is inconsistent with the historical origins of the corporation, contrary to the way in which corporations were successfully operated for much of the twentieth century, and is not only economically and legally unwarranted but is also demonstrably ruinous to the broader interests of society. We will return to this familiar debate in Chapter 5.

One must, however, tread cautiously here. There have been so many books and articles written on the topic of shareholder primacy, including articles about articles, books about books, articles about books, and books about articles that any discussion of the matter must be ring-fenced with a litany of humble apologies and exculpatory caveats. No attempt, therefore, will, could, or should be made to summarize, encapsulate, respond to, refute, recite, or

[2] Stephen Bainbridge notes that the term 'shareholder primacy' implies not only that the corporation ought to be operated for the benefit of the shareholders but also that the shareholders 'exercise ultimate control of the corporate enterprise'. See Stephen M Bainbridge, *The Profit Motive: Defending Shareholder Value Maximization* (Cambridge University Press 2023) 13. This distinction is especially significant for Bainbridge's 'directory primacy' view of corporate governance which emphasizes that it is directors, not shareholders, that have corporate decision-making power, although they must exercise that power in pursuit of the goal of shareholder wealth maximization.

[3] See eg D Gordon Smith, 'The Shareholder Primacy Norm' (1998) 23 Journal of Corporation Law 277, 278: 'This Article challenges the received wisdom and argues that the shareholder primacy norm is nearly irrelevant to the ordinary business decisions of modern corporations.'

indeed acknowledge even a fraction of the shelf-bending volumes of contributions that have been published on this subject. The diversity of opinions ventilated on the issue is matched only by the vitriol of many of the most prolific disputants. One may find equally dogmatic pronouncements on the timeless virtues and the irredeemable vices of shareholder primacy voiced by financial, economic, business management, and legal scholars as well as by legal practitioners, business executives, political commentators, and elected officials, not to mention Hollywood celebrities, Tik Tok influencers, soapbox buskers, and earnest university, high school, and elementary school students drawn from across the range of the political spectrum (if, indeed, a spectrum may be said to have a 'range').

A comprehensive literature review is therefore impossible. Nonetheless, a certain customary formulary of several famous authorities, both ancient and modern, seems to have become *de rigeur* for any legal work audaciously proposing to cloy the gazettes with further cant about the subject of Anglo-American shareholder primacy. For example, one must, it seems, make at least passing reference to the Michigan Supreme Court's 1919 *Dodge v Ford* decision;[4] add a serving of the 'cakes and ale' of *Dodge v Ford*'s English cousins[5] (appropriately qualified by enlightened references to the 'enlightened shareholder value' (ESV) /pluralist discussion in the UK Company Law Review,[6] and the Companies Act 2006[7]); unfold the pages of the 1931–32 Berle-Dodd *Harvard Law Review* 'debate';[8] gamely shed some light on *Shlensky v Wrigley*;[9] respectfully acknowledge, then adroitly recoil from, Milton Friedman's 1970 *New York Times Magazine* article[10] (and perhaps his earlier book);[11] and adopt a similarly detached perspective on the 1971 Lewis Powell Memorandum;[12]

[4] *Dodge v Ford Motor Co* 204 Mich 459, 170 NW 668 (1919).

[5] See eg *Hutton v West Cork Railway Co* (1883) 23 Ch D 654; *Parke v Daily News (No 2)* [1962] 3 WLR 566 (Ch D).

[6] See eg Company Law Review Steering Group, *Modern Company Law: For a Competitive Economy: Final Report*, vol 1, DTI (June 2001); House of Commons Trade and Industry Committee, *The White Paper on Modernising Company Law*, Sixth Report of Session 2002-03, HC 439 (13 May 2003).

[7] UK Public General Acts 2006 c 46.

[8] AA Berle Jr, 'Corporate Powers as Powers in Trust' (1931) 44 Harvard Law Review 1049; E Merrick Dodd Jr, 'For Whom Are Corporate Managers Trustees' (1932) 45 Harvard Law Review 1145; AA Berle Jr, 'For Whom Corporate Managers are Trustees: A Note' (1932) 45 Harvard Law Review 1365.

[9] 237 NE 2d 776 (Ill App 1968).

[10] Milton Friedman, 'The Social Responsibility of Business Is to Increase Its Profits' *New York Times Magazine* (13 September 1970) 32.

[11] Milton Friedman, *Capitalism and Freedom* (University of Chicago Press 1962).

[12] Lewis Powell, 'Confidential Memorandum: Attack on American Free Enterprise System' Memorandum to Eugene B Sydnor Jr, US Chamber of Commerce (23 August 1971) https://ia800303.us.archive.org/18/items/powell-memorandum-1971-ocr/Powell%20Memorandum%201971%20OCR.pdf.

engage with agency theory and the 'nexus of contracts' economic picture of the corporation, acknowledging economic scholars Michael Jensen and William Meckling[13] and legal luminaries Frank Easterbrook and Daniel Fischel;[14] chronicle both the corporate governance reports of the latter years of the twentieth century and the market-shaking governance debacles that followed shortly afterwards in the early years of the twenty-first; ruminate on the impact and legacy of Hansmann and Kraakman's seminal 'End of History for Corporate Law' paper;[15] take responsible account of the early rise of the concept of corporate social responsibility (CSR); cheer or sneer (or both) at the Business Roundtable's (BRT) 2019 'Statement on the Purpose of the Corporation'[16] while struggling to discern the significance of the BRTs subsequent qualifying (or was it clarifying?) release;[17] weigh the import of the 2022 hearing on shareholder primacy before the Joint Economic Committee of the US Congress;[18] review the American Law Institute's recent work on the Restatement of the Law of Corporate Governance; then marvel at how much impressive energy has been expended most recently expounding the significance of environmental, social, and governance issues (ESG).[19]

Indeed, each of these familiar matters will appear, even if briefly, in one of the following chapters. But as a preliminary matter, it is interesting to note two narrow aspects of shareholder primacy which are particularly intriguing yet are less commonly explored. These matters do not always engage the larger and more contentious political issues concerning the wisdom and fairness of capitalism, the appropriate role and scope of government, and the efficacy of promoting social justice within a robust competitive market economy—all issues about which technical squabbles over the proper goal of the business

[13] Michael Jensen and William Meckling, 'Theory of the Firm: Managerial Behavior, Agency Costs and Ownership Structure' (1976) 3 Journal of Financial Economics 305.

[14] Frank H Easterbrook and Daniel R Fischel, *The Economic Structure of Corporate Law* (Harvard University Press 1991).

[15] Henry Hansmann and Reinier Kraakman, 'The End of History for Corporate Law' (2001) 89 Georgetown Law Journal 439.

[16] Business Roundtable, 'Statement on the Purpose of a Corporation' (19 August 2019) https://www.businessroundtable.org/business-roundtable-redefines-the-purpose-of-a-corporation-to-promote-an-economy-that-serves-all-americans.

[17] See Business Roundtable, 'Redefined Purpose of a Corporation: Welcoming the Debate' (25 August 2019) https://www.businessroundtable.org/redefined-purpose-of-a-corporation-welcoming-the-debate (last accessed 11 September 2025).

[18] Examining the Impact of Shareholder Primacy: What it Means to Put Stock Prices First: Hearing Before the Joint Economic Committee of the Congress of the United States 117th Congress, Second Session (March 2022).

[19] This list of commonly-cited authorities is heavily tilted toward American sources. But the shareholder primacy theory is not an example of American exceptionalism. See eg Andrew Keay, 'Shareholder Primacy in Corporate Law: Can it Survive? Should it Survive?' (2010) 7(3) European Company and Financial Law Review 369.

corporation have become a kind of ideological proxy war. These two somewhat neglected matters are these. First, how did the concept of shareholder primacy (specifically, the notion of shareholder wealth maximization) emerge, evolve, and become differentiated, from earlier economic theories of firm profit maximization? Second, how did neoclassical[20]economic ideas of the firm migrate from abstract economic theory to the practical law and lore of modern corporate governance?

## Shareholder Primacy: Genesis and a Revelation

The origin of the term 'shareholder primacy' is somewhat uncertain. It appeared in articles by David Millon,[21] Lyman Johnson,[22] and Patrick Ryan[23] in 1989, of which Millon believes his paper and that of Professor Johnson—with whom he had been using the term in prior discussions—were the earliest.[24] However, Millon did not claim to have necessarily coined the term and acknowledged the possibility that the phrase may well have appeared earlier in books, although he was not specifically aware of any such earlier use. Indeed, one notes at least one earlier reference to the term in a published article from 1983, and the context in which the phrase was used there suggests that the author expected readers already to have had some acquaintance with it.[25] Brian Cheffins has identified an even earlier use by Phillip Blumberg in his 1975 work, *The Megacorporation in American Society: The Scope of Corporate Power.*[26]

[20] The label 'neoclassical economics' appears to have been coined by Thorstein Veblen in 'The Preconceptions of Economic Science' (1900) Quarterly Journal of Economics 240, 261. See Tony Aspromourgos, 'On the Origins of the Term "Neoclassical"' (1986) Cambridge Journal of Economics 265. Aspromourgos notes that the term 'became prominent in the literature of economics in the 1950s' (ibid 265). Aspromourgos argues that it was in the works of JR Hicks and George Stigler in the 1950s that the term came to acquire the sense in which it is used today and that the work of Alfred Marshall was identified as the first of the neoclassical economists. See also Tony Lawson, 'What Is this "school" Called Neoclassical Economics?' (2013) 37 Cambridge Journal of Economics 947.

[21] David Millon, 'State Takeover Laws: A Rebirth of Corporation Law?' (1988) 45 Washington & Lee Law Review 903, 904.

[22] Lyman Johnson, 'The Eventual Clash Between Judicial and Legislative Notions of Target Management Conduct' (1988) 14 Journal of Corporate Law 35.

[23] Patrick J Ryan, 'Rule 14a-8, Institutional Shareholder Proposals, and Corporate Democracy' (1988) 23 University of Georgia Law Review 97, 173.

[24] David Millon, 'Radical Shareholder Primacy' (2013) 10 University of St Thomas Law Journal 1013, 1015 n 7.

[25] See Donald E Schwartz, 'Shareholder Democracy: A Reality or Chimera?' (1983) 25 California Management Review 53.

[26] Brian R Cheffins, 'Stop Blaming Milton Friedman!' (2021) 98 Washington University Law Review 1607, 1639, n 211, citing Phillip I Blumberg, *The Megacorporation in American Society* (Prentice-Hall 1975). What is especially intriguing about the reference in Blumberg's work is that Blumberg was treating shareholder primacy not as a new notion of rising importance but rather as an old, declining

Whatever the etymology of the specific coinage 'shareholder primacy', certainly the broad proposition that the business corporation ought to be managed in the (usually financial) interests of its shareholders stretches back many decades and perhaps more than two centuries. Judd F. Sneirson suggests that the idea may even be said to have originated with Adam Smith,[27] although Smith's work was principally focused on the incentives and actions of the individual business proprietor rather than the corporate-run business. With respect to firms, Smith identified the rational apathy of the shareholders (whom he calls 'proprietors') of corporations or, to be more precise, of the joint-stock companies of his day that were the antecedents of the modern UK corporation.[28] He famously doubted whether such companies—even when they enjoyed the benefits of a state-granted monopoly—were likely to be astutely operated by directors who were, after all, merely 'managers of others people's money than of their own.'[29] Thus, Smith famously concluded:

> The only trades which it seems possible for a joint stock company to carry on successfully, without an exclusive privilege, are those, of which all the operations are capable of being reduced to what is called a routine, or to such a uniformity of method as admits of little or no variation.[30]

As some later economists confronted the apparent conflict between Smith's dismissive prognosis of the efficacy of most corporations and the unmistakable rise of the corporate form throughout the nineteenth century, Sneirson argues that neoclassical economics ultimately settled upon a shareholder-centric

concept: 'Shareholder primacy and profit-maximization appear to be on their way to interment as legal standards, at least insofar as the public corporation is concerned' (ibid 10).

[27] Judd F Sneirson, 'The History of Shareholder Primacy from Adam Smith through the Rise of Financialism' in Beate Sjåfjell and Christopher M Bruner, *The Cambridge Handbook of Corporate Law, Corporate Governance and Sustainability* (Cambridge University Press 2019).

[28] Adam Smith, *An Inquiry Into the Nature and Causes of the Wealth of Nations* (Edwin Cannan (ed), Max Lerner (Intro), Random House 1937, originally published in 1776) Bk V, ch 1 Pt III art 1, 699. Much has been written about the nature of the early 'joint-stock companies', including their similarities to and differences from the modern business corporation. Despite the institutional differences between the joint-stock companies of Smith's day and the modern business corporation, it is clear from Smith's description of the large joint-stock companies that they had a significant number of passive investors who, like the small shareholders of today's large publicly traded corporations, relied upon the corporation's managers to generate the profits upon which the gain on their investment depended.

[29] ibid 700. Cf Peter John de la Fosse Wiles, *Price, Cost and Output* (Basil Blackwell 1961) 201, arguing that, in fact, the separation of ownership and control in the modern corporation might not have such an adverse impact on profit-making after all since, among other things, 'it is easier to be avaricious on behalf of an absent third party than for oneself'. This idea is similar to Mitnick's 'fiduciary paradox' discussed in chapter 3.

[30] Smith, ibid 713.

view of the corporation as a way of comfortably squaring the venerated Smith's theory with observed reality.[31]

Sneirson, of course, is referring to economists' understanding of the corporation as it was actually presumed to operate. But economists cannot, and do not purport to, define or prescribe the scope of the distinctly legal obligations of a corporation or a corporation's directors. It is certainly possible that the economic depiction of the corporation might establish a business standard of practice, or as Sneirson suggests, 'a powerful social norm',[32] against which the actions of corporate officers and directors might ultimately come to be measured, just as developing knowledge in the medical sciences understandably conditions the standard of practice to which medical practitioners will be held in their interactions with patients. But such evolving knowledge and norms seem to be relevant to the evaluation of professional standards of care and competence, not to redefining the ultimate object to which the application of those standards ought to be directed. That is, we should certainly expect a modern physician to have her knowledge of medical technology and the treatment of disease evaluated against the demanding standards of modern medical knowledge and not the more limited base of medical science familiar to, say, a nineteenth century physician. However, these changing standards relate to means not to ends. And we presumably do not expect the overarching goal of the modern physician (ie to seek to restore a patient to health) to have changed in any material way from that of her nineteenth century counterpart.[33]

Is it inevitable, then, or even probable that an evolving conception on the part of economists or organizational theorists about the observed or normatively superior objective of a business corporation (as opposed to noted improvements in management technology, valuation techniques, and understanding of effective management practices) ought to determine the substantive content of the law of fiduciary duties in the corporate context? In particular, if the economists' corporate teleology does not accord with or reflect broader community standards or expectations about the modern corporation, is there any compelling reason to expect that the law should come to embody the consensus of economists rather than reflect or adopt the values of members of the broader (albeit non-expert) community? Or perhaps the legal obligations of directors

[31] Sneirson (n 27) 9.
[32] ibid 5.
[33] One recognizes that it could be argued that the goal of modern medical practitioners might now also be said to include the treatment of pain and relief of suffering, a goal about which there has evidently been considerable discussion within the medical profession. See eg Eric J Cassell, 'The Nature of Suffering and the Goals of Medicine' (1982) 306 The New England Journal of Medicine 639; Ben A Rich, 'Physicians' Legal Duty to Relieve Suffering' (2021) 175 Western Journal of Medicine 151.

are immaterial in any case if, as Lorsch and MacIver once asserted, directors' 'legal mandate often means little in the complex reality of governance'.[34]

## Is Profit-making Always Profit-maximizing?

Evaluation of the legitimacy, efficacy, and prevalence of the shareholder primacy norm as a legal concept must first involve consideration of precisely what might be understood to be implied by a doctrine of shareholder primacy.[35] For example, it was once common for commentators and critics to assert that business corporations do in fact—and perhaps are legally obliged to—maximize profits for the benefit of their shareholders. That specific 'profit maximization' (or 'net revenue maximization') formulation regularly appeared in some of the earliest economic discussions of the firm,[36] and was still routinely being invoked by economists in the 1960s, including in 1962 by Nobel-prize winning economist Milton Friedman in his provocative book *Capitalism and Freedom*[37] and (arguably[38]) later alluded to in 1970 in his provocative *New York Times Magazine* article.[39]

Economist Peter Wiles, in 1961, claimed the phrase 'profit maximization' was 'surprisingly new in economics, although something of this kind has always been implicit'.[40] By this, Wiles means that business enterprise was originally conceived by the classicists as owner-operated business where the owner was presumed to maximize 'utility'—a broader concept than money profit. It was not until economists in the early twentieth century—notably Chamberlin,[41] Robinson,[42] and Stackelberg[43]—began exploring the implications of monopoly and imperfect competition, that the theory of the firm

[34] Jay Lorsch and Elizabeth MacIver, *Pawns or Potentates: The Reality of America's Corporate Boards* (Harvard Business School Press 1989).

[35] See generally Sneirson (n 27).

[36] See eg Alfred Marshall, *Principles of Economics* (Macmillan and Co 1890), Bk V, ch VIII, 457.

[37] Milton Friedman, *Capitalism and Freedom* (University of Chicago Press 2020, originally published in 1962) 161.

[38] Brian Cheffins has noted that, although Friedman referred to 'increasing' profits in his 1970 article, he did not in fact use the word maximize. See Cheffins (n 26) 1640. This is correct. However, one notes that his article also incorporates by reference his earlier book, where he does expressly refer to maximizing (not merely increasing) profits.

[39] Friedman (n 10), who, of course, was writing here for a general audience, not a specialized one.

[40] Wiles (n 29).

[41] See eg Edward Chamberlin, *The Theory of Monopolistic Competition* (Harvard University Press 1933) 13.

[42] Joan Robinson, *The Economics of Imperfect Competition* (Macmillan & Co Ltd 1933).

[43] Heinrich von Stackelberg, *Market Structure and Equilibrium* (Damien Bazin, Lynn Urch, and Rowland Hill (trs), Springer-Verlag 2011, originally published as *Marktform und Gleichgewicht* in 1934).

began[44] and so the notion of profit maximization as the presumed firm goal was articulated. Wiles undertook systematically to '[destroy] the simpliste old-fashioned *assumption of the single maximand*.'[45] Indeed, even by the time Wiles made this statement, the recognized deficiencies of 'profit maximization' as a tractable corporate goal had led to the proposal of the alternative formulation of 'shareholder wealth maximization' in the financial economic literature.

Reference to corporations seeking to maximize profits is still frequently encountered in popular discussions of the business corporation, although, as we shall see, profit-maximization today, as a technical matter, is no longer (usually) identified as the putative goal of the corporation among specialized legal and financial shareholder primacy advocates. Even in an earlier era when economists uniformly framed the goal of the business corporation in terms of maximizing profits for the benefit of shareholders, the language used in judicial decisions was somewhat less explicit. Certain cases often cited as support for the proposition that shareholder primacy underlies a mandatory (if usually unenforced) legal duty to which corporate directors and managers are bound generally confirm only the less precise notion that corporations must operate primarily for the profit of the shareholders. They did not, in other words, specifically advert to any legal requirement to *maximize* such profits (or to maximize shareholder wealth, value, or anything else for that matter).

In the US, for example, consider the iconic 1919 decision of the Supreme Court of Michigan in *Dodge v Ford Motor Co.*[46] It is unlikely that a corporate law casebook in the United States published within at least the past forty years has failed to include *Dodge v Ford*,[47] although the case does not seem to have been regarded as particularly controversial at the time it was decided.[48] In fact, at least one scholar has argued that *Dodge v Ford* did not become a staple of law school casebooks because it was an influential case, but rather that it became an influential case because it began appearing in law school casebooks.[49] The central issue in this case, it will be recalled, was whether or not the Ford Motor

[44] ibid 88.

[45] Wiles (n 29) 208.

[46] 204 Mich 459, 170 NW 668 (1919).

[47] For a litany of statements from various corporate law scholars to the effect that *Dodge v Ford* is reproduced in virtually every (US) corporate law casebook see Mark J Roe, '*Dodge v. Ford*: What Happened and Why?' (2021) 74 Vanderbilt Law Review 1755, 1759–60 n 4.

[48] See eg Editorial in (1919–1920) 5 *Virginia Law Register* 566: 'We think there can be very little doubt that the action of the Ford Directors was certainly arbitrary and erroneous and that therefore the decision of the court was manifestly correct.'

[49] Robert J Rhee, 'The Neoliberal Corporate Purpose of Dodge v Ford and Shareholder Primacy: A Historical Context 1919-2019' (2023) Stanford Journal of Law, Business & Finance 202: '[*Dodge*] had minimal impact on legal scholarship for the first six decades. But from the 1980s, citations in law reviews exploded. *Dodge* became truly iconic—not in the courtroom but in the academy.'

Company could be compelled to pay a dividend to its shareholders rather than conserve its considerable stores of cash for the purpose of significantly expanding its production capacity by building a massive new factory on the River Rouge. The court ultimately agreed that Ford was obliged to pay a dividend, but rejected the plaintiffs' attempt to enjoin Ford from completing the River Rouge plant. Had Ford consistently defended the decision to limit dividends (a defence, it should be said, that was certainly advanced in Ford's written pleadings) as an exercise of business judgment, the plaintiffs' claim would surely have failed. But Henry Ford had made statements—including in his oral testimony—to the effect that his goal in expanding the scale of Ford's business was to reduce the price of automobiles—not to acquire greater market share and eventually larger profits—but to benefit the public, 'to help them build up their lives and their homes'.[50] Ostrander J rejected such an ostensibly public-spirited motivation as inappropriate for a for-profit business corporation. His famous declaration that 'A business corporation is organized and carried on primarily for the profit of the stockholders'[51] has become the *locus classicus* for the principle that, for American corporations at any rate, shareholder primacy describes a recognized legal standard, not merely an economic *desideratum*.[52]

Much has been written about the *Dodge v Ford* case in the years since it was decided. Insightful explorations have been made into important aspects of the historical context in which the dispute arose,[53] and the likely highly profit-motivated underlying explanation for Ford's ostensibly defiant claims of eleemosynary sentiments. Opponents of shareholder primacy have been especially critical of the decision and what they regard as the frustratingly inappropriate prominence it has assumed in the casebook canon of the legal academy.

[50] Henry Ford, quoted by Ostrander J in his opinion in 204 Mich 459 (9 April 1919). A somewhat less-frequently quoted passage from Ostrander J's opinion perhaps captures the notion of shareholder primacy as a legal duty even more explicitly: '[i]t is not within the lawful powers of a board of directors to shape and conduct the affairs of a corporation for the merely incidental benefit of shareholders and for the primary purpose of benefiting others, and no one will contend that if the avowed purpose of the defendant directors was to sacrifice the interests of shareholders it would not be the duty of the courts to interfere.'

[51] ibid 507.

[52] See eg Bainbridge (n 2) 33; Robert C Clark, *Corporate Law* (Aspen Law and Business 1986) 603. One frequently noted curiosity about the prominence of *Dodge v Ford* within the US corporate law universe is that it was rendered by a Michigan court, not the Delaware Supreme Court or the Delaware Court of Chancery and concerned a corporation incorporated under Michigan's, not Delaware's, corporate statute. In most other contexts, owing to the dominance of Delaware as the state of choice for the incorporation of more than half of America's largest public corporations, it is Delaware corporate law that is treated as a sort of de facto US corporate law.

[53] See eg Roe (n 47), arguing that the case arose from Henry Ford's need to preserve labour peace in order to sustain his monopoly position in the market, and is thus a key early example of a thesis he has developed elsewhere, that only firms with significant market power (or economic rents) can serve non-shareholder interests since competitive pressures otherwise prevent firms from doing so.

The late Lynn Stout, for example, cursorily dismissed the famous passage from *Dodge v Ford* as 'merely judicial dicta',[54] (an assertion, it must be said, with which other scholars staunchly disagree[55]). She went on to call, somewhat audaciously, for law professors to stop teaching the celebrated case altogether, declaring caustically that law professors 'are not in the business of imparting fables, however charming'.[56]

Even if more authoritative than merely a charming fable, the language of the *Dodge v Ford* decision must be studied with care. For example, though regularly invoked as authority for the proposition that, as a matter of law, a corporation must seek to maximize corporate profits, the decision does not use the language of 'maximizing' at all. This omission was identified decades ago by Merrick Dodd in the 1932 article that forms part of the famous Dodd-Berle debate[57] discussed below. This is surely not an inconsequential omission. The anodyne proposition that business corporations must earn profits for their shareholders hardly seems controversial either today or in the past. Victor Morawetz had declared in his nineteenth century book on private corporations that 'the ultimate object of every business corporation is the gain of money'.[58] And, again: 'Business corporations are formed for the pecuniary profit of their shareholders.'[59] In the UK, writing in 2001, L. S. Sealy observed that: 'It seems to have been accepted practically without question until only a decade or two ago that the sole purpose of any company was to make the greatest possible profits for its shareholders.'[60] Similarly, of Canadian companies, the leading corporate law textbook of the early twentieth century stated that: 'The fundamental purpose of every commercial company being to make gain or profit for its members, important questions are bound to arise as to the existence and disposition of such profit.'[61]

However, seeking gain does not necessarily imply seeking to *maximize* gain. One might glibly observe that parents' duty to feed their children does

[54] Lynn A Stout, 'Why We Should Stop Teaching *Dodge v Ford*' (2008) 1 Virginia Law & Business Review 163, 165. As Bainbridge (n 2) notes, several other scholars have also asserted that this aspect of the *Dodge v Ford* decision was *obiter dicta*.

[55] See eg Jonathan Macey, 'A Close Read of an Excellent Commentary on *Dodge v Ford*' (2008) 1 Virginia Law & Business Review 177, 180; Bainbridge (n 2) 51.

[56] Stout (n 54) 176.

[57] Dodd (n 8), 1145, 1158 n 31: 'Neither the language of the opinion nor the relief granted necessarily involves an unqualified acceptance of the maximum-profit-for-stockholders formula.' Roe has also made this observation. See Roe (n 47) 1761 n 6.

[58] Victor Morawetz, *A Treatise on the Law of Private Corporations* (2nd edn, Little, Brown, and Company 1886) §§ 363, 348.

[59] ibid §§ 364, 349.

[60] LS Sealy, *Cases and Materials on Company Law* (7th edn, Butterworths 2001) 173.

[61] FW Wegenast, *The Law of Canadian Companies* (Carswell 1979, originally published in 1931) 610.

not impose a duty to maximize the number of daily calories those children consume. One might well contend that corporate directors have a duty to seek an optimal (or reasonable), rather than a maximum, amount of profits.[62] Framing the corporate goal in such a way might incur the wrath of those economists who reject the concept of an objectively 'reasonable' or 'just price' as an incalculable and incoherent relic of the middle ages.[63] Such a goal would, nevertheless, not appear in principle to run afoul of the wording in *Dodge v Ford*, even assuming Ostrander J's opinion does indeed represent a binding legal standard.

Perhaps there is no practical reason to quibble over whether a duty on the part of corporate directors to seek to enhance corporate profits in the interest of financially benefiting a single constituency—the shareholders—does or does not imply a duty to maximize those profits. After all, as many commentators have noted, given the protective business judgment rule, it is all but unimaginable that directors would ever be found liable for failing to maximize profits even if one were to assume that they were unambiguously under a formal legal duty to do so.[64] But the maximization formulation is significant, at least from a symbolic or expressive perspective.

And certainly as an authoritative statement of the legal relationship of a corporation and its shareholders there are at least one or two puzzling technical aspects about *Dodge v Ford*, too. For example, the underlying theory on which the shareholder-plaintiffs evidently based their alleged entitlement to receive dividends from the Ford Motor Company was surely as erroneous in 1919 as it would be today. Specifically, in the 1916 letter first sent by the aggrieved

[62] 'Reasonable' in this context might, for example, be interpreted to mean such level of profits as is sufficient to induce shareholders in the future to invest more capital in the corporation as required. See eg Adolf A Berle and Gardiner C Means, *The Modern Corporation & Private Property* (Transaction Publishers 1991, originally published in 1932) 251. In this sense, the acceptable rate of profit would be estimated in much the same way that the market rate for labour is determined. As a law firm partner once facetiously observed about the compensation levels of the firm's associate lawyers: 'We pay them the "going rate": that is, the rate required to keep them from going.'

[63] See eg Raymond de Roover, 'The Concept of the Just Price: Theory and Economic Policy' (1958) 18 Journal of Economic History 41; Friedrich A Hayek, *Law, Legislation and Liberty, vol 2: The Mirage of Social Justice* (University of Chicago Press 1976) 75, discussing the related concept of 'reasonable wages', as a vestige of '[t]he futile medieval search for the just price and just wage'; even Adolf Berle, one of the principal architects of Franklin Roosevelt's New Deal, alludes in a comment on a paper by Abram Chayes, to 'canon-law thinking of the Middle Ages, when ethical considerations—notably that of a "just price"—were the imperatives'. Adolf Berle, 'Foreword' in Edward S Mason, *The Corporation in Modern Society* (Harvard University Press 1959) ix, xii. In that same volume see also Edward S Mason, 'Introduction' 1, 12: 'Then there are those . . . who seek the best of both worlds by equating long-run profit maximization with equitable treatment of all parties at issue. But to date no one has succeeded in working out of the logic of this modern rehabilitation of the medieval "just price".'

[64] See eg Gordon Smith (n 3) 286. But cf Bainbridge (n 2), who argues that this makes sense even if it is not readily enforceable.

plaintiffs to Henry Ford, in advance of the litigation, they asserted, among other things:

> [t]he fact is, however, that the assets of the company representing its surplus *is as much the property of the stockholders as the assets representing the capital stock* and the stockholders are as much entitled to a dividend that will give them returns on their surplus investment as their capital stock.[65]

Certainly then, as now, shareholders of a company with inordinately large cash reserves might well wish the company to take account of that store of cash when determining what size of annual dividend to pay, rather than have the company follow the more penurious practice—as Ford apparently had done—of limiting the dividend to a percentage of the shareholders' (much smaller) originally invested capital. Under certain, albeit rare, circumstances, one might even imagine that failure to pay a larger dividend could be considered oppressive to the minority shareholders. But in no case does there seem to be a legal basis for asserting that the payment of large dividends should be justified on the counterfactual basis that shareholders hold a property interest in the corporation's capital. And again, whatever sworn or unsworn general statements Henry Ford may have made about the purportedly altruistic operation of the Ford Motor Company, one point was clear. With respect to his insistence on maintaining large corporate cash balances, Ford's defence specifically maintained that 'the latter methods and policies ultimately redound to the best financial interests of the company and its stockholders'.[66]

Reference in the case to Ford Motor Company's attitude toward profits is also curiously contradictory. At one point in the opinion, the court reiterated its conclusion that: 'The purpose of any organization under the law is earnings—profit.'[67] But this pro-profit proposition was not invoked as a chastening reminder to Ford that his eponymous company had failed to focus upon earning profits. Rather, this remark occurs in the opinion as a statement offered by the court in clear *support* of one aspect of Ford's defence. Specifically, the court found it entirely lawful for Ford (the company) to capitalize its earnings even when the effect of doing so had resulted in the company's capital significantly exceeding the US$50,000,000 capital limit imposed by its incorporating statute. In effect, the court reasoned, the US$50,000,000 statutory capital

[65] Cited by Michigan Supreme Court (emphasis added).
[66] ibid.
[67] *Dodge v Ford* (n 4).

limitation could only properly be intended to apply to a corporation at the moment of its original incorporation. It could not have been intended that a profitable business was to be prevented from using its profits as business capital: 'It cannot be supposed that [the legislature] looked with disfavor upon a profitable corporate existence.'[68] The court thus concluded that, contrary to the plaintiffs' contention that Ford's public-spirited motives had led it to forsake its pursuit of profit, the corporation had succeeded rather splendidly at accumulating impressively large profits. And it was lawfully entitled to employ its large undistributed profits as capital even where this led to an increase in capital to an amount significantly in excess of the statutory cap. This conclusion was integral to the court's decision to deny the plaintiffs' plea for an injunction restraining Ford from making a capital investment in its planned massive River Rouge plant expansion.

*Dodge v Ford*, in short, says little, and implies less, about the specific question of whether a business corporation ought to be chastened for failing to *maximize* profits for the benefit of its shareholders. This perhaps should come as no surprise. The court could hardly have concluded that the Ford Motor Company had, in fact, failed in any way to earn or to seek significant profits. The plaintiffs' principal complaint, after all, was not that Ford was insufficiently profitable. It objected, rather, to the fact that that an appropriate portion of the undeniably extraordinary profits Ford had successfully earned had not yet been distributed to them. Accusing Ford of failing to *distribute* massive profits is a very different charge from accusing the company of failing to maximize profits in the first place. It is very probable that in 1919 equity investors viewed dividends, and not capital appreciation or capital gains, as the principal (although, to be sure, not the sole[69]) source of share value.[70] And,

[68] ibid.

[69] Edgar Lawrence Smith's influential 1928 book on stock investment observes that it is not dividend payments alone to which shareholders should look as a source of stock value: "Over a period of years ... directors [of conservatively managed corporations] will never aim to declare all the company's net earnings in dividends. They will turn back a part of such earnings to surplus account, and invest this increasing surplus in productive operation.' Edgar Lawrence Smith, *Common Stocks as Long Term Investments* (The MacMillan Company 1928) 77.

[70] Although published some twenty years after the *Dodge v Ford Motor Company* decision, John Burr Williams's book, *The Theory of Investment Value*, expressed the focus upon dividends as a determinant of share value that likely reflected a widespread view prior to the publication of Modigliani and Miller's paper on dividend irrelevance in 1958. Williams was adamant that dividends, and dividends alone, should be used in valuing stocks, explaining that: 'Earnings are only a means to an end, and the means should not be mistaken for the end. Therefore we must say that a stock derives its value from its dividends, not its earnings.' John Burr Williams, *The Theory of Investment Value* (Harvard University Press 1938) 57. Indeed, Williams defined an investor as a buyer of securities 'interested in dividends, or coupons and principal', as opposed to a 'speculator' whom he defined as 'a buyer interested in the resale price' (ibid 4). See also Benjamin Graham and David Dodd, *Security Analysis* (McGraw-Hill

of course, some commentators have argued that the plaintiffs in the case, the Dodge brothers, in bringing their action may well have been keen both to extract cash from Ford to fund their own rival auto manufacturer, and to constrain Ford from expanding operations to a scale that would thwart their own efforts to compete.[71] But considering the specifics of their legal claim, unencumbered by any assumptions or speculations about the plaintiffs' underlying motivations for launching their suit, it does appear that the only impugned action of the Ford Motor Company that could be said to have evidenced a possible (future) intention to favour the pocketbooks of Ford's customers over those of its shareholders was the decision to expand capacity by construction of the River Rouge plant. And it will be recalled that the Michigan Supreme Court ultimately permitted the corporation to proceed with this ambitious project.[72] In its effect, then, the judgment against Ford was ultimately based only on a failure to *distribute* unquestionably large profits, not on any lack of commitment to earn them in the first place. *Dodge v Ford* is still highly significant, however. It offers a clear vindication of the corporate profit-making function and a useful reminder (perhaps even more timely in the early twenty-first century than the early twentieth) that corporate directors focused upon financial gain rather than broader, but vaguely-defined, societal interests should be regarded as dutiful corporate stewards, not rapacious robber barons.

For students of American corporate law, discussion of *Dodge v Ford* is sometimes paired with consideration of the 1968 Illinois case *Shlensky v Wrigley*.[73] This case arose as a derivative action commenced against the directors of the Delaware corporation that owned and operated the Chicago Cubs baseball club. The Cubs, then as now, played their home games at Wrigley Field—named

1934) 325: 'Until recent years the dividend return was the overshadowing factor in common-stock investment. This point of view was based on simple logic. The prime purpose of a business corporation is to pay dividends to its owners.' But cf Edgar Lawrence Smith, *Common Stocks as Long Term Investments* (MacMillan 1928) 80: 'In the selection of securities for investment, we must consider more than the expected income yield upon the amount invested, and may quite properly weigh the probability of principal enhancement over a term of years without departing from the most conservative viewpoint.' It has in fact been suggested that in the nineteenth century, in the case of American corporations there was an expectation, and even a presumed 'right' of shareholders to receive dividends; in some cases corporations may have been required to distribute all profits as dividends. See Gordon Smith (n 3) 277, 298.

[71] See eg Todd Henderson, 'Everything Old is New Again: Lessons from *Dodge v Ford Motor Company*' in J Mark Ramseyer (ed), *Corporate Law Stories* (Foundation Press 2009).

[72] To be sure, in coming to this conclusion the court did not explicitly endorse the idea that directors may pursue actions that are detrimental to the financial success of the shareholders. Rather, it was suggested that the ultimate impact of the decision on the future financial success of the corporation was unknown and the court was thus 'not satisfied that the alleged motives of the directors, in so far as they are reflected in the conduct of business, menace the interests of the shareholders.'

[73] 237 NE 2d 776 (Ill App 1968).

for the eponymous chewing gum company of William Wrigley Jr,[74] whose son Philip K Wrigley held about 80 per cent of the shares of the corporation at the time of the litigation. The dispute revolved around whether or not Wrigley Stadium should be equipped with lights that would enable the Cubs to play night games on their home field. Philip Wrigley was opposed to night games. The plaintiffs alleged that Wrigley, who served as the president of the corporation, considered baseball a 'daytime sport', and also thought the conduct of night games would have a damaging effect on the residential north Chicago neighbourhood where Wrigley Stadium is located.[75] The plaintiffs, conversely, argued that more working people could attend night games, so they would increase ticket sales and thus enhance corporate revenue. Every other major league baseball team by that time was scheduling night games. According to statistics quoted in the case, in 1966 932 of the 1,620 major league baseball games played had been night games, and night games had become the norm for weekday games in other ball parks 'for the specific purpose of maximizing attendance and thereby maximizing revenue and income'.[76]

But the plaintiffs struck out. Their claim was dismissed, a decision that was upheld on appeal. Yet the opinion of the appellate court says nothing about how corporate directors ought to view the goal of maximizing corporate profits. Although the plaintiff had asserted that the directors were improperly motivated by considerations other than the financial interests of the corporation, the court did not accept that this was necessarily true as a matter of fact. It further noted that the plaintiff had not actually alleged any damage to the corporation or even that night games played by the other major league teams had, in fact, improved their profits. In short, the court in *Shlensky v Wrigley* found no reason explicitly to address the question of whether corporate directors are or are not obliged to maximize a corporation's profits since nothing in the plaintiff's case had sufficiently proved any failure to seek corporate profits in the first place. Since there was no evidence of fraud, illegality, or conflict of interest—indeed, the plaintiff had alleged no such improprieties—the court simply had no basis on which to interfere with the directors' decisions.

Explicit authority for a profit maximizing duty on the part of UK corporations is equally elusive. Two iconic English cases on the duty of directors to serve shareholder interests offer support for the idea that—at least prior to the

[74] Occasionally, defenders of the proposition that corporate directors can effectively balance the competing interests of multiple stakeholders will facetiously assert that they are well able to 'walk and chew gum at the same time'. Perhaps one might view this cliché is an unwitting reference to Mr Wrigley.

[75] ibid 778.

[76] ibid 777.

2006 changes to the English Companies Act—the corporation should operate in the interests of shareholders. Neither case makes mention of 'maximizing' profits, revenues, shareholder wealth, shareholder or enterprise value, or anything else. The first, *Hutton v West Cork Railway Co*,[77] is often considered one of the most unequivocal statements of the concept of 'shareholder primacy' in English common law (prior to statutory amendments referred to below). What is less often mentioned is that the action was actually brought not by a shareholder, but by a debenture holder of the West Cork Railway Company.

Debenture holders of the company had become entitled to vote pursuant to a scheme of arrangement under which debentures had been created to pay off the company's existing liabilities. The holders of those debentures were to be entitled to receive a distribution of the proceeds of the sale of the company that was proceeding under the terms of a special act of Parliament. The directors of the West Cork Railway Company had proposed that a sum of £4,000 should be reserved from the purchase proceeds. Part of that reserved amount would be used to remunerate certain directors for past services, although, evidently, those directors had never in the past sought remuneration. A further part would be used to pay officers of the company as compensation for loss of their employment, although no such payment was contractually required. The terms of this proposal were put to a vote at a meeting of the company. Although the proposal was passed 'by a large majority'[78] at the meeting, the plaintiff—a voting debenture holder—had dissented and brought an action to prevent the directors from applying the funds in the way proposed, despite receiving majority shareholder approval.

There is little in the language of the decision to suggest the court saw corporate profit-maximization as an affirmative legal duty, although the court did at one point refer, in a hypothetical, to 'the purpose of getting the greatest profit from the business of the company',[79] a phrase that could no doubt be read as a reference to profit maximization. The critical legal issue, however, was not about maximizing profits. It involved a narrower technical matter. The court concluded that neither the directors of the corporation nor the 'general meeting' (ie the majority of shareholders) were empowered to grant compensation to corporate officials when that compensation could not be linked to an inducement to earn profits for the company in the future. This aspect of the decision concerns no allegation of impropriety or breach of fiduciary duty

[77] (1883) 23 Ch D 654.
[78] ibid 657.
[79] ibid 666.

on the part of the directors but rather centres on the scope of the authority of the shareholders in general meeting to authorize the corporation to expend corporate funds in certain circumstances. And the conclusion is that they can, indeed, be prohibited from authorizing such payments where the expenditure, as Bowen LJ put it, is not 'reasonably incidental to, and within the reasonable scope of carrying on, the business of the company'.[80]

It is to Bowen LJ that we owe the iconic phrase with which this case has become indelibly associated. Acknowledging that it would be both unrealistic and inappropriate to insist that corporate directors could never agree to pay employees anything beyond what was strictly required by the terms of their employment contracts, Bowen LJ offers a hypothetical example of a permissible employer's bounty. He summons the hypothetical image of a magnanimous railway company that decides to arrange for all of its porters to have tea in the country at the company's expense:

> Why should they not? It is for the directors to judge, provided it is a matter which is reasonably incidental to the carrying on of the business of the company, and a company which always treated its employees with Draconian severity, and never allowed them a single inch more than the strict letter of the bond, would soon find itself deserted—at all events, unless labour was very much more easy to obtain in the market than it often is. *The law does not say that there are to be no cakes and ale, but there are to be no cakes and ale except such as are required for the benefit of the company.*[81] Charity has no business to sit at boards of directors *qua* charity. There is, however, a kind of charitable dealing which is for the interest of those who practise it, and to that extent and in that garb (I admit not a very philanthropic garb) charity may sit at the board, but for no other purpose.[82]

Despite the appetizing image of a pleasant tea service in an English country garden, the decision in *Hutton v West Cork Railway* did not turn on any finding of impropriety on the part of the corporation's directors, but on a conclusion that a resolution passed by a majority of shareholders improperly sought to bind the minority. The court at one point used the term ultra vires to describe this impugned resolution. But, as explained in a later case,[83] the term ultra vires, in its traditional sense, means that an action would be wholly beyond the

[80] ibid 671.
[81] ibid 672–73 (emphasis added).
[82] ibid 673.
[83] *Kaye v Croydon Tramways Co* [1898] 1 Ch 358 (CA).

powers of the company to perform—even if the shareholders unanimously resolved to perform it.[84] That is not quite how the term was used in *Hutton v West Cork Railway*. Instead, the court appeared to mean not that the corporation was wholly incapable of performing a certain act, but rather that the act was beyond the powers of a majority of the shareholders to impose upon dissenting shareholders.

The almost equally famous case of *Parke v Daily News Ltd*[85] also involved the efficacy of a shareholders' resolution rather than a challenge to the propriety of a directors' decision. A corporation had proposed to distribute to employees most of the purchase money to be received in the sale of its principal assets, although these employees had no contractual right to any such payments. A shareholders' meeting was to be called to authorize this essentially gratuitous distribution. One shareholder objected and brought an action to prevent the payment. In holding that a majority of shareholders did not, in fact, have the authority to ratify a payment of this sort, the court flatly rejected the notion that directors must take into consideration their duties to employees (beyond, of course, honouring the corporation's contractual obligations). After reciting the defendants' argument in favour of a putative duty to consider employees' interests, Plowman J curtly concluded: 'But no authority to support that proposition as a proposition of law was cited to me; I know of none, and in my judgment such is not the law.'[86] Thus, the payment of sums to employees beyond their contractual entitlements 'however laudable, and however enlightened from the point of view of industrial relations, were such as the law does not recognize as a sufficient justification.'[87]

This case has regularly been cited in support of the proposition that directors should not consider the interests of employees except as incidental to the long-term financial interests of shareholders.[88] This was not, however, a case about the object of directors' duties but rather about limits on the power of majority shareholders to impose their will on an objecting minority. In any event, as Davies and others have noted, the specific effect of both *Hutton* and *Parke* have now essentially been reversed in the UK by statute.[89]

[84] ibid 374, cited in *Parke v Daily News (No 2)* (n 5) 590.
[85] [1962] 2 WLR 566.
[86] ibid 593.
[87] ibid 594.
[88] See eg Sarah Worthington and Sinéad Agnew, *Sealy & Worthington's Text, Cases and Materials on Company Law* (Oxford University Press 2022) 337.
[89] Paul L Davies, Sarah Worthington, and Christopher Hare, *Gower's Principles of Modern Company Law* (11th edn, Sweet & Maxwell 2021) 288–89 n 183, citing Companies Act 2006 s 247. Section 247 even explicitly provides that directors have the power to make provision for a corporation's employees on a cessation or transfer of the business 'notwithstanding the general duty imposed by section 172' (duty to promote the success of the company.) The forerunner to s 247, s 719 of the Companies Act

Each of these famous cases offers proponents of shareholder primacy the comforting, if somewhat limited, assurance that, for at least a century, UK business corporations have, indeed, been expected to make profits, that those profits both economically and legally should benefit shareholders, at least indirectly, and that even where a majority of the corporation's shareholders are inclined to endorse a kinder, gentler policy of allowing some portion of the corporation's bounty to be shared gratuitously with non-shareholders, objecting minority shareholders may be able to restrain such an action as impermissible where it cannot be linked to ultimate shareholder financial benefit, except where the relevant corporate statute says otherwise. It thus may be said that these casebook warhorses are all roughly consistent with a corporate mandate to maximize profit (or shareholder or enterprise value or wealth), although none of them explicitly refers to such a 'maximizing' mandate.[90]

Although it thus seems that courts (absent statutory intervention) historically have been ready to forbid corporate munificence when directed toward employees, customers, and even perhaps the general public good, there is another line of authorities that suggests considerably more sympathy for outright charitable contributions by corporations. Yet, can it be said that these cases confirm, correct, or merely confuse the proposition that business corporations are to maximize profits or financial gain for their shareholders?

Consider, for example, the particularly well-known American case on this subject: *AP Smith Mfg Co v Barlow*,[91] a 1953 decision of the Supreme Court of New Jersey. The *AP Smith* case involved a New Jersey corporation that had made a modest donation[92] in 1951 to Princeton University. A number of the corporation's shareholders objected, prompting the corporation to seek a declaration of the court to ensure the lawfulness of the donation. The matter could not be decided solely by considering the common law rules applying to gratuitous payments by a for-profit corporation. The state of New Jersey had, in fact, enacted a statute explicitly authorizing corporations to make charitable

1985, similarly included an explicit statement that the power to make provision for such employees or former employees was exercisable even if 'not in the best interests of the company' (s 719(2)).

[90] One notes, however, that Moore and Petrin have argued that neither of these cases, properly read, stand for the unambiguous shareholder primacy norm for which they are typically cited. See Marc Moore and Martin Petrin, *Corporate Governance: Law, Regulation and Theory* (2nd edn, Edward Elgar Publishing 2025), 153ff.

[91] 98 A 2d 581 (NJ 1953).

[92] The donation of US$1,500 was specifically described as 'a very modest donation' by Stein JSC, the Chancery Division judge who heard the case at first instance. 26 NJ Super 106, 109 (1953). In the directors' resolution providing for the donation, the directors of the corporation described the sum to be donated as 'a moderate gift' (ibid 114).

donations; but that statute had been passed in 1930, many years after the incorporation of the corporation that was the subject of the case. The objecting shareholders therefore argued that the statute should not apply, and that, in the absence of such a statute, the common law would prohibit such a donation.

Characterizing as the 'common law rule' the notion that 'those who managed the corporation could not disburse any corporate funds for philanthropic or other worthy public cause unless the expenditure would benefit the corporation', the Court acknowledged that the growth of corporations in size and economic impact had led to an environment in which there was considerable public support and even public pressure for corporations to contribute to charities. Although the court reasoned that the statute would apply to permit the challenged donation, it went on to express the view that 'the corporate power to make reasonable charitable contributions exists under modern conditions, even apart from express statutory provision'.[93]

How is one, then, to interpret the relationship between charitable giving and a putative mandate to maximize financial gain for the benefit of shareholders? Was this decision a recognition that corporations may appropriately contribute to important societal institutions for the same reason that public-spirited citizens choose to do so, not from a sense of individual personal gain but from a broad recognition that the support of such institutions benefits society and so, at least indirectly, benefits the corporation? Or did it turn instead on the possibility that corporations may benefit more specifically and individually from such givings—in terms of improved public relations, for example? In such a case, donations would not be substantively different from advertising or public relations expenditures undeniably motivated by a desire to increase (and perhaps to maximize) profits. There is language in the opinion that might support either of these interpretations. Certainly, the lower court decision in *AP Smith* was based on a theory that a profit-making corporation would inevitably benefit—albeit indirectly—by supporting the operation of first-rate universities. That opinion includes repeated references to the long-term benefit to for-profit corporations of having a well-educated potential work force and to the presumed link between the public good and the corporation's success.[94] It also alludes to the broader pro-business ideological role of the university in preserving the American system of free enterprise, and 'erecting a strong breastwork against any onslaught from hostile forces which would

[93] ibid 590.

[94] 'What promotes the general good inescapably advances the corporate weal.' See 26 NJ Super 106 (1953) (n 92) 114 (Stein JSC).

change our way of life either in respect of private enterprise or democratic self-government'.[95] Yet, it must be said that the lower court does refer to the more firm-specific benefits of 'social licence' or perhaps the public relations aspect of charitable giving as well.[96] Yet, one may still note that there is no suggestion either in the lower court or in the opinion of the Supreme Court of New Jersey that the law demands of corporations that they operate to maximize profits or shareholder wealth. The reference to the presumed profit-making mandate of the business corporation is rather more equivocal, consisting only of the somewhat vague observation that, over time, the end of private profit became generally accepted as the controlling one in all businesses other than those classed broadly as public utilities.[97]

## Do Business Corporations Maximize Profits?

One may fairly conclude that early twentieth century judicial authorities in the UK and the US offered business corporations commendation, not condemnation, for pursuing profits.[98] And it seems equally clear that shareholders were understood to be the principal beneficiaries of corporate profit-making either because it is rising profits that were expected to facilitate the payment of larger dividends (which in some circumstances corporations might even be compelled to pay), or because the effect of rising profits would be to increase the value and trading price of the corporation's shares, or for some combination of both of these reasons. But although there is no serious doubt that business corporations should, and do, seek to earn profits, is it meaningful to assert that they do, or should (either as a matter of law or financial theory), *maximize* profits?

'*Profit* maximization', as a technical matter, is rarely seen today as the putative goal of the business corporation in the specialized economic, financial, or legal literature. This has been so for a number of years. So, for example, in

[95] ibid 112.

[96] For example, Stein notes: 'Anything that tends to promote with the public a company's good-will is a reasonable measure' (ibid 116).

[97] ibid 583, 584. It should also be noted that the question of corporate charitable donations has been dealt with in a similar way by UK courts. See eg *Evans v BrunnerMond & Co*, [1921] 1 Ch 359, in which a substantial corporate donation to Imperial College was also upheld by the English Chancery Court in circumstances where a shareholders' resolution purported to authorize the donation.

[98] As former Delaware Supreme Court Chief Justice Leo Strine Jr has pithily remarked, many commentators seem to have 'a continuing struggle with the idea that for-profit corporations seek profit.' Leo E Strine, Jr, 'Our Continuing Struggle with the Idea that For-Profit Corporations Seek Profit' (2012) 47 Wake Forest Law Review 135.

1978, legal scholar Henry Manne, in referring to the conduct of corporations in terms of maximizing profits, added the parenthetical '(or, more correctly, to maximize the present wealth position of the owners).'[99] Similarly, although legal scholar Stephen Bainbridge's recent book about the corporate objective is titled *The Profit Motive*,[100] the subtitle refers to the more conventional modern articulation of the corporate goal: 'shareholder value maximization.'

Today, the idea that shareholder primacy is understood to mean (or at least to include) that the corporate goal is specifically to maximize shareholder value is generally described as the 'traditional view.'[101] Indeed, a survey of widely used business school finance texts confirms that identifying the appropriate goal of the corporation as 'maximizing shareholder wealth' or 'value' (rather than 'maximizing profits') has become, quite literally, the 'textbook' articulation of the business corporation's goal.[102] As recently as 2011, in a survey by the Brookings Institution of leading US business and law schools, this 'maximizing shareholder wealth' version of shareholder primacy was found, overwhelmingly, to be the model taught to business and law students at the twenty leading law and business schools in the United States.[103] This finding was especially intriguing, because it was apparent that law professors' decisions to teach their students that the law required corporations to maximize shareholder value was not a reflection of each professor's preferred ideology, but rather represented occasionally grudging acceptance of what was understood to be settled US (or at least, Delaware) law: '[Law professors] cite federal court precedents and state rulings . . . as having resolved these issues, and believe they have a responsibility to teach what the law is, not what some would like it to be.'[104]

[99] Henry G Manne, 'Should Corporations Assume More Social Responsibilities' in M Bruce Johnson (ed), *The Attack on Corporate America* (McGraw-Hill 1978) 3.

[100] Bainbridge (n 2).

[101] Hart and Zingales (n 1) 196.

[102] See eg Richard A Brealey, Stewart C Myers, and Franklin Allen, *Principles of Corporate Finance* (10th edn, McGraw-Hill Irwin 2011) 9: 'The goal of maximizing shareholder value is widely accepted in both theory and practice'; Stephen A Ross, Randolph W Westerfield, and Bradford D Jordan, *Essentials of Corporate Finance* (7th edn, McGraw-Hill Irwin 2011) 10: 'The goal of financial management is to maximize the current value per share of the existing stock'; Zvi Bodie and Robert C Merton, *Finance* (Prentice Hall 2000), referring to a 'feasible rule' for managers to follow: 'To maximize the wealth of current stockholders is just such a rule.' Robert C Merton, *Continuous-Time Finance* (Basil Blackwell 1990) 4 n 3: 'Common practice in finance theory is to translate this obligation to shareholders into the simple operating imperative: maximize the current value of the equity of the firm.' In each case, these statements of shareholder primacy are qualified to make clear that they are subject to legal and ethical constraints and that there may also be sound practical reasons to consider the interests of other corporate stakeholders, each of whom can be expected to attempt to use whatever levers they may possess to influence corporate policy to favour their interests.

[103] Darrell West, 'The Purpose of the Corporation in Business and Law School Curricula' Governance Studies at Brookings (19 July 2011) 18.

[104] ibid.

The Aspen Institute undertook a similar survey[105] canvassing not only academics but also business executives and investors. The Aspen study likewise found that 'the vast majority of respondents, *regardless of their own opinions on the matter*, believe that the conventional wisdom in American business today is that businesses are either legally or ethically obliged to maximize shareholder value'.[106]

Whether the same result would have been obtained if a similar pool of respondents had been surveyed in 1960, or were surveyed in 2025, is unclear. Certainly, there is a widely held view that shareholder wealth maximization as a corporate goal did not come to dominate corporate boardrooms or law school classrooms until the 1970s or perhaps 1980s, and there are at least some indications that the dominance of that view in those same fora may have wobbled in the twenty-first century. Both of these propositions will be revisited in due course.

## Conclusion

Business corporations must pursue profits. Profit-seeking is the function that defines them, the activity that sustains them, the measure of their success, and the ultimate source of their value to society. How corporate managers navigate the essential profit-seeking function while recognizing the abiding need to fulfill their responsibilities as law-abiding citizens and enlightened and ethical members of a human community lies at the heart of the search for the optimal corporate goal. At various times and in various jurisdictions, an unapologetic shareholder primacy norm has been recognized and celebrated as the best, even if imperfect, corporate mission, At other times, and in many places, a carefully tempered, tactfully qualified profit-seeking mission has been heralded as the better, even nobler way.

Before exploring further the vicissitudes of possible bull and bear markets in shareholder primacy ideology, however, it will first be helpful to consider three foundational issues:

[105] Keller Fay Group, 'Unpacking Corporate Purpose: A Report on the Beliefs of Executives, Investors and Scholars' Aspen Institute Business & Society Program (May 2014).

[106] ibid 11 (emphasis added).

- the meaning of 'profit';
- how and why the putative corporate goal of 'profit maximization' evolved into the modern formulation of 'shareholder primacy', 'shareholder wealth', or 'shareholder value' maximization;
- how and why economic understandings of 'the firm' came to be adopted as supposed legal rules for the management of business corporations.

It is to these considerations that we turn in chapter 5.

# 5

# The Prophets and Profits of Shareholder Primacy Part II

## Introduction

Corporate directors have often been likened to trustees. The similarities are apparent. But the business corporation is not a trust; its directors and officers, although fiduciaries, are not trustees.[1] The best interests of a business corporation go well beyond ensuring the corporation's survival or safely preserving its assets for posterity.[2] Those would be conservative low risk strategies, but avoiding risk cannot be the guiding principle of business. Quite the contrary. The business corporation is distinguished from other bodies corporate (such as charities, churches, municipalities, and the British monarchy) by its profit-making function. Business profit-making must involve risk taking. If it were otherwise, business corporations would need to be prohibited from raising capital for any purpose other than investing in risk free government bonds.

[1] The influence of trust law upon the law of directors' duties has been significant throughout the common law world. In England, in particular, as FW Maitland observed many years ago, there are historical reasons for associating the role of corporate directors with the role of trustees since the ingenious form of business enterprise that preceded the introduction of general incorporation statutes in the mid-nineteenth century was the deed of settlement company, a structure that combined elements of general partnership and trust. Otto Gierke, *Political Theories of the Middle Age* (Frederic W Maitland tr, Cambridge University Press 1913). The parallel between directors and trustees has been drawn by commentators frequently in the early twentieth century See eg, AA Berle Jr, 'For Whom Corporate Managers are Trustees: A Note' (1932) 45 Harvard Law Review 1365; Harold Marsh, 'Are Directors Trustees? Conflict of Interest and Corporate Morality' (1966) 22 The Business Lawyer 35; CA Harwell Wells, 'Cycles of Corporate Social Responsibility: An Historical Perspective for the Twenty-First Century' (2002) 51 University of Kansas Law Review 77, 88. The historical significance of the trust as an alternative to the business corporation has also been explored by John Morley, 'The Common Law Corporation: The Power of the Trust in Anglo-American Business History' (2016) 116 Columbia Law Review 2145. The distinction between the fiduciary duty of trustees and the fiduciary duty of directors is discussed in Andrew S Gold, 'The Fiduciary Duty of Loyalty' in Evan J Criddle and others (eds), *The Oxford Handbook of Fiduciary Law* (Oxford University Press 2019) 384, 388.

[2] Tara Helfman has argued that the concept of fiduciary duty first arose in English law in the context of real property and that 'the concept of fiduciary duty . . . emerged as a means of moderating the tensions between current and future interests in land'. Tara Helfman, 'Land Ownership and the Origins of Fiduciary Duty' (2006) 41(3) Real Property, Probate and Trust Journal 651, 652.

*Corporate Governance and Enlightened Fiduciaries*. Christopher C. Nicholls, Oxford University Press.
 DOI: 10.1093/9780198904199.003.0005

But to paraphrase Tolstoy, 'How Much Profit Does a Corporation Need?'[3] How, precisely, can the profit-making function of the business corporation be specified and operationalized? Is there an untamed 'state of nature' for the business corporation? Is it natural or inevitable, for example, to expect that business corporations will seek not simply to earn but, more specifically, to *maximize* profit? Or is there some more refined (or proprietary) measure of financial success, such as enterprise value, 'Economic Value Added' (EVA),[4] or shareholder wealth, that the unbridled—and unregulated—corporation, subject to managerial fiat and market pressures alone, would be expected to enhance or maximize? The question of what firms did (or should 'maximize') has long been of interest to economists. Robin Marris posed the question this way: 'Are we justified in assuming that anything is *maximized* at all?'[5] Peculiar questions of this sort are relevant to the law and regulation of corporate governance, too. What the law does and should require of corporations and their managers will be conditioned by how we might expect corporations to behave in the absence of any particular legal mandates or legal constraints over the conduct of their managers or the operation of their business.

A legal regime that mandates merely what is inevitable would be ludicrous and superfluous; a regime that purports to prohibit outcomes ineluctably embedded in institutional definitions would be equally ludicrous and hopelessly ineffective. There is no legislation that decrees that human beings must regularly breathe oxygen. It is the very nature of human beings that they must do so. Nor could any sensible legal regime ever seek to regulate human behaviour through some absurd legislative directive purporting to ration, restrain, or prohibit the breathing of oxygen. Legislation mandating immutable characteristics is superfluous and fatuous, while legislation purporting to curb or vary those same characteristics must of necessity be ignored lest it lead to the obliteration of the very people or institutions subject to such pointless proscriptions. To define the fiduciary duties of corporate directors (and accordingly any supposed 'purpose' of the corporations they serve) sensibly, it is essential, from a legal perspective, to determine first to what extent a 'profit-making' or 'profit-maximizing' goal is or is not concomitant with the formation and operation of the business corporation itself under the command of its human leaders.

[3] See Leo Tolstoy, 'How Much Land Does a Man Need?' in Leo Tolstoy, *How Much Land Does a Man Need? And Other Stories* (Ronald Wilks tr, Penguin Books 1993) 96 (story originally published in 1886).

[4] EVA is a measure of economic profit (as opposed to accounting profit) developed and trademarked by Stern Stewart & Co. See Christopher C Nicholls, *Corporate Finance and Canadian Law* 2d edn (Carswell 2013), 448.

[5] Robin Marris, *The Economic Theory of 'Managerial' Capitalism* (Macmillan 1967) 107.

As Adolf Berle observed in 1965: 'Since economic theory is in preponderant measure dependent upon assumed motivations, to maintain an unchanged theory must involve assumption that the motivations and possibilities of action thereon are substantially similar under present conditions as those prevailing before its development.'[6]

## Profit

Businesses must earn profits, or at least attempt and reasonably expect to do so. And business corporations are created to carry on business. Some commentators have observed that: '[n]o statute, in Delaware or elsewhere, requires directors or officers to maximize [or, it may fairly be added, to earn any] shareholder profits.'[7] Certainly, the Delaware General Corporation Law,[8] for example, includes no such provision. Nor does the UK Companies Act 2006,[9] Australia's Corporations Act 2001,[10] or any of the thirteen Canadian federal and provincial incorporation statutes. Indeed, not only do none of these statutes expressly mandate that corporations *maximize* profit, wealth, or value, but they typically do not even explicitly require that corporations be operated on a for-profit basis. That is not quite the end of the story. The Model Business Corporations Act, for example, does define 'corporation' to mean 'a corporation for profit',[11] and there have also been important judicial decisions on the topic, including the cases discussed in Chapter 4. Those judicial decisions, however, do not typically rely on specific mandatory provisions of corporate statutes to draw their conclusions, but rather interpret the duties of corporate directors and officers within the context of the corporate statute as a whole.

The observation, then, that no statute in Delaware or in many other jurisdictions expressly requires business corporations to maximize profits is both undeniably accurate and singularly unhelpful. After all, one might also note that no statute, in Delaware or elsewhere, requires human beings to speak in prose, walk upright, eat when hungry, or engage in the pursuit of happiness. Should

[6] Adolf A Berle, 'The Impact of the Corporation on Classical Economic Theory' (1965) 79(1) The Quarterly Journal of Economics 25, 29.

[7] See eg Judd F Sneirson, 'The History of Shareholder Primacy from Adam Smith through the Rise of Financialism' in Beate Sjåfjell and Christopher M Bruner (eds), *The Cambridge Handbook of Corporate Law, Corporate Governance and Sustainability* (Cambridge University Press 2019) 73.

[8] 2021 Delaware Code Title 8.

[9] UK Public General Acts 2006 c 46.

[10] No 50 (2001).

[11] Model Business Corporations Act § 1.40: definition of 'Corporation', <https://www.americanbar.org/content/dam/aba/administrative/business_law/corplaws/mbca-202504.pdf>.

we therefore assume that human beings—in the absence of such express legal requirements—cannot be counted upon to do any of these things? People and the institutions they create behave according to their nature. The nature of business corporations means that, at all times, everywhere, they can be relied upon to operate with a view to profit—not because any lawyer, judge, economist, sociologist, legislator, or philosopher has declared that they are obliged to do so. But what, precisely, does characterizing corporations as 'for-profit' firms entail? It is to that question that we turn in this chapter.

As noted in Chapter 2, for neoclassical[12] economists, firms, including business corporations, were traditionally regarded merely as 'production functions' in which input and output levels are chosen to *maximize* profits.[13]

This simplified (one might say simplistic) picture was an old one. C.J. Hawkins has noted that '[a]lmost the whole of today's standard profit-maximization theory of the firm derived from the neo-classical models during the early part of [the twentieth] century',[14] by which he meant, in particular, models developed by neoclassical economists Edward Chamberlin and Joan Robinson.[15] Yet, the relative antiquity of the term 'profit maximization' is evidently a matter of debate, too. P.J.D. Wiles argued in 1961, for example, that the phrase 'profit maximization' 'is surprisingly new in economics',[16] and that '[t]

[12] It was Karl Marx who identified the 'classical' economists as those economists beginning with William Petty and Boisguillebert, through Adam Smith and Benjamin Franklin, and culminating with the work of David Ricardo and Sismondi. See Karl Marx, *A Contribution to the Critique of Political Economy* (NI Stone (tr), Charles H Kerr & Company 1904) 56 ff. John Maynard Keynes extended Marx's term to include, as Keynes put it, 'the *followers* of Ricardo, those, that is to say, who adopted and perfected the theory of the Ricardian economics, including (for example) J.S. Mill, Marshall, Edgeworth and Prof. Pigou'. See John Maynard Keynes, *The General Theory of Employment Interest and Money* (Harcourt, Brace and Company 1936) 3 (emphasis in original).

[13] See eg Oliver Hart, *Firms, Contracts, and Financial Structure* (Clarendon Press 1995) 15 (emphasis added). The important distinction between a putative duty to seek profits and a duty to *maximize* profits (or alternative metrics of financial gain) has occasionally been alluded to in the legal literature. See eg Edward B Rock, 'For Whom Is the Corporation Managed in 2020? The Debate Over Corporate Purpose' (2021) 76(2) The Business Lawyer 363, 377: 'While it is true that, outside of the sale-of-company context in which the interests of shareholders and other stakeholders inescapably diverge, there is no general legal duty to *maximize* shareholder value, there is a general legal duty to *pursue or promote* shareholder value' (emphasis in original). In Berle and Means there is a notion that the firm could be operated, not to maximize profits but rather to earn 'profits sufficient to keep the securityholders satisfied'. See Adolf A Berle and Gardiner C Means, *The Modern Corporation and Private Property* (Transaction Publishers 1991 (originally published in 1932)) 301. To this, Manne objected, claiming that it suffered from the deficiency that we 'manifestly' cannot know what constitutes a 'sufficient' amount of capital. See Henry Manne, 'The Higher Criticism of the Modern Corporation' (1962) 62 Columbia Law Review 399, 402.

[14] CJ Hawkins, *Theory of the Firm* (The Macmillan Press 1973) 11.

[15] ibid 16.

[16] Peter John de la Fosse Wiles, *Price, Cost and Output* (Basil Blackwell 1961) 182. Wiles did acknowledge that, while the verbal formulation 'profit maximization' was new, 'something of this kind has always been implicit' (ibid 182).

he maximization of profits is clearly never the same thing as the maximization of satisfaction'.[17]

More modern and sophisticated views of the corporation that explore the implications of intra firm incentives and operations have long since supplanted the economics primer stick-figure version of the infamous corporate 'black box'. But the original black box archetype has continued to cast a formidable intergenerational shadow, too. Remnants of this older economic model of the firm continue to resurface within modern analyses of the proper role and function of business corporations and the putative duties of the people who manage them.

The singular emphasis on the wealth-seeking (or profit-seeking/maximizing) goal of the corporation in the early economic literature is not surprising. The corporation is a human invention, and economists have fixed their attention on the extraneous, measurable factors that seem likely to motivate human action. We should hardly expect otherwise. Duty, hope, love, empathy, and charity are all undeniably powerful—perhaps ever the most powerful—determinants of human behaviour. But these forces of character, morality, sentiment, and emotion are internal, immeasurable, and largely immovable by the levers of legislation, regulation, or other instruments of hard or soft power. At the all-important 'margins',[18] then, it is the motivating power of external incentives, particularly the prospect of material gain—money—that can best explain those variations of human action or inaction that are most susceptible to changes in organizational protocols or broader public policy.

As John Stuart Mill observed,

> Political Economy . . . concerns itself only with "such of the phenomena of the social state as take place in consequence of the pursuit of wealth. It makes entire abstraction of every other human passion or motive; . . . Political Economy considers mankind as occupied solely in acquiring and consuming wealth; and aims at showing what is the course of action into which mankind, living in a state of society, would be impelled, if that motive, except in the degree in which it is checked by the two perpetual counter-motives above

[17] ibid163.

[18] The notion of 'marginal utility' that became one of the key defining elements of neoclassical economic theory is usually attributed to pioneering nineteenth century works by Léon Walras, Carl Menger, and William Stanley Jevons. See eg JR Hicks, 'Léon Walras' (1934) 2(4) Econometrica 338; Milton Friedman, 'Leon Walras and His Economic System' (1955) 45(5) American Economic Review 900, 901.

averted to [ie, aversion to labour and present enjoyment of indulgences], were absolute ruler of all their actions..."[19]

Mill fully understood and readily acknowledged that, in the case of individual human beings, the suggestion that gaining wealth was the sole motivation for actions was reductionist.[20] Of course human beings were moral creatures. Of course they were sensitive to the needs and wants of others. And of course they were capable of great acts of self-sacrifice, self-denial, and genuine altruism, especially—although surely not exclusively—within families and other closely knit communities. The economists' focus on the incentive effect of the prospect of material gain never suggested otherwise.

Alfred Marshall, in his classic 1890 text, *Principles of Economics*, also strongly defended economics against claims that it had wrongly normalized pursuit of self-interest, dismissing as a 'popular error' the suggestion that economists regarded it 'as "natural" or "normal," and in some sense even right that man should be governed only by selfish motives'.[21] The economist's focus on the pursuit of material gain, he insisted, did not imply any such gloomy belief that nobler sentiments were alien to human beings; but the pursuit of money must still be scrutinized precisely because it was money that could be seen as providing a significant external incentive to human behaviour.

Marshall, one of the early neoclassical economists, recognized the need to take proper account of ethical considerations in trying to construct a useful account of economics. And Marshall also was strongly of the view that, although much had obviously changed in the economic conditions of society throughout human history, there was no reason to believe 'that man is on the whole harder and harsher than he was, or that he was ever more willing than he is now to sacrifice his own happiness for the benefit of others'.[22] Surely the same could be said today. Marshall also rejected the suggestion that economics considered only those actions governed by selfish motives. The economist is concerned, Marshall said, with 'the quantities of measurable motives'.[23] Nor

[19] JS Mill, *Logic* (John W Parker 1843) Bk VI ch IX, 570–71. This passage Mill quoted from an earlier essay, 'On the Definition of Political Economy; and on the Method of Investigation Proper to it'. This essay was written between 1830 and 1832 and was first published in the *London and Westminster Review* in 1836. See Charles H Hinnant, 'The Invention of *Homo Oeconomicus:* A Reading of John Stuart Mill's "On the Definition of Political Economy"' (1998) 21(3) Prose Studies 51, 52.

[20] 'Not that any political economist was ever so absurd as to suppose that mankind are really thus constituted but because this is the mode in which science must necessarily proceed', cited in Hinnant (n 18) 59.

[21] Marshall, *Principles of Economics* (Macmillan and Co 1890), Bk I, Ch 6, 78.

[22] ibid Bk I, Ch 1, 7.

[23] ibid 79.

did Marshall confuse the positive and the normative aspects of economics. On the contrary, for Marshall:

> [f]ollowing our definition of an economic law, we may say that the course of action which may be expected under certain conditions from the members of an industrial group is the normal action of the members of that group relatively to those conditions . . . it is sometimes erroneously supposed that normal action in economics is that which is right morally. But that is to be understood only when the context implies that the action is being judged from the ethical point of view. When we are considering the facts of the world, as they are, and not as they ought to be, we shall have to regard as 'normal' to the circumstances in view, much action which we should use our utmost efforts to stop.[24]

It was important for economists to focus on the human pursuit of money, then, not because it was significantly more responsible for motivating human behaviour but rather because, even if ultimately far less significant overall, it was nevertheless a more quantifiable and—importantly—a more variable motivating factor. The pursuit of wealth was the measurable counterbalance to the complex and largely immutable psychological and moral forces that informed and constrained human decision-making. And, perhaps most fundamentally:

> When the motive to a man's action is spoken of as supplied by the money which he will earn, it is not meant that his mind is closed to all other considerations save those of gain. Even the most purely business relations of life assume honesty and good faith; while many of them take for granted, if not generosity, yet at least the absence of meanness.'[25]

Marshall also reminds that, even in the case of those (very few) individuals who are, indeed, motivated solely by the desire for money, one must recall that the uses to which money can be put need not necessarily be venal or dissipating, but can be ennobling and intellectually and artistically enriching. There is no reason to suppose that many people motivated by the desire for financial gain are not, in fact, ultimately seeking these nobler ends to which the acquisition of money is merely the means.[26]

[24] ibid Bk I ch III, 34–35.
[25] ibid 80.
[26] ibid 81.

For a slightly different reason, Hayek also objected to the somewhat misleading use of the term 'self-interest' in the classical economists' explication of the operation and social value of market exchange. As Hayek explained,

> The important point about the catallaxy[27] is that it reconciles different knowledge and different purposes which, whether the individuals be selfish or not, will greatly differ from one person to another.[28]

We need not, then, reduce all human motivation to a blinkered and Mammon-like obsession for 'trodden gold'[29] to concede that money incentivizes at least some human behaviour at least some of the time. Were it not so, labour strikes would be unheard of, compensation consultants would be working as—or for—baristas, and graduates of Ivy League colleges would be just as likely to seek employment as poets and sculptors as they are to compete for investment banking and management consultancy positions at Goldman Sachs and McKinseys.[30] But the mechanisms of material motivation are not straightforward. Certainly the pursuit of money cannot always be understood invariably as a proxy for, or a mere intermediate step on the road to, the ultimate enjoyment of hedonic pleasures. People do not strive to 'get' only so that they may prodigiously 'spend.'[31] Frank Knight observed a propensity of human beings to seek to accumulate wealth wholly unrelated to any desire for increased consumption. For Knight, this propensity to accumulate surplus wealth could not meaningfully be attributed to some human acquisitive 'instinct.' Rather, he preferred the explanation that human beings derive a certain 'pleasure of being

[27] Hayek coined the term 'catallaxy', deriving it from an earlier coinage, 'catallactics', which he attributed to Richard Whately, *Introductory Lectures on Political Economy* (London, 1855), and which he noted had also been invoked in the mid twentieth-century work of Ludwig von Mises, *Human Action* (Yale 1949). Hayek explained that 'catallaxy' was linked to a Greek word that implied not only 'exchange' but also 'to admit into the community' and 'to change from enemy into friend.' He used the term to refer to the spontaneous order 'brought about by the mutual adjustment of many individual economies in a market.' See Friederich A Hayek, *Law, Legislation and Liberty, Vol 2, The Mirage of Social Justice* (University of Chicago Press 1976) 108–09.

[28] ibid 110.

[29] John Milton, *Paradise Lost*, Book I, lines 679–83: 'Mammon, the least erected Spirit that fell/From Heaven; for even in Heaven his looks and thoughts/Were always downward bent, admiring more/The riches of heaven's pavement, trodden gold,/Than aught divine.'

[30] According to the *Economist*, 'in 2024 fully half of Harvard graduates who entered the workforce took jobs in finance, consulting or technology'. See 'Harvard Rules' *Economist* (21 December 2024) 40. (The title of the online version of this article is more blunt: 'Finance, Consulting and Tech are Gobbling Up Top Students' *The Economist* (19 December 2024).

[31] William Wordsworth's nineteenth-century lament about the alienating effects of materialism ('getting and spending, we lay waste our powers') was beautiful poetry but perhaps doubtful sociology. William Wordsworth, 'The World Is Too Much With Us' in *Poems in Two Volumes*, vol 1 (Longman, Hurst, Rees, and Ormes 1807).

a cause', a concept he evidently borrowed from CH Cooley, Gustav Gross, and others.[32] For Knight, irrespective of one's income level: 'A large part of the consumption of persons . . . does not yield satisfaction *as consumption*; the motives and cravings are social in their origin and nature.'[33]

However, it would be naïve and unrealistic to disregard the tangible advantages of wealth and the powerful lure the prospect of such advantages creates. Seeking greater material wealth has always been the most practical way to improve the physical conditions of one's life, a conclusion pithily observed by Adam Smith in his description of what he argued was an innate propensity of human beings to save:

> An augmentation of fortune is the means by which the greater part of men propose and wish to better their condition. It is the means the most vulgar and the most obvious; and the most likely way of augmenting their fortune, is to save and accumulate some part of what they acquire.[34]

## Is the System to Blame?

Are the personal motivating effects of the pursuit of wealth amplified or distorted by a capitalist system in which the business corporation plays such an essential role? Is capitalism, in effect, not merely a benign 'harness' of human impulses but a noxious 'spur'? Critics of capitalism certainly think so, fearing that the capitalist system, by celebrating material gain and even glorifying greed,[35] creates a distorted, loathsome, and destructive desire for the pursuit

[32] Frank H Knight, *Risk, Uncertainty, and Profit* (Houghton Mifflin 1921) 320–21 n 1.

[33] ibid 331. With respect to the critical influence of social influences on human desires, René Girard has articulated the provocative concept of 'mimetic desire'. Girard argues that 'Man is the creature who does not know what to desire, and he turns to others in order to make up his mind. We desire what others desire because we imitate their desires.' René Girard, 'Generative Scapegoating-Discussion' in Robert G Hamerton-Kelly (ed) *Violent Origins: Walter Burkhert, René Girard, and Jonathan Z Smith, on Ritual Killing and Cultural Formation* (Stanford University Press 1987) 73, 121–22.

[34] Adam Smith, *An Inquiry into the Nature and Causes of the Wealth of Nations* (Edwin Cannan ed, Methuen & Co 1904), Bk II ch III.

[35] Gordon Gekko, the screen villain portrayed by actor Michael Douglas in Oliver Stone's 1987 film *Wall Street* (Twentieth Century Fox 1987), in a much-quoted scene in that film, famously declared to the shareholders of a company whose managers he sought to unseat: 'Greed . . . is good. Greed is right. Greed works.' Although Gekko was a fictional character, this dramatized vindication of greed was reportedly based on a statement actually made in a 1986 commencement speech at the University of California, Berkeley's Haas School of Business by then-prominent arbitrageur Ivan Boesky: 'Greed is all right, by the way. I want you to know that. I think greed is healthy. You can be greedy and still feel good about yourself.' Quoted in Greg Farrell, 'Wall Street Titan, Who inspired Gordon Gekko's "Greed is Good" Screed Before Being Banned in One of the Biggest Financial Scandals and Sent to Prison, Has Died' *Fortune* (20 May 2024) https://fortune.com/2024/05/20/wall-street-titan-gordon-gekko-greed-is-good-ivan-boesky-dies/. Then UK Prime Minister Boris Johnson also reportedly told a meeting of

of wealth that far exceeds any natural innate human inclination to acquire through material gain the reasonable means for safety, comfort, or control.

There is good reason to doubt this pessimistic view. For individuals, the initial accumulation of wealth and its subsequent consumption or crass display involve distinctly different goals. These goals are not necessarily complementary nor are they both invariably pursued most aggressively by those who would conventionally be described as capitalists. In fact, sociologist Max Weber once insisted that 'the impulse to acquisition, pursuit of gain, of money, of the greatest possible amount of money, has in itself nothing to do with capitalism'.[36]

Weber went even further, suggesting, counter-intuitively, that '[c]apitalism *may* even be identical with the restraint, or at least a rational tempering' of an impulse of 'greed for gain'.[37] Nevertheless, he did insist that 'capitalism is identical with the pursuit of profit, and forever *renewed profit*, by means of continuous, rational, capitalistic enterprise'.[38] And, citing the writings of Benjamin Franklin as supposedly archetypal representations of the purest spirit of capitalism, Weber concluded that capitalism embodies 'the idea of a duty of the individual toward the increase of his capital, *which is assumed as an end in itself*'.[39] Amassing capital as an end in itself—not to fund a profligate lifestyle, or to gain social or political advantage—necessarily leads to productive activity and to an increase in societal wealth. Individual 'greed', provided it leads only to the accumulation, but not the profligate consumption, of wealth, could indeed, on this view, be 'good' for society as a whole, and the blessing of Adam Smith's invisible (perhaps rather tight-fisted) hand would attend over increasing prosperity for all.

There is another intriguing sense in which the pursuit of self-interest, understood specifically to mean the pursuit of material gain, may be seen not as a morally detestable vice, but as a desirable and useful motivator of human actions and even a powerful constraint on the excesses of other potentially dangerous anti-social impulses. Albert O. Hirschman has traced the evolution of

Tory MPs in 2021 that 'the reason we have the vaccine success is because of capitalism, because of greed, my friends'. This remark he evidently later dismissed as a flippant reference to the *Wall Street* movie quote noted above. See Pippa Catterall, '"Greed my friends": Has Boris Johnson Finally Revealed His Political Philosophy?' LSE British Politics and Philosophy (29 March 2021) https://blogs.lse.ac.uk/politicsandpolicy/greed-my-friends/.

[36] Max Weber, *The Protestant Ethic and the Spirit of Capitalism* (Talcott Parsons tr, Charles Scribner's Sons 1930) 17.

[37] ibid 17 (emphasis in original).

[38] ibid.

[39] ibid 51 (emphasis added).

philosophical and economic attitudes toward the pursuit of self-interest in this specific sense, noting, among other things, how the word 'interest' itself (and its equivalent in other Western European languages) developed through the seventeenth and eighteenth centuries to be viewed as a potent counterbalance to the destructive force of wilder and socially harmful passions.[40] During this period, Hirschman argues, the word 'interest' acquired not only a nuanced meaning as desire for material gain prudently tempered by reason, but also was heralded as an effective, pro-social counterweight and antidote to the risk of otherwise unrestrained pursuit of other passions. Indulging in these other passions, unlike the constructive pursuit of material interest, would serve no ultimate social good. Pursuit of one's own 'interest' (in this important seventeenth and eighteenth centuries sense) was, in other words, not a symptom of a sick society;[41] it was the very cure.

This concept of self-interest actually serving as a check on other more dangerous and destructive interests is found in Alexis de Tocqueville's nineteenth-century discussion of 'the principle of self-interest rightly understood',[42] or, as the idea is more commonly expressed today, 'enlightened self-interest'. De Tocqueville explains that:

> The principle of self-interest rightly understood produces no great acts of self-sacrifice, but it suggests daily small acts of self-denial . . . the principle of interest rightly understood perhaps prevents men from rising far above the level of mankind, but a great number of other men, who were falling far below it, are caught and restrained by it.[43]

To somewhat similar effect is Peter Drucker's observation that: 'To say that the profit motive is not inborn in man and the expression of his true nature is, however, something very different from asserting that it is vicious, unnatural, and socially undesirable.'[44] For Drucker, such an assertion is based on two fallacious beliefs: first, that 'man's 'creative instinct' is not only good in itself but alone sufficient to make man socially constructive', and, secondly, 'that, but for the profit motive, human society would be one of equality and peace, and that

[40] Albert O Hirschman, *The Passions and the Interests: Political Arguments for Capitalism Before Its Triumph* (Princeton University Press 1977).

[41] See Elton Mayo, who, in critiquing RH Tawney, famously stated that 'the problem is *not that of the sickness of an acquisitive society; it is that of the acquisitiveness of a sick society*'. Elton Mayo, *Human Problems of an Industrial Civilisation* (Macmillan 1933) 153 (emphasis in original).

[42] Alexis de Tocqueville, *Democracy in America*, vol II (Alfred A Knopf 1956 (originally published in 1838) ch VIII.

[43] ibid 123.

[44] Peter Drucker, *The Concept of the Corporation* (New American Library 1964) 196.

all drive for power and privilege, all conflict, and all inequality are the result of the lust for gain.'[45] He rejects both of these beliefs. Of the first, he simply declares:

> [t]hat no society can be based on man's 'creative instincts'. In order to make social life possible there must always be a principle of organization which reduces individual fulfillment and individual drive to a social purpose. Otherwise that coordinated human effort on which social life rests becomes impossible. If we do not use profit and profitability as the reduction gear, we would have to work out some other social mechanism to convert the subjective drive of the individual into the objective performance of society.[46]

The incentive provided to individuals by the prospect of increasing personal wealth can be fully understood only when integrated within a broader understanding of the complexity of human nature and human motivations. Man (or woman) does not live by bread alone. The desire for wealth is linked not simply to preferences for comfort and safety but also to a desire for social status, conspicuous signaling (both to others and to one's self) of success, and even some measure of empowering control over property or people. But when once we concede that at least some propensity for material acquisitiveness motivates most human beings in their individual capacities—to greater degree in some, to lesser degree in others—what might we expect to see when such propensities are compartmentalized within institutional structures (specifically, business corporations) created for the express purpose of carrying on profitable trade?

## Profit Motive and the Business Corporation

Whatever nuanced role money may play in motivating individual human action, it is reasonable to suppose this role will be narrowed and amplified when productive activity is conducted within the business corporation. A corporation has no desire for status and no need to enhance its self-esteem by displays of wealth. It has no human desires or preferences of any kind. It is entirely a tool of its human masters and a reflection (or perhaps a refraction) of their vision, competence, ambition, vanity, and insecurities. Individual human beings

[45] ibid.
[46] ibid 196.

might well eschew narrow materialism as they seek to maximize the uniquely complex bundle of wants or needs that comprise their personal satisfaction (or 'utility'). But 'utility' is a protean term that can be defined to include a combination of material goods together with irreconcilable non-material benefits and psychic rewards flowing from craftmanship,[47] virtuous behaviour, and even altruistic sacrifices. The classical economists' (or psychological egoists') assertion that human beings seek to maximize their own utility may therefore be unhelpfully reduced to an utterly incontrovertible but equally meaningless tautology: people always act to maximize their 'utility'; and 'utility' is simply defined as whatever it is people choose to maximize.

Business corporations are entirely different. They are institutional constructs. They are formed by human beings, managed by human beings, and operated by human beings. But they have no human interests of their own and no non-material 'utility' of their own to maximize.[48] They are initially created by entrepreneurs—primarily as a financing vehicle for business operations.[49] Those same entrepreneurs may themselves over time have been relegated to a subordinate role as their corporate creation grows and depends upon financial markets for its equity financing and professional managers for its operational decision-making.

[47] See Thorstein Veblen, 'The Instinct of Workmanship and the Irksomeness of Labor' (1898) 4(2) American Journal of Sociology 187, in which Veblen argues that—contrary to some economic assumptions—human beings do not, and could not, have a congenital aversion to work. Rather, 'when not harassed with the strain of overwork, men's common sense speaks unequivocally under the guidance of the instinct of workmanship. They like to see others spend their life to some purpose, and they like to reflect that their own life is of some use' (ibid 189).

[48] Some commentators have resisted the statement that corporations do not have their own interests. See eg Andrew Keay, *The Corporate Objective* (Edward Elgar Publishing 2011) 194. Keay's argument is based upon the significance placed by the courts on the concept that a corporation is a separate legal entity, and specific instances in which courts or legislation have appeared to recognize and protect a corporate interest that cannot meaningfully be regarded as the interest of any individual human actors. Yet, even in these examples no 'interest' in the sense of an alignment with preferences is involved. The corporation's supposed interests are projected onto it by human actors.

[49] Easterbrook and Fischel once dismissively declared that: 'The corporation is a financing device and is not otherwise distinctive.' See Frank H Easterbrook and Daniel R Fischel, *The Economic Structure of Corporate Law* (Harvard University Press 1991) 10. Jensen and Meckling had already dismissed the notion of the corporation having intention or objective in their famous 1976 paper. See Michael C Jensen and William H Meckling, 'Theory of the Firm: Managerial Behavior, Agency Costs and Ownership Structure' (1976) 3 Journal of Financial Economics 305, 311:'Viewing the firm as the nexus of a set of contracting relationships among individuals also serves to make it clear that the personalization of the firm implied by asking questions such as "what should be the objective function of the firm", or 'does the firm have a social responsibility" is seriously misleading. *The firm is not an individual.* [Emphasis in original.] It is a legal fiction which serves as a focus for a complex process in which the conflicting objectives of individuals (some of whom may "represent" other organizations) are brought into equilibrium within a framework of contractual relations. In this sense the "behavior" of the firm is like the behavior of a market; i.e., the outcome of a complex equilibrium process. We seldom fall into the trap of characterizing the wheat or stock market as an individual, but we often make this error by thinking about organizations as if they were persons with motivations and intentions.'

Shareholders of the business corporation are often colloquially described as the 'owners' of this vehicle, although as a matter of law, the corporation is not a thing that can be owned. Whatever Diceyan 'real entity'[50] may be identified with the large publicly traded business corporation, it is not an entity that may meaningfully be identified with the collective consciousness of the shareholders. Although the business corporation may once have been conceived of in many jurisdictions as a corporate body comprised of its shareholders, that is no longer formally the case under most corporate law statutes[51] and is not in any event particularly meaningful or realistic in the case of large publicly traded corporations, particularly corporations whose shares are held as part of diversified investment portfolios.

One might, perhaps, have thought that the identification of shareholders with the corporate entity might have been more robust in the UK than in the USA. As Gower noted in a 1956 article comparing US and British corporate law, '[t]he modern English business corporation has evolved from the unincorporated partnership, based on mutual agreement, rather than from the corporation, based on a grant from the state, and owes more to partnership principles than to rules based on corporate personality'.[52] Yet, as the same author had noted in the first edition of his seminal corporate law text just a few years earlier, the idea of companies implying 'an association of a number of persons for a common object' had become utterly unrealistic in the case of large public companies: '[i]t is fantasy to describe [a small shareholder of a large bank] as associating with the other members in running it . . . the shareholder, although a member, is in economic reality, but not in the eyes of the law, a mere lender of capital.'[53]

Shareholders, then, do not own corporations, nor do they—collectively—constitute the corporation. They are in all practical respects corporate outsiders: mere financial claimants who are unknown strangers to most of their fellow shareholders. They do not self-identify as constituent members comprising a corporation collective, but view the corporation, rather, as an external source of entirely passive and often fairly dimly understood investment. Thus, when we speak of the profit-seeking desire of the corporation, we must look beyond the acquisitiveness or avarice of the shareholders alone, although one can also not ignore the fact that it is the shareholders to whose

[50] See ch 2 n 128.
[51] See eg Keay (n 47) 196.
[52] LCB Gower, 'Some Contrasts between British and American Corporate Law' (1956) 69 Harvard Law Review 1369, 1371–72.
[53] LCB Gower, *The Principles of Modern Company Law* (Stevens & Sons 1954) 9.

benefit the corporation's profits indirectly accrue. In the economic literature of the late nineteenth and early twentieth centuries, the assumed narrow profit-maximizing function of the business corporation originally appeared in discussions of the consequences of monopoly. As Alfred Marshall observed, for example, in particular in the case of the 'owner' of a monopoly, such an owner's prima facie interest was to 'adjust the supply to the demand . . . in such a way as to afford him the greatest possible total net revenue'.[54] The great early twentieth century economist Joan Robinson similarly assumed 'that the individual firm will always arrange its affairs in such a way as to make the largest profits that can be made in the particular situation in which it finds itself'.[55] And Edward Chamberlin, another prominent economist of the early twentieth century, likewise premised his theory of monopolistic competition on the (wholly plausible) assumption that firms were operated so as to maximize profits.[56]

The profit-maximizing goal of the corporation was described by these economists as an intuitive economic assumption, not as a definitional characteristic and certainly not the result of any explicit or implicit legal mandate. Although actions taken by the profit-maximizing corporation might resemble those of the ambitious (or avaricious) individual business proprietor, the firm's narrow profit-seeking focus was presented as a neutral phenomenon—even one compelled by competitive forces—rather than as an object of moral condemnation. At times, indeed, corporate profit-seeking could be seen as socially beneficial. Peter Drucker, for example, a writer who is often viewed as an important champion of corporate social responsibility,[57] clarified in his book *Concept of the Corporation* the indispensable role played by profits in the modern corporation and warned that the motivating effect of money, although not 'inborn',[58] as the classical economists had assumed, should nevertheless not be vilified as 'vicious, unnatural, and socially undesirable'.[59] It is critical, he argued, that there be some 'social mechanism to convert the subjective drive of

[54] Marshall (n 21) Bk V ch 8, 457.
[55] Joan Robinson, *The Economics of Imperfect Competition* (Macmillan and Co Ltd 1938) 6.
[56] Edward Chamberlin, *The Theory of Monopolistic Competition* (Harvard University Press 1933) 13.
[57] See eg Peter F Drucker, 'The New Meaning of Corporate Social Responsibility' (1984) 26 California Management Review 53, in which Drucker argues that '[o]nly if business, and especially American business, learns that to do well it has to do good, can we hope to tackle the major social challenges facing developed societies today' (ibid 55). Significantly, Drucker asserted that: 'Government, the agency to which the generations after Carnegie and Rosenwald increasingly came to look for the solution to social problems, cannot tackle these challenges' (ibid 55). Drucker's view of corporate social responsibility was, however, based on a recognition of the importance of capital formation for the survival and flourishing of a modern economy. And his prescription for essential corporate social responsibility was for business 'to turn a social problem into economic opportunity and economic benefit, into productive capacity, into human competence, into well-paid jobs, and into wealth' (ibid 62).
[58] Drucker (n 44) 196.
[59] ibid.

the individual into the objective performance of society'.[60] That is precisely the role played by the profit motivation, and thus, in the absence of some alternative mechanism, the profit motivation remains indispensable.

Frank Knight, in 1921, made the uncontroversial observation that '[t]here is only one end, finally, to business activity, and this is already decided upon before the business is founded; that is, to make money.'[61] Or again: 'We can hardly over-emphasize the fact that the dynamic urge back of modern economic life is the desire to increase wealth.'[62]

It was assumed, plausibly enough, that the pursuit of profit was the business corporation's *raison d'être.* Since a corporation is an abstract conceptual creation,[63] it cannot 'enjoy' the profits its activities generate. A corporation neither eats cakes nor drinks ale. The unwavering corporate profit-making goal was, consequently, always understood to accrue ultimately to the benefit of some other natural persons: human beings—notably, the corporation's ultimate human quasi-'owners'—its shareholders.[64] Thus, long before the

[60] ibid.

[61] Knight (n 32) Pt III ch 10, 292.

[62] ibid 320. Knight also argued that the conventional economic narrative that goods were produced to satisfy wants was incomplete because, in fact, 'the economic process produces wants as well as goods to satisfy existing wants . . . [A]nd in business generally, [people] produce wealth to be used in producing more wealth with no view to any use beyond the increase of wealth itself' (ibid 319). In a limited sense, this sentiment may remind one of 'Say's Law', namely that 'supply creates its own demand'. See Jean-Baptiste Say, *A Treatise on Political Economy* (2nd US edn, CR Princep tr, Wells and Lilly 1824) Bk I ch XV, 86: 'It is worth while to remark, that a product is no sooner created, than it, from that instant, affords a market for other products to the full extent of its own value.'

[63] To those adherents to the modern version of 'real entity' theory, this statement may seem contentious. More will be said about 'real entity' and fiction theory in Chapter 6. For now, it need only be noted that even those who adhere to the most robust versions of the 'real entity' theory of the corporation would not suggest that, whatever sort of real person the corporation may be, it has an independent capacity to enjoy the consumption of the wealth its operations produce. The 'real entity' (or perhaps 'natural entity') theory of the corporation is often traced to the writings of Otto von Gierke whose works became especially influential among English language scholars owing to a translation of his work, *Political Theories of the Middle Age* by Cambridge scholar Frederic Maitland. See Otto Gierke, *Political Theories of the Middle Age,* (Frederic W Maitland (tr), Cambridge University Press 1913). In his introduction to this work, Maitland explains Gierke's real entity theory of the corporation this way: '[i]tself can will, itself can act; it wills and acts by the men who are its organs as a man wills and acts by brain, mouth and hand. It is not a fictitious person; it is a *Gesammtperson*, and its will is a *Gesammtwillle;* it is a group-person, and its will is a group-will' (ibid xxvi).

[64] It was common for early corporate statutes to prohibit one corporation from owning shares in another. A corporation's shareholders would, in such a case, invariably be human beings. The relaxation of those restrictions—a development in the United States often associated with the dawn of corporate competitive federalism. See, eg Joel Seligman, 'A Brief History of Delaware's General Corporate Law of 1899' (1976) 1(2) Delaware Journal of Corporate Law 249, 265, referring to New Jersey's initial decision to amend its corporate statute to permit inter-corporate share ownership in a deliberate attempt to attract to the state the large business enterprises that had previously attempted to avoid competition by circumventing common corporate law restrictions on maximum capitalization through the 'trust' device which became the focus of 'Anti trust' legislation. Once one corporation could own shares in another, to identify the proper beneficiary of the corporation's success, one would need to follow the corporate ownership trail through subsidiaries and holding companies to the door of human shareholders at the top of the corporate ownership pyramid.

term 'shareholder primacy' entered the corporate law lexicon, there was implicit recognition of the shareholders' status as principal beneficiaries of the corporation's financial success. Arthur Dewing observed, for example, in 1920 that, while business corporations are operated for profit, yet 'profit was possible only so long as they served real human need. This is the presupposition of the social justice of private property'.[65]

In their 1934 value investing bible, *Security Analysis*, Benjamin Graham and David Dodd left no doubt as to their view on the link between corporate profit-making and shareholder benefit: '[c]orporations are the mere creatures and property of the stockholders who own them; that the officers are only the paid employees of the stockholders; and that the directors, however chosen, are virtually trustees, whose legal duty is to act solely on behalf of the owners of the business.'[66] Nor can there be any question that Graham and Dodd fully comprehended the potential harshness to less favoured corporate stakeholders that their shareholder-oriented vision of the corporation implied. Considering, for example, the hypothetical problem facing a corporation that is unprofitable but whose liquidation would lead to painful unemployment for its employees, Graham and Dodd observed that while it may seem 'heartless in the extreme to discuss such a decision solely from the standpoint of what will be best for the stockholder's pocketbook . . . nothing is to be gained by confusing the issue . . . It is fair to point out that under our present economic system the owners of a business are not expected to dissipate their capital for the sake of continuing employment. In privately owned enterprises such philanthropy is rare.'[67]

In the meantime, Berle and Means, in their famous work *The Modern Corporation and Private Property*, discussed in Chapter 3, also adverted to the problem of what they termed, 'the traditional logic of profits', [68] a concept they conceive as developed in the context of proprietor owned businesses which becomes ill-suited to the large, modern publicly-traded corporation in which, as they famously chronicled, ownership has become separated from control.

That corporations would be operated to earn profits that would accrue to the benefit of their shareholders was certain. That corporations would somehow seek to maximize those profits was assumed. What calls for greater

[65] Arthur Stone Dewing, *The Financial Policy of Corporations*, vol 1 (Ronald Press Company 1920) ix. Anne Lipton has similarly argued that the concept of shareholder primacy was intended to depoliticize business management but in order for such depoliticized control of vast resources to be legitimate, shareholder primacy 'must not only channel corporate and managerial behavior in a pro-social direction, but it must be *seen* to do so.' Ann M Lipton, 'The Legitimation of Shareholder Primacy' (2025) 51(1) The Journal of Corporation Law 83, 88.

[66] Benjamin Graham and David Dodd, *Security Analysis* (McGraw-Hill 1934) 521.

[67] ibid 515.

[68] Berle and Means (n 13) 299.

scrutiny is the mechanism by which corporate profit-maximizing is supposed to occur. As Scitovsky noted more than eighty years ago: 'Many of us have been in the habit of regarding [the assumption that business maximizes profits] as similar in every respect to the assumption that the individual maximises his satisfaction.' But, as Scitovsky points out, for reasons to which we will return below: 'We have shown above that this is not so.'[69] To say that individuals maximize their satisfaction (or utility) can be reduced to a tautology. But to argue that one person (a corporate manager) can be relied upon to work to maximize the profits of another (a corporation) is neither intuitive nor inevitable. In fact, such extraordinary 'vicarious acquisitiveness'[70] calls for some additional explanation.

## Can There Be a Prescriptive Fiduciary Duty to Maximize Profits/Shareholder Wealth/Shareholder Value?

It is unlikely that early legal authorities drew directly on any of these early economic sources; it is, frankly, unlikely that they were even aware of them. But economic analysis and legal precedent emerge within a shared historical context. Corporate law must never be 'captured' by economics.[71] However, we should not be surprised—even before the emergence of the law and economics movement that began to flourish in the 1960s and 1970s—to see early legal authorities invoking assumptions and insights similar to those found in contemporary economic analyses as they are called upon—in the same historical period—to operationalize and contextualize the vague legal duty of corporate directors to act in the best interests of the company in specific legal disputes.

As discussed in Chapters 3 and 4, legal commentators in the 1930s well understood the theoretical gaps exposed when the traditional economic conception of profits originally formulated in the context of private, owner-managed firms, was applied to the large publicly traded corporations that had risen to prominence by the early decades of the twentieth century. The economic picture of the corporation could not remain static. And as a more refined economic understanding of the corporate maximand began to emerge

[69] TS Scitovksy, 'A Note on Profit Maximization and Its Implications' (1943) 11(1) The Review of Economic Studies, 57, 60.

[70] See Graham and Dodd (n 66).

[71] Lyman Johnson, 'Individual and Collective Sovereignty in the Corporate Enterprise' (1992) 92(8) Columbia Law Review 2215, 2217: '[e]conomics has not, will not, and should not *capture* corporate law.'

in the mid twentieth century, that refinement had important implications for lawyers' understanding of the corporation as well.

## What 'Profits' (If Any) Should Be Maximized?

When business managers today speak of 'profit', they are almost certainly referring to accounting earnings or income; that is, net income for a particular accounting period calculated by subtracting expenses incurred (or properly recognized) from revenues earned in that period, all in accordance with generally accepted accounting principles. Yet, historically when economists have described the role of firms within the economy, they referred to 'profit' (or occasionally to 'net revenue'), without necessarily intending to use these terms in any technical accounting sense. In fact, ambiguity surrounding the word 'profit' was a significant source of debate among economists in the early and mid-twentieth century,[72] as was the putative significance of profit maximization as a meaningful metric for assessing the motivation of corporate managers.[73]

It is not clear that lawyers and judges have always been sensitive to these terminological nuances. When some lawyers today characterize a firm as 'profit-maximizing', it is very possible that they simply mean that the business people managing the firm are more or less committed in some vague sense to pursuing financial gains as best they can, and that they will, perhaps, pursue that goal to the exclusion of other difficult to quantify pro-social objectives. But it is important to clarify the term. A more precise articulation of the financial goal of the business corporation as an institution is necessary because that goal defines the very economic relationship between the corporation and its shareholders that is embedded in the corporate legal form. It is also, of course, important in assessing the relationship between the corporation and its other 'stakeholders'[74] or 'constituencies'.

[72] See eg KE Boulding, 'Implications for General Economics of More Realistic Theories of the Firm" (1952) 42(2) *The American Economic Review* 35: '[t]he firm in the Chamberlin-Robinson theory of the firm] maximizes a curious income variable called net revenue, of which no accountant ever heard'; Gérard Debreu, *Theory of Value: An Axiomatic Analysis of Economic Equilibrium* (Yale University Press 1959) 37: '[t]he production plan is chosen, for given prices, so as to maximize profit, the sum of all receipts minus the sum of all outlays.'

[73] See eg C Addison Hickman, 'Managerial Motivation and the Theory of the Firm' (1955) 45(2) The American Economic Review 544.

[74] According to R Edward Freeman, the term 'stakeholder' in the corporate context is said to have originated in a 1963 Stanford Research Institute memorandum in which stakeholders were described as 'those groups without whose support the organization would cease to exist'. R Edward Freeman, *Strategic Management: A Stakeholder Approach* (Cambridge University Press 2010, originally published by Pitman in 1984) 31. The original Stanford Research Institute memorandum does not appear

## From Corporate Profit-making to Shareholder Wealth Maximization: A 'Special Type of Psychology'

By the early 1950s, economists had begun to explore with greater rigour how the concept of corporate maximization of profits should be understood and ultimately operationalized. It is this exploration that would lead to a refinement of the economic understanding of the corporate goal and the evolution of the notion that it is not actually profits (however they might be defined) but shareholder wealth—typically as represented by the current share price—that the corporation should dutifully maximize.

The trajectory of this conceptual evolution is illuminating. Let us begin with T.S. Scitovsky's 1943 observation: Thatthe entrepreneur aims at maximising his profits is one of the most fundamental assumptions of economic theory. So much so that it has almost come to be regarded as equivalent to rational behaviour, and as an axiom, which is self-evident and needs no proof or justification.'[75] Scitovsky identified a puzzle within this 'self-evident' proposition. He distinguished the 'profits' that entrepreneurs/owners receive as compensation for their management of the business (which are, really, more properly considered costs of the business) from the 'profits' represented by the business's entire net receipts less its costs (including, for this purpose, the 'costs' represented by the entrepreneur's compensation as manager). In other words, the neoclassical model of the firm assumes that the entrepreneur carrying on business through the firm seeks to maximize *not* the entrepreneur's own total income, but rather the firm's residual profit. This technical distinction is highly significant.

As Scitovsky points out, there is nothing intuitively obvious about the proposition that an entrepreneur would be motivated to maximize the firm's residual profit (rather than simply the entrepreneur's own personal total income). Under what conditions would this sort of firm profit maximization give the entrepreneur maximum personal satisfaction? The answer, for Scitovsky, must lie in the 'special type of psychology'[76] of the entrepreneur. One feature of this 'special type of psychology' is that the entrepreneur's choice between work and leisure must be independent of the entrepreneur's income. The entrepreneur simply must not be assumed to prefer leisure to work, regardless of the

to have been published, and Freeman himself noted in his book that: 'The precise origins of "stakeholder" were surprisingly difficult to track down' (ibid 49).

[75] Scitovksy (n 69) 57.
[76] ibid 59.

entrepreneur's income level. This is a rather remarkable conclusion that runs contrary to one of the premises of agency theory that would, several decades later, become so influential in modern theories of the firm. In their seminal 1976 paper on agency costs and the theory of the firm, for example, Michael Jensen and William Meckling suggested that perhaps the single most important conflict between the non-owner firm manager and the firm's shareholders was not the manager's extraction of pecuniary benefits or even the wasteful enjoyment of luxurious non-pecuniary perquisites, but rather the manager's increasing preference, the lower the level of his ownership stake falls, for the 'avoidance of trouble of effort' to engage in 'creative activities such as searching out new profitable ventures'.[77] This tendency—basically an understandable inclination to prefer leisure to work—is often colourfully described as an assumption that corporate managers would, in the absence of legal rules, market forces or other constraints, be disposed to indolent 'shirking', as well as nefarious 'sharking'.[78]

But Scitovsky insisted we are wrong after all to expect any such predictable preference of managers to eschew work for a 'quiet life'. He regarded it as highly plausible that entrepreneurs would be willing to continue to work regardless of income because they are 'so keen on making money that [their] ambition cannot be damped by a rising income'.[79] This conclusion derives from Scitovsky's assumption that an entrepreneur, unlike some other individuals, '[w]ill remain unaffected by a rise in his income if he makes money, not in order to have more to spend, but for its own sake, because it is an index and token of his success in life'.[80]

Although Scitovsky provided a rationale to explain why a satisfaction-maximizing individual might be expected to work almost tirelessly to maximize the financial success of a firm, commentators in the 1950s began

[77] Jensen and Meckling (n 49), 313. Ma and Shleifer note that, while Jensen and Meckling focused on managerial perquisites as the central agency problem, Jensen's later 1986 paper ('Agency Costs of Free Cash Flow, Corporate Finance and Takeovers' (1986) 76(2) American Economic Review 323) identified the key governance problem as excessive and economically destructive firm growth. See Yueran Ma and Andrei Shleifer, 'The Invention of Corporate Governance' (2025) 172 Journal of Financial Economics 4.

[78] The terms 'shirking' and 'sharking' are Dickensian. (See Charles Dickens, *Bleak House* (Macmillan and Co 1895) 5.) However, they have been colourfully invoked by corporate law scholars for decades. See eg Eric W Orts, 'Shirking and Sharking: A Legal Theory of the Firm' (1998) 16 Yale Law and Policy Review 265. My own preferred flippant terminology for the same concepts are 'lounging' and 'looting'. It might be mentioned that Peter Drucker pointed out, in his criticism of classical economists, a point that would also be relevant to agency theory. That is, '[t]hat the orthodox economists were completely mistaken when they used the 'utilitarian "pleasure-pain calculus" to equate "work" with "pain." The psychological and social ravages of unemployment have certainly shown that idleness, far from being pleasing, is destructive, and that work, far from being disagreeable, is a necessity of human existence and self-respect and in itself a source of pride and satisfaction.' See Drucker (n 44)196.

[79] Scitovksy (n 69) 59.

[80] ibid.

to challenge the proposition that such financial success would necessarily take the specific form of maximizing *profit*. Stephen Enke, for example, in an article published in 1951,[81] argued that 'it is quite unreasonable to suppose that each firm acts to maximize profits'.[82] By this, he did not mean that firms could not be expected to try to maximize financial gains of some kind. Nor was he suggesting that entrepreneurs do not desire for themselves, in their personal capacities, the greatest financial gains possible. His comment reflected a technical observation: the desire for maximum profit in the face of uncertainty 'does not constitute a clear and unique behavior prescription'.[83] Two hypothetical managers—one pursuing a mandate to maximize profits, the other pursuing a contrarian mandate to maximize losses—could well adopt exactly the same high-risk business strategy. Uncertainty makes the goal of maximization of profits incoherent and, accordingly, the actions of supposedly profit-maximizing firms wholly unpredictable.

Uncertainty, in short, changes everything. The effect of ubiquitous uncertainty on the feasibility of a profit-maximization goal appeared to have become well appreciated by financial economists by the end of the 1950s. By the time Franco Modigliani and Merton Miller's famous capital structure irrelevance paper was published, for example, among financial economists, the idea of 'profit maximization' as a workable corporate goal seems already to have been largely discarded. The technical reason for this was that profit maximization, as a corporate goal, would only lead to the maximization of the market value of the corporation in the unique case where there was no uncertainty—a case that would never be encountered in the real world. Under conditions of uncertainty, Modigliani and Miller explained:

> [t]here corresponds to each decision of the firm not a unique profit outcome, but a plurality of mutually exclusive outcomes which can at best be described by a subjective probability distribution. The profit outcome, in short, has become a random variable and as such its maximization no longer has an operational meaning.[84]

[81] Stephen Enke, 'On Maximizing Profits: A Distinction Between Chamberlin and Robinson' (1951) 41(4) American Economic Review 566.
[82] ibid 567.
[83] ibid.
[84] Franco Modigliani and Merton H Miller, 'The Cost of Capital, Corporation Finance and the Theory of Investment' (1958) 48 The American Economic Review 261, 263–64.

Firms could not meaningfully pursue a goal of 'profit-maximization' without attempting to assess the 'subjective "utility function" of the owners'[85]. This would involve, among other things, the intractable managerial task of having to 'ascertain the risk preferences of its stockholders and compromises among their tastes'.[86] This in turn would mean assessing investment opportunities at the firm level which would differ 'depending on precisely who happen to be the owners of the firm at the moment'.[87] Accordingly, the economists' firm 'profit-maximization' assumption must be abandoned.[88] In its place, financial economists provided an

> [a]lternative approach, based on market value maximization . . . Under this approach any investment project and its concomitant financing plan must pass only the following test: Will the project, as financed, raise the market value of the firm's shares? If so, it is worth undertaking; if not, its return is less than the marginal cost of capital to the firm. Note that such a test is entirely independent of the tastes of the current owners, since market prices will reflect not only their preferences but those of all potential owners as well. If any current stockholder disagrees with management and the market over the valuation of the project, he is free to sell out and reinvest elsewhere, but will still benefit from the capital appreciation resulting from management's decision.[89]

Thus, the very economic reasoning that led to the conclusion that 'shareholder wealth maximization' was the appropriate corporate goal did not ignore the fact that shareholders may have distinctly different investment horizons, objectives, or preferences. On the contrary, it was advanced as the only formulation of the corporate goal that could solve that very challenge. This fact is significant because modern critics of 'shareholder primacy' frequently make the erroneous claim that shareholder primacy is unattainable because of the diversity of shareholder preferences. The shareholder wealth maximization norm did not overlook that problem; it was proposed as the solution to address that very issue.

Did the proposed solution—that the corporation should seek to maximize shareholder value—reflect the actual practices of corporations of the time? Or,

[85] ibid 263.
[86] ibid 264.
[87] ibid 264.
[88] ibid 263.
[89] ibid 264.

alternatively, does this question miss the essential point? It is not necessary that one believes that real world firms do, in fact, maximize or even attempt to maximize profits, shareholder wealth, enterprise value, or anything else. As Machlup has argued, it is sufficient to ask 'whether the *assumption* that this is the objective of the theoretical firms in the artificial world of our construction will lead to conclusions . . . very different from those derived from admittedly more realistic assumptions'.[90]

Modigliani and Miller, although averring that the advantages of this approach 'have long been appreciated',[91] nevertheless bemoaned the fact that the use of the share value maximization approach in practice had been held back by 'the lack of an adequate theory of the effect of financial structure on market valuations, and of how these effects can be inferred from objective market data'.[92] Addressing these gaps was thus the motivation for their famous capital irrelevance paper.

In the same year Modigliani and Miller published the first of their famous 'irrelevance' papers, William Baumol contended that 'the typical large corporation in the United States seeks to maximize not its profits but its total revenues which the businessman calls its sales. That is, *once his profits exceed some vaguely defined minimum level,* he is prepared to sacrifice further increases in profits if he can thereby obtain larger revenues'.[93] This might seem anomalous since, as Baumol observed, it appeared that many businessmen after a certain level of profit was reached seemed to prioritize increasing sales (even at the cost of decreasing profits). So in his view 'oligopolists typically seek to maximize their *sales* subject to a minimum profit constraint'.[94] Baumol's theory differs critically from the notion of profit maximization. In his view, a certain minimum profit operates only as a constraint on the sales maximization goal.[95] This objective is consistent with the notion (to which Baumol refers) of a 'fair return'[96] to stockholders but not, of course, a maximum return. In other words, in Baumol's theory, seeking maximum profit is not an objective; instead, attaining a minimum profit is a constraint.

[90] Fritz Machlup, 'Theories of the Firm: Marginalist, Behavioral, Managerial' (1967) 57 The American Economic Review 1, 14–15. (One might note that Machlup also observed: 'Maximization of money profits is certainly the simplest "objective function," but it works only in the case of firms exposed to vigorous competition. The management of a firm that makes more than enough money need not go all out to maximize profits; it can afford to do a few other things that it likes, such as serving what by its own lights it regards as the national interest or indulging in other luxuries' (ibid 22).
[91] Modigliani and Miller (n 84) 264.
[92] ibid.
[93] William J Baumol, 'On the Theory of Oligopoly' (1958) 25 Economica 187 (emphasis in original).
[94] ibid 187.
[95] ibid.
[96] ibid 188.

Despite increasing convergence of opinion among financial economists, reference to 'profit maximization' as a presumed corporate goal did not abruptly end in the 1950s. For example, in a 1960 *Harvard Business Review* article titled 'The Trouble with Profit Maximization', Robert N Anthony argued that the 'trouble' was that: '[Profit maximization] is too difficult. It is unrealistic. It is immoral.'[97] Anthony asserts that students of his day were being taught that the sole goal of the corporation was to maximize profits. Reviewing the five largest selling economic texts, he observes that: 'All of them base their analysis of business decisions on profit maximization.'[98] However, he then goes on to conclude that, despite what students were taught, profit maximization was, in general, not the dominant objective of American business. Nor was any other sort of maximization. 'They are instead', he concluded, 'related to such notions as "balance," "equity," or "adequacy".'[99]

In his 1963 text, *The Theory of Financial Management*,[100] Ezra Solomon provides a detailed discussion of the distinction between 'profit-maximization' and 'wealth maximization' as corporate goals. He includes both technical distinctions and criticisms levelled against such goals including on moral grounds. But he concludes that the goal which ought to guide all financial decisions is one of net wealth maximization. Regardless of whether managers of any individual business ultimately seek to maximize shareholder wealth, he reasons, or whether, instead, they view their role as providing only a 'satisfactory' return to shareholders while distributing firm resources to other interests such as those of employees or charities, etc.—the net worth maximization goal will still serve to best benefit society's interests.[101]

The distinction between 'profit maximization' and 'shareholder wealth maximization' may be seen as deriving from the difference between 'traditional' economic analysis and the approach of financial economists whose work became increasingly influential beginning in the 1950s. Geoffrey Poitras discusses the distinction between the two putative corporate goals in his 1994 article, 'Shareholder Wealth Maximization, Business Ethics and Social Responsibility'.[102] Poitras identifies 'profit maximization' as the traditional microeconomic approach, which is appropriately suited to models based on

[97] Robert N Anthony, 'The Trouble with Profit Maximization' (1960) 38 Harvard Business Review 126.

[98] ibid 127.

[99] ibid 132.

[100] Ezra Solomon, *The Theory of Financial Management* (Columbia University Press 1963) 16, 19 ff.

[101] ibid 22–25.

[102] Geoffrey Poitras, 'Shareholder Wealth Maximization, Business Ethics and Social Responsibility' (1994) 13 Journal of Business Ethics 125.

assumptions of 'no uncertainty, the decision-maker is the owner of the firm, the capital stock is fixed and there is only one period'.[103] The shareholder wealth maximization goal, by contrast, is associated with financial economics (as opposed to traditional microeconomics), where uncertainty is necessarily an element since the distinguishing characteristic of finance is the allocation of resources through time, meaning that allocations require a consideration of expected future cash flows which are necessarily uncertain. Corporate finance also introduces the concept of the separation of ownership and control, assuming that managers are now not proprietors but agents for the proprietors and thus obligated to 'maximize the expected utility of the wealth of shareholders'.[104]

While Poitras recognizes that shareholder utility might well include, in addition to desire for wealth, consideration of the corporation's ethical principles (a notion developed in later work, for example, by Henderson and Malani[105] and Hart and Zingales,[106] discussed later in Chapter 7), the simplifying assumption of financial economists was that shareholders' utility could be usefully identified with wealth alone. Of course, as he observes, if market prices in fact reflect ethical preferences, then a share wealth maximization goal could actually prove to be ethically optimizing in any event.

Thus, profit maximization and shareholder wealth maximization are distinctly different corporate goals. But do technical or theoretical differences between them have any practical implications for the conduct of a corporation's operations or the interpretation of the duties of corporate managers? If the ultimate end of corporate law is to ensure that corporations provide more benefit to society than harm, should one expect the law of directors' duties to favour the pursuit of one of these goals over another?

In either case, the goal of the corporation would appear to be narrowly interpreted in terms of pursuing financial success for the ultimate benefit of equity holders, rather than balancing a broader range of corporate stakeholders' interests. In other words, both the traditional economists' 'profit maximizing' and the financial economists' 'shareholder wealth maximizing' goals appear to imply a 'shareholder primacy' view of the business corporation where the only relevant shareholders' interests are financial. Although some commentators do

[103] ibid 126.
[104] ibid.
[105] M Todd Henderson and Anup Malani, 'Corporate Philanthropy and the Market for Altruism' (2009) 109 Columbia Law Review 571.
[106] Oliver Hart and Luigi Zingales, 'Companies Should Maximize Shareholder Welfare Not Market Value' (2017) 2(2) Journal of Law, Finance, and Accounting 247.

occasionally refer to 'profit maximization' in critical discussions of corporate purpose, 'profit maximization' is less frequently identified today as the putative goal of the business corporation in the specialized economic, financial, or legal literature.

## Profit-maximization and the Era of Managerialism

Astute students of corporate governance will notice that this unforgivably brief account of the evolution of the concept of profit and wealth maximization conspicuously omits the well-documented 'shift' in the perceived balance struck between corporate profit-seeking and attentiveness to the non-pecuniary interests of non-shareholder corporate stakeholders that is said to have occurred at certain points during the twentieth century. The supposed trajectory has been frequently recounted.[107] According to this familiar narrative, after an early century period marked primarily by unapologetic bank-sanctioned corporate profit-seeking (punctuated in the 1920s and 1930s by the celebrated efforts of a handful of prominent pro-social executive outliers such as Owen Young[108] and Gerard Swope), corporations of the post-war period in the United States came to be characterized in the main by a 'managerial paternalism'[109] or 'heroic managerialism'.[110] The humanistic stewardship of this managerialist era was perhaps linked to the military service ethic of managers of the era,[111] perhaps to broader social-economic patterns, perhaps to a recognition among corporate executives that corporate statesmanship was essential for increasingly powerful corporations to maintain their public legitimacy, or perhaps simply to a more benevolent *zeitgeist*

[107] See eg Wells (n 1); Dorothy Lund, 'Toward a Dynamic View of Corporate Purpose' (2025) 109 Minnesota Law Review 2089; Lynn A Stout, 'On the Rise of Shareholder Primacy, Signs of its Fall, and the Return to Managerialism' (2013) 36 Seattle University Law Review 1169.

[108] Owen Young was widely celebrated in his lifetime. Young's progressive views were referenced by Adolf Berle in his 1928 book on corporate finance. (Adolf A Berle Jr, *Studies in the Law of Corporation Finance* (Callaghan and Company 1928), 1.) Ida Tarbell's biography of Owen Young reveals an almost fawning appreciation of the man. If he was a cynical greenwasher, Tarbell did not detect it. See Ida M Tarbell, *Owen Young: A New Type of Industrial Leader* (Macmillan 1932).

[109] Henry Hansmann and Reinier Kraakman, 'Reflections on the End of History for Corporate Law' in AA Rasheed and others (eds), *The Convergence of Corporate Governance* (Palgrave Macmillan 2012) 32.

[110] Harwell Wells, '"Corporate Law is Dead": Heroic Managerialism, Legal Change, and the Puzzle of Corporation Law at the Height of the American Century' (2013) 15 University of Pennsylvania Journal of Business Law 305.

[111] Andrew Smith, Kevin D Tennent, and Jason Russell, 'Berle and Means's *The Modern Corporation and Private Property*: The Military Roots of a Stakeholder Model of Corporate Governance' (2019) 42 Seattle University Law Review 535.

than that of the relentlessly pro-shareholder neoliberal approach that would soon follow.[112]

No matter why. The corporate executives of the 1950s have been at times idealized as the sort of interest-balancing statesmen that Merrick Dodd and Berle and Means had once imagined as the potential saviours of the corporate system, if not of capitalism itself.[113] Among the many early accounts of this supposed mid-century managerial turn are James Burnham's book, *The Managerial Revolution or What Is Happening in the World Now*;[114] Alfred D. Chandler's *The Visible Hand*;[115] Edward S. Mason's 'The Apologetics of Managerialism';[116] *Fortune* Magazine's *U.S.A.: The Permanent Revolution*;[117] Howard S. Bowen's *The Social Responsibilities of the Businessman*[118] and some, although not all,[119] of the essays in the 1959 publication *The Corporation in Modern Society*.[120] Indeed, Richard Eells, writing in 1960, alluded to the argument that the 'traditional' corporation in which managers' goals did 'not include any such objective as the promotion of the general welfare'[121] might be considered 'antiquated'.

Yet, curiously, it was during the very zenith of this age of supposed shareholder-sceptical managerialism when it is today routinely maintained that the idea of shareholder wealth maximization was largely unknown to corporate executives, that within the financial economic literature there was an emerging consensus that shareholder wealth maximization was the appropriate corporate goal, and that such a proposition might even be regarded as axiomatic terms. Why was this so? Were economists engaged in an exercise of counterfactual hypothesizing, constructing their own alternative realities, one supposes, that did not correspond to the real world stakeholder sensitive ideologies of the businessmen about whom they claimed to theorize? Herman Krooss made just such a claim: 'If economic theorists knew and taught that the businessman's objective was to maximize profits, that was more than most

[112] Harwell Wells has noted that the discussion of corporate social responsibility in the 1950s rarely involved economic concepts. See Wells (n 1) 109–10.

[113] Berle and Means (n 13 313.

[114] James Burnham, *The Managerial Revolution or What is Happening in the World Now* (Putnam & Company Limited 1942).

[115] Alfred D. Chandler, *The Visible Hand: The Managerial Revolution in American Business* (Belknap Press 1977).

[116] (1958) 31 Journal of Business 1.

[117] Editors of *Fortune, USA: The Permanent Revolution* (Prentice Hall 1951).

[118] Howard S Bowen, *The Social Responsibilities of the Businessman* (Harper 1953).

[119] See eg Eugene Rostow's strong endorsement of long-term profit maximization as the appropriate goal of the corporation in 'To What and For What Ends are Corporate Managements Responsible?' in Edward S Mason (ed), *The Corporation in Modern Society* (Harvard University Press 1959) 46.

[120] Mason (n 119).

[121] Richard Eells, *The Meaning of Modern Business* (Columbia University Press 1960) 40.

businessmen knew. Indeed, only a few were sure what their primary objective was; but most were quite sure it was not to maximize profits.'[122]

Or could there be another explanation? There is no doubt that there were throughout the early post-war period (as now) competing views about how if at all corporate directors and managers ought to balance the profit-making functions of the corporation against the demands of other non-shareholder constituencies. And certainly then, as now, corporate leaders recognized the public relations value of publicly and conspicuously declaring their commitment to be good corporate citizens, regardless of what actions they might actually be taking in the privacy of the C-suite or the corporate boardroom. But the suggestion that paternalistic managerialism truly was the 'dominant' view in the 1950s, and the shareholder primacy view, the clear 'loser'[123] seems difficult to verify. It is noteworthy that a contemporary study of corporate executives' views undertaken in 1956 identified managerialism as one of the competing corporate ideologies of the day, but did not appear to reveal any such 'dominant' view. Post-war corporations might not have been engaged in a single-minded pursuit to maximize profits; but it is far from clear that they were being managed with a view towards judiciously balancing the competing interests of the corporation's various financial and non-financial stakeholders either.

Economists of the time also seemed to be more equivocal in their assessment of what was widely regarded as the 'dominant' view of the era then many later writers. Edith Penrose, for example, discussed what she regarded as the most plausible explanation of the corporation's mission in her influential 1959 book, *The Theory of the Growth of the Firm*.[124] Her explanation had hints of perspectives that would gain prominence in the legal literature decades later. Describing her original perspective in the foreword to the third edition of her book, Penrose explained:

> I was not impressed by the reasoning behind, nor the evidence to support, the assumption that the managers or directors of large corporations in the modern economy saw themselves in business largely for the benefit of shareholders . . . Profits were treated as a necessary condition of expansion-or growth-and growth, therefore, was a chief reason for the interest of managers in profits.[125]

[122] Herman E Krooss, *Executive Opinion: What Business Leaders Said and Thought on Economic Issues 1920s-1960s* (Doubleday 1970) 333.

[123] See eg Lund (n 107) 2099.

[124] Edith T Penrose, *The Theory of the Growth of the Firm*, foreword by Martin Slater (Basil Blackwell 1959).

[125] Edith T Penrose, *The Theory of the Growth of the Firm* (3rd edn, Oxford University Press 1995), ix.

Legal scholar Eugene Rostow wrote, in 1959, that: '[a] clear acceptance of profit maximization as a legal principle might well do something, perhaps a good deal, to order the pattern of corporate policy... a clear-cut economic directive should help directors to discriminate more effectively among competing claims upon them, in carrying out their public trusteeship for the economic system as a whole.'[126]

In 1967, still well before the era in which shareholder wealth maximization is usually said to have supplanted the supposedly dominant post-war managerial ethic, Robin Marris asserted that: 'Business-school texts increasingly emphasize profit and shareholder-welfare maximization as normative axioms.'[127] And Rajan, Ramella, and Zingales have found, based on an analysis of 150 major American corporations' letters to shareholders during the 1955 to 2020 period[128] that, despite the frequently repeated claim that corporations prior to the 1970s were operated in a more pluralistic, less profit-focused manner than in the neoliberal era that followed, when corporations in the 1950s and early 1960s chose to indicate any goal at all in their letters to shareholders, '[t]he main goal often was to increase profits . . . The focus on profit maximization steadily increased from 1955 to 1990, *without any discontinuity or acceleration after 1970.* The novelty of the 1980s is that the goal of increasing profits is expressed in terms of maximization of shareholder value.'[129]

Whatever may be the most accurate understanding of the goals pursed by the publicly traded corporations of the post-war period, there is no doubt that at least by the early 1980s a consensus appeared to have emerged that such corporations *should* be managed with a view to maximizing shareholder value, and directors and officers of publicly traded corporations had by that time (if not earlier) certainly become overtly 'shareholder centric'.[130] The notion that the goal of the corporation was to maximize shareholder value as evidenced by the price of the corporation's shares became standard fare in corporate finance textbooks.[131] Cheffins says the phrase 'shareholder value' first appeared

[126] Rostow (n 119) 46, 71.
[127] Marris (n 4) 72, 73.
[128] Raghuram Rajan, Pietro Ramella, and Luigi Zingales, 'What Purpose Do Corporations Purport? Evidence from Letters to Shareholders' Working Paper No 2023-44, Becker Friedman Institute (2023).
[129] ibid 36.
[130] Edward B Rock, 'Adapting to the New Shareholder-Centric Reality' (2013) 161 University of Pennsylvania Law Review 1907,
[131] See eg Richard A Brealey, Stewart C Myers, and Franklin Allen, *Principles of Corporate Finance* (16th edn, McGraw-Hill Irwin 2011) 9: 'The goal of maximizing shareholder value is widely accepted in both theory and practice.'; Stephen A Ross, Randolph W Westerfield, and Bradford D Jordan, *Essentials of Corporate Finance* (7th edn, McGraw-Hill Irwin 2011) 10: 'The goal of financial management is to maximize the current value per share of the existing stock.'; Zvi Bodie and Robert C Merton, *Finance* (Prentice-Hall 2000) 12: '. . . the shareholder- wealth-maximization rule is the "right" rule for managers to follow in running the firm.'

in 1955,[132] but use of the term increased rapidly in the 1980s, popularized by proponents of the idea such as '"shareholder value" pioneer'[133] Alfred Rappaport.[134] The concept attracted particular attention from corporate executives over time as executive compensation policies increasingly emphasized an equity component, often through the generous granting of stock options.

To summarize, then, that business corporations were organized for the purpose of making profits was definitional. That such firms sought to 'maximize' those profits was considered by the neoclassical economists to be axiomatic. Finally, for the mid-twentieth century financial economists, the incoherence of a profit maximization goal under conditions of uncertainty called for the corporate goal to be reframed in terms of maximizing shareholder wealth as evidenced by the market value of the corporation's shares. This ultimate focus on maximizing shareholder value was expressed as an economically rational proposition, not as a legal requirement or a social norm. But it gradually came to be widely[135] (although by no means universally[136]) accepted as both. Once many corporation statutes had been modernized to eliminate mandatory objects clauses and altered to permit one corporation to purchase shares in another, the notion that a corporation existed to primarily or exclusively to maximize financial gain became as a matter of law much closer to the classical

[132] Brian Cheffins, 'Stop Blaming Milton Friedman!' (2021) 98 Washington University Law Review 1607, 1629.

[133] ibid 1628–29.

[134] ibid 1630.

[135] Edward B. Rock, for example, writing in 2013 canvasses a series of regulatory, structural, and corporate cultural changes that in his view altered the 'director ideology' such that, as he puts it: 'Companies, shareholders, business schools, corporate professors, and judges all seem to believe that the primary responsibility of directors is to maximize shareholder value.' Rock (n 130) 1923. See also Henry Hansmann and Reinier Kraakman, 'The End of History for Corporate Law' (2001) 89 Georgia Law Journal 439, 449 arguing that 'the shareholder-oriented model has emerged as the normative consensus . . . by force of *logic*, by force of *example*, and by force of *competition*'; Darrell West, 'The Purpose of the Corporation in Business and Law School Curricula' (Governance Studies at Brookings 2011), concluding following an analysis of the curricula of leading US law and business schools, that many business and law schools 'emphasize maximizing corporate profits and shareholder value' with the 'emphasis on shareholder value . . . especially prevalent in law schools' where 'a number of faculty view the focus on financial returns as "settled law"' (17, 18); Andrew C Inkpen and Anant K Sundaram, 'The Endurance of Shareholder Value Maximization as the Preferred Corporate Objective' (2022) 59 Journal of Management Studies 555.

[136] See eg Lynn A Stout, *The Shareholder Value Myth: How Putting Shareholders First Harms Investors, Corporations and the Public* (Berrett-Koehler 2012); D Gordon Smith, 'The Shareholder Primacy Norm' (1998) 23(2) Journal of Corporation Law 277, 279, where the author argues that—despite a prevailing view that the shareholder primacy norm had become widely accepted and even generally internalized by the managers of American corporations—in fact, 'the shareholder primacy norm is nearly irrelevant to the ordinary business decisions of modern corporations'. Oliver Weinstein, 'Understanding the Roots of Shareholder Primacy: the Meaning of Agency Theory, and the Conditions of Contagion' in Thomas Clarke, Justin O'Brien, and Charles RT O'Kelley (eds), *The Oxford Handbook of the Corporation* (Oxford University Press 2019) 139; Frank Partnoy, 'Shareholder Primacy is Illogical' in Elizabeth Pollman and Robert B Thompson (eds), *Research Handbook on Corporate Purpose and Personhood* (Edward Elgar Publishing 2021) 186. See also the authorities discussed in ch 6.

theoretical ideal. Indeed, Berle and Means allude to this development in *The Modern Corporation and Private Property*.[137]

There are, accordingly, at least three issues raised by the shareholder wealth maximization 'norm'. First, at the most general level, does *any* version of a corporate purpose that privileges shareholders over other corporate stakeholders reflect a positive economic view of the corporation, a normative economic view, or a legally enforceable principle? Second, does the specific formulation of corporate purpose in terms of maximizing shareholder value represent a viable legal standard against which the actions of corporate directors and officers can meaningfully be evaluated, let alone enforced[138]? Finally, to the extent that the law recognizes a shareholder value norm, how did this notion relate to the financial economic concept that firms need not be analysed as distinct enterprises with unique products and services that may align with the interests or preferences of investors, but may instead usefully be treated at least for economic purposes simply as sources of financial claims which should be considered financially fungible with any equity claims of other firms sharing the same risk/return profile? The essential fungibility of these claims, after all, is essential to the 'no arbitrage' method of proof offered offered for the Modigliani-Miller theorem by its authors, a method that was itself considered an important contribution at the time to the financial economic literature. Finance depends on valuation through equivalents and, in the case of corporate equity, that equivalency is found by treating firms as essentially interchangeable issuers of financial claims.

## Financial Economics and the Law

It is not certain how financial economic concepts of profit maximization/shareholder wealth maximization—which were matters of debate among economists—entered the law in what would prove to be such an influential and, at least for a time, a dominant fashion. It is possible that Brudney and Chirelstein's 1972 corporate finance casebook had much to do with the increasing impact economic literature began to have on corporate law both

[137] Berle and Means (n 1312) 235 n 43.

[138] See Melvin Eisenberg's analysis of the distinction between the stringent 'standard of conduct' for directors and the must less stringent 'standard of review' applied by courts when reviewing the performance by directors of their duties. Melvin Eisenberg, 'The Divergence of Standards of Conduct and Standards of Review in Corporation Law' (1993) 62 Fordham Law Review 437.

in law schools and the courts. Roberta Romano[139] has argued, for example, that the publication of the Brudney and Chirelstein casebook was a watershed event because it introduced some of the developments in modern finance to law students, connecting them to business law. However, it seems difficult to argue that Brudney and Chirelstein's work played the key role in persuading lawyers that the legal duty of corporate directors ought necessarily to accord with the economist's understanding of the corporation as a vehicle for maximizing shareholder value. As Brudney and Chirelstein themselves wrote in the preface to the first edition of their book:

> That hope [that legal problems could be solved by drawing on economic theory] has been largely disappointed, however. Financial theory does shed light on legal principles in many areas, but it does not provide a total framework for evaluating the law. The reason, perhaps, relates to an essential difference between the focus of the law and the focus of economics in this field. Conventionally viewed, the goal of corporate management is to maximize the wealth of the corporation's owners by maximizing the value of the enterprise and its securities. Accordingly, financial theory aims at developing an overall maximizing strategy for the firm. By contrast, legal regulation concentrates on fairly apportioning enterprise value among various interested parties who assert competing claims, and on identifying and vindicating investors' expectations when a restructuring of the corporate entity is sought. One field of study is concerned with making the pie as large as possible; the other worries about how to split it up.[140]

Perhaps the increasing salience of some financialized version of the shareholder primacy norm in legal literature, legal practice, and legal doctrine was also linked, as Professor Romano argues, to an explosion of hostile takeover bids, and the accompanying need to articulate a standard of fiduciary duty for the officers and directors of corporations subject to hostile bids.[141] Modern finance theory offered some reasoned answers to such questions, she notes, and that may well go some way to explain how often positive economic conceptions of the firm began to be advanced as normative settled legal standards, such as in the 1985 Delaware Supreme Court's endorsement of the proposition that

[139] Roberta Romano, 'After the Revolution in Corporate Law' (2005) 55 Journal of Legal Education 342.

[140] Victor Brudney and Marvin A Chirelstein, *Cases and Materials on Corporate Finance* (The Foundation Press 1972) xv, xvi.

[141] Romano (n 139) 348.

would come to be *Revlon*'s eponymous rule, that once the sale of a break-up of a company becomes inevitable, the directors have one goal: 'maximization of shareholder profit'[142] or 'maximization of the company's value'.[143]

## Conclusion

However significant the profit or shareholder wealth maximization goal might have been regarded within the economic and managerial literature, the legal obligations of corporate officers and directors had to account for a host of complex and competing human interests. Moreover, as we discuss further in Chapter 9, beginning in the early 1970s, rapid developments occurred in financial innovation as the convergence of macroeconomic and geopolitical developments, the proliferation of computer technology, and a breakthrough in option pricing theory made risk management a far more significant and far more sophisticated focus of corporations. In very short order, the distinction between defensive use of financial instruments such as swaps, options, futures, and forwards became a possible profit centre, and the line between expanding the 'pie' by maximizing value and ensuring a reasonable allocation of the slices became increasingly difficult to discern. The corporation's maximizing function had to be undertaken within an often unprecedented context of competing and often conflicting financial and non-financial interests and compelling social issues. It is to the corporation's role as an arbiter of such conflicts and interests that we turn in the following chapters.

142 *Revlon Inc v MacAndrews & Forbes Holdings* 506 A 2d 173 (Del SC 1986) 185.
143 ibid 182.

# 6
# The Corporation as a Nexus of Conflicts: Anomie of the People

## Introduction

The business corporation is a legislative product but was not a legislative invention. It was the culmination of an evolutionary process that resulted in a form of organization that legislatures and courts have subsequently tried to refine, regularize, and regulate.[1] Yet it retains a host of characteristics which, rather like the unwritten conventions of British constitutional law, have not been, and could never entirely be, reduced to a written document.

Students of corporate law, particularly in the United States, are very familiar with the contractarian economic model of the corporation. Under this model, theoretical ruminations about the nature of corporate 'personhood' are cast aside. Contract theory is brought in to do the heavy analytical lifting, and the corporate entity is ingeniously reduced to a functional piece of contracting machinery strategically fitted within the centre of a vibrant market of employees, suppliers, shareholders, creditors, and customers. It is the market-mimicking interplay of these various economic actors that defines the corporation's boundaries and the scope of its operations. They are both what the corporation does, and what the corporation is. The corporation is reimagined as a robust, somewhat fluid, free enterprise 'nexus of contracting relationships' or, more simply, a 'nexus of contracts'.

[1] Adolf Berle, in his 1928 book *Studies in the Law of Corporation Finance* (Callaghan and Company 1928), carefully traced the historical roots of the business corporation, strongly refuting the often-heard proposition (see eg William Blackstone, *Commentaries on the Laws of England*, vol 1 (University of Chicago Press 1979, originally published in 1765) 460) that the existence of the business corporation depended in any way on any governmental concession or decree. As he put it, 'corporations existed first, and if they wished to exercise governmental power, then asked for a franchise; but they could exist without the franchise and a considerable number had existed thus for several years'. (ibid 11). Thus, 'the essence of corporation lies in contract and not in governmental decree; and . . . the function of the state is limited to regulation with a view to protect itself' (ibid 23).

*Corporate Governance and Enlightened Fiduciaries*. Christopher C. Nicholls, Oxford University Press.
 DOI: 10.1093/9780198904199.003.0006

## Agency Theory

The 'nexus of contracts' model of the corporation emerged from agency theory. In Stephen Ross's pioneering 1972 paper on the theory of agency, he briefly introduced the idea that corporate managers could be conceived as agents of the corporate shareholders. He said nothing more about the implications or the analysis of this intriguing possibility.[2] Ross was not a lawyer, of course. His use of the term 'agency' was not wholly congruent with the well-defined legal concept of agency. But no matter. Ross's concept of economic agency was a significant contribution to the eventual evolution of the 'nexus of contracts' view of the firm that was forged in the economics literature but soon came to dominate the burgeoning law and economics approach to corporate law.[3]

The premise of the 'nexus of contracts' (or 'contractarian') view of the corporation is that the corporation is best understood not as an abstract, metaphysical, or mystical[4] entity, but as a practical hub of voluntary, contractual (or at least 'contract-adjacent') relationships. Through these actual and quasi-contracts, resources were combined to produce the goods and services delivered and sold to clients and customers. The corporate entity did not disappear entirely; it still had a formal technical role to perform as the common counterparty to these contracts or contract-like relationships, a function that facilitated the coordination of the voluntary economic relationships between suppliers, employees, managers, customers, shareholders, and creditors. But this coordinating role was ministerial and rather pedestrian; the corporation—as an entity—was not in itself a significant object of theoretical inquiry or study.

Corporate law statutes, on this view, were also matters of no great importance. They were regarded as helpful and potentially efficiency-enhancing, but not foundational. They were downplayed chiefly as 'enabling' rather than mandatory in nature. Their principal function was to provide a set of off the shelf default rules which were essentially intended to grease the wheels of business by establishing a user-friendly framework that most corporate participants would voluntarily choose to adopt for themselves if they were able to bargain costlessly. If particular corporations had idiosyncratic business requirements

[2] Stephen A Ross, 'The Economic Theory of Agency: the Principal's Problem' (1973) 63(2) The American Economic Review 134, 138.

[3] See also the discussion in Chapter 3 of the corporate governance implications of the somewhat lesser-known version of agency theory developed independently by Barry Mitnick.

[4] Adolf Berle once mocked the notion that the corporation was a 'mystic entity of some sort created by the fiat of the state'. Berle (n 1) 3. Berle's rejection of the 'mystic' concept of corporate personhood and of the concept that the corporation represented any sort of concession or franchise from the state was reiterated in a lengthy but often overlooked footnote in Adolf A Berle and Gardiner Means, *The Modern Corporation and Private Property* (Transaction Publishers 1991, originally published in 1932) 120 n 2.

that were not adequately reflected in the 'standard form' corporation provided by the corporate law template, a bespoke version could be crafted in place of the generic off-the-shelf model. Indeed, most of the key elements of the standard form were easily varied by individual tailor-made additions to the corporate constitution.

If corporate statutes performed no critical constitutive role, then the initial act or process of incorporation did not represent the bestowing of any particularly valuable state-conferred benefit, franchise, or concession.[5] The state was, at most, a minor supporting actor.[6] The market was the star featured player, and whatever remaining mandatory features of corporate statutes were not subject to modification or contracting-out were dismissed as 'trivial'.[7]

The 'nexus of contracts' approach was originally formulated, championed, and developed in two seminal economics articles in the 1970s, the first by Armen Alchian and Harold Demsetz in 1972,[8] the second by Michael Jensen and William Meckling in 1976.[9] In short order, the concept had crossed disciplinary boundaries and was embraced, popularized, and virtually canonized by many influential legal scholars as well. In particular, Frank Easterbrook and Daniel Fischel's 'groundbreaking'[10] 1981 article on the role and legal duties of the management of a target company subject to a takeover bid[11] and their later 1991 book, *The Economic Structure of Corporate Law*[12], both owed significant intellectual debts to Jensen and Meckling.[13]

[5] See eg Paul G Mahoney, 'Contract or Concession? An Essay on the History of Corporate Law' (1999) 34 Georgia Law Review 873.

[6] Recent scholarship, however, has provided important new perspectives on the significance of the state to the success of the corporation. Taisu Zhang and John D Morley have argued that the modern corporation would have been impossible without the rise of a modern state with the ability to 'enforce uniformity among the corporation's various owners'. Taisu Zhang and John D Morley, 'The Modern State and the Rise of the Business Corporation' (2025) 132(7) Yale Law Journal 1970.

[7] See Bernard S Black, 'Is Corporate Law Trivial? An Economic and Political Analysis' (1990) 89(4) Northwestern University Law Review 542, concluding that: 'Apparently mandatory rules, however, may be trivial because they are market mimicking, avoidable, changeable, or unimportant. I have explored the triviality hypothesis that, with limited exceptions for changes in law and the benefits and costs of paternalism, state corporate law is trivial' (ibid 593).

[8] Armen A Alchian and Harold Demsetz, 'Production, Information Costs, and Economic Organization' (1972) 62(5) American Economic Review 777.

[9] Michael C Jensen and William H Meckling, 'Theory of the Firm: Managerial Behavior, Agency Costs and Ownership Structure' (1976) 3(4) Journal of Financial Economics 305.

[10] See eg Roberta Romano, 'After the Revolution in Corporate Law' (2005) 55 Journal of Legal Education 342, 348.

[11] Frank H Easterbrook and Daniel R Fischel, 'The Proper Role of a Target's Management in Responding to a Tender Offer' (1981) 94 Harvard Law Review 1161, 1169 n 24.

[12] Frank H Easterbrook and Daniel R Fischel, *The Economic Structure of Corporate Law* (Harvard University Press 1991).

[13] Roberta Romano has discussed the impact of the influence of agency theory on legal scholarship in Romano (n 10).

Easterbrook and Fischel's use of economics to illuminate legal analysis was an important part of a larger intellectual movement. Economic perspectives had become of increasing interest to corporate law scholars in the United States in the decade preceding their 1981 paper. It is possible that Brudney and Chirelstein's 1972 corporate finance casebook[14] had much to do with hastening the importation of economic ideas into the American corporate legal academy. Roberta Romano[15] has argued, for example, that the publication of the Brudney and Chirelstein casebook was a watershed event because it introduced some of the groundbreaking and thought-provoking developments in modern finance theory to law students, connecting them to both the traditional principles and the modern practice of business law. Along with transaction costs economics, discussed later in this chapter, Professor Romano maintains that beginning in the mid-1970s, agency theory in particular came to have a 'lasting impact on the thinking of corporate law academics.'[16]

The impact of the contractarian perspective of corporate law, particularly on American legal scholarship, was profound. A likely catalyst or perhaps accelerant for the rapid diffusion of economic theory into legal thinking was the pioneering summer programme in economics for law professors launched by Professor Henry Manne beginning in 1971 and offered until 1995.[17] Manne said of this programme that many of the law professors who attended took the advice offered by the programme organizers to go back and teach a course in economics at their own respective law schools. Manne noted that: 'Quite a few followed that advice', which may explain causally why a number of law schools began to offer a law and economics course, often co-taught with an economist.'[18] Manne also observed that: 'It is a little-known [aspect] of the whole law and economics movement that it greatly encouraged broad ranging cooperation between professional economists and lawyers, both in and outside of corporations.'[19] Nor was the impact of the programme limited to academic lawyers. In addition to the programmes Manne ran for law professors, he also launched an Economics Institute for Federal Judges programme through the Law and Economics Center at the

[14] Victor Brudney and Marvin A Chirelstein, *Cases and Materials on Corporate Finance* (The Foundation Press 1972).
[15] Romano (n 10).
[16] ibid 347.
[17] Henry G Manne, 'How Law and Economics Was Marketed in a Hostile World: A Very Personal History' in Francesco Parisi and Charles K Rowley (eds), *The Origins of Law and Economics: Essays by the Founding Fathers* (Edward Elgar Publishing 2005) 309, 313.
[18] ibid 315.
[19] ibid.

University of Miami School,[20] a programme that ran for seventeen years beginning in 1976.

Embedded in the contractarian view of the corporation, for reasons explored later in this chapter, was a shareholder primacy norm. Perhaps the increasing salience of some financialized version of that shareholder primacy norm in legal literature, legal practice, and legal doctrine was also linked, as Professor Romano argues, to an explosion of hostile takeover bids in the 1980s and the accompanying need to articulate a novel standard of fiduciary duty for the officers and directors of corporations subject to hostile bids. Hostile takeovers, Professor Romano points out, were a form of transaction for which there were few judicial precedents because they had been exceedingly rare prior to the 'junk bond' leveraged buy-out era of the 1980s.[21] Modern finance theory offered some reasoned answers to the legal questions posed by such deals, Romano notes. That may well go some way to explain how often positive economic conceptions of the firm began to be advanced as normative legal standards.[22]

The economic takeover of American corporate law scholarship was soon all but complete, and resistance seemed as futile as the efforts of recalcitrant corporate directors facing a bear hug hostile takeover offer. Former Yale Law Dean Anthony Kronman in 1995 was prepared to declare (not without regret) that the law and economics movement 'continues and remains the single most influential jurisprudential school in this country'.[23] In the corporate law context, the 'nexus of contracts' model, specifically, soon became the dominant paradigm in American corporate law scholarship.[24]

But it generated considerable criticism[25] and scepticism, too. For example, writing in 2006, Michael Klausner pronounced a withering judgment on the contractarian approach to corporate law: 'A generation of scholarship,

[20] ibid 319.

[21] Romano (n 10) 348.

[22] In 1985, for example, the Delaware Supreme Court endorsed the proposition that would come to be *Revlon*'s eponymous rule, that once the sale or 'break-up' of a company becomes inevitable, the directors have one goal: 'maximization of shareholder profit' or 'maximization of the company's value'. See *Revlon Inc v MacAndrews & Forbes Holdings* 506 A 2d 173, 182,185 (Del SC 1986).

[23] Anthony Kronman, speaking at 'The Second Driker Forum for Excellence in the Law', reported in (1995) 42 Wayne Law Review 115, 160.

[24] See Brian R Cheffins, *Corporate Governance Law and Regulation* (Edward Elgar Publishing 2024) 25.

[25] See eg William W Bratton Jr, 'The Nexus of Contracts Corporation: A Critical Appraisal' (1989) 74(3) Cornell Law Review 407. See also Lyman Johnson, 'After *Enron*: Remembering Loyalty Discourse in Corporate Law' (2003)28 Delaware Journal of Corporate Law 27, 29 lamenting, in his view, the corporate law field 'largely being colonized by the law and economics perspective'. More recently see Simon Deakin and others, 'Legal Institutionalism: Capitalism and the Constitutive Role of Law' (2017) 45 Journal of Comparative Economics 188.

however, suggests that the contractarian theory is not, and never was, an accurate description of reality or a basis for policy prescription. The theory was based largely on perfect market assumptions and lacked empirical support.'[26] The shortcomings of the basic contractarian perspective of the firm were identified in the economic literature, and alternative theories of the firm were formulated emphasizing such things as the allocation of property rights[27] and minimizing transaction costs to address the inevitability of contract incompleteness and the possibility of guile and 'hold up' opportunism.[28] These alternative approaches did have an impact on legal theory as well,[29] although they did not displace the prominence of the contractarian model in the legal literature.

The emphasis on voluntary exchange and individual contract-like relationships minimized the significance of the role of government in the creation and regulation of the corporation. But it did something more. It rendered the search for higher corporate purpose irrelevant and even somewhat incoherent. If the corporate entity is merely a functional common-counterparty, searching for a corporation's purpose is as fruitless a task as seeking to divine the dreams and ambitions of a table lamp or a desk stapler. The corporation can have no discernible interests distinct from the interests of the various parties who make use of it and whose contractual exchanges define its existence. Thus, as Easterbrook and Fischel once declared, 'What is the goal of the corporation? . . . Our response to such questions is: who cares?'[30]

However, the contractarian perspective is not entirely irrelevant to the question of the corporate objective either because, despite the objections of some commentators,[31] its conventional version supported a 'shareholder

[26] Michael Klausner, 'The Contractarian Theory of Corporate Law: A Generation Later' (2006) 31 Journal of Corporation Law 779, 781.

[27] See eg Sanford Grossman and Oliver Hart, 'The Costs and Benefits of Ownership: A Theory of Vertical and Lateral Integration' (1986) 94 Journal of Political Economy 691; Oliver Hart, *Firms, Contracts, and Financial Structure* (Oxford University Press 1995).

[28] See eg Oliver Williamson, *The Economic Institutions of Capitalism* (The Free Press 1985).

[29] See eg John Armour and Michael J Whincop, 'The Proprietary Foundations of Corporate Law' (2007) 27(3) Oxford Journal of Legal Studies 429.

[30] Easterbrook and Fischel (n 12) 36, 37. See also Jensen and Meckling (n 9) 311: '[t]he personalization of the firm implied by asking questions such as "what should be the objective function of the firm" . . . is seriously misleading. The firm is not an individual. It is a legal fiction which serves as a focus for a complex process in which the conflicting objectives of individuals . . . are brought into equilibrium within a framework of contractual relations.'

[31] Dorothy Lund has argued that the 'malleability' of agency theory makes it possible to argue that it could support a 'public primacy' view under which directors would be obliged to promote corporate value for the public interest. See Dorothy Lund, 'Public Primacy in Corporate Law' (2024) 47 Seattle Law Review 365. Professor Lund contends that the shareholder primacy view of the corporation was

primacy' view of the corporation.[32] Shareholders are assumed, alone among those contributing corporate resources, to lack the protection of a genuine, legally enforceable contract. Their relationship to the corporation may be embodied in the corporation's constating documents and the particular statute under which the corporation has been incorporated, but their financial claims are unusually fragile. They can sue for neither return of their capital nor any regular distribution of corporate profits. They are merely the 'residual risk bearers'. The fixed, contractual, potentially actionable claims of all other suppliers of corporate inputs—creditors, employees, and suppliers—must be satisfied or adequately provided for before shareholders may realize any gain on their investment at all. If, therefore, the value of the interests of these most precarious corporate constituents is increased, then *ex hypothesi* the interests of all those claimants ranking higher on the corporate financial hierarchy must also be enhanced.

To induce shareholders to commit their capital to an enterprise—to facilitate the all-important characteristic of 'capital lock-in'—and accept financial claims (if they may be considered 'claims' at all) ranking last in priority, corporate law furnishes two sorts of safeguards. The first, limited liability, provides downside protection. The second, shareholder primacy (coupled with voting rights), offers potential upside.

largely owing to the influence of agency costs theory as filtered through a conflation of agency law and economic agency theories first in the work of Fischel and Easterbrook. In her view, Delaware courts had also not clearly adopted a shareholder-primacy approach prior to the 1980s when forced to confront the issue in the context of the wave of hostile takeover bids. Lund has elsewhere argued that shareholder primacy is now seen in terms of enhancing long-term shareholder value rather than share price maximization. See Dorothy S. Lund, 'Enlightened Shareholder Value, Stakeholderism, and the Quest for Managerial Accountability' in Elizabeth Polman and Robert B Thompson (eds), *Research Handbook on Corporate Purpose and Personhood* (Edward Elgar Publishing 2021) 91. But the supposed dichotomy between share price maximization and the pursuit of long-term shareholder value is based on assumptions about market inefficiency that seem to make all decisions about maximizations little less random than a roll of the dice: if financial markets (even if imperfect) are not the best available estimate of long-term value increases, then what is the point of them? As Stephen Ross has argued, even allowing for inefficiencies (estimated by tallying the average excess risk adjusted returns of hedge funds and applying a significant multiple to those returns to ensure no undercounting of inefficiencies), such inefficiencies prove to be very small indeed. Ross concludes that 'on average, prices are "off" or inefficient to about . . . less than 0.1 percent.' See Stephen A Ross, *Neoclassical Finance* (Princeton University Press 2005) 64.

[32] Bratton and Wachter have claimed that shareholder primacy 'descends from the Jensen and Meckling model'. See William W Bratton and Michael L Wachter, 'Shareholder Primacy's Corporatist Origins: Adolf Berle and The Modern Corporation' (2008) 34 Journal of Corporation Law 99, 145. But it is surely older—much older—and, as discussed in Chapter 4, in fact seems to have been developed in the financial economic literature in the 1950s as a modification (or perhaps 'correction') of the firm profit maximization goal that had been a standard part of the neoclassical model of the firm since Alfred Marshall.

## Capital Lock-in

The nexus of contracts theory is linked to the identification of shareholders as 'residual risk bearers', a position that not only explains the unique vulnerability of shareholders but also serves as the rationale for endowing shareholders alone with voting power and identifying them as the proper ultimate, if indirect, beneficiaries of the directors' fiduciary duties. The shareholder's unique position—both unusually fragile (as financial claimants) and unusually powerful (as voting securityholders)—is, in turn, a function of the critical corporate feature of 'capital lock in'. If shareholder capital were not 'locked in', the rationale for conferring upon shareholders their exclusive voting rights and the justification for the corporation's focus upon the promotion of shareholder wealth as an overarching objective would be eviscerated.

The fact that corporations effectively 'locked in' shareholder capital may, historically, have been the single most fundamental organizational characteristic distinguishing corporations from ordinary partnerships: more significant, even, than limited liability. Margaret Blair, for example, has argued:

> Investors in corporate shares could subscribe in small units, but once the funds paid to purchase those shares had been committed, limits were imposed—sometimes severe ones—on the ability of investors to withdraw funds from the business. The commitment of capital by shareholders, I argue, helped protect the at-risk investments made by other corporate participants. To again use a phrase from Hansmann and Kraakman, the capital contributed or pledged in the form of equity shares helped secure a pool of 'bonding assets,' which made it easier to draw in other risky contributions to the enterprise.[33]

In Blair's view, it was this ability to lock in capital and so offer visible protection as an inducement to other potential resource contributors—and not limited liability—that was historically the chief attraction of incorporation.[34] In fact, in the United States, limited liability was not even available to shareholders of corporations for many years after American independence; in certain states limited liability for corporate shareholders was still unavailable

[33] Margaret Blair, 'Locking in Capital: What Corporate Law Achieved for Business Organizers in the Nineteenth Century' (2003) UCLA Law Review 387, 392.
[34] ibid 437 ff.

more than a century later. Most notably, the state of California did not provide for corporate limited liability until 1931.[35]

The importance of 'capital lock-in' as a defining characteristic has also been emphasized by legal scholar, the late Lynn Stout:

> This quality of corporate entities—whether called affirmative asset partitioning, capital lock-in, or the absence of a repurchase condition—may come closer than any other to capturing the essential difference between incorporated and unincorporated business forms. It may also go a long way towards explaining why the corporation has evolved into the dominant business form for pursuing certain kinds of large, long-term economic projects.[36]

Stout goes so far as to argue 'that corporations exist primarily to lock in capital',[37] a sweeping claim which, one should note, has been disputed by other scholars including Larry Ribstein.[38]

Hansmann and Kraakman also advert to the importance of locking in shareholder capital in arguing that the 'essential role' of organizational law was 'asset partitioning'.[39] Certainly, Hansmann and Kraakman note the importance of the corporate form in offering different types of asset partitioning, including protecting shareholders' assets from the corporation's creditors by providing limited liability to a corporation's shareholders. But they attach especial significance to that particular version of asset partitioning—'affirmative asset partitioning'—that involves shielding a corporate entity from the liabilities of its shareholders: a result that depends upon capital lock-in. Limited liability, they observe, at least with respect to voluntary creditors, would not necessarily require corporate legislation. It could be achieved contractually, albeit at significant cost. Locking in shareholder capital could not. Shielding contributed corporate capital from the potential claims of shareholders' creditors, with whom the corporation has no contractual relationship, requires specific

[35] Mark I. Steinberg, 'Share Price Changes and the Arrival of Limited Liability in California' (2003) 32 Journal of Legal Studies 1.

[36] Lynn Stout, 'On the Nature of Corporations' (2005) University of Illinois Law Review 253, 258. The term 'asset partitioning' was coined by Hansmann and Kraakman and discussed further below.

[37] ibid 260.

[38] See eg Larry E Ribstein, 'Should History Lock in Lock-in?' (2005) 41 Tulsa Law Review 523. Although the late Professor Ribstein challenged the strength of Stout's claim about the unparalleled importance of capital lock-in, Ribstein's disagreement relates primarily to the presumed historical significance of capital lock-in as a distinctly corporate (as opposed to possible partnership) feature and the resulting policy implications of Stout's analysis. But he does not dispute that locking in capital is important. As he puts it, 'Plainly lock-in *is* an important feature of modern business' (ibid 537).

[39] Henry Hansmann and Reinier Kraakman, 'The Essential Role of Organizational Law' (2000) 110 Yale Law Journal 387.

organizational law. Capital lock-in may thus, historically, have been more a more essential characteristic of corporate statutes than limited liability.[40]

In fact, Hansmann, Kraakman, and Squire have argued that the very availability of limited liability itself typically requires 'entity shielding' which, in its 'strong' form, is characterized by the lack of any right on the part of equity investors to withdraw their capital from the corporation. In their view, limited liability for shareholders and 'strong entity shielding' (essentially, locking in capital), 'are highly complementary; the presence of one generally calls for the other.'[41]

## Limited Liability[42]

Limited liability—insulating shareholders from the debts and other liabilities of the corporation—is often regarded, particularly by legal practitioners, as the principal advantage of incorporation over other organizational forms such as partnership.[43] Not surprisingly, some consider this particular characteristic

[40] Hansmann and Kraakman provide a convincingly detailed explication of this point, although it is noteworthy that the English corporate law scholar LCB Gower made a similar, albeit much more brief and less carefully developed observation several years earlier. See LCB Gower, *Gower's Principles of Modern Company Law* (5th edn, Sweet & Maxwell 1992) 23.

[41] Henry Hansmann, Reinier Kraakman, and Richard Squire, 'The New Business Entities in Evolutionary Perspective' (2005) University of Illinois Law Review 5, 12.

[42] This brief section on limited liability draws on Christopher C. Nicholls, *Corporate Law* (Emond-Montgomery 2005) 77–82.

[43] A frequently overlooked aspect of limited liability is that it provides one of the most compelling arguments in support of treating the shareholders, and the shareholders alone, as the most fundamental constituents of the business corporation. If statutorily granted limited liability has any economic or legal significance, then we must assume that, in the absence of such statutory provision, shareholders would face some risk of exposure to the debts or other liabilities of the corporation to an unlimited degree. But why should this be? The answer appears to be that, as constitutive members of the corporation, they would be exposed to liability for their corporation's obligations just as partners are exposed to unlimited liability for the partnership's debts and other obligations. And as partners in a general partnership, it will be recalled, they would each be owed a fiduciary duty by their fellow partners in the conduct of the business. If employees, creditors, or other 'stakeholders' were equally considered members—equally entitled, for example, to be beneficiaries of directors' fiduciary duties and to enjoy benefits from the corporation exceeding their strict contractual entitlements—then presumably they too ought to face the prospect of unlimited liability for the corporation's debts in the absence of any statutory provision to the contrary. If, after all, such important 'stakeholders' are, as some opponents of shareholder primacy insist, as much 'owners' of the corporation as the shareholders, then they must surely be subject both to the benefits and the burdens of such putative 'ownership' interests. Yet, unlike shareholders, no such stakeholders do enjoy such statutory liability protection. What, then, might a robust 'stakeholder constituency' theory of the corporation imply? Should the employees of Enron, for example, as corporate stakeholders (if truly as much 'members of the company' as the shareholders, but sadly unprotected by statutory limited liability) have been found liable for the misdoings of their disgraced corporate employer? Such a conclusion is, of course, outrageous, but is a reminder that employees—and other non-shareholder corporate constituents—do have a distinctly different, and decidedly more external relationship to the corporation than shareholders.

of incorporation the corporation's *sine qua non*. For example, in 1926 the *Economist* asserted that 'the economic historian of the future . . . may assign to the nameless inventor of limited liability, as applied to trading corporations, a place of honor with Watt and Stephenson, and other pioneers of the Industrial Revolution'.[44]

Most business people are apt to defend the need for limited liability by claiming it is necessary to encourage risk-taking. But such an explanation is incomplete at best. Entrepreneurs are surely among the least risk averse of people. Many businesses thrive as sole proprietorships or partnerships where limited liability is not available, and the shareholders of many smaller corporations are not infrequently compelled, by market conditions, personally to guarantee the obligations of the corporations they control particularly to bank lenders, making the formal protection of limited liability a very thin veil of protection. In the case of potential tort liability, insurance can very often provide entrepreneurs adequate protection, rendering the immunity of limited liability largely redundant. And, in any event, even if limited liability does uniquely encourage and facilitate 'risk taking', that explanation alone cannot justify the easily-available grant of statutory limited liability since there can be no assurance that more business risk taking will necessarily ensure a socially optimal level of risk taking. If the devastating global financial crisis of 2007–2009 taught us nothing else, it surely demonstrated with abundant clarity that too much business and financial risk is at least as hazardous for a nation as too little.

A more nuanced economic justification for limited liability has been advanced by Easterbrook and Fischel.[45] Among other things, they identify the crucial role limited liability plays in allowing for large, anonymous trading markets. Their insight is simple but powerful: when shareholders' liability is limited, shareholders need not worry about the financial capacity of their fellow shareholders. Thus, shareholdings and share trading may be anonymous—the price of shares on public markets will not be affected by the identity (and thus the perceived wealth) of any specific current shareholder. This also implies, however, that share value will not be affected by other individual shareholder attributes either—such as, for example, shareholders' differing views towards competing corporate goals, such as wealth maximization, on the one hand, or corporate social responsibility on the other. The efficiency of anonymous trading markets, then, depends in part on an implicit assumption that the

[44] *Economist* (18 December 1926), cited in Bishop Carleton Hunt, *The Development of the Business Corporation in England* (Harvard University Press 1936) 116.

[45] Frank H Easterbrook and Daniel R Fischel, 'Limited Liability and the Corporation' (1985) 52 University of Chicago Law Review 89.

interests of the shareholders are homogeneous and do not vary from one day to the next even as shares rapidly change hands on securities exchanges. It is assumed that, however various their individual tastes, preferences, and priorities may otherwise be, shareholders have a common interest in seeing the value of their shares enhanced. This conclusion, it may be added, seems to accord with Henry Hansmann's general observation that the control and 'ownership' of corporations by shareholders is efficient precisely because the interests of shareholders (investors), unlike the interests of all other corporate constituents, are homogeneous, and based quintessentially on a desire for economic gain.[46]

## Shareholders: Pooling and Primacy

The corporation, then, is a pooling device through which it becomes possible first to aggregate and then permanently to lock-in capital contributions for the pursuit of large scale, indivisible enterprise, enticing investors with the twin promises of limited liability and a managerial commitment to shareholder primacy. The shareholder primacy goal is typically framed strictly in financial terms; the directors' efforts are to be focused upon maximizing shareholder wealth. This narrow financial formulation of the 'shareholder primacy' goal necessarily disregards the very real possibility that individual shareholders are not homogeneous. Many may have other non-financial priorities and might well have preferred any corporations over which they exercised complete control to pursue those non-financial priorities, even at the risk of seeing the price of their shares stumble and fall.

Many commentators have assumed that individual corporations might theoretically seek to amend the terms of their standard 'off the shelf' corporate charters to reflect a recognition of alternative priorities in place of, or in addition to, a shareholder value enhancement goal. Corporations, on this view, could, if they chose, prioritize other stakeholders' interests instead, provided that such alternative priorities were explicitly set out in the corporation's constating documents so that prospective shareholders could take full account of such unusual corporate priorities when assessing the price at which they were willing to purchase the corporation's shares. Occasionally, however,

[46] Henry Hansmann, *The Ownership of Enterprise* (Harvard University Press 1996). I am grateful to Bengt Holmström for this observation.

doubts had been raised about whether or not Delaware law in particular would indeed allow for the voluntary abnegation of shareholder primacy in this way.[47]

## Alternative Corporate Forms

While some detractors contended that the US Supreme Court itself had weighed in against the concept of a mandatory, non-waivable shareholder primacy norm in *Burwell v Hobby Lobby Stores Inc*,[48] that claim may perhaps

[47] Among the Delaware judicial decisions most frequently cited in support of the proposition that directors had a positive duty to enhance (or maximize) shareholder value were *Revlon Inc v MacAndrews & Forbes Holdings Inc* 506 A 2d 173 (Del 1986) (albeit, the duty in this case was limited to situations where a sale or change of control had become inevitable, and the nuances of what would constitute a change of control event that triggered this Revlon duty was subject to later judicial refinement and considerable scholarly debate), and *ebay Domestic Holdings Inc v Newmark* 16 A 3d 1 (Del Ch 2010). Perhaps the most explicit endorsement of the wealth maximization norm came in the 2024 case *McRitchie v Zuckerberg* 315 A 3d 518 (Del Ch 2024), in which Laster VC of the Chancery Court of Delaware declared: 'The fiduciary duties owed by directors of a Delaware corporation require the directors to seek to maximize the value of the corporation over the long-term for the benefit of the stockholders as residual claimants to the value created by the specific firm that the directors serve.' This decision is discussed further in Chapters 8 and 9. The ubiquity of the shareholder primacy norm among US corporate law scholars is evinced in the 2011 Brookings Institution Study surveying the curricula of leading law and business schools in the United States finding that most professors in those schools—especially leading law schools—taught their students that the corporate obligation to focus on financial returns was 'settled law', a conclusion that even professors ideologically opposed to such an outcome felt themselves obliged to teach as their responsibility was to tell students what the law is, not what it ought to be. Darrell A West, *The Purpose of the Corporation in Business and Law School Curricula* (Governance Studies at Brookings 2011) https://www.brookings.edu/wp-content/uploads/2016/06/0719_corporation_west.pdf.

[48] 573 US 682 (2014). The most direct reference to profit maximization in the *Hobby Lobby* decision appears in the opinion of Justice Alito: 'Not all corporations that decline to organize as nonprofits do so in order to maximize profit. For example, organizations with religious and charitable aims might organize as for-profit corporations because of the potential advantages of that corporate form, such as the freedom to participate in lobbying for legislation or campaigning for political candidates who promote their religious or charitable goals. In fact, recognizing the inherent compatibility between establishing a for-profit corporation and pursuing nonprofit goals, States have increasingly adopted laws formally recognizing hybrid corporate forms. Over half of the States, for instance, now recognize the "benefit corporation," a dual-purpose entity that seeks to achieve both a benefit for the public and a profit for its owners.' This statement, of course, is not a statement about the corporate law of Oklahoma (where Hobby Lobby Stores Inc was incorporated), let alone Delaware, but a general observation of background facts. Moreover, *Hobby Lobby* was not a case in which shareholders were challenging the conduct of the corporation's directors. Quite the contrary. It was the shareholders' support of the directors' conduct to which the Secretary of Health and Human Services objected. Finally, Justice Alito's final comment about benefit corporation legislation is very telling. If it were genuinely the case that conventional business corporations in every state need not be concerned about focusing on profit (or shareholder wealth maximization), then what conceivable purpose would benefit corporation legislation serve? Those who argue that *Hobby Lobby* rejects corporate profit (or share wealth) maximization proceed from the false premise that shareholder primacy demands maximizing value *above all else*,that is without legal or ethical restraint. As discussed in Chapter 2, this is not an accurate articulation of the corporate goal as it has been framed by neoclassical economists. Share value maximization is to be pursued within the boundaries of the law and ethical constraints and, in a pluralist society, those ethical constraints could well overlap with religious convictions. A director would not be in breach of his or her fiduciary duties for refusing to work on a religious holiday—notwithstanding that the corporation might make a greater profit if the director had agreed to do so. Nor could a corporation or its directors

be regarded more as creative advocacy than genuinely disinterested scholarship. Among more careful commentators, it was noted that strong doubts about the latitude of directors ever to depart from a shareholder primacy objective had sparked and initiated the drive for the enactment of legislation providing for the creation of a new and different kind of business corporation, one that would not only be permitted but also expressly mandated to pursue some public benefit in addition to (and judiciously balanced against) the goal of seeking financial gains for shareholders.

In the United States, since 2007, it has been possible for for-profit corporations that choose to undertake commitments to certain broader social interest mandates to obtain a 'B Corp' certification from B Lab, a non-profit certificating organization.[49] B Lab is expressly opposed to the notion of shareholder primacy on normative grounds. Its website, for example, declares: 'B Lab considers shareholder primacy to be an obstacle to creating long-term value for all stakeholders, including the owners and shareholders themselves. We believe overturning shareholder primacy is integral to making our economy work for everyone.'[50] But a certified B Corp is not a distinct type of business organization. It is simply an ordinary business corporation that had been accorded a third-party seal of ethical approval. And if—as some cautious lawyers feared—courts in at least some US jurisdictions (including Delaware) might view express denial of unequivocal shareholder primacy as a breach by corporate directors of their fiduciary duty, perhaps the B Corp certification model would not provide the ethical constraint on corporate excesses that its founders hoped for.

A proposed solution to this potential legal limitation came with the introduction of legislation providing for an entirely new kind of for-profit business corporation—the benefit (or public benefit) corporation. Maryland was the first state to introduce benefit corporation legislation, in 2010. As of 2024, at least forty-one US states and the District of Columbia had introduced some version of benefit corporation legislation.[51] Although benefit corporation legislation varies from state to state, every version of the new organizational form is required to pursue some general public benefit (in addition to pursuing

be sued for declining to shift the corporation' sits business from, say, the sale of bibles to the sale of alcohol or tobacco because the latter might be more profitable.

[49] See B Lab, online: https://www.bcorporation.net/en-us/movement/about-b-lab/.

[50] See https://www.bcorporation.net/en-us/about-b-corps/legal-requirements/.

[51] See Grunin Center for Law and Social Entrepreneurship, *The State of Social Enterprise and the Law 2024-2025*, 6 https://socentlawtracker.org/wp-content/uploads/2025/08/Grunin-2024-25-Social-Enterprise-and-Law-Report_V2-1.pdf.

profit) and may also pursue specific public benefits. These public benefit goals are typically subject to reporting obligations using appropriate credible and independent third-party standards.[52] However, although benefit corporations are mandated to pursue some non-shareholder interests, typically the requirement of directors of public benefit corporations to balance the interests of shareholders and non-shareholders is a requirement that may be enforced only by the shareholders.[53] Accordingly, the viability of the structure depends not only on an initial interest on the part of shareholders to invest in a vehicle with an overarching social mandate but also upon such an enduring commitment to that goal that shareholders would be willing to initiate legal action against the directors if need be for failure to pursue it. And shareholders' enthusiasm to pursue such actions, it must be presumed, would prevail even when those shareholders benefit financially from the directors' impugned behavior.

US states were not the first jurisdictions to introduce legislation providing for organizational alternatives to the traditional corporation that would allow for explicit blending of objectives of private gain and public service. In the UK, for example, since 2005, it has been possible for socially minded entrepreneurs to operate businesses through community interest companies (CICs), a hybrid profit/community-directed entity of which there are now more than 37,000 in existence.[54] Although they are profit-making firms, CICs are also required to satisfy a broad 'community interest' test and are subject to a series of reporting, regulatory, and asset-transfer restrictions. Additionally, the cooperative movement, involving profit-seeking firms operating in accordance with stakeholder-sensitive cooperative principles, has enjoyed a distinguished history in many parts of Europe, Asia, and South America.[55]

Even 'traditional' business corporations in many jurisdictions operate under a variety of legislative and judicial frameworks, not all of which unambiguously embrace shareholder primacy. However, it appears that the extent to which some jurisdictions mandate or permit corporate consideration of non-shareholder interests may occasionally be overstated.[56]

[52] See eg Delaware General Corporation Law, Delaware Code Title 8 ch 1 subch XV.

[53] ibid § 367.

[54] See Regulator of Community Interest Companies Annual Report 2024–2025, 4 https://assets.publishing.service.gov.uk/media/68809f4f28f29c99778a7504/cic-25-01-community-interest-companies-annual-report-2024-2025.pdf.

[55] See eg Mary Hilson, Silke Neunsinger, and Greg Patmore (eds), *A Global History of Consumer Co-operation Since 1850* (Brill 2017).

[56] For example, in a recent book by Sir John Kay, *The Corporation in the 21st Century* (Yale University Press 2024) the author cites a provision he identifies as s 4.1.1 of 'the German commercial code' (ibid 180) and s 172 of the UK Companies Act 2006 (ibid 178–79) as examples of corporate law regimes that depart from an express shareholder primacy norm. The provision he identifies as the 'German commercial code', in particular, he tells his readers, states 'an unambiguous stakeholder position'. (ibid

Interest in forms of business organization that attempt to integrate a profit motive with broader non-financial social goals reflects the frustration of many activists and prospective investors over what they perceive at times as a dangerous, irresponsible, and dehumanizing materialism fomented by the relentless and unapologetic profit-maximizing missions of business corporations, particularly the largest business corporations. The rationality of shareholder primacy and the financial economic perspective of the business corporation in general have been resisted by progressive corporate scholars, too, who seek, among other things, to promote a more socially beneficial 'communitarian' approach to corporate law.[57]

It is no easy matter to graft benevolent branches onto a profit-driven root. Appeals to the demands of conscience are questionable guides for the management of a business corporation because to insist that corporate directors do 'the right thing' [58]implies that there is universal agreement about what the 'right thing' is. Robin Marris once noted that: 'All ethics conflict with

181). He goes on to contend that, unlike the non-mandatory 'comply or explain' approach of the UK's Combined [corporate governance Code (to which we will return in due course), 'Since Germany is a civil law jurisdiction, the commercial code is legally binding.' (ibid 181). There are, unfortunately, a few problems with this analysis. First, it is not the German 'commercial code' that Sir John has cited, but rather the German Corporate Governance Code (the 'Code'). Further, the version of the Code he cites is an outdated version that has been superseded. Finally, while the Code does indeed have a legal basis, the Code's provisions are not, in fact, all mandatory. While the broad 'Principles' set out in the Code are said to 'reflect material legal requirements for responsible governance', (see 'The Deutscher Corporate Governance Kodex (the German corporate governance code), Foreword', online: https://www.dcgk.de/en/code//foreword.html), the 'recommendations' are in fact implemented on a 'comply or explain' basis only, and the third type of Code provisions--'suggestions'—may be ignored by corporations without even triggering such a disclosure requirement. Thus, although the current version of the Code does include some *recommendations* for the consideration of broad non-shareholder interests (with which companies subject to the Code must either comply, or explain their non-compliance), the relevant 'Principle' governing Management Board's management duties contains far more ambiguous language than the provision quoted by Sir John, stating only:

> The Management Board is responsible for managing the enterprise in its own best interests. Its members are jointly accountable for managing the enterprise. The Chair or Spokesperson of the Management Board coordinates the work of the Management Board members. (Code A. I. Principle 1, online: https://www.dcgk.de/en/code/current-version/a-management-and-supervision.html).

As for the implications of s. 172 of the UK Companies Act 2006, which Sir John rightly describes as 'a masterpiece of ambiguity and compromise,' we will return to consider in chapter 7. One also notes that Canada is often heralded as a jurisdiction in which shareholder primacy has been purged from corporate law. Andrew Keay, for example, states in *The Corporate Objective* (Edward Elgar 2011) that, in Canada, the Canadian Supreme Court has 'unequivocally rejected shareholder primacy.' (ibid 168) To the constructively ambiguous Canadian federal corporate law provisions dealing with these issues, we will also briefly turn in chapter 7.

[57] See eg Matthew T Bodie, 'The Next Iteration of Progressive Corporate Law' (2017) 74 Washington & Lee Law Review 739; David Millon, 'Communitarians, Contractarians, and the Crisis in Corporate Law' (1993) 50 Washington & Lee Law Review 1373.

[58] See eg Leo E Strine Jr, 'Making it Easier for Directors to "Do the Right Thing"' (2104) 4 Harvard Business Review 235.

self-interest, and few societies rely on the effectiveness of conscience alone',[59] precisely because one person's moral cause may be another person's moral violation. Morality in a pluralist society is so highly contestable that it is easy to understand the appeal of asserting that corporations would do best to focus on generating material wealth within the bounds of the law and let moral debates surrounding the appropriate content of the law occur at the political level.

## Nexus of Conflicts

We will return to consider these alternative perspectives in Chapter 7. The point to be noted here is that the corporation necessarily serves as an important mechanism for integrating resources and mediating competing interests among its various stakeholders. The corporation may thus be considered not only as a 'nexus of contracts' but also as a 'nexus of conflicts'. This latter characterization may indeed more aptly explain the unique contribution of the corporation than the former.[60] Even before Berle and Means, indeed even before Veblen, Alfred Marshall recognized the conflicts necessarily at work in joint stock companies as a result of the separation of ownership and control: 'Joint Stock companies are hampered by internal frictions', he said, 'and conflicts of interest between shareholders and debenture holders, between ordinary and preferred shareholders, and between all these and the directors; and by the need for an elaborate system of checks and counterchecks'.[61]

In the face of inevitable conflict, corporations help facilitate the success of the improbable miracle that is modern organized civil society. Accumulating capital from widespread, unrelated investors (whether directly or through the intermediation of asset managers) to facilitate millions of anonymous trading transactions amongst billions of human beings, the corporation represents one of the greatest triumphs of human ingenuity.

One of the remarkable attributes of the shareholder primacy norm is that it facilitates this organizational wonder by rendering irrelevant what might otherwise be paralysing conflicts among shareholders with divergent personal interests. No common idea of 'the good' among shareholders is necessary; no agreement on any divisive political matters is required. People from

[59] Robin Marris, *The Economic Theory of 'Managerial' Capitalism* (Macmillan 1967) 55.

[60] As[Williamson has observed the formation of the firm can be seen as an alternative way of mitigating disputes and thus, in effect, a more efficiacious and more efficient alternative in many circumstances to relying upon resort to the courts. See Williamson (n 28) 32, 154, 166.

[61] Alfred Marshall, *Principles of Economics* (Macmillan and Co 1890), Bk VII ch 8, 639.

all backgrounds, with the most diverse and irreconcilably conflicting views whether on the profound social and political matters of our time or the most trivial questions of taste may nonetheless pool their resources anonymously and productively. Divided on many matters, or even on most, shareholders stand united in the simple shared goal of increasing corporate wealth. That wealth, once acquired and unlocked by individual shareholders, through dividends, share buy-backs, collateralized borrowings, or liquidating sales, may then be deployed by each shareholder in accordance with his or her own individual values, beliefs, preferences, and priorities. The shareholder primacy norm thus triumphs over the deepening polarization that elsewhere threatens to rock society and paralyse political institutions. Shareholder primacy, in this idealized form, becomes the great peacemaker of our time. And, as Stephen Bainbridge has argued, shareholder primacy *is* pro-social, too, because it is the best means for allocating resources efficiently and spurring innovation, thus increasing social wealth, and enhancing personal freedom.[62]

Or so it might. But the shareholder primacy norm (in its rarefied legal context) may never have been intended to function as any such decision rule for resolving the competing demands of diverse corporate stakeholders. It may rather have been a principle (or a norm) developed for the much more modest task of ensuring ensuring even-handedness in contests between the conflicting interests of majority and minority shareholders.[63]

There is an additional complicating nuance. Since even the most ardent proponents of the shareholder primacy norm acknowledge that pursuit of this goal must always be subject to legal and ethical constraints, could these qualifications not open the door to the possibility that corporate directors might properly be called upon to balance any number of other competing interests against the goal of increasing shareholder value?[64] For that matter, could commitment to shareholder primacy oblige corporate directors and the officers they appoint to dedicate themselves to enhancing shareholder *welfare*, not merely shareholder *wealth*, since it is surely beyond debate that for some shareholders, if not for most, their personal satisfaction and welfare depend less on crass and transitory financial considerations than on the achievement of important

[62] Stephen M Bainbridge, *The Profit Motive: Defending Shareholder Value Maximization* (Cambridge University Press 2023) 166–68.

[63] D Gordon Smith, 'The Shareholder Primacy Norm' (1998) 23(2) Journal of Corporation Law 277.

[64] There is, of course, an extensive body of academic literature which insists that one need not necessarily balance shareholder wealth maximization against due consideration for non-shareholder interests since the proper consideration of such interests will, in the long term, enhance shareholder value as well. This approach is often referred to as the 'enlightened shareholder value' approach. See eg Lund, 'Enlightened Shareholder Value" (n 31) 91. This topic is discussed further in Chapter 7.

and enduring social goals such as, perhaps, a commitment to combat climate change or to ensure the payment of fair wages and the safe and dignified treatment of all employees.[65] Perhaps, therefore, the modern 're-emergence of corporate purpose provisions in corporate constitutions could mark the end of unbridled shareholder primacy'.[66] To arguments of this sort we will also return in Chapter 7.

## Shareholder Primacy and Social Division

One other troubling consideration deserves mention. The corporation may well be an ingenious device for balancing or mediating competing interests and focusing productive activity in order to thrive in a competitive marketplace. But in an economic system that depends so mightily upon competition—lavishly rewarding success and indifferent to the consequences of failure—what may happen if a critical mass of people come to feel—and not without reasons—that they will never be able to triumph and win more than a meagre share of society's 'prizes' under the current terms of competition? It is understandable enough that such discouraged souls might well seek to change the rules of engagement altogether.

Almost a century ago, sociologist Robert K. Merton, in an insightful article,[67]explored this possibility and noted the importance of ensuring that social rewards flow to participants in the capitalist system even where those participants were not the victors in the competitive race for wealth and social position:

> Continuing satisfactions must derive from sheer participation in a competitive order as well as from eclipsing one's competitors if the order itself is to be sustained. The occasional sacrifices involved in institutionalized conduct must be compensated by socialized rewards. The distribution of statuses and roles through competition must be so organized that positive incentives for conformity to roles and adherence to status obligations are provided for every position within the distributive order.[68]

[65] See eg Oliver Hart and Luigi Zingales, 'Companies Should Maximize Shareholder Welfare Not Market Value' (2017) 2 Journal of Law Finance and Accounting 247; Oliver Hart and Luigi Zingales, 'The New Corporate Governance' (2022) 1(1) The University of Chicago Business Law Review 195.

[66] Susan Watson and Lynn Buckley, 'Directors' Positive Duty to Act in the Interests of the Entity: Shareholders' Interests Bounded by Corporate Purpose' (2024) 24 Journal of Corporate Law Studies 233, 235.

[67] Robert K Merton, 'Social Structure and Anomie' (1938) 3(5) American Sociological Review 672.

[68] ibid 674.

In the worst cases, Merton warned, a society that fails to ensure that there is intrinsic fulfilment in competing for society's rewards can foster 'anomie'—lawlessness—which in turn can lead to social disruption and a breakdown in social order:

> In the extreme case, the latter may be so vitiated by the goal-emphasis that the range of behavior is limited only by considerations of technical expediency. The sole significant question then becomes, which available means is most efficient in netting the socially approved value? The technically most feasible procedure, whether legitimate or not, is preferred to the institutionally prescribed conduct. As this process continues, the integration of the society becomes tenuous and anomie ensues.[69]

Consider Merton's ideas in their starkest form. If one wishes to sustain a social and economic system that will generate exceedingly generous rewards for the few and meagre rewards for the many, those perennially deprived of the richest rewards must be given good reasons—satisfactory and persuasive to them—to continue to participate. Competition itself must involve some intrinsic fulfilment, irrespective of success. Without such intrinsic reward, there is grave risk that the disaffected may come to react in ways that are undesirable and potentially destructive—to themselves or others.

Many years after he wrote his 'Anomie' paper, in 1960, Professor Merton participated in a symposium to mark the occasion of the tenth anniversary of the Graduate School of Industrial Administration of the Carnegie Institute of Technology. Participants in this symposium included several other noted thinkers who are mentioned elsewhere in this book including Adolf Berle, Friedrich Hayek, and Herbert Simon. Although he was evidently unable to complete his formal paper for the occasion, his brief statement on the subject 'The Corporation: Its Coexistence with Man' included this poignant observation:

> Although an indispensable objective of every business corporation is to maintain itself and improve its competitive position, managers have a strange way of becoming dissatisfied with this as an exclusive goal . . . [The large corporation's] very economic success has led our society to hold the corporation accountable not only for the creation and distribution of goods and services, but for all the ensuing consequences that inevitably follow when

[69] Ibid 674.

> economic activity is carried on by massive, concentrated organizations . . . Today, the accumulation of fiction that centers on the manager as an object of interest reflects not only his increasingly strategic place in society, but a sensing of the value conflicts to which he is subject by virtue of his job and, even more important, the value consequences of what he does or fails to do.[70]

## Conclusion

Perhaps one of the least appreciated virtues of the modern business corporation is the role it can play in mitigating conflict by facilitating productive activity employing resources pooled from contributors between whom cooperation would otherwise be impossible. This conflict-soothing function is enabled by many of the traditional features of corporate law: limited liability, capital lock-in, and, perhaps counter-intuitively, a shareholder wealth maximization norm. However, the wealth generated by modern corporations is by no means evenly shared among all members of society. And the resentment engendered by significant disparities of wealth and income, conjoined with rising anxiety about a cascade of social and environmental threats including climate change, racism, and increasing political polarization, have focused critical attention on the proper purpose corporate form. In the following chapter, we consider the demands socially-conscious critics have made upon business corporations and how corporations have sought to respond to the critics from across the political spectrum.

[70] Robert K Merton, 'The Corporation: Its Coexistence with Men' in Melvin Anshen and George Leland Bach (eds), *Management and Corporations 1985* (McGraw-Hill 1960) 57, 58, 59.

# 7

# How Does a Corporation Do? CSR and ESG: Doing Well by Doing Good? Doing Good by Doing Well?

## Introduction

Business corporations are formed for the purpose of carrying on for-profit businesses.[1]As we have seen, for the neoclassical economists, business corporations, like other 'firms', were treated as production functions and were assumed to operate with the goal of maximizing those profits. The simple 'profit maximization' assumption was later refined in the financial economic literature. Uncertainty was a stubborn fact of business life, and since corporations must invariably operate under conditions of uncertainty, 'profit maximization' unravels as a coherent goal. By the 1950s an alternative had been proposed: corporations ought to maximize shareholder wealth or value (as reflected in the current market price of the corporation's shares). Pursuit of this objective was later dubbed 'shareholder primacy'.[2] It was assumed by the financial economists of the time that corporations were, in fact, operating with this shareholder wealth maximization goal in mind. It was the only rational thing to do. Whether contemporary business leaders themselves—especially those enjoying dominant market position—actually shared the economists' certainty (or were even aware of it) is a mystery best left to business historians to unravel. Certainly, by the 1980s (or perhaps a little earlier), the so-called corporate 'shareholder primacy norm' had become widely accepted not only

[1] Portions of this chapter draw on material from an earlier book chapter: C Nicholls, 'The Corporation and Modern Capitalism: Folk, Broke and Woke' in Oonagh E Fitzgerald (ed), *Corporate Citizen: New Perspectives on the Globalized Rule of Law* (CIGI 2020).

[2] The term 'shareholder primacy' can also be used as a term distinct from shareholder value or wealth maximization to refer more broadly to the objective of enhancing shareholder welfare, which could include both financial and non-financial interests. The implications of this broader view are discussed later in this chapter.

*Corporate Governance and Enlightened Fiduciaries*. Christopher C. Nicholls, Oxford University Press.
 DOI: 10.1093/9780198904199.003.0007

among financial economists but also among legal scholars, corporate managers, and courts, particularly in the influential US jurisdiction of Delaware.

This modern version of shareholder primacy was regarded by many law and economics scholars as a sensible development, perhaps even an inevitable one. Maximizing shareholder wealth, from this perspective, is seen not as contrary to serving societal interests but rather as the specific and most efficient means by which business corporations serve those very interests. Corporations' role is to increase the economic 'pie' and so, within the boundaries of socially protective regulation and with the wise ex-post intervention of appropriate governmental income and wealth distribution initiatives, more generous slices may be enjoyed by all.

Is this moral alchemy? Can private 'greed' really be transmuted into public good? Lawyers, in particular, should understand how an apparently morally ambiguous sub-goal can actually prove essential to a beneficial social outcome. Consider how criminal lawyers' single-minded vigorous defence of, or 'resolute advocacy' for, their clients—regardless of whatever personal views such lawyers might entertain about the likely moral innocence of those clients—is celebrated as the crucial means by which society's interest in criminal justice is pursued. The lawyer's arguably amoral sub-goal operates within the broader context of the criminal justice system. We do not expect—indeed, we do not permit—defence lawyers to indulge their own individual sense of what is best for society, for example by prejudging ostensibly 'guilty' clients and betraying them to conviction rather than vigorously defending them. We demand, instead, that the lawyer adhere to the parameters of a more narrow, specialized role. That role is constrained by 'rules of the game' which require honesty and forbid the advocate from misleading the court. But subject to those ethical boundaries, the lawyer is duty bound to advocate vigorously on behalf of the client's interests alone, regardless of how morally 'undeserving' that client might otherwise appear.

To the layperson, the lawyer's unwavering commitment to protect the interests of apparent 'criminals' (to help 'criminals get off scot-free', to quote a familiar refrain) may seem troubling, unethical, and contrary to the long-term interests of society. It is none of these things. As other participants in the criminal justice system faithfully perform their designated roles as well, the interests of society are successfully advanced after all. Justice is served. Equally important, the alternative is unacceptable. Suppose a socially conscious defence lawyer were improperly to forego her single-minded 'fixation' or 'obsession' on advocacy in favour of adopting a self-righteous goal of what might be dubbed 'lawyers' social responsibility': an earnest commitment to serve the public interest by ensuring guilty clients answered for their crimes. Those clients adjudged by their lawyers as morally 'innocent' would still receive the benefit of the lawyer's zealous advocacy, but matters would be very different when the lawyer concluded that a client was probably blameworthy. Then the lawyer's assessment of the interests of society would prevail and the lawyer would not hesitate to betray the guilty client to ensure conviction.

The results of such hypothetical 'lawyer social responsibility' would be disastrous. The integrity of the adversarial system of justice would be subverted, the candour of the lawyer/client relationship exploded, and the genuine long-term interest of society seriously and irreparably undermined.

So, too, it might be argued, that the shareholder wealth maximization norm—although seemingly a soulless celebration of materialism and greed—properly understood, is altogether more, not less, socially responsible than an alternative view that insists that business corporations abandon their singular focus upon financial performance in favour of pursuing explicitly pro-social goals instead. Where corporations must compete for capital, shareholder wealth maximization may be the only corporate goal that may be expected in the long run to succeed in any case.[3] A defunct corporation employs no labour, purchases no supplies, produces no goods or services, and supports no community organizations.

Nor, on this view, is this corporate objective likely to lead to any kind of distortive or 'myopic' focus on short-term gains at the expense of the long term, as critics frequently, but often mistakenly, claim.[4] (It is intriguing to note in this regard, that the complaint about the imminent dangers of corporate short-termism have been around for many decades,[5] yet, somehow, these 'short-sighted' corporations have survived and prospered and economic growth

[3] See eg Henry Hansmann and Reinier Kraakman, 'The End of History for Corporate Law' (2001) 89 Georgetown Law Journal 439.

[4] There is no shortage of examples of critics who assail the 'short-termism' of the modern corporation. See eg Dominic Barton, Jonathan Bailey, and Joshua Zoffer, 'Rise to the Challenge of Short-Termism' https://www.fcltglobal.org/docs/default-source/default-document-library/fclt-global-rising-to-the-challenge.pdf; Rebecca Carr and Tim Koller, 'How to Build an Alliance Against Corporate Short-Termism' https://www.fcltglobal.org/docs/default-source/default-document-library/fclt-global-rising-to-the-challenge.pd; Wachtell, Lipton, Rosen & Katz, 'The Threat to the American Economy and Society from Activism and Short-Termism' https://corpgov.law.harvard.edu/2015/01/27/the-threat-to-the-economy-and-society-from-activism-and-short-termism-updated/; The Aspen Institute, *Overcoming Short-Termism: A Call for a More Responsible Approach to Investment and Business Management* (15 December 2009) https://assets.aspeninstitute.org/content/uploads/files/content/images/BSPonlineBroch.pdf; Lynne L Dallas, 'Short-Termism, the Financial Crisis and Corporate Governance' (2012) 37 Journal of Corporate Law 265; Kent Greenfield, 'The Puzzle of Short-Termism' (2011) 46 Wake Forest Law Review 62.

[5] See eg Michael C Jensen, writing in 1991: 'Some even point to such gains as evidence of a "short-term" orientation that is said to be destroying American business.' Michael C Jensen, 'Corporate Control and the Politics of Finance' (1991) 4(2) Journal of Applied Corporate Finance 13.

worldwide has been unimaginably large.[6] Perhaps, there is less to the corporate 'short-termism' complaint than meets the eye.)

A corporation's current stock price is, by definition, a price that impounds the market's assessment of *all* future earnings. It is, necessarily, an estimate of long-term prospects. Maximizing shareholder wealth, as reflected in the current market price for the corporation's shares, therefore ensures that all shareholders—irrespective of individual investment horizons—share a community of interest.[7] That wayward corporations are undoubtedly capable of engaging in egregious anti-social behaviour (as are wayward human beings) is never denied by advocates of shareholder primacy. However, it is argued that constraining such objectionable behaviour is better achieved by robust enforcement of legislation or regulation than by relying in vain on vague and unenforceable norms of ethical managerial behaviour.[8]

It hardly needs mentioning that even the most ardent proponents of the shareholder primacy norm have never argued, suggested, or hoped that corporations should pursue this goal above all else. Of course, the corporation is properly subject to legal and ethical constraints.[9] But ethical considerations are

[6] As noted by David E Levari and others, 'Prevalence-induced Concept Change in Human Judgment' (2018) 360 Science 1465, the percentage of the human population living in poverty has decreased monumentally over the past 200 years, with particularly dramatic reductions in world poverty since the late twentieth century. Curiously, however, the majority of people surveyed on this issue mistakenly believe it is getting worse, a cognitive error the authors attribute to what they deem 'prevalence-induced concept change'—ie the very fact that poverty has decreased makes the remaining instances of poverty seem more acute and severe. Levari and others cite Max Roser's 2016 article 'The short history of global living conditions and why it matters that we know it' (https://ourworldindata.org/a-history-of-global-living-conditions-in-5-charts, cited in Levari and others, 1466) showing that in 1820 more than 89 per cent of the world's population lived in extreme poverty. By 1950, that number had fallen to 36.65 per cent and the number continued to fall for the next sixty-five years, such that by 2015 less than 10 per cent of the world's population lived in extreme poverty.

[7] See eg Robert C Clark, *Corporate Law* (Aspen Law and Business 1986) 18 note 46. For a detailed critique of the short-termism perspective see Mark J Roe, 'Stock Market Short-Termism: Impact' (2018) 167 University of Pennsylvania Law Review 71. Reconciling the interests of 'short term' versus 'long term' investors is one of the key advantages of defining the corporate goal in terms of maximizing current shareholder wealth rather than the largely undefinable goal of maximizing profits. See Stephen A Ross, Randolph W Westerfield, and Bradford D Jordan, *Essentials of Corporate Finance* (7th edn McGraw-Hill/Irwin 2011) 10. For a recent reminder of why the most elementary principles of corporate finance make clear that shareholder value necessarily involves the pursuit of long-term, not short-term, gains see Alex Edmans, 'Applying Economics—Not Gut Feel—to ESG' (2023) 79(4) Financial Analysts Journal 16, 17 ff.

[8] See eg Stephen M Bainbridge, 'In Defence of the Shareholder Wealth Maximization Norm: A Reply to Professor Green' (1993) 50 Washington & Lee Law Review 1423. Critics note, however, that large corporations themselves play an important role in the process of creating the very laws to which they are subject. See eg Christopher Stone, *Where the Law Ends* (Harper & Row 1975) 94 ff.

[9] See eg Friedrich A Hayek, 'The Corporation in a Democratic Society: In whose Interest Ought It to and Will It Be Run?' in *Studies in Philosophy, Politics and Economics* (Simon & Schuster 1967) 300, originally published in M Anshen and GL Bach (eds), *Management and Corporations 1985* (McGraw-Hill 1960) 300–12. Hayek first advances the thesis that: '[i]f we want effectively to limit the powers of corporations to where they are beneficial, we shall have to confine them much more than we have yet done to one specific goal, that of the profitable use of the capital entrusted to the management by the stockholders. I shall argue that it is precisely the tendency to allow and even to impel the corporations

essential to create boundaries, and must not to be used to swallow up the shareholder wealth goal itself or to camouflage attacks on the underlying premises of the free enterprise system.[10]

The corporation's proposed singular focus on economic gain (even within appropriate legal and ethical boundaries), and the particular focus on enhancing the wealth of shareholders have always been the subject of controversy and debate. There has never been universal agreement that business corporations exist solely to produce economic value for the benefit of their shareholders (or for their shareholders along with other financial claimants for that matter).[11] Nearly a century ago, Adolf Berle observed that the 'tremendous development of the corporation as an engine of finance and as an instrument

to use their resources for specific ends other than those of a long- run maximisation of the return on the capital placed under their control that tends to confer upon them undesirable and socially dangerous power'. He then goes on to explain 'this does not mean that in the pursuit of this end they ought not to be restrained by general legal *and* moral rules'. See also Milton Friedman, 'The Social Responsibility of Business Is To Increase Its Profits' *New York Times Magazine* (13 September 1970) 32, arguing, as the article's title indicates, that a corporation must 'increase its profits so long as it stays within the rules of the game, which is to say, engages in open and free competition without deception or fraud'. See also American Law Institute, *Principles of Corporate Governance: Analysis and Recommendations*, vol 1 (ALI 1994) comment (g) to § 2.01, in which the suggestion that corporations might engage in a cost-benefit analysis in determining whether or not to comply with applicable laws is unequivocally rejected: 'With few exceptions, dollar liability is not a "price" that can properly be paid for the privilege of engaging in legally wrongful conduct. Cost-benefit analysis may have a place in the state's determination whether a given type of conduct should be deemed legally wrongful. Once that determination has been made, however, the resulting legal rule normally represents a community decision that the conduct is wrongful as such, so that cost-benefit analysis whether to obey the rule is out of place.' See also Robert C Merton, *Continuous-Time Finance* (Blackwell Publishers 1990) 4: '[m]anagers are viewed as fiduciaries, which implies an even stronger legal obligation to shareholders than if they were simply the owners' agents. This stronger legal bonding does not, of course, obligate managers to benefit owners by violating other laws, nor does it prohibit managers from giving due consideration to other stakeholders of the firm.' This accords with former Delaware Supreme Court Chief Justice Leo E Strine Jr's warning that 'Delaware law does not charter law breakers'. See *In re Massey Energy Co* 2011 WL 2176479, *20 (Del Ch 31 May 2011). What remains curious is that it appears to be the opponents of corporate capitalism, not its supporters, who are convinced that corporations must relentlessly maximize profit (or shareholder wealth) at the cost of all else. Joel Bakan, for example, in his book *The Corporation: The Pathological Pursuit of Profit and Power* (Viking Canada 2004) makes the surprising statement that: 'The corporation's legally defined mandate is to pursue, relentlessly and without exception, its own self-interest, regardless of the often harmful consequences it might cause to others' (ibid 1–2). Or, again: 'The irony in all of this is that the corporation's mandate to pursue its own self-interest, itself a product of the law, actually propels corporations to break the law' (ibid 80). Yet, this does not appear to be a legal requirement anywhere, is contrary to the pronouncements of the very economists who are usually said to support shareholder primacy, and seems highly improbable as a description of what is, or ever could be, the express goal of a corporation's officers and directors.

[10] Thus, for example, Milton Friedman, in his famous attack on corporate social responsibility, says of business people who claim that business has a 'social conscience' or various social or environmental responsibilities: 'In fact they are—or would be if they or any one else took them seriously—preaching pure and unadulterated socialism.' See Friedman (n 9).

[11] See eg Michael C Jensen, 'Value Maximization, Stakeholder Theory, and the Corporate Objective Function' in Donald H Chew and Stewart L Gillan (eds), *US Corporate Governance* (Columbia University Press 2009) 3.

of economic organization' had led to a 'radical change in the popular conception of the relationship between management and stockholders'.[12] Berle referred in particular to a then-recent statement by Owen Young of The General Electric Company who asserted that his corporation 'owed its first duty to its labor, its next to the public it served, and its third obligation in rank to its stockholders'.[13] This view, Berle suggested, would only a few years earlier 'have been high socialism'.[14]

Yet, Berle himself in his legendary *Harvard Law Review* exchange with E. Merrick Dodd[15] had championed the view that all corporate powers granted to a corporation or to its management are powers in trust and 'are necessarily and at all times exercisable only for the ratable benefit for all the shareholders as their interest appears'.[16] This statement also appears, *verbatim,* in a chapter of Berle and Means's book, *The Modern Corporation and Private Property.*[17] Berle was an ally of Franklin Delano Roosevelt, an unapologetic 'New Dealer' and no conservative icon. His evolving views of the corporate mission have therefore been a matter of considerable interest and study among his many modern admirers.[18] Within *The Modern Corporation and Private Property* itself the authors recognized that the growing power of the modern corporation would call for a 'new concept of the business enterprise'.[19] The 'new concept' they envisioned would emerge from 'insistence that power in economic organization shall be subjected to the same tests of public benefit which have been applied in their turn to power otherwise located'.[20] The pressure that Berle and Means described to make the power of the modern giant corporation, like the dominant institutions of earlier eras, 'the servant of the bulk of the individuals it affects',[21] is an apt description of the premise on which many modern critiques of corporate power are based.

[12] Adolf A Berle Jr, *Studies in the Law of Corporation Finance* (Callaghan and Company 1928) 1.
[13] ibid 1.
[14] ibid. Owen Young's legacy as a progressive corporate leader has been the subject of considerable commentary. A contemporary account of his enlightened approach to management is found in Ida M Tarbell, *New Ideals in Business* (The Macmillan Company 1917, first published in 1916, reprinted in 1917).
[15] AA Berle Jr, 'Corporate Powers as Powers in Trust' (1931) 44 Harvard Law Review 1049; E Merrick Dodd Jr, 'For Whom Are Corporate Managers Trustees' (1932) 45 Harvard Law Review 1145; AA Berle Jr, 'For Whom Corporate Managers Are Trustees: A Note' (1932) 45 Harvard Law Review 1365. See further discussion of this exchange in Chapter 4.
[16] Berle, 'Corporate Powers as Powers in Trust' (n 15).
[17] Adolf A Berle and Gardiner C Means, *The Modern Corporation and Private Property* (Routledge 2017, originally published in 1932) 220.
[18] See eg William W Bratton and Michael L Wachter, 'Shareholder Primacy's Corporatist Origins: Adolf Berle and the Modern Corporation' (2008) 34 Journal of Corporate Law 99.
[19] Berle and Means (n 17) 309.
[20] ibid 310.
[21] ibid 310.

Although some commentators have challenged the empirical accuracy of Berle and Means's study of American corporations in 1932,[22] the broad observation of the growing size and significance of America's largest corporations seems irrefutable. However, the staggering size of today's largest modern corporations would surely have stunned even Berle and Means. Consider, for example, that the total market capitalization of America's 3,577 largest publicly traded companies as of August 2025 was approximately US$66.115 trillion. The market capitalization of the ten largest of those companies (that is, less than one-third of one per cent in number of those companies) accounted for more than 34 per cent of the total.[23] Of the 500 companies included in the S&P 500 index, the market capitalization of the largest ten accounts for more than 42 per cent of the total.[24] Of the thirty stocks included in the Dow Jones Industrial Average, the market capitalization of just five corporations accounts for almost 70 per cent of the total.[25]

The vast 'footprint' of America's largest corporations means that their potential social and environmental impact has been similarly scaled up. The turn of the century accounting scandals involving Enron,[26] WorldCom,[27] Tyco,[28] Adelphia,[29] and a host of other large firms, the excesses associated with the financial crisis of 2007–2009,[30] and such recent debacles as the Volkswagen 'Dieselgate' emissions scandal[31] or the Purdue Pharma OxyContin disgrace[32] all stand as salient examples not only of the

[22] See eg George J Stigler and Claire Friedland, 'The Literature of Economics: The Case of Berle and Means' (1983) 26(2) Journal of Law and Economics 237.

[23] See 'Largest American Companies by Market Capitalization' https://companiesmarketcap.com/usd/usa/largest-companies-in-the-usa-by-market-cap/.

[24] See S&P 500 Index Stock list https://stockanalysis.com/list/sp-500-stocks/.

[25] See 'Largest Dow Jones Companies by Market Cap' https://companiesmarketcap.com/usd/dow-jones/largest-companies-by-market-cap/.

[26] See eg John C Coffee Jr, 'What Caused Enron? A Capsule Social and Economic History of the 1990s' (2004) 89(2) Cornell Law Review 269.

[27] See Dennis R Beresford, Nicholas de B Katzenbach, and CB Rogers Jr, *Report of Investigation by the Special Investigative Committee of the Board of Directors of Worldcom Inc* (11 March 2003) https://www.sec.gov/Archives/edgar/data/723527/000093176303001862/dex991.htm.

[28] SEC Press Release, 'SEC Brings Settled Charges Against Tyco International Ltd Alleging Billion Dollar Accounting Fraud' (17 April 2006) https://www.sec.gov/news/press/2006/2006-58.htm.

[29] SEC Press Release, 'SEC Charges Adelphia and Rigas Family with Massive Financial Fraud' (24 July 2002) https://www.sec.gov/news/press/2002-110.htm.

[30] For a detailed and persuasive explanation of the financial crisis see Gary B Gorton, *Slapped by the Invisible Hand: The Panic of 2007* (Oxford University Press 2010). See also Financial Crisis Inquiry Commission, *The Financial Crisis Inquiry Report* (PublicAffairs 2011).

[31] For a detailed discussion of the timeline of the Volkswagen emissions scandal along with an analysis of the impact of the scandal on the collective reputations of German auto manufacturers see R Bachmann and others, 'Firms and Collective Reputation: a Study of the Volkswagen Emissions Scandal' (2023) 21(2) Journal of the European Economic Association 484.

[32] See eg Art Van Zee, 'The Promotion and Marketing of OxyContin: Commercial Triumph, Public Health Tragedy' (2009) 99(2) American Journal of Public Health 221.

disheartening frequency of incidents of corporate negligence or malfeasance but also of the magnitude of harm that can be inflicted upon shareholders, creditors, employees, and society as a whole when governance failures occur in the largest corporations.

Even in the absence of any criminal or civil wrongdoing, the vast resources commanded by large corporations can still play a role in the exacerbation of income and wealth inequality, an issue of increasing political salience and popular unrest.[33] The growing emphasis on shareholder value, for example, has been criticized by progressive scholars who link this corporate desideratum to growing income inequality among other things. O'Sullivan and Lazonick, for example, argue that US corporations moved from a constructive philosophy of 'retain and reinvest' to one of 'downsize and distribute' with significant adverse consequences for working class Americans.[34]

One highly visible example of the contribution of massive corporations to widening economic disparity is the ever-increasing levels of compensation of chief executive officers (CEOs), many of whom now receive pay packages beyond the capacity of any human being to consume in a lifetime or, indeed, in many lifetimes. The disputed compensation arrangements for Tesla Inc's CEO Elon Musk have probably attracted the most public attention and outrage.[35] Those arrangements ultimately became the subject of a court challenge,[36] followed by an even more extraordinary pay proposal that, albeit subject to Herculean performance targets, could potentially enable Musk to receive compensation of US$1 trillion.[37] But although Elon Musk's compensation may be in a class of its own, as Table 7.1 indicates, the total reported compensation for CEOs (and other senior officers) of several of America's other largest

[33] See eg Richard G Wilkinson and Kate Pickett, *The Spirit Level: Why More Equal Societies Almost Always Do Better* (Allen Lane 2009); Thomas Piketty, *Capital in the Twenty-First Century* (Harvard University Press 2014). Not all commentators agree that rising economic inequality should necessarily be regarded as a self-evident sign of a failed economic system. See eg Harvard Psychology professor Steven Pinker, *Enlightenment Now* (Penguin 2018) 120; 'An increase in inequality is not necessarily bad: as societies escape from universal poverty, they are bound to become more unequal, and the uneven surge may be repeated when a society discovers new sources of wealth.'

[34] William Lazonick and Mary O'Sullivan, 'Maximizing Shareholder Value: A New Ideology for Corporate Governance' (2000) 29(1) Economy and Society 13.

[35] See eg Theo Francis, 'Elon Musk Gets $23.7 Billion Stock Award to Stay Focused' *Wall Street Journal* (4 August 2025).

[36] *Richard J Tornetta v Elon Musk and Ors (I)* 310 A 3d 430 (Del Ch 2024); and *Richard J Tornetta v Elon Musk and Ors (II)* 2024 WL 4930635 (Del Ch Dec 2 2024).

[37] See Tesla Inc, 2025 Proxy Statement (September 2025) sch 14A https://www.sec.gov/ix?doc=/Archives/edgar/data/0001318605/000110465925087598/tm252289-4_pre14a.htm; Nick Lichtenberg, '"Yes, You Read That Correctly": Tesla Pay Committee Pitches $1 Trillion Pact to Keep Elon Musk as CEO for Long Term' *Fortune* (5 September 2025).

**Table 7.1** CEO Compensation for Selected Large American Corporations

| **Corporation** | **CEO** | **Total Annual Compensation (both cash and non-cash)** |
|---|---|---|
| Nvidia Corporation[a] | Jen-Hsuan Huang | $32,000,000 |
| Microsoft Corporation[b] | Satya Nadella | $79,106,183 |
| Apple Inc.[c] | Tim Cook | $74,609,802 |
| Amazon.Com, Inc.[d] *Note: The highest paid executive at Amazon in 2024 was Douglas J. Herrington, CEO of Worldwide Amazon Stores whose total compensation in 2024 was $34,193,958.* | Andrew R. Jassy | $1,596,889 |
| Alphabet Inc.[e] *Note: The highest paid executive at Alphabet in 2024 was Philipp Schindler, Senior Vice President, Chief Business Officer, Google whose total compensation in 2024 was $47,024,009.* | Sundar Pichai | $10,725,043 |
| Meta Platforms, Inc.[f] | Mark Zuckerberg | $27,219,874 |
| Broadcom Inc.[g] *Note: The highest paid executive at Broadcom Inc. in 2024 was Mark D Brazeal, Chief Legal and Corporate Affairs Officer, whose total compensation in 2024 was $28,981,943.* | Hock E. Tan | $2,634,542 |

[a] Nvidia 2025 Annual Report.

[b] Microsoft 2024 Proxy Statement.

[c] Apple Inc 2025 Proxy Statement.

[d] Amazon.Com Inc 2025 Proxy Statement.

[e] Alphabet Inc 2025 Proxy Statement.

[f] Meta Platforms Inc 2025 Proxy Statement.

[g] Broadcom Inc 2025 Proxy Statement.

corporations also demonstrate how the burgeoning size of firms can contribute to expanding executive pay packages further aggravating public perceptions of growing income inequality.

Many corporations have become unfathomably large, and the compensation of their senior managers has outstripped the lofty ascent of a SpaceX rocket during a period when the real wages of most working Americans have, at least on many measures, been stagnating.[38] Yet, concerns about the possible excesses of executive compensation are not new. Livingston, in 1958, identified extravagant managerial compensation as a central problem in the large business corporation,[39] a refrain that has persisted and, in recent years, in the legal academic literature has been frequently associated with the research of Lucian Bebchuk and Jesse Fried of the Harvard Law School.[40]

Is it envy alone that causes many readers of corporate proxy statements to rail at the sight of these vertigo-inducing compensation figures? Was René Girard right to insist that human desires are mimetic,[41] or to use older and less morally neutral language, covetous? (And are corporate CEOs, when it comes to that, convenient Girardean scapegoats?) Or is there a larger political issue at stake? Does the modern large corporation contribute to political polarization by aggravating a class divide that leaves a great mass of workers living economically precarious lives while their labour enriches a managerial class increasingly out of touch with the daily struggles and fears of their unknown and largely unacknowledged labouring benefactors?

It is not concern for workers and the dangers of income inequality alone that have prompted critics of the modern mega corporation to argue that a single-minded corporate commitment to shareholder wealth maximization may well have led to more harm than good. The rising threat of climate change (even an impending 'climate emergency'[42] or 'climate crisis'[43]), it has been argued, also reflects, at least in part, the inevitable result of a reckless pursuit of profits by large corporations at the cost of immeasurable, and irreversible environmental degradation.

The presumed net benefit to society to be derived from the operation of corporations depends upon corporations internalizing any harmful third party effects (or 'negative externalities') created by their business operations. This internalization could, in theory, be achieved through government regulation,

[38] See eg Laura Harvey and James Rockey, 'Long-Run Stagnation in US Real Wages: An Unconditional Quantile Approach' (2025) https://papers.ssrn.com/sol3/papers.cfm?abstract_id=5080401; Lenore Palladino, 'Financialization at Work: Shareholder Primacy and Stagnant Wages in the United States' (2021) 23 Competition & Change 382.

[39] JA Livingston, *The American Stockholder* (JB Lippincott Company 1958) 222 ff.

[40] See eg Lucian A Bebchuk and Jesse M Fried, *Pay Without Performance: The Unfulfilled Promise of Executive Compensation* (Harvard University Press 2004).

[41] See R Girard, *Deceit, Desire, and the Novel: Self and Other in Literary Structure* (Johns Hopkins University Press 1965).

[42] See UN Secretary General António Guterres, 'Remarks at 2019 Climate Action Summit' (23 September 2019) https://www.un.org/sg/en/content/sg/speeches/2019-09-23/remarks-2019-climate-action-summit.

[43] See eg United Nations, UN 75, 'Climate change is the defining crisis of our time' from 'The Climate Crisis: A Race We Can Win' https://www.un.org/en/un75/climate-crisis-race-we-can-win.

the judicious use of a Pigouvian tax,[44] or—in an ideal world of perfect information and no transaction costs—resolved through Coasean bargains[45] struck between corporations and those adversely affected by their operations. But transaction costs in the real world are never zero and are rarely negligible. Pigouvian taxes are politically unpopular, administratively intractable, and impossible to calibrate with precision. And governments, critics insist, have utterly failed in their role to regulate. Corporations are thus not adequately constrained by external forces to internalize their negative externalities. Accordingly, it cannot be assumed that profitable corporations—delivering products and services that people want and need at prices they are willing to pay—do, indeed, provide a net benefit to society. The social costs of their operations might well equal or exceed the private benefits gained by the corporation itself and the consumers of its products or services. If the world is to be saved from injustice, inequality, and imminent disaster, then, critics argue, it falls to corporations themselves to step in where governments fear to tread and assume responsibility for mitigating the harms they create or to compensate the victims of those harms.

For some, like former Delaware Supreme Court Chief Justice Leo Strine Jr, the claim by financial economists that the corporation's single-minded pursuit of shareholder value best ensures that the corporation will also provide net social benefit has eroded protection for non-shareholder corporate constituents, particularly employees, and undermined efforts at implementing beneficial regulation that would protect the interests of the vulnerable.[46]

Students of corporate law are familiar—some might suggest fatigued—with the endless debate over whom business corporations do (or ought to) serve: shareholders alone, or some broader group of 'constituents' or 'stakeholders' including not only shareholders, but also others whose interests are intertwined with or affected by the corporation, such as creditors, employees, customers, suppliers, the local community, the natural environment, and so on.

[44] A Pigouvian tax refers to a proposed method of ensuring that the negative externalities generated by the market activities of a business are internalized by imposing a tax on the business such that the social costs of its activity become equal to its private cost. The concept of the Pigouvian tax was introduced by British economist AC Pigou in his book *The Economics of Welfare* originally published in 1920. See AC Pigou, *The Economics of Welfare* (4th edn, Macmillan & Co 1932) 192: 'It is, however, possible for the State, if it so chooses, to remove the divergence [between private and social net product] in any field by "extraordinary encouragements" or "extraordinary restraints" upon investments in that field. The most obvious forms which these encouragements and restraints may assume are, of course, those of bounties and taxes.'

[45] RH Coase, 'The Problem of Social Cost' (1960) 3 Journal of Law and Economics 1.

[46] See eg Leo E Strine Jr, 'Restoration: The Role Stakeholder Governance Must Play in Recreating a Fair and Sustainable American Economy: A Reply to Professor Rock' (2021) 26(2) Business Lawyer 397.

So familiar is this debate, so long its legacy, and so dogmatic its noisiest participants, there may seem to be little prospect of finding new common ground or generating fresh insights on the subject, and even less hope of persuading partisans with firmly entrenched positions to consider re-examining their views. Yet, no discussion of the potential impact on the duties of the modern corporate director of broad notions of corporate social responsibility or, as discussed below, integration of environmental, social, and governance (ESG) factors in corporate decision-making can avoid at least a cursory review of certain distinct versions of earlier appeals to business corporations to be 'responsible' or 'socially responsible'.

First, corporations may be urged to embrace some version of stakeholder or constituency theory that departs from the shareholder primacy norm. The usual non-shareholder constituents identified as especially deserving of such care and attention are creditors, employees, suppliers, and customers. But the list may be extended to include, for example, retired employees, the local community, and, of course, the natural environment.

At least two practical difficulties are routinely identified with the broad-minded corporate stakeholder approach. The first is the accountability problem flagged by Adolf Berle almost a century ago.[47] Corporate directors and officers who are not strongly accountable to a single identifiable constituency (such as the shareholders) are effectively accountable to no one, since it is always possible for directors and officers to justify virtually any action by pointing to its potential benefits to at least one group of stakeholders. It's an ill wind (and a rare one) that blows nobody any good. The second well-understood problem is that there is no way to calibrate and thereby fairly balance competing loyalties. If a corporation shuts down a polluting factory, hundreds of hard-working employees may be thrown out of work. How is the genuine suffering of these employees and their families—along with the potential economic harm to the local community—to be balanced against the possible benefit to the natural environment? How much personal hardship to working families equals one less tonne of $CO_2$?

It is sometimes suggested that because shareholders, like their fellow human beings, care about far more things than simply enriching themselves, a corporate goal to maximize 'shareholder welfare' would effectively unify the shareholder primacy and stakeholder constituency views.[48] However, while

[47] AA Berle Jr, 'Corporate Powers as Powers in Trust' (n 15); AA Berle Jr, 'For Whom Corporate Managers Are Trustees: A Note' (n 15).

[48] See eg Oliver Hart and Luigi Zingales, 'Companies Should Maximize Shareholder Welfare Not Market Value' (2017) 2 Journal of Law Finance and Accounting 247; Oliver Hart and Luigi Zingales, 'The New Corporate Governance' (2022) 1(1) The University of Chicago Business Law Review 195.

it is certainly true that people have complex preferences, this does not necessarily mean that most shareholders—in their capacity as shareholders—should be understood to be seeking anything except material gain. It is the nature of human experience to compartmentalize. The satisfaction of one genuine preference or want may necessarily require the denial or deferral of another. A shopper—choosing to pay for a pair of shoes, a luxurious watch, or a streaming service subscription—is not, at the moment of purchase, attempting to generate revenue (even though the same person at other times, in other places may well see earning and saving money, not spending it, as her single highest priority). A person may love dogs and also adore the opera. But when she is at the opera, she does not want to see any dogs, and when she is at the dog park, she may not want to watch the performance of an opera (not even *Barkouf*).

Human beings are certainly not interested in money alone. But is it unreasonable to suggest that most human beings—as investors[49]—do, indeed, seek primarily (even exclusively) to maximize their financial gain? How they choose to use the wealth they so acquire will no doubt reflect their many other interests, goals, and values. Some may choose to join an exclusive golf club, others to buy original works of art, while others may use their investment gains to support a local homeless shelter, contribute to much-needed medical research, or fund relief work in war-torn parts of the world. All of these important expressions of individual preference—and individual munificence—share in common the need first to acquire enabling financial resources.

In this respect, shareholders are actually in a rather different position from corporate managers. Managers may, too, desire many different things from their managerial positions in addition to money: perquisites, prestige, satisfaction from craftsmanship, a stimulating and collegial work environment, and so on. An employment relationship is nothing like a passive financial investment. That is precisely why, although it is reasonable to propose a simple mathematical formula for valuing shares based entirely on financial inputs like projected future cash flows, and appropriate risk-adjusted discount or capitalization rates, no similarly simple metric can be used to assess the value of a job. Managers, then, like all employees must routinely seek a balance between tangible and intangible rewards and they must do so by applying not only their

[49] One notes that recent research by Hirst and others indicated that, while individuals do indeed seem to be willing to sacrifice some financial gains in favour of promoting social interests, they seem to be willing to forego greater gains in their capacity as donors and consumers than in their capacity as investors. See Scott Hirst, Kobi Kastiel and Tamar Krickeli-Katz, 'How Much Do Investors Care About Social Responsibility?' (2023) Wisconsin Law Review 977.

knowledge, business experience, and specialized training but also their ethical values and broader interests as members of a human community. This is not an impossible managerial undertaking; this is, literally, all in a day's work.

Still, as Hansmann and Kraakman emphasized, reflecting on their well-known 2001 paper 'The End of History for Corporate Law',[50] a decade after its publication, their conception of shareholder primacy 'does not impose upon corporate managers a legal obligation to maximize financial returns to shareholders without any regard to the consequences for third parties'.[51] Rather, they argue, 'managers should do what the shareholders, as a group would prefer them to do. And it's reasonable to assume that most shareholders prefer that their corporations behave according to the same ethical norms that guide shareholders themselves in their own activities as individuals. Shareholders presumably do not want their corporate managers to cheat customers, abuse workers, or foul the environment even if doing so would be both legal and profitable'.[52] This formulation is similar to Henderson and Malani's suggestion that there is a 'market' for corporate philanthropy or altruism that the for-profit corporation can fulfill while still pursuing a shareholder primacy norm[53] or Hart and Zingales's argument that it is shareholder welfare, not shareholder wealth, that corporations should seek to maximize.[54] As Hansmann and Kraakman explain, 'what distinguishes [their preferred model (the standard shareholder-oriented model)] from the labor-oriented model (or stakeholder models in general) is not that managers can be generous toward employees only under the latter, but rather that it is the norms of the shareholders, and not those of the employees, that determine the appropriate level of this generosity'.[55] Indeed, advocates of an unbridled 'pure' wealth maximization corporation are more likely to be found as villains in popular motion pictures and cartoons than in the 'C-suite' of real corporations.[56]

[50] Hansmann and Kraakman (n 3).

[51] Henry Hansmann and Reinier Kraakman, 'Reflections on the End of History for Corporate Law' in Abdul Rasheed and Toru Yoshikawa (eds), *Convergence of Corporate Governance: Promise and Prospects* (Palgrave-MacMillan 2012) 32.

[52] ibid.

[53] M Todd Henderson and Anup Malani, 'Corporate Philanthropy and the Market for Altruism' (2009) 109 Columbia Law Review 571.

[54] Oliver Hart and Luigi Zingales, 'Companies Should Maximize Shareholder Welfare Not Market Value' (2017) 2 Journal of Law Finance and Accounting 247.

[55] Hansmann and Kraakman, 'Reflections on the End of History for Corporate Law' (n 51) 36.

[56] The uncontentious recognition that shareholder wealth maximization is only socially optimal if the corporation fully internalizes the costs of its activities is sometimes misunderstood or mischaracterized as equivocation. Lynn Stout, for example, has characterized the Hansmann and Kraakman view as 'highly qualified'. Lynn A Stout, 'New Thinking on Shareholder Primacy' (2012) 2 Accounting, Economics, and Law 4, note 9. Lord Wedderburn once spoke of the 'fudge' approach to the issue of choosing between shareholder primacy and attention to broader social interests. See Lord Wedderburn, 'Trust, Corporation and the Worker' (1985) 23 Osgoode Hall Law Journal 203. Jean

## Doing Well by Doing Good?

Adam Smith famously sneered at the suggestion that businesses did, or could, effectively engage in acts explicitly intended to benefit the public interest:

> By pursuing his own interest he frequently promotes that of society more effectually than when he really intends to promote it. I have never known much good done by those who affected to trade for the public good. It is an affectation, indeed, not very common among merchants, and very few words need be deployed in dissuading them from it.[57]

Yet, it is occasionally suggested that the pursuit by corporations of non-financial goals will, paradoxically, enhance their financial performance, too. Generously paid and respectfully treated employees will work harder and be less likely to quit. Clean air and water, modern hospitals, excellent schools, and a socially cohesive and prosperous community all benefit the corporation's business in the long-run. Might we not, therefore, reasonably suppose that there is no real conflict between the goals of maximizing financial value in the long-run and behaving as a good corporate citizen by generously supporting the interests of employees, creditors, and the corporation's non-financial stakeholders as well? Do pro-social actions by business corporations represent such a serendipitous 'win-win' or, as Bénabou and Tirole once put it, a 'free lunch'?[58] In short, have the bumper sticker slogans had it right all along: Corporations will 'do well by doing good'?

While most would agree that the interests of shareholders and other corporate stakeholders frequently—perhaps even commonly—align at least over the long-run, the principal purpose for seeking to articulate a corporate purpose from a legal perspective is precisely for the task of guiding the actions of directors and officers when dealing with those situations (hopefully rare) where conflict does occur. One cannot, therefore, assume away the problem by

Tirole has wryly suggested that the most anodyne articulations of the proper corporate goal were the result of 'some management gurus' who have 'surfed the stakeholder society wave and have argued that "stakeholding" makes commercial sense'. See Jean Tirole, *The Theory of Corporate Finance* (Princeton University Press 2006) 57.

[57] Adam Smith, *An Inquiry into the Nature and Causes of the Wealth of Nations* Edward Cannan (ed) (Methuen & Co 1904) Bk IV ch 2.

[58] Roland Bénabou and Jean Tirole, 'Individual and Corporate Social Responsibility' (2010) 77 Economica 1, 9.

blissfully asserting that no conflict between shareholder and non-shareholder interests should ever be expected to arise.

One also recalls the poignant warning of Alfred Marshall's classic 1890 text, *Principles of Economics* to modern hopeful advocates of the notion that those businesses that undertake good works may also expect to thrive financially. As Marshall reminds, '[t]he fact that a thing is beneficial to its environment will not by itself secure its survival either in the physical or in the moral world. The law of "survival of the fittest" states that those organisms tend to survive which are best fitted to utilize the environment for their own purposes; not those which are best fitted to benefit the environment, except in so far as, by benefiting it, they may increase the support which they derive from it'.[59]

Thus, we must look for principles for decision-making, and for evaluating the content of corporate directors' and officers' fiduciary duties, that not only will ensure the corporate enterprise will thrive but that can also be applied in those very situations where conflict between financial gain and non-financial interests cannot be avoided.

And perhaps it is all for the best that corporations do not pursue ostensibly pro social goals merely as an indirect method of increasing shareholder wealth. Ida Tarbell, a famous investigative journalist of the early twentieth century, admired the progressive business leaders of her day, in particular Owen Young of the General Electric Company of whom she wrote a fawning biography.[60] In her 1917 book, *New Ideals in Business*,[61] Tarbell presents the story of how a new progressive approach to industrial management was overcoming the former 'industrial evils' as the science of management was successfully combined with a sense of humanity leading to business that was not only more efficient than ever before, but also more humane and responsible. One of the more intriguing aspects of Tarbell's exploration of the supposed progressive modern employers of her day that she favoured is that the notion of what might be dubbed by some commentators today as 'enlightened self-interest' is doomed to fail. The self-interest, she insisted, will inevitably undermine the enlightenment:

> It is idle for an employer to think that he can win labour by welfare machinery, by high wages, by profit sharing; unless his reasons for attempting these things are something more than selfish interest, they won't work. No

[59] Alfred Marshall, *Principles of Economics* (Macmillan and Co 1890) Bk IV ch VIII, 302.
[60] Ida M Tarbell, *Owen Young: A New Type of Industrial Leader* (The Macmillan Company 1932).
[61] Ida M Tarbell, *New Ideals in Business* (The Macmillan Company 1917, first published in 1916, reprinted in 1917).

> one is quicker to detect the intent and spirit behind a new practice than a body of workers. They know the *scent* of reality. A good thing undertaken for a mean purpose or undertaken half-heartedly and because some competitor succeeds with it is almost surely sterile.[62]

## CSR Point and Counterpoint

If we may not fairly assume that the pursuit by a corporation of pro social ends may be happily relied upon to enhance long-term financial performance as well, then the embrace by some business corporations of broader social concerns, in addition to, or even in lieu of, enhanced financial performance, must transcend the money grubbing considerations of the marketplace. A corporate commitment to 'responsibility', to the concerns of 'people, and planet', to 'sustainability', 'triple bottom lines', 'good corporate citizenship' and 'giving back' (or even 'paying it forward') seems to signal civilized enlightenment and modernity. Indeed, the 'heartless' pursuit of mere economic gain has never been very marketable, and highly unlikely to garner image-conscious CEOs honorary degrees, lavish after-dinner testimonials, the highest national civilian honours, or prestigious international accolades.

We have canvassed in Chapters 4 and 5 some highlights in the punctuated equilibrium that characterized the evolution of the concept of corporate profit maximization and shareholder wealth maximization through the late nineteenth and early to mid-twentieth century. There is a view, commonly held among many corporate law commentators, that at some point in the 1930s—perhaps in response to the grinding conditions of the Great Depression, perhaps in tandem with the New Deal reforms enacted in an attempt to ameliorate these conditions, or perhaps simply as the result of a changing zeitgeist—corporate managers began to see their mission as one of serving a broad range of interests of which shareholders were only one of many, and perhaps not even the most important among them. How common this view was in practice[63] or how credible it was regarded in theory remain a subject of some conjecture and debate.[64]

[62] ibid 323.

[63] See eg text accompanying notes 11 to 13 above.

[64] Graham and Dodd's classic 1934 investment text asserted that 'directors, however chosen, are virtually trustees, whose legal duty is to act solely on behalf of the owners of the business'. See Benjamin Graham and David L Dodd, *Security Analysis* (McGraw-Hill 1934) 521. In 1938, John Burr Williams, the author of *The Theory of Investment Value*, a book that has been described as 'the authoritative work on how to value financial assets' (Peter L Bernstein, *Capital Ideas* (Free Press 1992)46), referred in that book, with apparent disapproval, to the fact that it had become 'commonplace that large

In the early and mid-twentieth century, a number of scholars and business leaders asserted that large corporations should consider their privileged status wholly contingent not upon their successful ability to deliver goods and services to satisfied consumers and clients, but upon their adherence to an unwritten pro social code of corporate social responsibility (CSR).[65]

Following the second world war, as discussed in Chapter 5, it is said that the management of large American corporations was increasingly characterized by the 'managerial paternalism'[66] of munificent corporations, sharing their bounty more equitably, in particular, with workers and demonstrating benevolent sensitivity to the needs of other non-shareholder corporate stakeholders as well.[67]

Economist Robin Marris's 1963 article, 'A Model of the "Managerial" Enterprise,'[68] and his subsequent book, *The Economic Theory of 'Managerial' Capitalism*[69] advanced the provocative theory that in the absence of perfect competition, and where corporate managers were not themselves the personal

corporations . . . are not governed by the stockholders but rather by a clique of officers and directors who feel nearly as much responsibility toward workers, customers, and the public, as toward the stockholders.' John Burr Williams, *The Theory of Investment Value* (Harvard University Press 1938) 251, 252.

[65] Among the most prominent of these advocates in the 1920s were Owen Young and Gerald Swope at General Electric. See Berle (n 12) and Tarbell (n 14). In that same era, Wallace Donham, the Dean of the Harvard Business School from 1919 to 1942, also insisted that 'The social responsibility of the business man, therefore, is inescapable.' See Wallace R. Donham, 'The Social Significance of Business' (1927) 5(4) Harvard Business Review 406, 411. Donham, though himself a graduate of the Harvard Law School, not the Harvard Business School, nevertheless dismissed the possibility that the social leadership he regarded as essential could come from the legal profession, a profession which in his view had lost its 'social point of view' and become 'largely an auxiliary business rather than a learned profession.' ibid 410-411.

[66] Hansmann and Kraakman, 'Reflections on the End of History for Corporate Law' (n 51) 32.

[67] For examples of the many published contemporary accounts chronicling this supposed managerial era, see Chapter 5, notes 111-118. Among these sources, of particular interest, perhaps, is Howard S. Bowen's work, *The Social Responsibilities of the Businessman* (Harper & Brothers 1953). Bowen's work is particularly noteworthy for the reaction it provoked at the time. See Aurélien Acquier, Jean-Pascal Gond, and Jean Pasquero, 'Rediscovering Howard R Bowen's Legacy: The Unachieved Agenda and Continuing Relevance of Social Responsibilities of the Businessman' (2011) 50 Business and Society 607. Some have argued that Bowen was the founder of the concept of corporate social responsibility. Bowen was forced to resign from his post as Dean of the College of Commerce and Business Administration of the University of Illinois in 1950 following a fiery dispute within the faculty in which the allegation that he was 'anti-business' (and thus, inferentially, at least a New Deal liberal if not an actual communist) featured prominently. See Winton U. Solberg and Robert W Tomilson, 'Academic McCarthyism and Keynesian Economics: The Bowen Controversy at the University of Illinois' (1997) 29 History of Political Economy 55, 73. Faculty members at the time included future Nobel prize winning economist Franco Modigliani who, with several other faculty members, wrote to the University's president, George D Stoddard, to complain about the conduct of a faculty meeting in September 1950 in which Bowen was pilloried. ibid 69. Modigliani's own resignation from the University of Illinois seemed to have been linked, at least in part, to his profound disagreement with the controversy surrounding Bowen's ouster. ibid 80.

[68] Robin Marris, 'A Model of the "Managerial" Enterprise' (1963) 77 Quarterly Journal of Economics 185.

[69] Robin Marris, *The Economic Theory of 'Managerial' Capitalism* (Macmillan 1967).

recipients of corporate profits, not only would corporations not be profit maximizers, in fact, 'profits need not represent even one dimension of motivation'.[70] Marris's work was ultimately motivated by the need to revisit neoclassical assumptions about the firm in light of the undeniable significance of the separation of ownership and control chronicled by Berle and Means,[71] drawing, among other things, on Herbert Simon's famous notion of 'satisficing'[72]—that is, the hypothesis that human beings faced with uncertainty do not seek to 'maximize' (as the classical economists assumed) but instead settle for some sub-optimal goal that is 'good enough'.

In the context of assessing decision-taking processes within firms, an approach such as Marris's offers a valuable reality check. As Sidney Winter once observed,[73] neoclassical views that firms maximize shareholder value (or, at least, behave *as if* they were seeking to do so) seem to rely on deterministic assumptions that what a firm aspires to do (its objective) and what it is effectively compelled to do (its environment) are more important than actual decision-making processes. But when we consider the possibility that explicitly non-financial goals are somehow weighed by managers against more conventional value-increasing objectives, then the mechanics of the decision-making process merit closer scrutiny. The details of decision-making are particularly important from the perspective of determining what legal standards are to be applied to corporate decision-making.

The supposed pursuit by firms of socially responsible goals in the mid twentieth century rather than strict adherence to a shareholder-wealth maximization norm attracted criticism from many quarters. Milton Friedman's attack[74] is perhaps the most well-known. But Friedman was by no means the only CSR skeptic.

Consider, for example, Theodore Levitt, a professor of marketing at the Harvard Business School widely credited today with coining the term 'globalization' in 1983.[75] Many years before Professor Levitt expounded his theory of globalization—explaining why the global corporation was very different from the multinational corporation that had preceded it—he had raised some eyebrows with another provocative theory. In 1958, at the supposed height of

[70] Marris (n 68) 186.
[71] See Robin Marris, *The Economic Theory of Managerial Capitalism* (n 69) xi.
[72] Herbert A Simon, 'Rational Choice and the Structure of the Environment' (1956) 63(2) Psychological Review 129.
[73] Sidney G Winter, 'Satisficing, Selection, and the Innovating Remnant' (1971) 85(2) The Quarterly Journal of Economics 237.
[74] Friedman (n 9).
[75] Theodore Levitt, 'The Globalization of Markets' Harvard Business Review (1 May 1983) 92.

the era of corporate paternalistic managerialism in the United States, Levitt published an article in the *Harvard Business Review* entitled, 'The Dangers of Social Responsibility'.[76] Twelve years before Milton Friedman's famous 1970 indictment of the dangers of corporate social responsibility in his short New York Times magazine essay,[77] and four years, even, before Friedman had made a similar argument in his book *Capitalism and Freedom*,[78] Levitt was sounding an alarm bell. The rise in corporate social responsibility Levitt saw as a growing menace to American diversity, individualism, and freedom. It threatened to turn America into a monolithic, feudal-like society, he warned. At one point, he even invoked the spectre of fascism as the ultimate end of unbridled corporate social responsibility.[79] His proposed remedy was clear: let business be business:

> Welfare and society are not the corporation's business. Its business is making money, not sweet music. . . .Government's job is not business and business's job is not government.[80]

Like Friedman, Levitt also made clear that he by no means advocated profit-seeking above all else. Business was, of course, to be restrained—like all worthwhile human activity—by 'the elementary canons of everyday face-to-face civility (honesty, good faith, and so on)'.[81] But subject to those important constraints, he insisted, business should not shrink from advancing its profit-seeking goals. The survival not merely of capitalism, he contended, but of democracy itself relied upon it.

There were other explorations of the perceived threat to American business posed by, among other things, the notion of corporate social responsibility, ranging from the provocative philosophical fiction of Ayn Rand[82] to the methodical research of J.D. Glover,[83] and including the unmitigated condemnation of the idea by legal scholar Henry Manne,[84] who derisively 'credited' early

[76] Theodore Levitt, 'The Dangers of Social Responsibility' Harvard Business (September–October 1958) 41.
[77] Friedman (n 9).
[78] Milton Friedman, *Capitalism and Freedom* (University of Chicago Press 1962).
[79] Levitt (n 76) 46.
[80] ibid 47.
[81] ibid 49.
[82] In her novel *Atlas Shrugged*, Ayn Rand portrays a fictional executive, James Taggart, a self-righteous devotee of corporate social responsibility, as an ineffectual, inept, destructive, and contemptuous failure and villain. See Ayn Rand, *Atlas Shrugged* (Random House 1957).
[83] JD Glover, *The Attack on Big Business* (Graduate School of Business Administration, Harvard University 1954).
[84] Henry Manne, 'Should Corporations Assume More Social Responsibilities?' in M Bruce Johnson (ed), *The Attack on Corporate America: The Corporate Issues Sourcebook* (McGraw-Hill 1978) 3.

public relations pioneer Ivy Ledbetter Lee with first promulgating the notion that business ought to pursue social welfare rather than profit.[85]

The idyllic era of 'managerial paternalism' is usually said to have ended sometime in the 1970s or 1980s with the emergence of the corporate doctrine of 'shareholder pre-eminence' or 'shareholder primacy', discussed earlier. This supposed shift in corporate management philosophy was, according to some, somehow 'connected to the well documented post-1980 rise in levels of income inequality in the United States'[86] This latter observation is intriguing. While one might readily envision how shareholder primacy could contribute to *wealth* inequality, it is less obvious how it would necessarily contribute to *income* inequality, unless it may be assumed that corporations were not only pursuing profits at all costs but were also, with similar abandon, paying lavish dividends to their shareholders from these exorbitant profits. Though high managerial salaries might be said to contribute to income inequality, such salaries needless to say, are by no means a symptom of shareholder primacy. Quite the contrary, they come at the expense of the corporation and thus are more consistent with the failure of the corporation to maximize shareholder wealth. One might also reasonably ask how, exactly, had companies of an earlier managerial era shared more of their revenues with their workers? Were they magnanimously paying them above-market wages? On what basis, and by what metrics did they determine such above-market wages?[87] If this practice was generally pursued, how were economically harmful distortions in the overall labour market avoided? For that matter, without the reliable signal of demand provided by market-determined compensation levels, how did people make rationally informed decisions about what careers to train for or embark upon?

## From CSR to ESG

As discussed in Chapter 6, the corporate shareholder-centric norm is usually said to have dominated the American corporate landscape beginning some

[85] Ivy Ledbetter Lee is often considered, along with Edward Bernays, to be one of the founding fathers of public relations. He is especially well known for his work attempting to restore the public image of the Rockefellers in the early twentieth century. Ray Eldon Hiebert, *Courtier to the Crowd: The Story of Ivy Lee and the Development of Public Relations* (Iowa State University Press 1966).

[86] Andrew Smith, Kevin D Tennent, and Jason Russell, 'Berle and Means's *The Modern Corporation and Private Property*: The Military Roots of a Stakeholder Model of Corporate Governance' (2019) 42 Seattle University Law Review 535.

[87] For a discussion of this problem as a modern iteration of 'the futile medieval search for the just price and just wage' see Friederich A Hayek, *Law, Legislation and Liberty, vol 2: The Mirage of Social Justice* (University of Chicago Press 1976) 75.

time in the 1970s, and culminating in various judicial decisions,[88] scholarly explications (by professors[89] and judges[90]), and institutional pronouncements.[91] But the countervailing call for business corporations to take account of interests beyond financial performance was reinvigorated in the twenty-first century owing in a significant degree to increasingly urgent warnings about the dangers of climate change,[92] the turn-of-the-century accounting scandals discussed above, and the fear and disillusionment engendered by the Global Financial Crisis in 2007–2009.

This confluence of events created the context from which emerged the concept of ESG (environmental, social, and governance) factors or issues. It has been suggested that ESG represents a very different approach to the incorporation of non-financial matters into corporate decision-making and investment evaluation. The acronym (or, more precisely, the initialism) ESG was first coined in 2004.[93] The term originally appeared in the 2004 UN Global Compact document, *Who Cares Wins*,[94] a report described as a 'joint effort of financial institutions which were invited by United Nations Secretary-General Kofi Annan to develop guidelines and recommendations on how to better integrate environmental, social and governance issues in asset management, securities brokerage services and associated research functions'.[95] Some critics have come to dismiss the novelty of the term ESG as merely the most recent incarnation of the older concept of 'corporate social responsibility'. Others, however, argue that there are compelling reasons to consider ESG a distinct concept that is, by design, necessarily intended to focus attention upon factors correlated with a corporation's long-term financial performance and, in

[88] See eg *Revlon Inc v MacAndrews & Forbes Holdings Inc* 506 A 2d 173 (Del 1986); *eBay Domestic Holdings Inc v Newmark*, 16 A 3d 1 (Del Ch 2010); *McRitchie v Zuckerberg* 315 A 3d 518 (Del Ch 2024).

[89] See eg Edward B Rock, 'Adapting to the New Shareholder-Centric Reality' (2013) 161 University of Pennsylvania Law Review 1907.

[90] See eg Leo E Strine Jr, 'Our Continuing Struggle with the Idea that For-Profit Corporations Seek Profit' (2012) 47 Wake Forest Law Review 135.

[91] See eg American Law Institute (n 9) § 2.01: '[a] corporation should have as its objective the conduct of business activities with a view to enhancing corporate profit and shareholder gain.' This statement is subject to qualification in the case of certain actions taken in the face of a hostile takeover bid, and is further subject to legal and ethical boundaries and charitable considerations. See also, The Business Roundtable, *Statement on Corporate Governance* (September 1997).

[92] See eg Intergovernmental Panel on Climate Change, *Third Assessment Report (TAR) Climate Change 2001 Synthesis Report* https://www.ipcc.ch/report/ar3/syr/. The most recent IPCC Synthesis report is the *AR6 Synthesis Report Climate Change 2023* https://www.ipcc.ch/report/ar6/syr/

[93] Elizabeth Polman, 'The Making and Meaning of ESG' (2024) 14 Harvard Business Law Review 403. In particular, Paul Clements-Hunt, then the head of the United Nations Environment Programme Finance Initiative, is credited with coining the term ESG,

[94] Global Compact, *Who Cares Wins* (2004) https://documents1.worldbank.org/curated/en/280911488968799581/pdf/113237-WP-WhoCaresWins-2004.pdf.

[95] ibid i.

particular, to provide a decision-useful metric for corporations and their investors for classifying and quantifying key sources of firm risk.

Certainly, the origin of the term supports the argument that ESG was not merely intended to be little more than CSR 2.0. Although the drafters of the *Who Cares Wins* document do identify the Global Compact as a 'social responsibility initiative',[96] they go on to distance the new initialism from the conceptual legacy of CSR. Specifically, the report '[refrains] from using terms such as sustainability, corporate citizenship, etc., in order to avoid misunderstandings deriving from different interpretations of these terms'.[97]

The report then expressly draws a connection between attention to ESG factors and investment value:

> [m]any studies confirm that the way a company manages ESG issues is often a good indicator of overall risk levels and general management quality—which are both strong determinants of companies' long-term success . . . Companies with better ESG performance can increase shareholder value by better managing risks related to emerging ESG issues.[98] This report focuses on issues which have or could have a material impact on investment value. It uses a broader definition of materiality than commonly used—one that includes longer time horizons (10 years and beyond) and intangible aspects impacting company value. Using this broader definition of materiality, aspects relating to generally accepted principles and ethical guidelines (e.g. the universal principles underlying the Global Compact) can have a material impact on investment value.[99]

The report also stresses the importance of incorporating consideration of ESG factors into 'mainstream'[100] financial research and analysis of corporations. And, indeed, ESG factors are, apparently, 'increasingly being integrated into investment analysis'.[101] This should not be altogether surprising. Corporate directors in the current environment of economic and geopolitical uncertainty are bound to serve, in many ways, as a plenary corporate risk management committee. And the risks facing all major business corporations now include

[96] ibid vii.
[97] ibid 1, 2.
[98] ibid 9.
[99] ibid 2.
[100] ibid v.
[101] Deborah S Kidd, Young Lee, and Johan Vanderlugt, 'Environmental, Social, and Governance (ESG) Considerations in Investment Analysis' in Michelle R Clayman and others (eds), *Corporate Finance: Economic Foundations and Financial Modeling* (Wiley 2022) ch 15.

significant social and political elements—a fact especially highlighted in the United States in recent years. In 2024, for example, KPMG, issued its *Top Risks Forecast* emphasizing the importance of geopolitical risks for corporate directors and, in particular, corporate CEOs.[102]

ESG, evidently, was created to be a less 'confrontational' concept than CSR,[103] although recent disavowal or avoidance of the term ESG by leading asset managers[104] and corporations[105] suggest that, perhaps, that goal has not been entirely achieved. One might note, though, the admonitions of commentators such as Robert Eccles who has argued that 'The fundamental misconception of ESG critics on the right is that single-materiality ESG is a liberal political agenda. It is nothing so ambitious. It is simply about sustainability issues that matter to value creation'.[106]

At least one commentator has also suggested that the shift in attention from the earlier concept of CSR (usually considered to involve the sacrifice of financial gains in favour of the non-financial goals) to ESG (a concept that purports to focus on pro social factors as an aspect of risk reduction contributing to long-term financial gains) could be seen as a function of the increasing financialization of the corporation and of the goals of sustainability.[107]

If ESG factors are, from the perspective of corporations as opposed to their investors, important risk considerations that are ultimately linked to financial performance, is positive performance on ESG metrics correlated with financial performance? A recent report by NYU Stern Center for Sustainable Business and Rockefeller Asset Management[108] examined more than 1,000 research

[102] https://assets.kpmg.com/content/dam/kpmgsites/xx/pdf/2024/05/top-risks-forecast-2024.pdf.; Curtis J Milhaupt, 'Corporate Governance in an Era of Geoeconomics' (2025) 25 Journal of Corporate Law Studies DOI: 10.1080/14735970.2025.2549601.

[103] Mariana Pargendler, 'The Rise of International Corporate Law' (2021) 98 Washington University Law Review 1763, 1794.

[104] In 2023, BlackRock CEO Larry Fink declared that he had stopped using the term ESG because it had become 'weaponized'. Isla Binnie, 'BlackRock's Fink Says He's Stopped Using Weaponized Term ESG' Reuters (26 June 2023) https://www.reuters.com/business/environment/blackrocks-fink-says-hes-stopped-using-weaponised-term-esg-2023-06-26/.

[105] Elon Musk notoriously denounced ESG as 'the devil incarnate'. Michael Baxter, 'Musk Calls ESG the Devil Incarnate' *GRC Forums* (8 April 2022) https://www.grcworldforums.com/esg/musk-calls-esg-the-devil-incarnate/4727.article; See also See Chip Cutter and Emily Glazer, 'The Latest Dirty Word in Corporate America: ESG' Wall Street Journal (9 January 2024) (suggesting, among other things, that American executives were opting to use phrases such as 'responsible business' as alternatives to the increasingly controversial moniker, ESG).

[106] Robert Eccles, 'Moving Beyond ESG' (2024) Harvard Business Review 101, 104–105.

[107] See eg Stefanie Hiss, 'The Financialization of Sustainability' (2013) 17(3) Competition & Change 234.

[108] Tensie Whelan and others, 'ESG and Financial Performance: Uncovering the Relationship by Aggregating Evidence from 1,000 Plus Studies Published between 2015–2020 (2021) Rockefeller Asset Management/NYU Stern Center for Sustainable Business https://www.stern.nyu.edu/sites/default/files/assets/documents/ESG%20Paper%20Aug%202021.pdf.

papers written in the period from 2015 to 2020 and concluded that 58 per cent of those papers did show a positive connection between ESG and traditional financial performance metrics such as return on assets (ROA), return on equity (ROE), or stock price. Needless to say, if those firms with the highest ESG ratings also consistently achieve superior financial performance, then the traditional neoclassical goal needs no amending: Corporations should simply seek to maximize shareholder wealth and, evidently, to achieve that goal they will likely need to be leaders in ESG as well.

Whatever the correlation between ESG and corporate performance might be, one might note that at least one source of financial gain that may certainly be linked to ESG is the ESG cottage industry itself. There has been a proliferation of ESG metrics, ESG measurements, and ESG 'rankings' and scores such as those of MSCI, Refinitiv, Sustainalytics, Vigeo-Eiris, The Upright Project and others. Regrettably, as has often been noted, ESG ratings or rankings are by no means consistent.[109] Worse still, recent research has indicated that greater ESG disclosure by firms actually increases, rather than decreases, the inconsistency of ESG ratings.[110]

## Is Shareholder Primacy in Retreat? Greenwashing and Greenhushing

In August 2019, the Business Roundtable—a group of more than 200 leading American CEOs—with much fanfare and self-congratulation, issued its new 'Statement on the Purpose of a Corporation'.[111] Signatories to this statement trumpeted their newfound commitment 'to deliver value' to all of their stakeholders, 'for the future success of our companies, our communities and our country'. The statement itself was constructively ambiguous. It was the press release accompanying the statement that really drew the headlines. That release clearly signaled that the Business Roundtable, which had embraced 'principles of shareholder primacy' since 1997, had turned over a new leaf.[112] Their

[109] See eg Florian Berg, Julian F. Kölbel, and Roberto Rigobon, 'Aggregate Confusion: The Divergence of ESG Ratings' (2022) Review of Finance 1315.

[110] Dane Christensen, George Serafeim, and Anywhere Sikochi, 'Why Is Corporate Virtue in the Eye of the Beholder? The Case of ESG Ratings' (2022) 97(1) The Accounting Review 147.

[111] See https://opportunity.businessroundtable.org/wp-content/uploads/2019/09/BRT-Statement-on-the-Purpose-of-a-https://www.businessroundtable.org/business-roundtable-redefines-the-purpose-of-a-corporation-to-promote-an-economy-that-serves-all-americansCorporation-with-Signatures-1.pdf.

[112] See News Release, 'Business Roundtable Redefines the Purpose of a Corporation to Promote "An Economy that Serves All Americans"' (19 August 2019) https://www.businessroundtable.org/busin

powerful corporate overlords had come over from the dark side, it seems, and joined the modern people-before-profit camp of enlightenment. This corporate epiphany has been viewed by some as part of a wave of 'new capitalism' that has been embraced as contemporary orthodoxy.[113] (The uncomfortable fact, of course, as Professor Stephen Bainbridge was quick to point out in a wry tweet to the Business Roundtable, is that the Business Roundtable simply has no authority to 'redefine the purpose of the corporation'):

> Only the Delaware courts can change the law of corporate purpose. And, as you ought to know, Delaware comes down square on the side of shareholder wealth maximization.[114]

Just days later, the Business Roundtable issued an explanation and clarification of their updated corporate purpose statement.[115] Among other things, this clarification assured readers that 'The new Statement is not an abandonment of capitalism, but a call to action to ensure the benefits of capitalism are shared more broadly'.[116] It also rejected the proposition that the Business Roundtable CEOs were abandoning shareholders.

The recent American Law Institute Restatement of the Law Corporate Governance, Tentative Draft No 1 also expressly includes reference to non-shareholder interests in its description of the objective of American corporations. Specifically, it describes alternative versions of the objective of American corporations, depending on whether such corporations are incorporated in 'common law' jurisdictions, such as Delaware, or in one of the many American 'stakeholder' jurisdictions, that have adopted constituency statutes, as discussed in Chapter 6. Even in the case of common law jurisdictions, the description includes an important qualification. While the objective of such a corporation 'is to enhance the economic value of the corporation, within the boundaries of the law . . . for the benefit of the corporation's shareholders', in pursuing that objective, the draft provides that the corporation may consider

ess-roundtable-redefines-the-purpose-of-a-corporation-to-promote-an-economy-that-serves-all-americans.

[113] See eg 'The Next Business Revolution' *Economist* (2 November 2019) 55; Marc Benioff, 'We Need a New Capitalism' *New York Times* (14 October 2019): 'Capitalism, as we know it, is dead.'

[114] See Stephen Bainbridge https://www.professorbainbridge.com/professorbainbridgecom/2019/08/a-tweet-to-the-business-roundtable-re-the-law-of-corporate-purpose.html.

[115] Business Roundtable, 'Redefined Purpose of a Corporation: Welcoming the Debate' (25 August 2019) https://www.businessroundtable.org/redefined-purpose-of-a-corporation-welcoming-the-debate.

[116] ibid.

a host of non-shareholder interests, too, including those of its employees, its business relationships with suppliers, customers and others, its impact on the community and the environment, and 'ethical considerations related to the responsible conduct of business'. It also specifically acknowledges that the corporation may allocate a 'reasonable amount of resources' to various charitable purposes 'whether or not doing so enhances the economic value of the corporation'.[117]

Many other jurisdictions provide for the consideration of non-shareholder interests in the corporate statute itself, though often with studied ambiguity. The UK Companies Act 2006, for example, requires each company director to 'have regard' to the interests of various non-shareholder constituents, but to do so in the course of acting 'in the way he considers, in good faith, would be most likely to promote the success of the company *for the benefit of its members* [ie, its shareholders] *as a whole*.'[118] That this statutory duty differs from the duty of corporate directors at common law there can be little doubt.[119] But there is reason to be cautious about offering extravagant claims about the ultimate significance of a requirement to 'have regard' to non-shareholder interests, while remaining duty bound to promote the success of the company for the benefit of the shareholders alone.[120] Section 122.1 of Canada's federal corporate statute, the *Canada Business Corporations Act*,[121] and the two Supreme Court

[117] American Law Institute, Restatement of the Law Corporate Governance, Tentative Draft No 1 (April 2022) § 2.01 (a)(1), (b).

[118] UK Companies Act 2006, s. 172(1) (emphasis added). For a provocative explication of this language, in the context of a case exploring the putative duty of directors to consider or act in the interests of the creditors of the company when the company is in the vicinity of insolvency, see *BTI 2014 v Sequana SA*, [2022] UKSC 25.

[119] See eg Paul L Davies, Sarah Worthington and Christopher Hare, *Gower Principles of Modern Company Law* (11th ed Sweet & Maxwell 2021), 275: 'The historical common law formulation differs in significant ways from what is now found in s. 172(1) of the Act.' The principles differences are, first that directors' duties are based on '[promoting] the success of the company for the benefit of its members as a whole' rather than acting in what the directors considered to be the best interests of the company. Secondly, s. 172(1) requires directors, in promoting the success of the company, to have regard to a number of matters, including such things, among others, as the interests of the company's employees and the impact of the company's operations on the community. See also *BTI 2014 v Sequana SA*, ibid, especially the judgments of Lady Arden and Lord Briggs.

[120] The UK Companies Act 2006 does allow companies to specify 'purposes' that involve something other than the benefit of its members and, where a company has adopted such purposes (presumably in its corporate constitution), the duty of the directors becomes a duty to achieve those purposes. Although this language appears to allow for corporations incorporated under the Companies Act 2006 to depart from a shareholder primacy objective, David Kershaw and Edmund Schuster have argued that recourse to this provision is 'rarely used and is typically viewed as a means of adapting the corporate form for charitable bodies and nonprofits.' See David Kershaw and Edmund Schuster, 'The Purposive Transformation of Corporate Law' (2021) 69 The American Journal of Comparative Law 478, 498. See also Davies and others, ibid 278.

[121] *Canada Business Corporations Act*, RSC 1985, c. C-44 (CBCA). Every Canadian province and territory also has its own business corporation statute and no provincial or territorial corporate statute, other than in the comparatively small province of Saskatchewan, includes provisions equivalent to s. 122.1 of the CBCA. (See *The Business Corporations Act* (Saskatchewan), SS. 2021, c. 6, s. 9-23(2).)

of Canada cases that are understood to have inspired s. 122.1,[122]may offer directors welcome assurance that they are unlikely to be exposed to liability for any alleged failure to relentlessly pursue the goal of maximizing shareholder wealth. But there is equally little doubt that directors who are, indeed, determined to maximize shareholder wealth are likewise unlikely to be exposed to liability, provided they do not behave in a way that is oppressive, unfairly prejudicial, or that unfairly disregards relevant interests of non-shareholders.[123]

Do these sort of recent reframings signal a significant general change in the law or the practice of business corporations? Or do they allow for such significant flexibility that managers could, in good faith, find support for any preferred managerial bias from the most zealous shareholder primacy mandate to the most 'stakeholder-friendly' corporate purpose?

Dorothy Lund has suggested that it may well be most sensible to think of the most appropriate corporate mandate to be somewhat protean, to be determined based on important situational factors. Specifically, she suggests that the neoclassical shareholder primacy approach is premised on the notion that the corporation operates within a legal and regulatory environment that ensures that the corporation must internalize its negative externalities. Since that assumption is frequently (perhaps typically) violated in the real world, there is an inverse relationship between the robustness of government regulation of corporate negative externalities and the aptness of shareholder wealth maximization as the primary corporate goal. Where regulation is lax, she suggests, there are compelling reasons for the business corporation to adopt broader corporate 'mandates' to address the resulting gaps that might otherwise endanger important social or environmental interests. On this view, the optimal goal of the corporation, from a social welfare perspective, would vary depending on the prevailing regulatory environment.[124] Thus, Lund in particular argues that current economic conditions account for the recent rise in interest in stakeholderism:

As a practical matter, Canadian businesses can choose to incorporate either under the CBCA or under any one of the 13 provincial or territorial statutes, regardless of the province or territory in which they operate. No clear corporate champion, equivalent to Delaware in the United States, has emerged in Canada, although it appears that a majority of large, publicly-traded corporations in Canada are incorporated under the CBCA. See Christopher C Nicholls, *Corporate Law* (Emond Montgomery 2005) 34-35.

[122] *Peoples Department Stores (Trustee of) v Wise*, [2004] 3 SCR 461; *BCE Inc v 1976 Debentureholders*, [2008] 3 SCR 560.

[123] This language is drawn from the typical Canadian corporate 'oppression' remedy. See eg CBCA, s. 241.

[124] Dorothy Lund, 'Toward a Dynamic View of Corporate Purpose' (2025) 109 Minnesota Law Review 2089.

> In particular, the external economic factors discussed above—corporate concentration, inequality, and the absence of adequate externality regulation—are currently at extreme points, which explains the increased appetite for a governance system that privileges stakeholders'.[125]

But has the actual approach adopted by corporations changed at the 'moments' she describes? Or has the rhetoric simply changed? Did the real 'change' in the understanding of the corporate goal come only when the financial economic conception of the corporation became mainstream, at around the same time that financial markets were being dramatically transformed following the international economic upheavals of the early 1970s and the unprecedented wave of financial innovation that followed? For that matter, how should one understand or interpret the supposed decline of externality regulation? Is there some objectively optimal level of regulation? Or are regulatory approaches matters on which reasonable people may well disagree based on differing economic, political, and ideological beliefs?

It is difficult to be certain how to evaluate the extent to which corporations, past or present, have actually committed resources to the pursuit of non-financial, pro-social objectives. Financial success is readily measurable. Non-financial 'success' is not. It is well recognized that some firms have attempted to gain the public relations benefits of 'good corporate citizenship' by laying claim to a heartfelt commitment to 'people and planet' that amounts to no more than ensuring the corporation's annual report is generously adorned with glossy stock photographs of lush forests and smiling employees. When the vacuity of such claims is exposed, duplicitous companies may be condemned as notorious 'greenwashers.'[126] But recently, as corporations struggle to conduct their operations in a socially responsible way while avoiding the ire of shareholders and even political leaders loathe to accede to any departure from shareholder wealth maximization, a new form of corporate disingenuousness has emerged: 'greenhushing', ' whereby [firms] deliberately engage in fewer

[125] ibid 2145.

[126] In 2023, for example, the US SEC brought a 'greenwashing' enforcement action against DWS Investment Management Americas Inc (DIMA), a subsidiary of Deutsche Bank AG, finding, among other things, that 'DIMA marketed itself as a leader in ESG that adhered to specific policies for integrating ESG considerations into its investments; however, . . . DIMA failed to adequately implement certain provisions of its global ESG integration policy as it had led clients and investors to believe it would. . . . DIMA also failed to adopt and implement policies and procedures reasonably designed to ensure that its public statements about the ESG integrated products were accurate.' The enforcement action led to a settlement in which DIMA agree to pay $25 million in penalties. See SEC, Press Release, 'Deutsche Bank Subsidiary DWS to Pay $25 Million for Anti-Money Laundering Violations and Misstatements Regarding ESG Investments' (25 September 2023) https://www.sec.gov/newsroom/press-releases/2023-194.

pro-sustainability communications than they actually practice.'[127] Indeed, according to Maibaum and others, a July 2025 study revealed that a remarkable 39% of US companies surveyed 'had reduced or stopped publicly promoting their sustainability investments even while maintaining or increasing them relative to 2024.'[128] It is thus no longer entirely clear that corporations believe they may expect to enjoy a green premium (or 'greenium') from activities aimed at social rather than merely financial ends. Quite the contrary. Good deeds, it seems, are now sometimes best done in the dark.

## Doing Bad by Doing Poorly?

Changing public sentiment, then, may materially influence corporate social mandates, but formal corporate law has not proved to be a very harsh taskmaster. In the absence of wrongdoing, bad faith, or clear conflict of interest—none of which may be present when a director takes steps to expend corporate resources in furtherance of the interests of some 'deserving' non-shareholder constituency—successful legal actions against corporate directors have, historically, been rare.[129] In some jurisdictions, as we have seen, corporate statutes expressly invite or mandate directors to consider a range of non-shareholder interests, although the interpretation of these mandates can be challenging and controversial.

What seems abundantly clear is that directors are highly unlikely to be exposed to the risk of personal liability when considering the impact of the corporation's actions on non-shareholders, provided they are not personally conflicted or self-interested. If corporate social responsibility advocates demand no more of corporate law than this reassuring level of pro social director immunity, there is really no hill left to fight for. Accordingly, as Tirole has noted, as a practical matter, the dispute between those who advocate for some version of shareholder primacy and those who favour the corporate pursuit of broader social goals is less a disagreement over the goals themselves and more a matter of whether explicit 'noisy' pursuit of

[127] Whitney Ginder, Wi-Suk Kwon and Sang Eun-Byun, 'Effects of Internal–External Congruence-Based CSR Positioning: An Attribution Theory Approach' (2021) 169 Journal of Business Ethics 355, 356.

[128] Frederik Maibaum, Manuel Reppmann, Laura Marie Edinger-Schons, and Johann Nils Foege, 'The Greenhushing Trap' (2026) 67(2) MIT Sloan Management Review 6.

[129] See Brian R Cheffins and Bernard S Black, 'Outside Director Liability Across Countries' (2006) 84 Texas Law Review 1385.

non-shareholder interests by for-profit businesses is, in fact, the best way to achieve those broader goals.[130]

Of course if the explicit pursuit, or at least thoughtful consideration, of non-shareholder interests is merely a high level risk management tool that ultimately promotes long-term financial success, then public-spirited directors should have little to fear even from the most avaricious and litigious shareholders. Yet, despite some potentially encouraging links between strong ESG metrics and positive corporate financial performance referred to above, doubts about the use and consistency of ESG metrics abound. Accordingly, reporting positive correlation between high ESG 'scores' and financial performance may not necessarily indicate a meaningful correlation between unequivocally clear and beneficial social initiatives and corporate financial success. It may still be the case, then, that a well-intentioned departure from the shareholder primacy norm does, indeed, adversely affect financial performance.

In a recent paper,[131] Bennett et al report the results of a 'natural experiment' (or, as they term it, a 'quasi natural experiment') on the effects of weakening shareholder primacy. The natural experiment to which they refer relates to the introduction of unusual legislation in Nevada in 2017, essentially forbidding courts from relying on the law of other jurisdictions when interpreting the fiduciary duties of the directors of Nevada corporations. The context for the enactment of this unique legislation was this. Nevada's corporate law had

[130] Tirole (n 56) 57. Of course, a number of arguments have been raised against the proposition that corporate directors ought to pursue a corporate social responsibility agenda. It has been argued, for example, that: effective managerial accountability requires managers to have a clear and singular corporate goal and to undermine that goal is to risk managerial entrenchment and inefficiency; corporate managers are not chosen for their expertise in identifying and pursuing appropriate non-financial goals and so are not qualified for the task; corporate social responsibility distorts the allocation of resources and so is likely to destroy value; corporate social responsibility is dangerous because it empowers the corporation at the expense of other institutions better suited to the task of filling less materialistic demands and so risks expanding the monolithic influence of corporate power and ideology fuelling a kind of modern feudalism. See eg Levitt (n 75). Hayek raised an additional concern. If corporations were permitted to divert resources to socially desirable (non-business) purposes, Hayek argues, 'this would turn corporations from institutions serving the expressed needs of individual men into institutions determining which ends the efforts of individual men should serve.' Hayek (n 9) 305. In the long term, he suggests, this practice would lead to an additional insidious result: '[i]f the management is supposed to serve wider public interests, it becomes merely a logical consequence of this conception that the appointed representatives of the public interest should control management.' ibid 305–06. Even worse, he suggests, 'the more it comes to be accepted that corporations ought to be directed in the service of specific "public interests", the more persuasive becomes the contention that, as government is the appointed guardian of the public interest, government should also have power to tell the corporations what they must do.' ibid 311–12. See Hayek (n 9).

[131] Benjamin Bennett, René M Stulz, and Zexi Wang, 'What Are the Costs of Weakening Shareholder Primacy? Evidence from a U.S. Quasi-Natural Experiment' (2025) ECGI Finance Working Paper No 1064/2025.

long included provisions expressly permitting directors, when exercising their powers, to consider various interests other than those of the corporation's shareholders. Yet, despite these apparently clear provisions, some Nevada courts had apparently chosen to import into Nevada, and rely upon, shareholder primacy principles found in Delaware jurisprudence.[132]

The question Bennett et al thus posed was this: what impact, if any, did this new legislation (which was expressly intended to loosen the perceived requirement for corporations to pursue a shareholder primacy goal) have on the performance of Nevada companies? The results of this 'quasi natural' experiment are disheartening. The authors find that the effect of insulating directors from the fiduciary demands of shareholder primacy appeared to be a weakening of many traditional indicia of good corporate governance. There was a decline in board independence, a decline in director meeting attendance, an increase in director entrenchment indices, and an increase in accounting issues and auditors' concerns. Excess CEO pay increased and the link of executive compensation to performance decreased. Worse still, the effect of allowing managers to consider the interests of non-shareholders did not even appear to benefit these other stakeholders. In fact, the authors found that ESG performance of these companies following the change actually weakened, 'significantly'. The unsettling conclusion appears to be precisely what the agency theorists have long warned: giving directors more latitude to consider the interests of stakeholders other than shareholders simply provides directors cover to enhance their own interests at the expense not only of shareholders, but indeed of all corporate stakeholders.

List and Momeni reported equally gloomy results from their research on the potential adverse performance effects of CSR.[133] Their research indicated that the use by an employer of CSR messaging and incentives increased employee misbehaviour and shirking. One plausible explanation they offer for this result is a 'moral licensing' effect: people who believe they are acting morally in one aspect of their life feel 'liberated' to behave unethically in some other aspect.

Doing good, it seems, or at least having the freedom to do so, does not necessarily lead to 'doing well'

[132] See eg Jim Penrose and Paul Young, 'Nevada State Bill No 203: An Important Development for Nevada Corporations and Their Counsel' *Nevada Lawyer* (January 2019) 18, citing, in particular, *Hilton Hotels Corp v ITT Corp* 978 F Supp 1342 (D Nev 1997) and *Shoen v SAC Holding Corp* 122 Nev 621 (2006).

[133] John A List and Fatemeh Momeni, 'When Corporate Social Responsibility Backfires: Evidence from a Natural Field Experiment' (2021) 67(1) Management Science 8.

## Disclosure, Exposure, or Composure

Perhaps the most important channels through which ESG and other proxies for pro social corporate 'citizenship' operate are disclosure obligations. The European Union has, in particular, attempted to integrate traditional disclosure obligations with non-financial metrics. The European Corporate Sustainability Reporting Directive (CSRD), for example, a major step in the regulation of non-financial disclosure, came into effect on January 5, 2023,[134] although implementation of the directive was to occur in 'waves' with the original implementation schedule recently postponed by an 'omnibus' proposal introduced in 2025.[135] The CSRD replaced the earlier, more limited European Non-Financial Reporting Directive.[136] The European Directive was intended to implement aspirational commitments of the 'European Green Deal'.[137] The European Green Deal explicitly identified fighting climate change and related environmental problems as 'this generation's defining task'. This, in turn, reflects a European goal, as expressed in a March 2018 Commission Communication, 'Action Plan: Financing Sustainable Growth' (the 'Action Plan on Financing Sustainable Growth'), that expressed, among other things, the goal of '[reorienting] capital flows towards sustainable investment in order to achieve sustainable and inclusive growth . . . '[138] Of potentially even greater significance is the EU's Corporate Sustainability Due Diligence Directive (CSDDD)[139] which entered into force July 25 2024. The CSDDD, to be implemented through laws in EU Member states to be adopted by July 2026, will introduce significant requirements on corporations not only to report on various environmental and human rights matters but also to identify, assess, prevent and mitigate adverse environmental and adverse human rights impacts. The application of the new provisions is to be phased in over three years beginning initially with the largest companies, with more than 5,000 employees and more than €1.5 billion in turnover, and eventually extending, by July 2029, to companies with more than 1,000 employees and more than €450 million in turnover.

[134] See https://eur-lex.europa.eu/legal-content/EN/TXT/?uri=CELEX:32022L2464.

[135] See European Commission, Press Release, 'Commission Adopts "Quick Fix" for Companies Already Conducting Corporate Sustainability Reporting' (11 July 2025) https://finance.ec.europa.eu/publications/commission-adopts-quick-fix-companies-already-conducting-corporate-sustainability-reporting_en

[136] Directive 2014/95/EU https://eur-lex.europa.eu/legal-content/EN/TXT/PDF/?uri=CELEX:32014L0095.

[137] See https://eur-lex.europa.eu/legal-content/EN/TXT/?uri=CELEX%3A52019DC0640.

[138] European Commission, *Action Plan:Financing Sustainable Growth* COM/2018/097 final, 2 https://eur-lex.europa.eu/legal-content/EN/TXT/?uri=CELEX:52018DC0097.

[139] Directive (EU) 2024/2760 https://eur-lex.europa.eu/eli/dir/2024/1760/oj.

These climate-spurred regulatory initiatives confirm the overarching importance of the 'E' in ESG. Environmental issues, and, in particular, widely shared fears of the implications of climate change are the most significant elements motivating support for the concept. International pressures for companies, and countries, to make additional progress in combatting climate change continue to build. Yet, the results of environmental advocacy have been mixed. There was great initial excitement, for example, over the May 26 2021 decision of the Hague District Court ordering Royal Dutch Shell to reduce the volume of its $C0_2$ emissions by 45 per cent.[140] However, the celebrations were short-lived. The Hague Court of Appeal subsequently overturned the decision in 2024.[141]

The endorsement of measures to confront climate change and commitment of such measures has also varied from jurisdiction to jurisdiction. On 23 July 2025, for example, the International Court of Justice issued its Advisory Opinion on the Obligations of States in Respect of climate change.[142] That opinion concluded, among other things, that: States have obligations under international human rights law to respect and ensure the enjoyment of human rights by taking necessary measures to respect the climate system and other parts of the environment.'[143]

In the United States, however, the recent transition to a new presidential administration in 2025 has also had implications for the development of ESG initiatives in general and climate-related disclosure law in particular. For example, in *Iowa v Securities and Exchange Commission*[144] the legality of certain SEC climate disclosure rules had been challenged. However, on 27 March 2025, after President Trump took office, the SEC notified the court (the Eighth Circuit Court of Appeals) that it wished to withdraw its defence of the Climate Disclosure rules,[145] stating that a majority of the SEC's Commissioners now were of the view that these rules exceeded the SEC's authority.

[140] *See Milieudefensie and Ors v Royal Dutch Shell plc* C/09/571932/HA ZA 19-379, The Hague District Court (26 May 2021) ECLI:NL:RBDHA:2021:5339 https://climatecasechart.com/wp-content/uploads/non-us-case-documents/2021/20210526_8918_judgment-2.pdf.

[141] *Royal Dutch Shell plc v Milieudefensie and Ors.* Hague Court of Appeal (12 November 2024) ECLI:NL:GHDHA:2024:2099) https://climatecasechart.com/wp-content/uploads/non-us-case-documents/2024/20241112_8918_judgment.pdf. Milieudefensie has appealed the decision of the Hague Court of Appeal to the Supreme Court.

[142] Opinion made pursuant to a submission by Secretary General of the UN to the International Court of Justice of questions set forth in resolution 77/276 adopted by the United Nations General Assembly on 29 March 2023. https://www.icj-cij.org/sites/default/files/case-related/187/187-20250723-adv-01-00-en.pdf.

[143] International Court of Justice, Advisory Opinion, 'Obligations of States in Respect of Climate Change' (23 July 2025) 131 https://www.icj-cij.org/case/187/advisory-opinion.

[144] *State of Iowa v SEC* 24-1522 (8th Circuit).

[145] Letter from Tracy A Hardin SEC to Acting Clerk of Court, US Court of Appeals for the Eighth Circuit https://climatecasechart.com/wp-content/uploads/case-documents/2025/20250327_doc

The contrast between the relative robustness of the EU's approach to climate change and public company disclosure obligations and the US approach is significant. And these differences may have knock-on effects on other matters as well. For example, on 21 August 2025 the US and the EU issued a joint statement on a United States-European Union framework on an agreement on reciprocal, fair, and balanced trade.[146] That statement included the following commitment:

> The European Union commits to undertake efforts to ensure that the Corporate Sustainability Due Diligence Directive (CSDDD) and the Corporate Sustainability Reporting Directive (CSRD) do not pose undue restrictions on transatlantic trade. In the context of CSDDD, this includes undertaking efforts to reduce administrative burden on businesses, including small- and medium-sized enterprises, and to propose changes to the requirement for a harmonised civil liability regime for due diligence failures and to climate-transition-related obligations. The European Union commits to work to address US concerns regarding the imposition of CSDDD requirements on companies of non-EU countries with relevant high-quality regulations.

## Is Disclosure Enough? Can Directors Be Relied Upon to Do 'the Right Thing'?

Mandatory disclosure of corporations' adherence to or deviation from purported standards of exemplary behaviour does not seem to provide a sufficient check on corporate nimiety, at least to many shareholder primacy skeptics. Something more, they suggest, may be necessary to bring venal and recalcitrant corporations to heel. Colin Mayer has argued that 'it is unlikely that human norms and principles are sufficient on their own to restrain corporate

ket-24-1522-24-1623-24-1624-24-1626-24-1627-24-1628-24-1631-24-1633-24-1634-24-1685_letter-1.pdf. These rules had been adopted on 6 March 2024. (See SEC Release Nos 33-11275, 34-99678.) Although the rules were characterized at the time of their adoption as 'decision-useful' information for investors, the particular emphasis on climate-related risks is difficult to interpret as politically neutral, financially-oriented investor-protection regulation. On 23 July 2025, the SEC filed a status report in which, among other things, it requested the court to proceed with deciding the petition before it.

[146] Seehttps://policy.trade.ec.europa.eu/news/joint-statement-united-states-european-union-framework-agreement-reciprocal-fair-and-balanced-trade-2025-08-21_en.

conduct'.[147] By this he presumably means that such norms and principles are insufficient to restrain corporate conduct in the way that he believes it would best be restrained. He may well, of course, be right; but the difficulty with attempting to mandate greater 'morality' in the corporate boardroom is that one must be able to settle on a version of morality or pro social action upon which there is universal agreement. In a pluralist society, that is a very significant challenge indeed.

Moreover, as Masconale and Sepe have argued,[148] unlike earlier notions of CSR, which involved corporations seeking to contribute to the *means* of realizing non-financial social goals on which there was already broad social consensus (such as fighting poverty or ending pollution), the new activist corporation is more than a vehicle for realizing aims. Now, they argue, it performs the citizen's role in defining aims—by taking stands on issues, such as gun control, for which there is not broad social consensus. The activist causes of the modern corporation, they suggest, are, in fact, necessarily divisive. Yet, the divisive aims pursued by corporations do not reflect a broad range of political preferences. Instead, the specific economic pressures that motivate this corporate activism, they warn, can reflect only majoritarian preferences—specifically the preferences of a small group of wealthy investors, the dominant asset managers. Nevertheless, Kershaw and Schuster have argued that it would be mistaken for corporate law to inflexibly forestall all corporations from adopting what they dub a 'mission-purpose' that may transcend narrow shareholder primacy. Instead, they maintain, corporate law should facilitate 'zones of insulation' for corporate directors allowing them to pursue such broader 'mission-purposes,' free from pressing shareholder demands. Within such protective zones of insulation, directors would have sufficient opportunity to prove the long-term benefits to be derived from the faithful pursuit of broader 'mission-purposes' and the productive bonds with diverse corporate stakeholders to which a commitment to such mission purposes may lead.[149] Yet, will a 'mission-purpose' genuinely believed by certain directors to facilitate what they have determined is in the best long-term interests of society necessarily accord with society's interests as envisioned by others?

[147] Colin Mayer, 'Success, Law and ESG' European Corporate Governance Institute (ECGI) Law Working Paper No 795/2024 (2024).

[148] Saura Masconale and Simone Sepe, 'Citizen Corp-Corporate Activism and Democracy' (2022) 100 Washington University Law Review 257.

[149] Kershaw and Schuster (n 126).

## Conclusion

It would be impossible here to summarize or even catalogue the vast number of scholarly and popular articles and books that have been written about ESG.[150] No attempt has been, or will be, made to do so. It is enough to observe that the same competing economic and social forces have, in every decade for as long as the business corporation has existed, battled over how best to ensure that its necessary pursuit of profit does not blind its managers to the broader needs and vulnerabilities of the human communities and the natural environment in which they operate. Perhaps, in the end, as Alex Edmans has suggested: 'If ESG is a set of value-relevant factors, then it's both extremely important and nothing special.'[151]

Lawyers have always been important participants in the corporate shareholder/stakeholder debate. This is entirely appropriate, since the corporate goal is inextricably linked to the legal role and responsibilities of corporate officers and directors. But the parameters of the corporate purpose question seem more often to reflect considerations of economics and of sociology rather than of law. Debates over the content of corporate managers' powers and obligations too often depart from diligent and disinterested efforts to discern the contours of the law of fiduciary duty. Instead, disagreement over corporate ends are too frequently characterized by vitriol, self-righteousness, and spleen as champions of one view or another seek to wage a kind of proxy political battle in which the business corporation serves as a convenient embodiment of a particularly favoured, or particularly despised, economic system. Champions of the free market insist that corporations must be seen as dutiful wealth-maximizing exemplars of the capitalist system. Critics of that system insist that the corporation—much like the modern state itself—must unapologetically promote and protect the common good, and not simply serve as a vehicle for enriching shareholders by imposing externalities on others. To advocates of both positions, their opponents' arguments are frequently condemned as the intellectually flawed product of incomplete understanding, ideological bias, or both. Today's large publicly-traded corporation must, however, confront the challenges of powerful institutional shareholders—some of which are motivated by an uncompromising commitment to improving financial performance,

[150] For recent surveys of ESG literature see Pedro Matos, 'ESG and Responsible Institutional Investing Around the World' (2023) CFA Institute Research Foundation; and Bruno Buchetti, Francesa Romano Arduino, and Salvatore Perdichizzi, 'A Literature Review on Corporate Governance and ESG Research' (2025) 97 International Review of Financial Analysis 103759.

[151] Alex Edmans, 'The End of ESG' (2023) 52 Financial Management 3.

others of whom contend that their own fiduciary obligations oblige them to press the corporations in which they invest to consider the impact of their business on climate change, human rights, and other compelling non-financial issues. The implications of this institutional shareholder/corporation dynamic will be explored in Chapter 8.

# 8

# Whose Corporation Is it Anyway? Myopic Gadflies and Institutional Share Ownership: Is Shareholder Activism a Short-sighted Solution?

'The annual meeting of the large American corporation is perhaps our most elaborate exercise in popular illusion.'[1]

-John Kenneth Galbraith

## Introduction: The 'Gadflies'

Wilma Soss, Lewis D. Gilbert with his younger brother John, and J. A. Livingston were among the most famous of the shareholder activist 'gadflies'[2] of the 1950s. Livingston[3] and Gilbert[4] each wrote somewhat self-congratulatory books about their exploits as perennial thorns in the smartly tailored sides of the directors of large American corporations. Wilma Soss has been the

[1] John Kenneth Galbraith, *The New Industrial State* (Princeton University Press 2007) 106.

[2] The term 'gadfly' in the colloquial sense of someone who pesters or seeks to rouse up people in power to change the status quo traces its origin to a passage in the *Apology* by Plato in which Socrates, speaking in his own defence, explains: 'For if you kill me you will not easily find a successor to me, who, if I may use such a ludicrous figure of speech, am a sort of gadfly, given to the state by God; and the state is a great and noble steed who is tardy in his motions owing to his very size, and requires to be stirred into life. I am that gadfly which God has attached to the state, and all day long and in all places am always fastening upon you, arousing and persuading and reproaching you.' See Plato, 'Apology' in B Jowett (ed), *Dialogues of Plato: Translated into English, with Analyses and Introduction* (Cambridge University Press 2010) 319, 345. The Greek word used by Plato that is translated in this passage as 'gadfly' is μύωψ ('myops'). The word is used in this passage as a noun. But, as an adjective, the same word could also mean short-sighted. See Laura A Marshall, 'Gadfly or Spur? The Meaning of μύωψ in Plato's *Apology of Socrates*' (2017) 137 Journal of Hellenic Studies 163. It is the root of the English word 'myopia'. Thus, one might facetiously say that the corporate gadflies were the original myopic shareholders.

[3] Lewis D Gilbert, *Dividends and Democracy* (American Research Council 1956).

[4] JA Livingston, *The American Stockholder* (J B Lippincott Company 1958).

*Corporate Governance and Enlightened Fiduciaries*. Christopher C. Nicholls, Oxford University Press.
 DOI: 10.1093/9780198904199.003.0008

subject of a recent biography,[5] and was said to have been the inspiration for Howard Teichman and George Kaufman's 1954 Broadway play, *The Solid Gold Cadillac*.[6] The shareholder democracy movement associated with these 1950s shareholder activists and others like them was very much a product of an era in which millions of small shareholders of large American Berle-Means corporations felt rather powerless, disenfranchised, frequently patronized, and, more frequently, ignored. Executive compensation was a regular target of their wrath, and improved financial performance generally their goal. Livingston, for example, mocked the idea that corporate managers should trumpet themselves and the corporations they served as 'good citizens' rather than as faithful profit-making stewards of their shareholders' capital:

> A good citizen! The corporation now has a new identify apart from profit-making . . . It is Good Citizen Inc! And the Corporate Executive comports himself to reflect that corporate citizenship . . . In his paneled office, in his travels about the country, in his community relations, he represents, not himself, but The Corporation. He represents not the stockholder, but The Corporation.[7]

Lewis Gilbert declared the corporation's shareholders to be 'the owners, legally, morally, historically',[8] and so insisted that they were deserving of a more effective voice in the management of corporations.

Wilma Soss was perhaps the most interesting of all the early corporate gadflies. Although she shared with her fellow prominent activists a commitment to holding to account corporate directors and officers—whom, she insisted, the shareholders employed as a form of labour[9]—she also had broader equitable goals. For example, she founded the Federation of Women Shareholders,[10] and campaigned, among other things, to have more women on the boards of American corporations.

[5] Janice M Traflet and Robert E Wright, *Fearless: Wilma Soss and American's Forgotten Investor Movement* (All Seasons Press 2022).

[6] Sarah C Haan, 'Corporate Governance and the Feminization of Capital' (2022) 74(3) Stanford Law Review 515, 564; Howard Teichmann and George S Kaufman, *The Solid Gold Cadillac: A Comedy* (Random House 1954).

[7] Livingston (n 4) 219–20.

[8] Gilbert (n 3) 11.

[9] See Richard Gehman, 'Guardian Angel of Shareholders' *Cosmopolitan Magazine* (April 1963) 64, quoting Soss at the 1961 annual meeting of General Electric addressing General Electric Chair of the Board, Ralph Cordiner: 'I am your employer today. I am representing those who employ you. You are not an act of God. You are a form of labor.'

[10] Gilbert (n 3) 30.

There have been a number of modern successors to the corporate gadflies of the 1950s. Among the most well known, perhaps, are the late Evelyn Davis, John Chevedden, Gerald R. Armstrong, Myra Young, Emil Rossi and family, William Steiner and family, and James McRitchie.[11] In fact, James McRitchie's recent unsuccessful action against Mark Zuckerberg and other directors of Meta attempted to invoke modern portfolio theory in a novel way to impugn the actions of the members of the Meta board. McRitchie advanced an argument evocative of an observation once made by Professor Jeffrey Gordon,[12] that since a diversified investor cares about the overall performance of his portfolio, not the performance on any single stock within that portfolio, an asset manager (or, in Mr McRitchie's case, any diversified investor) seeking to maximize wealth would have an incentive to lobby companies in which they invest to adopt pro-social policies if the negative externalities resulting from the operations of those companies would otherwise lead to harmful effects that would lower the overall performance of the portfolio. The opinion granting the motion to dismiss this action gave the Delaware Court of Chancery the opportunity to articulate a particularly explicit version of the shareholder primacy norm under Delaware corporate law.[13]

## From Gadflies to Goliaths: The Rise of Institutional Shareholders

The gadfly activists of the mid-twentieth century emerged within the context of the original Berle-Means corporation. Managers of such corporations were generally free from effective shareholder scrutiny, discipline, and accountability because of the rational apathy of the widely dispersed shareholders, none of whom had an economic interest in any single corporation large enough to justify spending either time or money seeking to monitor or discipline lacklustre, self-serving, or overpaid managers. The costs of actively monitoring managers would not only be disproportionate to the size of the economic interests held by small shareholders but also, since any benefits to be gained from such vigilance would be shared by all other shareholders, the prospect of free-riding would create an additional disincentive to engage in shareholder activism.

[11] See Kobi Kastiel and Yaron Nili, 'The Giant Shadow of Corporate Gadflies' (2021) 94 Southern California Law Review 569, 590–91.
[12] Jeffrey N Gordon, 'Systematic Stewardship' (2002) 47 Journal of Corporate Law 627, 659–60.
[13] *McRitchie v Zuckerberg* 315 A 3d 518 (Del Ch 2024).

But this old Berle-Means model, as Gilson and Gordon have noted, has become 'factually obsolete and now provides a misleading framework for contemporary corporate governance theorizing.'[14] The obsolescence of the model arises from the increasing importance now played in securities markets by institutional investors such as pension funds, mutual funds, and other collective investment vehicles.

Recent research by Dasgupta and others[15] has identified the four types of institutional investor with the most significant share ownership of US public corporations today: mutual funds, exchange traded funds (ETFs), public pension funds, and private pension funds. Although the holdings of hedge funds[16] are not as large as any of those four classes of institutions, it is also recognized that hedge funds, often among the most active of institutional investors, have come to have a particularly important voice in modern corporate governance.

The increase in institutional share ownership of publicly traded corporations over the past 50 years has been dramatic. In the 1950s, it has been estimated that institutional share ownership accounted for only 7 or 8 per cent of market capitalization in the US.[17] These were the companies of which Berle and Means wrote, in which there was an unmistakable separation of ownership and control. By 2017, the percentage of shares of US public companies held by institutions had increased to an estimated 73%.[18] While the percentage of shares held by institutions is particularly high in the case of the largest US corporations, increasing institutional share ownership is also a global

[14] Ronald J Gilson and Jeffrey N Gordon, 'The Agency Costs of Agency Capitalism: Activist Investors and the Revaluation of Governance Rights' (2013) 113 Columbia Law Review 863, 864.

[15] Amil Dasgupta, Vyacheslav Fos, and Zacharias Sautner, 'Institutional Investors and Corporate Governance' (2021) 12(4) Foundations and Trends in Finance 276.

[16] The term 'hedge fund' is said to have been originally coined by Carol Loomis in a 1966 story in *Fortune* magazine profiling Alfred Winslow Jones, usually regarded as the creator of the first hedge fund (or, as he evidently preferred to describe it, 'hedged fund'). See Carol Loomis, 'The Jones Nobody Keeps Up With' *Fortune* (April 1966) https://fortune.com/article/hedge-funds-fortune-1966/. The term 'hedge fund' (or 'hedged fund') refers to the fundamental hedging strategy of the original funds, which used a 'long/short' investment approach to protect investors from general market downturns, while attempting to provide them with above market returns. The basic insight behind these original funds was to buy (go long) on stocks which the fund manager forecast would outperform the market, then concurrently sell (short) a basket of stocks intended to be representative of the market as a whole. As long as the fund was, in fact, able to identify stocks that would generate above-market ($\alpha$) returns, fund investors would profit, whether the market as a whole rose or fell. Modern hedge funds employ an array of sophisticated 'alternative investment strategies' including, notably, activist strategies involving acquiring shares in a target company and using a combination of voting power, negotiating prowess, and persuasive influence among fellow shareholders (including traditional institutional investors) to 'agitate for change' of some kind to enhance or unlock value.

[17] Luis A Aguilar (US Securities and Exchange Commission) 'Institutional Investors: Power and Responsibility' (19 April 2019) https://www.sec.gov/news/speech/2013-spch041913laahtm.

[18] Jonathan Lewellen and Katharina Lewellen, 'Institutional Investors and Corporate Governance: The Incentive to be Engaged' (2022) 77 Journal of Finance 213.

phenomenon.[19] A 2019 report by the OECD reported that, as at the end of 2017, 'institutional investors hold 41 per cent of global market capitalisation'.[20]

Of particular note has been the steady rise in stature of the so-called 'Big Three' asset managers: BlackRock, State Street, and Vanguard (or the 'Big Four', including Fidelity.) The assets under management of the Big Four institutions—albeit through a myriad of separate funds—totals in excess of US$31 trillion, of which BlackRock alone accounts for some US$11 trillion.[21] So it is that we appear to have entered an age, as former Delaware Supreme Court Chief Justice Leo E. Strine, Jr. has aptly remarked, in which we have witnessed the 'separation of ownership from ownership'.[22] How much power do large institutional investors—especially the Big Three—really have, and how do they use such power? Determining the scope of the voting power of the Big Three is challenging for a number of reasons. Evaluating the significance of this voting power involves even more variables.[23]

The rise in institutional share ownership has been accompanied by an evolving understanding of the relationship between institutional shareholders, the corporations in which they invest, and the ultimate beneficiaries of the investing institutions. In particular, it is apparent that the shifting pattern of shareholdings could have important implications for conceptions of corporate governance and the interpretation of directors' and officers' fiduciary duties. When the corporation is viewed through an agency theory lens, the key issue is ensuring that managers are subject to sufficient checks, and one of those checks could involve effective shareholder monitoring. Large institutional shareholders have the means and, potentially, sufficient incentive to monitor managers, unlike the widely dispersed shareholders of the Berle-Means corporation. As Roberta Romano indicated in her 2001 review of the role and efficacy of institutional investors, prior to 1986, most shareholder activism in the

[19] See eg Iris H-Y Chiu and Dionysia Katelouzou, 'From Shareholder Stewardship to Shareholder Duties: Is the Time Right?' in Hanne S Birkmose (ed), *Shareholders' Duties* (Kluwer Law International 2016) 131.

[20] A De La Cruz, A Medina, and Y Tang, 'Owners of the World's Listed Companies' OECD Capital Market Series, Paris (2019) 5 https://www.oecd.org/corporate/Owners-of-the-Worlds-Listed-Companies.pdf.

[21] See eg WTW Investments, 'World's Largest Asset Managers' AUM Surges to Record $140 Trillion, Driven by North America and Passives' (10 November 2025) https://www.wtwco.com/en-gb/news/2025/11/worlds-largest-asset-managers-aum-surges-to-record-dollars-140-trillion-driven-by-north-america.

[22] Leo E Strine Jr, 'Toward Common Sense and Common Ground? Reflections on the Shared Interest of Managers and Labor in a More Rational System of Corporate Governance' (2007) 33 Journal of Corporate Law 1, 6–7; Leo E Strine Jr, 'Can We Do Better by Ordinary Investors? A Pragmatic Reaction to the Dueling Ideological Mythologists of Corporate Law' (2014) 114 Columbia Law Review 449.

[23] See eg John D Morley, 'Too Big to be Activist' (2019) 92 Southern California Law Review 1407.

United States was undertaken by individual investors, but the role of individuals was later supplanted by pension funds and unions.[24]

But do the incentives of large institutional shareholders align with those of other investors? For example, if asset managers explicitly exercise their shareholder voting power to maximize the value of their holdings on a portfolio basis, rather than on a company-by-company basis, how can, or should, managers of individual firms respond? Further, although a number of judicial and regulatory authorities seem to support the notion that institutional investors, such as pension funds, should concentrate solely on the financial performance of the companies in which they invest,[25] there are competing arguments that fiduciary duties 'evolve over time according to social norms and the values of society and to a degree, technological and market changes'.[26] This evolution, it has been suggested, may now favour the proposition that institutional investors, in some circumstances, may be obliged to look beyond the financial performance of corporations in which they invest and consider broader environmental, social and governance factors as well.[27]

The nature of shareholder activism has, in any event, certainly evolved. Wolf-Georg Ringe has said that 'in recent years, shareholder activism has reinvented itself to become a mainstream business'.[28] Ringe also identifies an important distinction between activists in companies with strong controlling shareholders and activists in companies with widely dispersed shareholders and powerful managers. In the first case, the activists are 'usually acting or purporting to act on behalf of all *other* [non-controlling] shareholders'[29] as opposed to the 'traditional' activists who purported to act on behalf of shareholders as a whole against an imperial management. Ringe also distinguishes between formal and informal activism, pointing to certain legal and institutional factors that make the former more prevalent in the United States and the latter more prevalent in the UK. He observes that: 'It appears that shareholder activism is more adversarial in nature in nations that offer minority

[24] Roberta Romano, 'Less Is More: Making Institutional Investor Activism a Valuable Mechanism of Corporate Governance' (2001) 18 Yale Journal on Regulation 174, 176.

[25] See eg US Department of Labor, 'Fiduciary Duties Regarding Proxy Voting and Shareholder Rights' https://www.dol.gov/sites/dolgov/files/ebsa/temporary-postings/fiduciary-duties-regarding-proxy-voting-and-shareholder-rights.pdf; *Cowan v Scargill* [1984] 3 WLR 501.

[26] Freshfields Bruckhaus Deringer/UNEP Finance Initiative, *A Legal Framework for the Integration of Environmental, Social and Governance Issues Into Institutional Investment* (October 2005) 9.

[27] ibid 3.

[28] Wolf-Georg Ringe, 'Adaptive Advocacy: The Reinvention of Shareholder Activism' in Jeffrey N Gordon and W Georg Ringe (eds), *Oxford Handbook of Corporate Law and Governance* (2nd edn, Oxford University Press 2025) section 1.

[29] ibid section 2.1.

shareholder protection against managerial and controlling shareholder influences.'[30]

Many commentators have even suggested that perhaps the fiduciaries most in need of scrutiny today are no longer corporate directors at all, but the fund managers.[31] Thus, just as the 1990s witnessed the framing of 'governance codes' for widely held business corporations in many jurisdictions, in the twenty-first century, attention began increasingly to turn to 'stewardship codes', dealing with the duties of asset managers who have become major shareholders of publicly traded corporations. In the UK, for example, the UK Stewardship Code was first promulgated in 2010 by the Financial Reporting Council. Although not mandatory, it has attracted about 300 voluntary signatories.[32] The current version of the Stewardship Code, the UK Stewardship Code 2026,[33] defines stewardship as 'the responsible allocation, management and oversight of capital to create long-term sustainable value for clients and beneficiaries'.[34] It then sets out six broad principles for signatories who are asset managers and asset owners and four broad principles for signatories that are service providers. When applying the principles, asset managers are counselled to take a number of considerations into account, including not only matters related to corporate governance such as directors' duties under the UK Companies Act 2006 and the UK Governance Code, but also such considerations as 'diversity, remuneration and workforce interests' and 'environmental and social issues, including climate change'.[35]

## From Passive (Funds) to Active(ism)

One of the major developments in the asset management industry has been the significant shift of invested assets from actively managed funds to passive, index funds.[36] The pouring of investors' money into index funds in

[30] ibid. section 2.2.

[31] See eg John C Bogle, 'The Fiduciary Principle: *No Man Can Serve Two Masters*' (Fall 2009) The Journal of Portfolio Management 15, 19: 'The failure of our money manager agents represents not only a failure of modern-day capitalism, but a failure of modern-day capitalists.'

[32] UK Stewardship Code signatory list (11 February 2025) https://media.frc.org.uk/documents/Signatory_List_at_11-02-2025.pdf.

[33] UK Stewardship Code 2026 (Financial Reporting Council 2025) media.frc.org.uk/documents/UK_Stewardship_Code_2026.pdf.

[34] ibid 5.

[35] ibid 9.

[36] Jan Fichtner, Eelke M Heemskerk, and Javier Garcia-Bernardo, 'Hidden Power of the Big Three? Passive Index Funds, Re-concentration of Corporate Ownership, and New Financial Risk' (2017) 19(2) Business and Politics 298; Lucian Bebchuk and Scott Hirst, 'Big Three Power, and Why it Matters' (2022) 102 Boston University Law Review 1547.

particular—mutual funds or ETFs designed to track or replicate the returns on some broad-based stock market index such as the S&P 500—seems to represent the triumph of investors' faith in efficient market theory and even perhaps some version of the capital asset pricing model. Indeed, William Sharpe, the Nobel-prize winning creator of the capital asset pricing model, long advocated investing in index funds.[37] Even legendary value investor Warren Buffett, who has regularly dismissed the efficient market theory as 'foolish',[38] has acknowledged that at least for the non-professional retail investor a passive investment in an index fund is usually the most sensible investment strategy.[39]

Investors' increasing preference for passive index funds rather than actively managed alternatives may reflect increasing skepticism about the ability of active fund managers reliably to outperform the market. That skepticism is, perhaps, fueled by financial economic research and a perception that long-term fund performance is most significantly affected by the level of fund management fees, which are lowest for passive funds. Investors may also, justifiably, believe that the principal benefit of pooled investment for smaller retail investors is the opportunity to achieve portfolio diversification at a modest cost.

One implication of the rise in index investing, however, is that it has called for a reassessment of disgruntled shareholders' investment strategies. The traditional method by which disappointed investors responded to inadequate performance on the part of the corporations in which they held securities was to follow the so-called 'Wall Street Rule': they would sell their underperforming shares, and thus 'exit' their unsatisfactory investment.[40] The ability to exit, however, becomes impractical in the case of very large ownership stakes because of potential market impact,[41] and impossible in the case of index funds that are obliged to hold shares in corporations included in the relevant index.

[37] See eg William F Sharpe, 'The Arithmetic of Active Management'(1991) 47(1) Financial Analysts Journal 7.

[38] See eg Warren Buffett, 'The Essays of Warren Buffett: Lessons for Corporate America' (1997) 19(1) Cardozo L Review 1, 72: 'In my opinion, the continuous 63-year arbitrage experience of Graham-Newman Corp., Buffett Partnership, and Berkshire illustrates just how foolish [the efficient market theory] is.'

[39] For example, in answer to a question about how a young non-professional investor should invest posed at the 2008 Annual Meeting of Berkshire Hathaway, Buffett responded: 'Under the conditions you name, I'd probably have it all in a very low-cost index fund.' This advice was then echoed by Buffett's long-time business partner Charlie Munger: '[i]f you don't have any rational prospects of being a very skilled professional investor of course you should compromise on some simple thing like an index fund.' See Berkshire Hathaway 2008 Annual Meeting, Warren Buffett Archive, CNBC http://buffett.cnbc.com/2008-berkshire-hathaway-annual-meeting/. Buffett has reiterated similar advice many times, often specifying the desirability of investing in an S&P 500 index fund.

[40] Albert O Hirschman, *Exit, Voice and Loyalty: Responses to Decline in Firms, Organizations and States* (Harvard University Press 1970).

[41] Simply put, an attempt to sell a large block of shares could, itself, drive down the price of those shares.

Accordingly, institutional shareholders who are displeased with the performance of the corporations in their portfolios must consider exercising their 'voice'[42] rather than heading for the exit.

In any event, how effective a role traditional institutional investors can play in the governance of corporations is difficult to discern. Former Delaware Supreme Court Chief Justice Leo E. Strine, Jr[43] has argued that institutional investors face pressures that he regards as 'irrational' to compete on short term performance metrics that are fundamentally at odds with the long-term interests of the individual investors for whom they ultimately hold their shares. He argues, in particular, that index funds ought to be required to exercise their votes from the specific perspective of a buy-and-hold investor for whom exit is not a practical option and with a view of what is in the long-term interests of their investors. But matters may be more complicated than they first appear. John Morley[44] has argued that, in fact, the very size of the share holdings of the largest investment managers may actually impede their ability to engage in effective activism because they are not monolithic shareholders; the shareholdings attributed to them in fact represent holdings in a large number of individual, disparate investment vehicles which means that activism aimed at benefiting one of those vehicles could have the effect of harming another. Nevertheless, Hu and Hamermesh have noted that at least some major asset managers do, indeed, operate on the basis of what they dub 'host share value maximization': that is, a policy under which shares held by the asset manager's various funds will be voted in each case with a view to maximizing the value of that individual corporation, not with a view to maximizing the overall portfolio of the relevant fund, let alone the overall portfolio of the asset manager itself.[45]

Hedge funds, although typically much smaller shareholders in large corporations than the major asset managers, may have considerably more latitude, and much higher-powered incentives, to engage in shareholder activism. Certainly, the incidence of shareholder activism has risen sharply since the early years of the twenty-first century.[46] And hedge fund activism, in particular,

[42] Hirschman (n 40).

[43] Leo E Strine Jr, 'Who Bleeds When Wolves Bite? A Flesh-and-Blood Perspective on Hedge Fund Activism and Our Strange Corporate Governance System' (2017) 126 Yale Law Journal 1870.

[44] Morley (n 23).

[45] Henry T C Hu and Lawrence A Hamermesh, 'Reconceptualizing Stockholder "Disinterestedness": Transformative Institutional Investor Changes and Motivational Misalignments in Voting' (2025) 80 The Business Lawyer 311.

[46] Coffee and Palia cite a survey indicating that 1,115 activist campaigns occurred between 2010 and early 2014. John C Coffee Jr and Darius Palia, 'The Wolf at the Door: The Impact of Hedge Fund Activism on Corporate Governance' (2016) 41(3) Journal of Corporation Law 545, 554.

has attracted considerable industry and academic attention.[47] Hedge funds and other activist investors regularly challenge public company managers, waging aggressive campaigns frequently culminating in proxy contests seeking to replace directors and to implement changes purporting to improve corporate financial performance and increase shareholder value. Occasionally these 'performance activists' will enlist the support of more conventional 'governance activists' such as pension funds and other so-called 'long only' institutional shareholders. Gilson and Gordon, accordingly, see activist shareholders, such as hedge funds, as 'governance intermediaries'[48] who can propose strategies to which traditional institutions can then respond (though they are unlikely to originate such proposals). The need for hedge fund activists (who typically hold relatively small stakes in the firms in which they seek change) to persuade other institutional investors to support them, allows for what has been dubbed 'a hybrid internal-external role in a middle-ground form of corporate governance'.[49]

## Performance or Impact Activism

Recent research suggests that hedge fund activism seems to improve corporate financial performance[50] and does not harm corporate social performance (at least based on ESG ratings),[51] although it may be linked to the unwanted loss of valuable employees in targeted firms.[52]

The unprecedented rise in shareholder performance activism is not, however, unidimensional. It has been accompanied by the emergence of another powerful cross current: corporate social responsibility (CSR) and environmental, social and governance (ESG) concerns, discussed in Chapter 7. Unlike

[47] See eg Alon Brav and others, 'Hedge Fund Activism, Corporate Governance and Firm Performance' (2008) 63 Journal of Finance 1729; Marcel Kahan and Edward B Rock, 'Hedge Funds in Corporate Governance and Control' (2007) 155 University of Pennsylvania Law Review 1021; Lucian A Bebchuk, Alon Brav, and Wei Jiang, 'The Long-Term Effects of Hedge Fund Activism (2015) 115 Columbia Law Review 1085; Coffee and Palia (n 46); Brian R Cheffins and John Armour, 'The Past, Present, and Future of Shareholder Activism by Hedge Funds' (2011) 37(1) The Journal of Corporation Law 51.

[48] Gilson and Gordon (n 14) 867.

[49] Alon Brav, Wei Jiang, and Rongchen Li, 'Governance by Persuasion: Hedge Fund Activism and Market-Based Shareholder Influence' ECGI Working Paper No 797/2021 (2022) 1.

[50] ibid; Saikat Sovan Deb and others, 'Does Hedge Fund Activism Improve Investment Efficiency?'(2024) 29 Review of Accounting Studies 2551.

[51] Jiaying Wei and Shan Zhao, 'Does Hedge Fund Activism Harm Corporate Social Performance? Evidence from ESG Ratings' (2025) 94 Journal of Corporate Finance 102801.

[52] Guoli Chen, Philipp Meyer-Doyle, and Wei Shi, 'Hedge Fund Investor Activism and Human Capital Loss' (2021) 42(12) Strategic Management Journal 2193.

performance activists, CSR and ESG advocates have urged corporations to reject the single-minded pursuit of profit (or shareholder wealth maximization) in favour of advancing diverse social goals, and to embrace the broader aims of 'stakeholder capitalism'. There have been several high profile activist campaigns that seem to have been motivated, in whole or in part, by such broader non-financial considerations, such as:

- Engine No. 1's 2021 campaign at ExxonMobil;[53]
- Carl Icahn's 2022 animal-welfare proxy fight against McDonald's Corporation[54] and his aborted animal welfare and employee rights campaign at Kroger Co;[55]
- As You Sow's successful 2021 proposal resolution at DuPont de Nemours seeking greater disclosure about plastics released by the company into the environment;[56]
- Follow This's successful 2021 proposal resolution at ConocoPhillips seeking to have the company set emission reduction targets;[57]
- the successful shareholder proposal passed at Chevron's 2021 Annual Meeting seeking to have the company reduce 'Scope 3' emissions.[58]

One challenge that has been identified, however, is that, even if corporate directors do, indeed, want to consider broader social interests, institutional investors are often prohibited—in their own capacity as fiduciaries—from

[53] See eg Bernard S Sharfman, 'So Much for Engine No 1's Climate Activism at ExxonMobil' *Wall Street Journal* (22 March 2022); Engine No 1, 'We Energized ExxonMobil—And Drove a Dramatic Increase in Shareholder Value' https://engine1.com/transforming/articles/engagement-with-exxon-strengthened-company-value-for-shareholders/.

[54] Amelia Lucas, 'Carl Icahn Loses Proxy Fight with McDonald's Over Animal Welfare' (26 May 2022) CNBC https://www.cnbc.com/2022/05/26/carl-icahn-loses-proxy-fight-with-mcdonalds-over-animal-welfare.html.

[55] Reuters, 'Carl Icahn Drops Proxy Fight Against Kroger After McDonald's Defeat' (6 June 2022) https://www.reuters.com/business/retail-consumer/carl-icahn-drops-proxy-fight-against-kroger-withdraws-nominees-2022-06-06/.

[56] Kevin Crowley, 'DuPont Loses Plastic Pollution Vote with Record 81% Rebellion' (3 May 2021) https://news.bloomberglaw.com/environment-and-energy/dupont-loses-plastic-pollution-vote-with-record-81-rebellion.

[57] Jennifer Hiller, 'ConocoPhillips Shareholders Back Proposal to Set Scope 3 Targets' (11 May 2021) Reuters https://www.reuters.com/business/environment/conocophillips-shareholders-back-proposal-set-scope-3-targets-2021-05-11/. The following year, however, ConocoPhillips shareholders rejected a proposal to set emissions reductions targets to align with the Paris Agreement, the 2015 international treaty on climate change. See Liz Hampton, 'ConocoPhillips Shareholders Vote Against New Emissions-reductions Targets' (10 May 2022) Reuters https://www.reuters.com/business/sustainable-business/conocophillips-shareholders-vote-against-scope-3-emissions-reduction-targets-2022-05-10/.

[58] Sergio Chapa, 'Chevron Investors Back Climate Proposal in Rebuke to Management' (26 May 2021) Bloomberg https://www.bloomberg.com/news/articles/2021-05-26/chevron-investors-back-climate-proposal-in-rebuke-to-management.

considering anything other than financial performance. How practical a barrier this apparent restriction poses is, however, unclear. Geczy and others, for example, found that institutional investors with 'especially strict fiduciary duties' to seek only monetary returns (what they dub 'high fiduciary duty institutions') were not significantly deterred from investing in firms even after the passage of constituency statutes that would permit those firms to consider non-shareholder interests.[59] Moreover, the 2019 PRI[60] Report, 'Fiduciary Duty in the Twenty-first Century'[61] asserts that investors in fact have fiduciary duties to 'incorporate environmental, social and governance (ESG) issues into investment analysis and decision-making processes, consistent with their investment time horizons'.[62] Assertions of this sort do run directly counter to the language of US President Donald Trump's recent Executive Order relating to proxy advisory firms, discussed later in this chapter.

In this context it is intriguing to recall the evolution of BlackRock CEO Larry Fink's public ruminations on the social objectives of business corporations. In his 2020 'Letter to CEOs', he expressed bold public commitment to the importance of battling climate change, and building a more 'sustainable and inclusive capitalism.'[63] He also offered a strong endorsement of the value of ESG in his 2021 'Letter to CEOs.'[64] These provocative statements were then followed by his 2023 announcement that: 'I don't use the word ESG any more, because it's been entirely weaponised . . . by the far left and weaponised by the far right.'[65]

What role, in particular, should index funds have in holding corporations responsible either for better financial performance or for more socially responsible stewardship of their resources? Since they are not active managers but have no choice but to hold shares in the companies that comprise major stock

[59] Christopher Geczy and others, 'Institutional Investing When Shareholders Are Not Supreme' (2015) 5 Harvard Business Law Review 73. However, as the authors note, constituency statutes merely permit—they do not require—directors to consider non-shareholder interests. And the finding could simply reflect an assumption that such statutes would not, in fact, have any material impact on the profit-orientation of the companies in question.

[60] The PRI ('principles for responsible investment') describes itself as 'an investor initiative in partnership with [UN Environment Programme] Finance Initiative and UN Global Compact' www.unpri.org/about-us/about-the-pri.

[61] PRI, *Fiduciary Duty in the Twenty-First Century Final Report* (22 October 2019) https://www.unpri.org/investor-duties/fiduciary-duty-in-the-21st-century-final-report/4998.article.

[62] ibid 8.

[63] Larry Fink, 'A Fundamental Reshaping of Finance' (2020 Annual Letter to CEOs) www.blackrock.com/corporate/investor-relations/2020-larry-fink-ceo-letter.

[64] Larry Fink's 2021 Letter to CEOs www.blackrock.com/corporate/investor-relations/2021-larry-fink-ceo-letter. See also Giovanni Strampelli, 'Can BlackRock Save the Planet? The Institutional Investors' Role in Stakeholder Capitalism' (2020–2021) 11 Harvard Business Law Review 1.

[65] Quoted in Isla Binnie, 'BlackRock's Fink Says He's Stopped Using "Weaponised" Term ESG' *Reuters* (26 June 2023) www.reuters.com/business/environment/blackrocks-fink-says-hes-stopped-using-weaponised-term-esg-2023-06-26/.

indices such as the S&P 500, do they have either an obligation or any incentive to use their position as major shareholders to agitate for change or improvement in the corporations in which they invest? What competitive advantage could any such actions have? They hold the same shares as their indexing competitors. They can scarcely gain performance advantages by improving the financial gains of their portfolio investments. Is there some additional basis upon which they might seek to compete which might also explain their support for non-financial ESG metrics?

Barzuza and others[66] have shown that, although index funds are generally passive with respect to traditional performance or accountability-related corporate governance issues, they are highly active with respect to ESG issues. Their explanation for index funds' eagerness to lead on ESG issues is that these index funds are playing the long game; they are essentially courting the good will of the millennial generation knowing that 'in the next two decades, somewhere between $12 trillion and $30 trillion will pass to the millennial generation in what BlackRock CEO Larry Fink has called "the largest transfer of wealth in history"'.[67] Barzuza and others also considered the potential impact of this development on corporate law. Their argument, essentially, is that the matter of whether the corporation ought to take account of social values along with profit-seeking goals should be decided by the shareholder franchise: investors who favour pro social values should feel free to elect directors who share such goals.[68] They consider their approach distinct from an 'other constituency' approach to corporate law because it would, in fact, represent the faithful pursuit of shareholder interests. It would simply (as in the case of the Hart and Zingales approach, discussed in Chapter 7[69]) interpret shareholder interest more broadly than simply an interest in financial gain. Yet, this proposal appears to suffer from the same weakness as the Hart and Zingales model. It undermines one of the fundamental advantages of the modern publicly traded corporation that the shareholder wealth maximization norm facilitates—the ability to trade shares on anonymous exchanges at market-determined prices that do not vary depending on who one's fellow shareholders are or might prove to be.[70]

[66] Michal Barzuza, Quinn Curtis, and David H Webber, 'Shareholder Value(s): Index Fund ESG Activism and the New Millennial Corporate Governance' (2020) 93 Southern California Law Review 1243.

[67] ibid 1249.

[68] ibid 1319.

[69] Oliver Hart and Luigi Zingales, 'Companies Should Maximize Shareholder Welfare Not Market Value' (2017) 2 Journal of Law Finance and Accounting 247.

[70] Ann Lipton, in a review essay on Stephen Bainbridge's book, *The Profit Motive,* offers an intriguing counterpoint. She argues that values or ESG-based investing is valuable precisely because it facilitates

In the end, in any event, financial performance in the business world cannot be too readily disregarded even by the most ardent and committed advocates of socially responsible business. A sobering reminder of this fact came with the 2021 replacement by Danone S.A. of its CEO, Emmanuel Faber, less than a year after he declared to Danone shareholders that they had '[toppled] the statue of Milton Friedman'.[71] Although Faber was replaced by the board of directors, not directly by the shareholders, it was widely reported that the board's action was taken following increased pressure by activist investors, and in reaction to the company's weak sales data, not its failure to achieve ESG goals.

## Proxy Advisory Firms

Much has been written and much more said about the role and influence of proxy advisory firms, private companies providing advice to institutional investors regarding how to vote shares they hold in publicly-traded corporations. Institutional investors in the US first turned to such firms in reaction to a 1988 US Department of Labor (DOL) 'opinion letter' to Avon Products Inc., in which the DOL expressed the view that 'the fiduciary act of managing plan assets which are shares of corporate stock would include the voting of proxies appurtenant to those shares of stock'.[72] Later, in 2003, the US Securities and Exchange Commission promulgated two rules relating to proxy voting by funds, the first requiring funds to publish their votes,[73] and the second requiring investment advisers that had authority to vote proxies on behalf of

the expression of heterogeneous shareholder preferences rather than reinforce the corporate structural features that are traditionally defended on the basis of an assumption of homogeneous shareholder preferences for wealth maximization. Thus, she argues, 'ESG may fracture the unitary vision that has given the corporate form such power. From a shareholder primacist perspective, that is precisely why it should be stamped out; but if one is concerned that the legal technology of the corporation is *too efficient* in overcoming societal guardrails, this is a virtue to be cultivated.' See Ann M Lipton, 'Will the Real Shareholder Primacy Please Stand Up' (2024) 137 Harvard Law Review 1584, 1615.

[71] Editorial, 'Danone is a case study in the pitfalls of purpose; CEO's departure shows need to marry sustainability with profitability' *Financial Times* (19 March 2021) 22. One might also contrast the broad support offered by some managers for non-financial ESG initiatives with Fundsmith's acerbic 2022 observation that: 'A company which feels it has to define the purpose of Hellmann's mayonnaise has in our view clearly lost the plot.' See Fundsmith's 2022 Investor Letter https://d2gr5kl7dt2z3t.cloudfront.net/blog/wp-content/uploads/2022/01/15235630/Fundsmith-Equity-Funds-Q4-2021-Investor-Letter.pdf.

[72] See Federal Register, 'Fiduciary Duties Regarding Proxy Voting and Shareholder Rights: A Proposed Rule by the Employee Benefits Security Administration' (4 September 2020) www.federalregister.gov/documents/2020/09/04/2020-19472/fiduciary-duties-regarding-proxy-voting-and-shareholder-rights.

[73] SEC, 'Disclosure of Proxy Voting Policies and Proxy Voting Records by Registered Management Investment Companies' 68 Fed Reg 6,563 (7 February 2003) 17 CFR §§ 239, 249, 270, 274.

clients to adopt policies and procedures reasonably designed to ensure those votes were cast in the best interests of clients.[74] Institutions seeking to comply with these obligations without incurring the inordinate expense of hiring full-time staff to undertake the necessary voting due diligence with respect to every company in their entire investment portfolios and to avoid conflicts of interest turned to proxy advisory firms for advice, a practice that was effectively endorsed by the SEC in two 'no-action' letters issued in 2004.[75]

Since that time, the power of proxy advisory firms, in particular the two dominant firms in the United States, Institutional Shareholder Services (ISS) and Glass Lewis & Co LLC (Glass Lewis), has been a frequent source of controversy. In 2014, an SEC Staff Legal Bulletin warned investment advisers that retained proxy advisory firms about their ongoing responsibilities to ensure that the proxy advisory firms they retained had the capacity and competence to provide reliable advice and to identify and manage any conflicts of interest.[76] In 2018, the SEC repealed the two no-action letters from 2004 referred to above as it undertook a review of many aspects of the proxy process, including the appropriate role of proxy advisers.[77]

Regulatory interests in proxy advisors is by no means confined to the United States.[78] The reach of proxy advisors is global and the attention of regulators is global as well. However, it is in the United States where there has been perhaps the most notable controversy surrounding the ideological influence of proxy advisors in corporate America. In his 2023 Annual Report to shareholders, for

[74] SEC, 'Registered Management Investment Companies' 68 Fed Reg 6,563 (7 February 2003) 17 CFR §§ 239, 249, 270, 274.

[75] SEC, No-Action Letter, 'Investment Advisers Act of 1940-Rule 206(4)-6 Egan-Jones Proxy Services' (27 May 2004) https://www.sec.gov/divisions/investment/noaction/egan052704.htm; SEC, No-Action Letter, 'Investment Advisers Act of 1940-Rule 206(4)-6 Institutional Shareholder Services, Inc (15 September 2004) https://www.sec.gov/divisions/investment/noaction/iss091504.htm.

[76] SEC, Staff Legal Bulletin No 20 (IM/CF),'Proxy Voting: Proxy Voting Responsibilities of Investment Advisers and Availability of Exemptions from the Proxy Rules for Proxy Advisory Firms' (30 June 2014) https://www.sec.gov/rules-regulations/staff-guidance/staff-legal-bulletins/proxy-voting-proxy-voting-responsibilities-investment-advisers-availability-exemptions-proxy-rules.

[77] SEC, 'Statement Regarding Staff Proxy Advisory Letters' (13 September 2018) https://www.sec.gov/divisions/investment/imannouncements/im-info-2018-02.pdf.

[78] See eg European Securities and Markets Authority (ESMA) and European Banking Authority, *Report: Implementation of SRD2 [the second Shareholders Rights Directive] on Proxy Advisors and the Investment Chain* (27 July 2023) https://www.esma.europa.eu/sites/default/files/2023-07/ESMA32-380-267_Report_on_SRD2.pdf; Best Practice Principles Oversight Committee, *2025 Report.* https://bppgrp.info/wp-content/uploads/2025/11/BPP-Oversight-Committee-2025-Annual-Report.pdf. The Best Practices Principles Group is a collective initiative of major proxy advisory firms formed following the publication in 2013 of ESMA's *Final Report and Feedback Statement on theConsultation Regarding the Role of the Proxy Advisory Industry;* UK *The Proxy Advisors (Shareholders Rights) Regulations 2019,* SI 2019, 926; Australian Government, The Treasury, Consultation Paper, *Greater Transparency of Proxy Advice* (April 2021) https://treasury.gov.au/sites/default/files/2021-04/c2021-169360_consultation_paper.pdf.; Canada, CSA, National Policy 25-201, *Guidance for Proxy Advisory Firms,* (2015), 38 Ontario Securities Commission Bulletin 4121.

example, the CEO of JP Morgan Chase took aim at proxy advisory services in general and at ISS and Glass Lewis in particular. After noting that both of these two dominant firms are foreign owned (ISS by Deutsche Borse, and Glass Lewis by a Canadian firm), the CEO questions 'whether American corporate governance should be determined by for-profit international institutions that may have their own strong feelings about what constitutes good corporate governance.' He then goes on to declare that 'it is increasingly clear that proxy advisors have undue influence.'[79]

Proxy advisory firms regularly issue proxy voting guidelines, indicating how they intend to vote their proxies based on various corporate governance metrics.[80] In addition to these general voting polices, proxy advisory firms may also provide their clients so-called 'customized proxy advice'. Recent research indicates that some 80 per cent of institutional investors receive customized proxy advice and recommendations from proxy advisory firms.[81] Indeed, proxy advisory firm Glass Lewis announced in 2025 that it will cease to issue its standard benchmark voting guidelines as of 2027.[82] To the extent that proxy advisory firms recommend that institutions vote their proxies not only in support of performance-based corporate governance matters but also in accordance with broader CSR or ESG metrics, the corporate 'purpose' may come increasingly to be influenced by the proxy advisers, rather than remain wholly under the control and stewardship of the corporation's directors and officers. The significant influence of proxy advisory services, in particular ISS and, to a lesser extent, Glass Lewis, have attracted the attention of practitioners, academic commentators, and regulators. However, despite the strong claims that have been made about the power wielded by proxy advisory firms, it is not clear how strong the evidence of such power really is.[83] However, it became clear in December 2025 that the President of the United States had determined that the two leading proxy advisory firms wielded considerable influence over the voting practices of institutional shareholders and, in the President's view, too often that influence was being used to promote interests other than increasing investors' financial returns. Accordingly, on December 11 2025, President

[79] JP Morgan Chase Letter from CEO and Chairman to Shareholders, from Annual Report 2023 (April 2024).

[80] See eg ISS Voting Polices (2025) www.issgovernance.com/policy-gateway/voting-policies/; Glass Lewis, Proxy Voting Policies (2025) www.glasslewis.com/policy-guidelines.

[81] Edwin Hu, Nadya Malenko, and Jonathon Zytnick, 'Custom Proxy Voting Advice' ECGI Working Paper Working Paper No 975/2024 (2025).

[82] Glass Lewis, News Release, 'Glass Lewis Leads Change in Proxy Voting Practices' (15 October 2025) https://www.glasslewis.com/news-release/glass-lewis-leads-change-in-proxy-voting-practices.

[83] Stephen Choi, Jill Fisch, and Marcel Kahan, 'The Power of Proxy Advisors: Myth or Reality?' (2010) 59 Emory Law Journal 869.

Trump issued Executive Order 14366, 'Protecting American Investors from Foreign-Owned and Politically-Motivated Proxy Advisors.'[84] The President's Executive Order was unequivocal in its assessment of the role of proxy advisors: they had regularly and, in the President's view, improperly '[used] their substantial power to advance and prioritize radical politically-motivated agendas—like "diversity, equity, and inclusion" and "environmental, social, and governance"—even though *investor returns should be the only priority.*'[85] If proxy advisors and the institutional investors who retain them are indeed constrained directly or indirectly by government regulation to focus upon financial performance alone, how will broader, explicitly pro social mandates be expected to fare in the future?

## Conclusion

The modern role of institutional shareholders and the phenomenon of shareholder activism are significant, still evolving, and have been carefully and methodically studied by others. As Coates has noted: '[t]he channels through which institutions affect public companies have multiplied.'[86] This short chapter has touched only briefly on a few aspects of activism that seem likely to be relevant to the motivation and role of corporate directors in a world in which corporations are increasingly viewed not only as a source of shareholder wealth but also of social duty. The two distinct types of activism—impact or social activism and performance activism—and their aims are frequently difficult or impossible for corporate managers to reconcile.[87]

[84] Exec Order 14366, 90 FR 58503 (16 December 2025).

[85] ibid (emphasis added).

[86] John C Coates IV, 'Thirty Years of Evolution in the Roles of Institutional Investors in Corporate Governance' in Jennifer G Hill and Randall S Thomas (eds), *Research Handbook on Shareholder Power* (Edward Elgar Publishing 2015) 79, 94.

[87] For purposes of the rather broad overview in this chapter, we have avoided delving into technical regulatory matters that affect the ability or incentive for shareholders to influence a corporation's attentiveness to non-financial measures such as, for example, the SEC's updated compliance and disclosure interpretation guidance on Regulation 13-D-G beneficial ownership reporting issued on 11 February 2025. See SEC, Compliance and Disclosure Interpretations, 'Exchange Act Sections 13(d) and 13(g) and Regulation 13D-G Beneficial Ownership Reporting' https://www.sec.gov/rules-regulations/staff-guidance/compliance-disclosure-interpretations/exchange-act-sections-13d-13g-regulation-13d-g-beneficial-ownership-reporting. This new guidance could have the effect of compelling institutions that engage on matters relating to ESG to report on Schedule 13D (the much more detailed form required to be filed by active investors) instead of Schedule 13G (the less extensive form passive investors are permitted to file). In addition, In addition, SEC staff legal bulletin (SLB) 14Mpublished February 12 2025, rescinded previous staff guidance in SLB 14L (from 2021) that had limited the ability of companies to exclude shareholder proposals that raised issues with 'broad societal impact' and so reinstates older SEC guidance that had been repealed by SLB 14L and thus once again makes it easier for

The impact of shareholder activism on corporate performance, whether undertaken by traditional 'long only' institutions such as pension funds or by activist hedge funds, is a complex empirical question. It would not be possible in this brief chapter to propose an answer to the putative value of such activism or even to survey the considerable academic literature surrounding this question. There is a litany of concerns associated with the rise of activist hedge funds in particular, including, among others, that corporations may be pushed by activist hedge funds to de-emphasize long term investments, including in R&D, that they may be incentivized to increase leverage significantly, and that they may be prompted to distribute corporate cash holdings especially in the form of share buy-backs rather than reinvest those earnings. Further, as Coffee and Palia have noted, the potential harms of excessive leverage or distributions at the expense of long-term investment are not limited to firms that are actually the target of activist campaigns but may also be pursued by other firms fearing the possibility of becoming such targets.[88]

Finally, proxy advisory firms have assumed an importantly influential role and the recommendations of proxy advisory firms has also come to include a mix of both performance and social objectives. The prominence of such organizations and the potential impact of their pro social mandates on the financial performance of major American corporations was dramatically spotlighted by President Trump's December 2025 Executive Order purporting to protect American investors from these 'politicall-motivated' firms.

Even as directors and officers of publicly traded corporations struggle to discern how to prioritize the interests of shareholders in seeking to fulfil their fiduciary duties, the interests of those shareholders—as represented by votes cast in person or by proxy—may themselves be an imperfect or even distorted reflection of the preferences of the human beings whose material interests ultimately stand to be affected by the financial performance of the company. If this ambiguity were not enough, managers must also contend with the machinations and manipulations of interests made possible by the modern tools of financial innovation. To that additional complication we turn in Chapter 9.

companies to exclude such proposals. See SEC, 'Shareholder Proposals: Staff Legal Bulletin No. 14M (CF) https://www.sec.gov/about/shareholder-proposals-staff-legal-bulletin-no-14m-cf.

[88] Coffee and Palia (n 46) 552.

# 9
# The Deconstructed Corporation: Financial Innovation and the Clouding of Corporate Duties

## Introduction: Corporate Personality

For centuries, lawyers and judges have conceptualized the corporation invoking the familiar metaphor of an artificial person.[1] This is a synthesizing metaphor. The elaborate processes, complex relationships, and quotidian operations that define the corporation's business and affairs are conveniently bundled for analytical and legal purposes into a simplified, anthropomorphic picture. Out of the many, comes 'the one'.

The legal personality or 'personhood' of the corporation was not always warmly embraced, even before the rise in prominence of the economic 'nexus of contracts' conception of the corporation discussed in Chapter 6. As early as 1910, Woodrow Wilson called upon American lawyers to abandon in certain circumstances 'the fatuous, antiquated and quite unnecessary fiction which treats it as a legal person'.[2] But the entity concept appears to endure in many jurisdictions worldwide,[3] and its utility and versatility seem likely to ensure its continuing survival as a legal artifact and at times a useful, but no longer unrivalled, legal tool.

[1] See eg William Blackstone, *Commentaries on the Laws of England*, vol 1 (The University of Chicago Press 1979, originally published in 1765) 455.

[2] Woodrow Wilson, 'The Lawyer and the Community' (1910) 192 The North American Review 604, 611.

[3] John Armour and others, 'What Is Corporate Law?' in Reinier H Kraakman and others, *Anatomy of Corporate Law* (3rd edn, Oxford University Press 2017) 1, 5.

*Corporate Governance and Enlightened Fiduciaries*. Christopher C. Nicholls, Oxford University Press.
 DOI: 10.1093/9780198904199.003.0009

## From Person to Particles[4] to Precision[5]

In the twentieth and twenty-first centuries, 'financialization' has challenged the boundaries of this synthesizing person metaphor. A growing array of financial contracts have made it possible to unbundle and repackage the aggregation of claims that historically would have been understood to define and constitute the corporation itself. What were once ineluctably intertwined commercial or financial relationships may now be reduced to financial transactions to be packaged, bought, and sold in contractual form on specialized markets like other commodities. Much has been written about the increasing impact of 'financialization' in general, a phenomenon sometimes linked to a rise in the emphasis placed by corporations upon shareholder value.[6] In the context of financial innovation, the notion of financialization has special significance.

Three important conceptual developments provide the background for the unbundling of key corporate functions made possible by modern financial contracting technology. First, at the most general level, increasing financialization of the large business corporation, and the emergence of 'finance capitalism' encouraged characterization of the relationship of shareholders to publicly held corporations as that of (mere) cash flow claimants or passive 'rentiers'[7] rather than as business owners. Secondly, as discussed in Chapter 6, a de-emphasis of the significance of corporate 'personhood' or the concept of the 'corporate entity'[8] in the early twentieth century and the later widespread

[4] The term 'particle finance' is usually attributed to the late Charles S Sanford Jr, formerly chief executive officer (CEO) of Bankers Trust. See Charles S Sanford Jr, 'Financial Markets in 2020' in *Changing Capital Markets: Implications for Monetary Policy*, A Symposium Sponsored by the Federal Reserve Bank of Kansas City (August 1993) 227, 235 ff https://www.kansascityfed.org/Jackson%20Hole/documents/6850/FullPublication_JH93.pdf.

[5] See Alexander S Blum, 'Precision Finance: What It Could Mean for Financial Securities' *Forbes* (5 March 2019). The term 'precision finance' draws on the concept of 'precision medicine'. It has been used by Nobel laureate Robert C Merton to refer to the use of financial engineering to eliminate the adverse 'side-effects' of specific financial investments, while retaining the advantage of those investments. See eg Robert C Merton, 'Financial Engineering and Derivatives to Manage Country Risks and Improve Sovereign Policy Implementation' 8th Lindau Nobel Meeting in Economic Sciences (29 August 2025) https://mediatheque.lindau-nobel.org/recordings/42688.

[6] For a survey of research on financialization see Natascha van der Zwan, 'Making Sense of Financialization' (2014) 12 Socio-Economic Review 99. For a more recent review of the corporate financialization literature see Tobias Klinge, Rodrigo Fernandez, and Manuel B Aalbers, 'Whither Corporate Financialization? A Literature Review' (2021) 15 Geography Compass e12588.

[7] Paddy Ireland, 'Company Law and the Myth of Shareholder Ownership' (1999) 62 Modern Law Review 32.

[8] Morton Horwitz has written that: 'For almost forty years after 1890, American jurists, like their German, French and English counterparts, were preoccupied with the theory of corporate personality.' See Morton J Horwitz, *The Transformation of American Law, 1870-1960: The Crisis of Legal Orthodoxy* (Oxford University Press 1992) 67. Cheffins, and others, have suggested that the early twentieth-century scholarly rumination over the concept of corporate personhood came to an end, thanks, in no small part, to John Dewey's influential 1926 article, 'The Historic Background of Corporate Legal

adoption by corporate law scholars of the contractarian or 'nexus of contracts'[9] theory of the firm facilitated a view of the corporation as an instrumental bundle of contractual relationships among transient interest holders rather than a stable, monolithic entity. Although many of the specific implications of that theory have subsequently been questioned doubted by a number of scholars,[10] the functional characterization of the corporation as a bundle of contracts remains a powerful theme in economic analyses of the corporation. Finally, in 1972, Black and Scholes's rightly famous option pricing formula introduced, together with their eponymous option pricing model, the concept of contingent claims analysis, a way of formally modelling corporate equity and debt claims as financial contracts—specifically, options[11]—challenging traditional perspectives of 'ownership' in the corporate context and paving the way to conceptualize virtually any financial asset—including a corporate share—as a financial derivative contract.

## Financial Innovation and Shareholder Primacy

For reasons canvassed in Chapter 5, I am somewhat sceptical about the frequently repeated claims that business corporations in the early post-Second World War period were predominantly characterized by a pro-social managerial paternalism. However, there can be no doubt that a shift did occur at least in the corporate rhetoric beginning sometime in the 1970s or early 1980s marked by the explicit, unapologetic adoption by many major corporations in the United States of a shareholder wealth maximization goal. Many explanations for this development have been offered. Brian Cheffins, for example, has pointed to the political turmoil and macroeconomic challenges in the United States that created the conditions for the American electorate's conservative

Personality' (1926) 35 Yale Law Journal 655. See Brian R Cheffins, 'The Trajectory of (Corporate Law) Scholarship' (2004) 63 Cambridge Law Journal 456, 479.

9 See Michael Jensen and William Meckling, 'Theory of the Firm: Managerial Behavior, Agency Costs and Ownership Structure' (1976) 3 Journal of Financial Economics 305. Roberta Romano has described the development of agency costs theory as one of the 'two lines of development [in the economics research agenda that] have had a lasting impact on the thinking of corporate law academics'. Roberta Romano, 'After the Revolution in Corporate Law' (2005) 55 Journal of Legal Education 342, 347.

10 See eg Michael Klausner, 'The Contractarian Theory of Corporate Law: A Generation Later' (2006) 31 The Journal of Corporation Law 779, 781.

11 Fischer Black and Myron Scholes, 'The Pricing of Options and Corporate Liabilities' (1973) 81 Journal of Political Economy 637, 649 ff.

turn and the 1980 election of Ronald Reagan as president.[12] Martin Gelter has suggested that the shift from defined benefit to defined contribution pension plans triggered by the enactment of the Employment Retirement Income Security Act of 1974 (ERISA) was a significant, if not the most significant, contributor to the adoption by American corporations of an express shareholder value (or shareholder wealth maximization) norm.[13] Other explanations, of varying degrees of plausibility, have also been proffered both by those who support shareholder primacy on ideological grounds and by those who abhor it.

As discussed in earlier chapters, there were certainly many contemporary hints that unabashedly pro-profit conservative voices were arising in America in the 1970s in an apparent backlash to a perceived wave of progressivism seen in some conservative circles as the leading edge of a dangerous move towards socialism. Thus, for example, in Lewis Powell's confidential 1971 memo to the Chair of the Education Committee of the US Chamber of Commerce,[14] the soon-to-be appointed Supreme Court Justice declared that: 'No thoughtful person can question that the American economic system is under attack.'[15] The sources of the attacks on the free enterprise system, according to Powell, 'include, not unexpectedly, the Communists, New Leftists and other revolutionaries who would destroy the entire system, both political and economic.'[16]

As we have seen in Chapters 4 and 5, the economists' view of the centrality to the corporate mission of increasing (if not necessarily maximizing) either profit or share value has not significantly wavered in more than a century. It is corporate law, of course—embodied both in statutory provisions and in judicial decisions—that defines and is 'constitutive'[17] of the business corporation in every jurisdiction in which that form of organization exists,[18] and delimits

[12] Brian Cheffins, *Advanced Introduction to Corporate Governance Law and Regulation* (Edward Elgar Publishing 2024) 4.

[13] Martin Gelter, 'The Pension System and the Rise of Shareholder Primacy' (2013) 43 Seton Hall Law Review 909. The shift from defined benefit to defined contribution pension plans has been linked materially to the enactment of the Employee Retirement Income Security Act of 1974 ('ERISA') Pub L 93-406. Among other things, the ERISA introduced a number of regulatory burdens on the sponsors of defined benefit pension plans including minimum funding rules and requirements to pay premiums to the Pension Benefit Guaranty Corporation. See Edward A Zelinksy, 'The Defined Contribution Paradigm' (2004) 114 Yale Law Journal 451, 469 ff.

[14] Lewis F Powell Jr, 'The Memo' (1971) *Powell Memorandum: Attack On American Free Enterprise System*, 1 https://scholarlycommons.law.wlu.edu/powellmemo/1.

[15] ibid.

[16] ibid 2.

[17] See eg Katharina Pistor, 'A Legal Theory of Finance' (2013) 41 Journal of Comparative Economics 315.

[18] One may say the law is formally constitutive of the corporation without concluding that the corporation owes its existence to a state concession or franchise. The concession issue involves very different considerations. See eg Paul G Mahoney, 'Contract or Concession?: An Essay on the History of Corporate Law' (2000) 34 Georgia Law Review 873.

fundamental elements of its business and affairs. And Roberta Romano has demonstrated how the convergence of economic theory reinvigorating legal scholarship and an unprecedented wave in the 1980s of novel corporate transactions (namely, hostile takeovers) prompted American courts to look to economic theory to illuminate the analysis of directors' duties under these novel circumstances.[19]

This same period also coincided with the beginning of an era of explosive growth in financial innovation. This concurrent development had an impact both on the theoretical conception of the firm and the practical implementation of financial technologies that challenged traditional understandings of the corporation and its relationship to shareholders.

The rapid explosion of financial innovation is usually thought to have been ignited in the early 1970s. A link has been drawn between the escalating pace of financial innovation at that time and specific concurrent changes in markets, technology, regulation, and financial theory.[20]

President Nixon's dramatic decision on 15 August 1971 to halt the convertibility of the US dollar to gold effectively marked the end of the era of relatively stable international currency exchange rates that had been established by the Bretton Woods Agreement.[21] One result of Nixon's decision (which had reportedly been made 'with strong prodding from academic economists, notably Milton Friedman'[22]) was that international currency exchange rates became much less stable. Because of the link between currency exchange rates and interest rates in currency markets,[23] among other things, interest rates also became much more volatile. Businesses now faced significant financial risks from which they had largely been spared during the Bretton Woods era of fixed currency exchange rates.

[19] Romano (n 9).

[20] See eg James C Van Horne, 'Of Financial Innovation and Excesses' (1985) 40(3) Journal of Finance 620, 622; William L Silber, 'The Process of Financial Innovation' (1983) 73 American Economic Review 89. Silber, in particular, stresses the idea that financial innovations would be likely to arise in response to sustained external conditions that increased the constraints under which firms were operating in pursuit of maximizing their utility. The reason Silber argued that such external conditions must be sustained to induce financial innovation was the recognition that innovation was costly and so would not be pursued in response to transitory conditions.

[21] See 'Nixon and the End of the Bretton Woods System 1971-1973' US Department of State, Office of the Historian https://history.state.gov/milestones/1969-1976/nixon-shock. Under the Bretton Woods system, member countries agreed to peg their currencies to the US dollar. The United States, separately, made the US dollar convertible into gold at a price of US$35 per ounce. The obligation of participants to maintain fixed exchange rates was contained in Article IV of the original 22 July 1944 version of the Articles of Agreement of the International Monetary Fund https://www.elibrary.imf.org/display/book/9781451972511/ch008.xml.

[22] Merton H Miller, 'Financial Innovation: Achievements and Prospects' (1992) 4 Journal of Applied Corporate Finance 4.

[23] See eg Ian H Giddy, *Global Financial Markets* (DC Heath and Company 1993) 60–65.

Other major macroeconomic events added to uncertainty and price volatility in world commodities markets. In particular, in October 1973, members of the Organization of Petroleum Exporting Countries (OPEC) announced a cut to oil production and a limit of exports, in particular to the United States. This prompted the US government to introduce a series of restrictions and reductions in oil use (and a planned rationing program) which culminated in a disruptive 'energy crisis'.[24] Crude oil prices surged from roughly US$4.31 per barrel in September 1973 to US$10.11 per barrel by September 1974,[25] with corresponding jumps in consumer prices for petroleum products such as gasoline.

These unusual and unprecedented shocks to financial and commodities markets stimulated demand on the part of many corporations for innovative financial risk management products such as futures, forwards, options, and swaps.[26]

Many of these risk management contracts, or financial derivatives,[27] had (with the exception of swaps[28]) existed for years, in some cases, for millennia.[29] However, the markets for such instruments had always been limited by the practical need for rare and specialized trader knowledge and valuation complexity and uncertainty. Several concurrent developments addressed these limitations:[30] advances in computing technology, improvements in communications, and breakthroughs in financial economic theory, in particular the

[24] See President Richard Nixon, 'Address to the Nation About Policies to Deal with the Energy Shortages' (7 November 1973) https://www.presidency.ucsb.edu/documents/address-the-nation-about-policies-deal-with-the-energy-shortages.

[25] The prices referred to here were for West Texas Intermediate Crude Oil. See 'Crude Oil Prices 1946 to 2025' https://www.macrotrends.net/1369/crude-oil-price-history-chart.

[26] For an overview of these basic derivative contracts see Christopher C Nicholls, *Corporate Finance and Canadian Law* (2nd edn, Carswell 2013) 253–72.

[27] The term 'derivative' refers to financial contracts that 'derive' their value from some other underlying asset or index. So, for example, an option to purchase shares, or a call option, derives its value from the value of the underlying share.

[28] Swaps are usually thought to have originated in the 1970s in Great Britain, developing from back-to-back loan transactions that were used to facilitate foreign investment at a time of currency controls. The first formal swap agreement is usually said to be a 1981 transaction between IBM and the World Bank. See GMS Hammond, 'Recent Developments in the Swaps Market' Bank of England Quarterly Bulletin 1987, 66 https://www.bankofengland.co.uk/-/media/boe/files/quarterly-bulletin/1987/recent-developments-in-the-swap-market.pdf.

[29] It is often suggested that Aristotle's story of the philosopher Thales of Miletus, who supposedly 'cornered' olive presses, is an illustration of an ingenious use of options more than 2,000 years ago. See eg Mihir A Desai, *The Wisdom of Finance* (Houghton Mifflin Harcourt 2017) 42–43, citing Aristotle, *Politics*, vol 1 (H Rackham tr, Harvard University Press 1944) Bk 1.

[30] Scott Mason and others, *Cases in Financial Engineering* (Prentice Hall 1995) 51. Van Horne credits the burgeoning academic work in that period in the fields of 'asset pricing, options, interest rates, futures markets, and derivative securities' along with the increasing number of MBA students studying finance with increasing the receptivity of the financial community to increasing innovation. Van Horne (n 20) 624.

publication of the Black–Scholes (Merton) option pricing model.[31] The launch of the Chicago Board Options Exchange in April of 1973 was also no doubt an important catalyst for the rapid expansion of the derivatives industry, an event that occurred as the US equity markets were entering what would prove to be a period of dismal performance. The value of the S&P 500 index, for example, fell almost 33 per cent from April 1973 to August 1974.[32]

There is a voluminous financial economic literature on financial innovation: its meaning,[33] its history,[34] its mechanisms,[35] its practical applications,[36] appropriate frameworks for its regulation,[37] whether it is (or could be) socially valuable,[38] or whether it is merely rent-seeking[39] and a source of dangerous financial market fragility.[40] Since the Global Financial Crisis (GFC) of

[31] Black and Scholes (n 11); Robert C Merton, 'Theory of Rational Option Pricing' (1973) 4 Bell Journal of Economics and Management Science 141. Scholes and Merton were honoured with the 1997 Nobel Prize in Economics 'for a new method to determine the value of derivatives'. See https://www.nobelprize.org/prizes/economic-sciences/1997/press-release/. Fischer Black had, regrettably, died in 1995 and the Nobel Prize is not awarded posthumously. Though the option pricing model they developed is generally called the 'Black-Scholes Option Pricing Model', many financial economists also refer to it as the Black-Scholes (Merton) Option Pricing Model, in recognition of the important contribution to the model made by Robert C Merton. Merton's influence in the development of the final derivation of the model was explained by Fischer Black in 'How We Came Up with the Option Formula' (1989) 15 The Journal of Portfolio Management 4; and in 1988 Black said of Merton's contribution, 'Bob gave us that [arbitrage argument for deriving the formula.] It should probably be called the Black-Merton-Scholes paper.' Fischer Black, quoted in Peter L Bernstein, *Capital Ideas* (The Free Press 1992), 223.

[32] See S&P 500 100 Year Historical Chart and Data https://www.macrotrends.net/datasets/2324/sp-500-historical-chart-data.

[33] See eg Peter Tufano, 'Financial Innovation' in George M Constantinides and others, *Handbook of the Economics of Finance*, vol 1A: *Corporate Finance* (Elsevier 2003) 307, 310 ff.

[34] Peter Tufano, 'Securities Innovations: A Historical and Functional Perspective' (1995) 7 Journal of Applied Corporate Finance 90; Merton H Miller, 'Financial Innovation: The Last Twenty Years and the Next' (1986) Journal of Financial and Quantitative Analysis 459.

[35] Robert C Merton and Zvi Bodie, 'A Conceptual Framework for Analysing the Financial Environment' in Dwight Crane and others, *The Global Financial System* (Harvard Business School Press 1995) 3, 20 ff.

[36] See eg Josh Lerner and others, 'Financial Innovation in the Twenty-First Century: Evidence from US Patents' (2024) 132(5) Journal of Political Economy 1391; John D Finnerty, 'Financial Engineering in Corporate Finance: An Overview' (1988)17(4) Financial Management 14.

[37] See eg Dan Awrey, 'Regulating Financial Innovation: A More Principles-Based Approach' (2011) 5(2) Brooklyn Journal of Corporate, Financial and Commercial Law 273; Eric A Posner and E Glen Weyl, 'An FDA for Financial Innovation: Applying the Insurable Interest Doctrine to Twenty-First Century Financial Markets' (2013) 107 Northwestern University Law Review 1307.

[38] See eg Robert J Shiller, *The New Financial Order: Risk in the 21st Century* (Princeton University Press 2003); Boris Vallee, 'The Power of Financial Innovation' (2024) https://papers.ssrn.com/sol3/papers.cfm?abstract_id=4741077.

[39] Paul Volcker, former chair of the Federal Reserve, once wrote: 'I cannot detect any connection between the enormous development of the financial markets in the past ten years and the economy's performance', and recounted a conversation he had had with an unnamed Nobel-prize winning financial economist who, he claimed, conceded that financial engineering did nothing for productivity but merely 'moves around the rents in the financial markets and, intellectually, it's a lot of fun'. See Paul A Volcker, 'Keynote Address: The Financial Crisis in Perspective' in Roger B Porter and others (eds), *New Directions in Financial Services Regulation* (MIT Press 2011) 201, 207.

[40] Nicola Gennaoili, Andrei Shleifer, and Robert Vishny, 'Neglected Risks, Financial Innovation and Financial Fragility' (2012) 104 Journal of Financial Economics 452; Anjan V Thakor, 'Incentives to Innovate and Financial Crises' (2012) 103 Journal of Financial Economics 130.

2007–2009, the interest of lawyers and legal scholars in the innovative financial instruments which became the subject of scrutiny during the crisis[41] significantly increased. (If 'War is God's way of teaching Americans geography',[42] then, as I have mused elsewhere, perhaps a financial crisis is the devil's way of teaching lawyers economics.)

Although the cause of the GFC remains the subject of considerable debate,[43] there is little disagreement that at least two key innovative financial devices—securitization and credit default swaps—played particularly important roles. These techniques at their core involve, in one case (securitization), isolating and permitting investment in the cash flows of specific corporate assets (rather than an investment in the corporation as an integrated entity)[44] and, in the other (credit default swaps), allowing parties to acquire synthetic credit exposure to corporate debt instruments without, in fact, owning those instruments.[45] The proliferation of financial derivatives more generally has also attracted some share of the blame for the GFC. Accordingly, there has been a substantial body of academic, professional, and popular commentary denouncing financial innovation and the financial engineers responsible, and more broadly probing the implications of the financialization of the modern corporation.[46] Some have criticized use of innovative financial instruments for

[41] Financial Crisis Inquiry Commission, *The Financial Crisis Inquiry Report* (Public Affairs 2011) chs 3, 8.

[42] The provenance of this humorous quotation is uncertain. As noted in Christopher C Nicholls, 'Open Banking and the Rise of FinTech: Innovation, Finance, and Functional Regulation' (2019) 35 Banking and Finance Law Review 121, 141 n, the quotation is frequently ascribed to American writer Ambrose Bierce. However, Bierce scholars have maintained that it is not found in his extant written works. A report of a comic performance in 1987 credits comedian Paul Rodriguez with a very similar line, 'War is God's way of teaching us geography', quoted in Lawrence Christon, 'Comic Relief: An HBO Tradition' *Los Angeles Times* (16 November 1987) G1, G7. However, similar phrases long predate Rodriguez. See eg 'Editorial Statecraft', *Chicago Daily Tribune* (22 March 1915) A4: 'If the European war is teaching Americans geography, it is also sprinkling our thought with picturesque dashes of European history and politics.' Mr Rodriguez, in correspondence with the author, indicates that he first used his version of the line on the Tonight Show in 1986 after returning from a USO show in Eastern Europe, but that he 'really [loses] no sleep over who thought this up first' (email correspondence from Paul Rodriguez, 18 November 2013, on file with author).

[43] The bipartisan Financial Crisis Inquiry Commission, for example (n 41), was unable to arrive at a bipartisan conclusion, with four members of the ten member panel dissenting from the final report, and offering two dissenting statements.

[44] For a more complete explanation of securitization see Nicholls (n 26) ch 7.

[45] For an explanation of credit default swaps see Donald A Bendernagel, 'Common Derivatives and their Uses: Credit Derivatives' in Practising Law Institute, *Swaps and Other Derivatives in 2006* (PLI 2006) 85.

[46] Paddy Ireland, 'Financialization and Corporate Governance' (2009) 60 Northern Ireland Legal Quarterly 1. Ireland has decried what he has called the 'deeply dysfunctional nature of the highly financialized corporate culture', and asserts that: 'American corporate governance in particular, is in need of radical rather than ameliorative reform.' Ireland's objection to financialization relates to the broader and more familiar debate between those who insist that the corporation's primary (or exclusive) mission is to serve the interests of its shareholders, and those who argue, instead, that the corporation is obliged to pursue broader social goals. He links the increasing financialization of the corporation

their excessive complexity[47] and resulting opacity,[48] their inherent fragility,[49] their socially undesirable use as mere instruments of speculation, gambling,[50] or rent shifting,[51] and their distortive effect on shareholder voting[52] and bankruptcy resolution.[53] It is often suggested that legislators and regulators, subject to unwise or perhaps reckless deregulatory impulses beginning in the 1980s, unwound previously protective legislation and so spawned a destructive proliferation of financial innovation that caused or at least exacerbated the financial crisis,[54] although this deregulatory narrative has been strongly challenged by some scholars.[55]

It is beyond the scope of this chapter to assess the relative merits or demerits of innovation within the financial sector, either before, during, or after the GFC. It must be observed, however, that despite the criticism levelled against many specific financial techniques associated with the GFC—including the use of asset securitization[56] and over-the-counter (OTC) derivatives—those

beginning in the early part of the twentieth century with a recognition that the logic underpinning the corporate mission had changed. If shareholders were no longer true 'owners' in a meaningful sense, then corporate managers should not be serving their interests alone. To do so, would be to substitute the production of mere money for the production of better goods and services for the betterment of society. Ireland cites, among others, Keynes, who argued that there was 'no clear evidence from experience that the investment policy which is socially advantageous coincides with that which is most profitable'. See ibid 14, quoting Keynes.

[47] See Dan Awrey, 'Complexity, Innovation and the Regulation of Modern Financial Markets' (2012) 2 Harvard Business Law Review 235, 238, arguing that 'conventional financial theory failed to adequately account for both the complexity of modern financial markets and the nature and pace of financial innovation'.

[48] Henry TC Hu, 'Too Complex to Depict? Innovation, "Pure Information" and the SEC Disclosure Paradigm' (2012) 90 Texas Law Review 1601.

[49] Gennaoili, Shleifer, and Vishny (n 40).

[50] Lynn A Stout, 'Derivatives and the Legal Origins of the 2008 Credit Crisis' (2011) 30(12) Banking and Financial Services Policy Report 13, 15. Interestingly, Donald Mackenzie has indicated that the introduction of sophisticated mathematical pricing models, notably the Black–Scholes option pricing model, was used by participants in derivatives markets to legitimize their activities and distinguish them from mere gambling. See Donald Mackenzie, *An Engine Not a Camera: How Financial Models Shape Markets* (MIT Press 2006).

[51] Volcker (n 39).

[52] See Henry TC Hu and Bernard S Black, 'Hedge Funds, Insiders and the Decoupling of Economic and Voting Ownership: Empty Voting and Hidden (Morphable) Ownership' (2007) Journal of Corporate Finance 343; Henry TC Hu and Bernard S Black, 'The New Vote Buying: Empty Voting and Hidden (Morphable) Ownership' (2006) 79 Southern California Law Review 811; Henry TC Hu and Bernard S Black, 'Equity and Debt Decoupling and Empty Voting II: Importance and Extensions' (2008) 156 University of Pennsylvania Law Review 625.

[53] Douglas G Baird and Robert K Rasmussen, 'Anti-Bankruptcy' (2010) 119 Yale Law Journal 648. See also Michael Frierman and PV Viswanath, 'Agency Problems of Debt, Convertible Securities and Deviations from Absolute Priority in Bankruptcy' (1994) 37 Journal of Law and Economics 455.

[54] See eg Financial Crisis Inquiry Commission (n 41) ch 4.

[55] See eg Paul G Mahoney, 'Deregulation and the Subprime Crisis' (2018) 104 Virginia Law Review 235.

[56] The securitization market experienced, in the words of Gorton and Metrick, 'decimation during the financial crisis'. See Gary Gorton and Andrew Metrick, 'Securitisation' in George M Constantinides and others, *Handbook of the Economics of Finance*, vol 2A (Elsevier 2013) 60. However, within just a

techniques survive and continue to be widely used.[57] Although some have argued that the GFC provides evidence that even sophisticated market players may somehow be duped into using dangerous financial instruments and financial models they do not fully understand, it is not tenable to suggest that instruments that have continued to thrive following the harrowing but undoubtedly edifying experience of the GFC—and that today constitute multi-trillion-dollar markets—are not somehow fulfilling genuinely important business needs.

Advances in finance and financial engineering would also come to have an important impact on corporate law and corporate legal theory. As Roberta Romano has observed, it was in 1972 that law professors Victor Brudney and Marvin Chirelstein published their innovative law school casebook, *Corporate Finance Cases and Materials*.[58] The book was unusual because, instead of restricting themselves to the explication and analysis of the somewhat tedious details of trust indentures and preferred share conditions, the authors chose to introduce their law school readers to the world of modern financial theory in a legal context. Their rationale was that, through their experience in teaching corporate finance law, they had come to the conclusion that it was 'increasingly difficult to consider the policy and probable effect of legal constraints without a systematic understanding . . . of why a corporation or an investor chooses a particular course of action'.[59] In particular, their book emphasized the importance of valuation of corporations and of corporate securities, a theme, they explained, 'that pervades and loosely unifies'[60] the materials presented in their book.

The 'proper goals of the large, publicly-held, professionally managed corporation', Brudney and Chirelstein told their readers, 'have been debated by social theorists for many years'.[61] Yet, they seemed to entertain no serious doubt

few years of the crisis, the continuing importance of the securitization market was still widely recognized. See eg Hans J Blommestein, Ahmet Keskinler, and Carrick Lucas, 'Outlook for the Securitisation Market' (2001) 1 OECD Journal: Financial Market Trends 259, 261: '[i]t seems likely that in the long run, structured-finance securitization will once again become an important channel for debt markets.'

[57] The Bank for International Settlements, for example, notes that, as of the end of June 2024, the total outstanding notional principal of over-the-counter derivatives worldwide significantly exceeded US $600 trillion. See BIS OTC Derivatives Statistics at End June 2024, 5 https://www.bis.org/publ/otc_hy2411.pdf. According to Data Horizzon research: 'The asset securitization market is valued at USD 2.45 trillion in 2024 and is anticipated to reach around USD 4.82 trillion by 2033' https://datahorizzonresearch.com/asset-securitization-market-42493

[58] Victor Brudney and Marvin A Chirelstein, *Corporate Finance Cases and Materials* (The Foundation Press 1972).

[59] ibid xv.

[60] ibid 1.

[61] ibid.

about the goal of investors and, accordingly, about the goal those investors expect corporations to pursue: 'It is to maximize the value of the corporation to its stockholders, subject to whatever constraints may be imposed by law and public policy.'[62]

Thus, four years before Jensen and Meckling's agency costs paper, discussed in Chapter 6, and with no mention of Milton Friedman to be found, these two eminent legal authors recognized that the conventional goal of corporate managers should be presumed to be the maximization of the value of the corporation for the benefit of their shareholders. Brudney and Chirelstein do include, however, some qualifying language not only suggesting that it is not clear that managers always actually pursue this goal but also acknowledging that 'a substantial body of opinion supports a contrary assumption'.[63]

The financial derivatives created in the 1970s and 1980s were principally marketed as tools for hedging risk. But these same financial products also allowed corporations not simply to hedge but also to acquire specific risks they were willing to bear, and to leverage their exposure to risky positions in ways that could be impossibly difficult to finance otherwise.[64]

Financial innovations of this period performed another role as well. They dramatically increased the power of the markets to discipline corporations more frequently and more aggressively than had been possible in earlier eras. In particular, the development of a large market for original issue high-yield bonds (the instruments colloquially dubbed 'junk bonds') made it possible for 'raiders' to acquire, or threaten to acquire, virtually any corporation regardless of size. Historically, junk bonds (that is, bonds with a below (or significantly below)-investment-grade credit rating from the major credit rating agencies such as S&P and Moody's) had consisted mainly of debt instruments originally issued as investment-grade bonds. Such bonds became 'junk' only some time later when the issuing corporations suffered financial setbacks that reduced their creditworthiness and so prompted the rating agencies to downgrade their outstanding debt instruments. Junk bonds of this sort were thus colourfully

[62] ibid.

[63] ibid 1–2.

[64] Embedded leverage characterizes many common financial derivatives. For example, as Merton has demonstrated, a levered position (that is, a position financed by debt) in all of the stocks comprising the Standard & Poor's 500 index could be replicated in a number of different ways without, in fact, borrowing any money in a number of different ways using derivatives contracts such as a futures contract on the S&P 500 or by simultaneously buying call options and selling put options on the S&P 500. These alternative derivative positions would behave economically in the same way as a leveraged position in the stock, although for legal, tax, and other purposes they could be treated very differently. See Robert C Merton, 'Financial Innovation and the Management and Regulation of Financial Institutions' (1995) 19 Journal of Banking & Finance 461, 474.

referred to as 'fallen angels'. (There were some bonds, however, even decades before the 1970s 'junk bond era', that were originally issued as high-risk, high-yield bonds.)[65]

In the mid-twentieth century, several financial market watchers and participants, including, in particular, W. Braddock Hickman, discovered that, in fact, junk bonds actually tended to outperform investment grade bonds over time on a risk-adjusted basis.[66] As an MBA student in the late 1960s, Michael Milken, whose name would later become synonymous with the junk bond market,[67] became aware of Hickman's work and undertook research that built on Hickman's insights.[68] After joining the investment firm that would become Drexel Burnham Lambert, Milken began applying his research to the development of an original issue junk bond market.[69]

The first Drexel issue of an original issue high-yield (junk) bond occurred in 1977.[70] The market rapidly evolved. Beginning some time in 1984,[71] junk bonds began to be used to finance takeovers—including some notable leveraged buy-outs (LBOs) and hostile takeovers.[72] The LBO takeover technique involved financing a proposed corporate acquisition using the assets of the target company itself to secure the acquisition financing (rather like a home mortgage, in which the house being acquired becomes the asset against which the prospective home buyer's mortgage loan comes to be secured). This new financing tool, adapted to implementation of the LBO technique, made possible credible takeover offers for even the largest firms. The implications were dramatic. Suddenly, the theoretical role of disciplining managers through the

[65] See Peter F Basile and others, 'Toward a History of the Junk Bond Market, 1910-1955' NBER Working Paper No 21559 (2015) 3 http://www.nber.org/papers/w21559.

[66] See, in particular, W Braddock Hickman, *Corporate Bond Quality and Investor Experience* (Princeton University Press 1958).

[67] Michael Milken was convicted of securities fraud in 1990 but was eventually pardoned by President Trump in February 2020. See 'Statement from the Press Secretary Regarding Executive Grants of Clemency' (18 February 2020). For a provocative and highly critical account of Milken's prosecution see Daniel R Fischel, *Payback: The Conspiracy to Destroy Michael Milken and His Financial Revolution* (Harper Business 1995).

[68] Glenn Yago, *Junk Bonds: How High Yield Bonds Restructured Corporate America* (Oxford University Press 1991) 20.

[69] For a discussion of Milken and the junk bond market see William W Bratton and Adam J Levitin, 'A Transactional Genealogy of Scandal: From Michael Milken to Enron to Goldman Sachs' (2013) 86 Southern California Law Review 783.

[70] Yago (n 68) 23.

[71] *Corporate Mergers and High Yield (Junk) Bonds: Recent Market Trends and Regulatory Developments: A Report*, prepared by the Congressional Research Service for the Use of the Subcommittee on Telecommunications, Consumer Protection, and Finance of the Committee on Energy and Commerce (US House of Representatives US GPO 1986) 4.

[72] One of the largest, and most notable, deals of the era involved the leveraged buy-out of RJR Nabisco. For a popular account of the RJR Nabisco transaction see Bryan Burrough and John Helyar, *Barbarians at the Gate: The Fall of RJR Nabisco* (Harper & Row 1990).

threat of acquisition—or 'the market for corporate control'—that had been identified two decades earlier by Robin Marris[73] and by Henry Manne[74] had become a very practical, very powerful reality. The impact on the management of large American corporations was profound. Within a few years, Macey and Miller were able to declare that 'the market for corporate control lies at the heart of the American system of corporate governance'.[75]

The growth of the junk bond market in the 1980s and the proliferation of takeovers also had another salutary effect. As Holmström and Kaplan have argued, takeovers of this era readily facilitated the shifting of capital 'from declining industries to emerging industries',[76] a process, they suggest, at which 'markets are more effective than managers'[77] of firms.

Disruptive change predictably encounters resistance. As intra-corporate relationships were reordered in an increasingly financialized environment, there were understandable calls for a return to what were perceived to be more traditional and benign business relationships, governance structures, and commercial values. Occasionally, opponents of change single out for particularly trenchant criticism the innovations that have made transformative changes possible. Such criticism of the 'newest financial thing' became especially salient and intuitively appealing in light of the GFC. Robert Shiller has suggested that there is a human inclination to blame recent financial technology for crises: 'People seem to want to return to their moral roots after a crisis, and that seems to imply, to a certain extent, a return to old ways of doing things'.[78] Financial markets and products that existed before the GFCs, thus, remained safe and acceptable—no populist attack, for example, was ever launched insisting that all markets should be shut down because of the financial crisis. However, as Shiller puts it, 'progress has to stop there'.[79]

Even some of the most thoughtful and carefully reasoned contributions to recent corporate law and governance debates occasionally exhibit hints of such a nostalgic longing for a kinder and gentler (if romanticized) past, when corporations were thought to be benign and respectful lifetime employers,

[73] Robin Marris, 'A Model of the Managerial Enterprise' (1963) 77 Quarterly Journal of Economics 185, 205.

[74] Henry G Manne, 'Mergers and the Market for Corporate Control' (1965) 73 Journal of Political Economy 110.

[75] Jonathan R Macey and Geoffrey P Miller, 'Corporate Governance and Commercial Banking: A Comparative Examination of Germany, Japan, and the United States' (1995) 48 Stanford Law Review 73.

[76] Bengt Holmström and Steven N Kaplan, 'Corporate Governance and Merger Activity in the United States: Making Sense of the 1980s and 1990s' (2001) 15 Journal of Economic Perspectives 121, 137.

[77] ibid 137.

[78] Robert J Shiller, *Finance and the Good Society* (Princeton University Press 2012) 63.

[79] ibid.

reliable producers of top quality goods and services, honourable borrowers, attentive stewards of the needs of the community, and committed to offering investors a 'fair and reasonable' (although not necessarily a maximum) financial return. These idealized avuncular managers of the corporations of yesteryear, it is presumed, were not hostages to the destructive pressure of shareholder-driven 'short-termism'. They were equally free from the supposedly unreasonable and avaricious demands of predatory acquirors and selfish activist shareholders willing to shamelessly manipulate corporate voting mechanisms through incomprehensible financial legerdemain, looking to make a 'fast buck', all the while callously indifferent to the long-term costs their insatiable greed would impose upon employees, creditors, the community, and the spotted owl.

This distorted caricature, of course, unfairly characterizes the many sophisticated, thoughtful, and constructive contributions many leading scholars have made to our understanding of corporate social responsibility, the proper goal of the corporation, the perceived dangers of corporate 'short-termism',[80] the proper role of corporate directors of a company subject to a contested control transaction,[81] and the corporate governance impact of activist financial investors such as hedge funds.[82]

The principal point for our purposes is neither to celebrate nor decry the impact of financial innovation that began in the latter decades of the twentieth century. It is only to note that, as it became increasingly possible and at times commercially desirable, to deconstruct or unbundle corporate financial interests, the distinction between intra-firm relationships and market transactions frequently became difficult to draw. From an economic perspective this difficulty may not have been regarded as important. But from a legal perspective it could be highly significant. The parties to market transactions are assumed to act in their own individual interests; they are subject to no fiduciary obligations towards their counterparties nor do they have any expectation that their counterparties owe such duties to them. But within the corporation, matters are very different. The legal duties of directors and officers must be first order considerations.

[80] For a few examples of the extensive literature on the alleged dangers of corporate short-term thinking, see the sources cited in Chapter 7, n 4.

[81] See eg Christopher C Nicholls, *Mergers, Acquisitions and Other Changes of Corporate Control* (3nd edn, Irwin 2020) 244 ff.

[82] See eg John Armour and Brian Cheffins, 'The Rise and Fall(?) of Shareholder Activism by Hedge Funds' (Winter 2012) The Journal of Alternative Investments 17; Stuart L Gillan and Laura T Starks, 'The Evolution of Shareholder Activism in the United States' (2007) 19 Journal of Applied Corporate Finance 1. See also the discussion of this issue in Chapter 8.

## Black–Scholes–Merton and Contingent Claims Analysis

There are two distinct aspects to the deconstruction of the corporate entity into a set of disparate financial claims: one is conceptual, the other practical. The conceptual aspect originates in an insight contained in the original Black–Scholes option pricing paper itself.[83] After deriving their option pricing formula, Black and Scholes go on to observe that: '[i]t is not generally realized that corporate liabilities other than warrants may be viewed as options.'[84] They then proceed to demonstrate how, economically, the shareholders of a corporation that also has outstanding debt 'have the equivalent of an option on their company's assets. In effect, the bondholders own the company's assets but they have given options to the stockholders to buy the assets back.'[85]

In the context of the Black–Scholes article itself, this observation is significant because it indicates how their pricing formula—derived with respect to a specific financial contract—can actually be applied more broadly to the valuation of a much wider range of financial claims. In the corporate law context, however, their suggestion that bondholders could be characterized economically as the owners of a company's assets, rather than shareholders, has been seized upon by some opponents of the shareholder primacy norm as further evidence (if any were needed) that there is no sound justification for treating shareholders alone as 'owners' of the corporation. And if not owners, then shareholders should hardly be entitled to expect the corporation's directors, acting in accordance with their fiduciary duties, to place their financial interests above the interests of other corporate constituents or stakeholders.[86]

Analysing the interests of shareholders as economically equivalent to the position of holders of call options certainly offers many useful insights. For example, since option pricing theory indicates that the value of a call option is unambiguously increased when the risk of the underlying asset is increased,[87] *if* one assumes that directors do, indeed, have a duty to maximize share value, then this duty could be interpreted as a mandate for corporate directors to increase the volatility of the corporation's assets to the greatest degree possible. Needless to say, such a strategy would be highly undesirable from the

[83] Black and Scholes (n 11).
[84] ibid 649.
[85] ibid 649–50.
[86] See eg Lynn A Stout, 'Bad and Not-so-Bad Arguments for Shareholder Primacy' (2002) 75 Southern California Law Review 1189, 1191-92.
[87] See eg Richard A Brealey, Stewart C Myers, and Franklin Allen, *Principles of Corporate Finance* (10th edn, McGraw-Hill 2011) 516–17. 'Risk' refers here to the volatility of the share price as represented in the Black-Scholes formula by the standard deviation ($\sigma$) of the rate of return on the underlying stock.

perspective of the corporation's bondholders and perhaps for employees, too. If bondholders were aware at the time of making their original investment that the issuing company intended to ratchet up the riskiness of its assets, they could demand a high interest rate to compensate them for this increased risk. Alternatively, they could seek to protect themselves contractually by including asset substitution clauses in their loan agreements (or trust indentures, in the case of public bondholders) thus prohibiting the issuing company from taking on additional risk in an attempt to enhance the trading price of its outstanding shares.

But does the fact that the interest of a shareholder may be regarded, economically, as equivalent (or substantially equivalent) to the holder of a call option on the corporate assets really undermine the rationale upon which the shareholder primacy norm is based? Does the argument for shareholder primacy rest so significantly on the proposition that shareholders ought to be considered the corporation's 'owners'?[88]

It should not. The Black and Scholes's theoretical recharacterization of the interests of shareholders and bondholders is based on the authors' observation of the behaviour or economic performance of these financial claims: shares of a corporation with outstanding debt can be modelled as call options on the corporation's assets with a strike price equal to the outstanding principal amount of the corporation's debt precisely because of the presumed financial relationship between equity holders and debt holders implied by, or embedded in, existing law. Thus, this economic recharacterization cannot be used to undermine or vary these very premises. In particular, to characterize bondholders as 'owners' of the company's assets (subject to a call option 'written' in favour of the corporation's shareholders) overlooks the fact that the

[88] As emphasized in earlier chapters, shareholders are not owners of the corporation, as the corporation is not something that can be owned. But their relationship to the corporation is closer to ownership than that of other corporate stakeholders. Many scholars have roundly denounced the proposition that shareholders may be considered 'owners' of the corporation. See eg Jill E Fisch, 'Measuring the Efficiency of Corporate Law: The Role of Shareholder Primacy' (2006) 31(3) Journal of Corporation Law 637, 648 ff. D Gordon Smith has linked the early notion in American law that shareholders became the corporation to the origins of the shareholder primacy norm in the United States. D Gordon Smith, 'The Shareholder Primacy Norm' (1998) 23(2) Journal of Corporation Law 277, 297. Smith ultimately concludes that shareholder primacy is actually irrelevant to most corporate decision-making and may be 'one of the most overrated doctrines in corporate law' (ibid 323). It is also interesting to note that, as Andrew Keay has pointed out, in the UK, one actually observes a 'subtle but critical' shift in the conception of the corporation in the mid nineteenth century such that, by the time of the framing of the Companies Act of 1862, the theory was no longer that members (shareholders) were themselves 'incorporated' to become a company. The law correspondingly came to endorse the notion—analogizing the role of corporate directors to that of trustees—that the duty of the directors was to act in the best interests of the company of shareholders, a concept that denoted the shareholders in general meeting expressing their collective will. See Andrew Keay, *The Corporate Objective* (Edward Elgar Publishing 2011) 188.

bondholders lack the residual rights essential to such an ownership interest; there is no state of the world in which the bondholders will ever capture any value of the corporation's assets in excess of their outstanding debt. A genuine owner who had written a call could, at least in theory, potentially capture such an excess if the call holder (albeit irrationally) failed to exercise its call at maturity when it was in the money. Of course, the recharacterization also disregards other elements of debt and equity securities, including the voting rights attached to shares and the creditor protections that are customarily included not only in the debt contract but also in corporate law statutes themselves, such as express prohibitions against making distributions to shareholders that would render the corporation insolvent.[89]

Although contingent claims analysis illuminated by option pricing theory would thus not appear to be quite the knock-out blow to shareholder primacy that some commentators have contended, the use of financial derivatives nevertheless poses an altogether different challenge to the traditionally shareholder-oriented conception of corporate governance. Financial derivatives may be used to unbundle, deconstruct, or disaggregate the various rights and obligations historically packaged together inextricably within a corporate share.

Some uses of financial derivatives for these purposes are wholly benign and even beneficial. A corporate officer who is restricted from selling shares in his corporate employer might use put options to obtain needed liquidity or portfolio diversification while still retaining title to the shares themselves. Or again, to use an example offered by Robert C. Merton, an asset manager with an uncanny ability consistently to earn above-market returns (or 'alpha') in the fixed income market, could use total return swaps to synthesize an equity holding so that—remarkably—without owning a single corporate share, the asset manager could provide a market-beating *equity* product to their investors.[90]

[89] See eg Delaware General Corporation Law, §§160, 170, 173; UK Companies Act 2006, s 831; Canada Business Corporations Act, s 42, ss 34–36; Australia Corporations Act 2001, s 254T, s 256B.

[90] The mechanics of this ingenious transaction would involve investing the client's funds entirely in a bond portfolio on which, we assume, the asset manager (AM) is able to achieve an above average fixed income return. Then, the AM would enter into a swap with a counterparty in which the AMr agrees to pay the counterparty a return equal to the return on a standard bond index and to receive, in exchange, amounts equal to the return on a standard equity index such as the S&P 500. As long as the AM is able to 'beat' the bond index' by some amount ($\alpha$), it will be possible to provide the client with a return equal to the return on the S&P 500 plus $\alpha$, without holding even a single share of stock of an S&P 500 company. See Robert C Merton, 'Financial Innovation and the Management and Regulation of Financial Institutions' (1995) 19 Journal of Banking and Finance 461, 467–68. In a recent speech, Professor Merton explained how this same technique could be used by sovereign wealth funds based in countries subject to exchange controls to achieve international diversification of their portfolios, while still complying with domestic exchange controls. Robert C Merton, 'Financial Engineering and Derivatives to Manage Country Risks and Improve Sovereign Policy Implementation' (29 August 2025) Lecture at Lindau Nobel Laureate Meetings https://mediatheque.lindau-nobel.org/recordings/42688.

Other uses, however, may be considerably more controversial. Contentious examples of such innovations might include the use of financial derivatives by corporate shareholders or creditors to amplify their voting power in conjunction, for example, with a proxy battle, without assuming any additional financial exposure to the corporation. Such tactics have frequently been condemned as improper 'empty voting',[91] 'vote buying',[92] or misleading 'morphable ownership'.[93] While they undoubtedly can be the source of abuse, sweeping denunciation of these methods may be both unfair and imprudent. It is very possible that such techniques, at least in some circumstances, may be used effectively to enhance corporate value,[94] notwithstanding the discomfort they may cause to complacent managers and to other beneficiaries of corporate institutional stability.[95]

More fundamentally, however, if a corporate shareholder has, for example, entered into a total return swap the effect of which is to transfer all of the future economic returns on their shares to someone else—while, nevertheless, retaining title to the shares—on what rational basis may it be said that the corporation ought to be managed primarily, or exclusively, in the interests of such shareholders? Such shareholders are not owners; they are not residual risk bearers; they may not be presumed to have the strongest incentive to ensure the corporation is efficiently and properly run. In short, they seem to be deserving of no particular managerial consideration at all.

Several commentators have considered the question of how the decoupling or unbundling of voting and economic interests of shares now made possible through the use of financial derivatives might affect the traditional analysis of

[91] The terms 'empty voting' and 'decoupling' (of voting and economic interest) were coined by Bernard Black and Henry Hu. See Hu and Black (n 52).

[92] Hu and Black, 'The New Vote Buying' (n 52).

[93] Hu and Black, 'Hedge Funds, Insiders and the Decouplilng of Economic and Voting Ownership' (n 52).

[94] See eg Alon Brav and Richmond D Matthews, 'Empty Voting and the Efficiency of Corporate Governance' (2011) 99 Journal of Financial Economics 289; Renée Adams and Daniel Ferreira, 'One Share-One Vote' (2008) 12 Review of Finance 51; Jordan M Barry, John William Hatfield, and Scott Duka, 'On Derivatives Markets and Social Welfare: A Theory of Empty Voting and Hidden Ownership' (2013) 99 Virgina Law Review 1103; M Burkhart and S Lee, 'The One Share-One Vote Debate: A Theoretical Perspective' (2008) 12 Review of Finance 1.

[95] See eg Henry T C Hu and Lawrence A Hamermesh, 'Reconceptualizing Stockholder "Disinterestedness": Transformative Institutional Investor Changes and Motivational Misalignments in Voting' (2025) 80 The Business Lawyer 311 in which the authors warn against applying a simplistic definition of 'disinterested shareholders' in the context of determining the effectiveness of shareholder votes to approve or 'cleanse' proposed corporate transactions. Hu and Hamermesh note that in certain cases shareholder votes cast on such resolutions seeking to approve or cleanse a corporate transaction by institutional investors who might initially appear to have an overall financial interest that does not align with that of the corporation should, nevertheless, be counted as 'disinterested' votes. For reasons they explain, 'factors unique to institutional investors have emerged that can systematically cause them to vote in ways that deviate from what their share ownership would seemingly motivate.' ibid 319.

corporate directors' fiduciary duties.[96] As Henry Hu once bluntly observed, financial innovation makes the shareholder primacy norm 'intolerably ambiguous'.[97] Indeed, Professor Hu had declared in an earlier paper in 1990 that: 'The law pertaining to the pecuniary objectives of the corporation has been rendered obsolete by modem financial theory.'[98] Gilson and Whitehead, drawing on the work of Myron Scholes, even posited that the general risk 'cushion' provided by equity capital could be replaced in its entirety by a more precise transfer of specific risks using innovative financial instruments.[99] In other words, all corporate shares could one day be rendered extinct. In whose interests would the corporation be managed then?

Needless to say, the 'common agency'[100] problem presented by stakeholder-constituency models of corporate governance offers sufficient challenges to the corporate governance model even without the additional complication potentially posed by financial innovation. If corporate managers are permitted or expected to balance the interests of their financial investors against those of other non-financial stakeholders because (i) they are, or believe themselves to be, under some duty to serve such interests; (ii) they are attempting to preserve a social licence; (iii) they are, in fact, satisfying the interests of non-financial stakeholders in the instrumental pursuit of long-term shareholder value (ie, they are actually pursuing what has sometimes been dubbed 'enlightened shareholder value'[101]); or (iv) they are indirectly satisfying what they perceive to be the likely public-spirited wishes of their shareholders[102]—how is this already formidable balancing act to occur in a context where the interests of

[96] See eg Frank Partnoy, 'Financial Innovation in Corporate Law' (2006) Journal of Corporation Law 799; Henry TC Hu, 'New Financial Products, the Modern Process of Financial Innovation, and the Puzzle of Shareholder Welfare' (1991) 69 Texas Law Review 1273.

[97] Hu (n 94) 1286–87.

[98] In this case, Professor Hu was referring not to the implications of financial innovation within the corporation but to the more general implications of modern finance theory, in particular the capital asset pricing model. See Henry TC Hu, 'Time, Risk and Fiduciary Principles in Corporate Investment' (1990) 38 UCLA Law Review 277, 295. It was a similar implication that formed the basis for the plaintiff's (ultimately unsuccessful) claim in *McRitchie v Zuckerberg* 315 A 3d 518 (Del Chancery 2024).

[99] Ronald J Gilson and Charles K Whitehead, 'Deconstructing Equity: Public Ownership, Agency Costs, and Complete Capital Markets' (2008) 108 Columbia Law Review 231.

[100] See eg BD Bernheim and M Whinston, 'Common Agency' (1986) 54 Econometrica 923.

[101] See eg UK House of Commons Trade and Industry Committee, *The White Paper on Modernising Company Law*, Sixth Report of Session 2002-03 HC 439 (2003) 12: 'The [enlightened shareholder value] approach towards defining directors' duties maintained that the primary duty of a company director was to maximise value for the company's shareholders. However, it added that other relationships were significant in this and therefore needed to be taken into account when judging how to carry out this duty.'

[102] See eg Henry Hansmann and Reinier Kraakman, 'Reflections on the End of History for Corporate Law' in Abdul A Rasheed and Toru Yoshikawa, *The Convergence of Corporate Governance: Promise and Prospects* (Palgrave Macmillan 2012) 32, as discussed in Chapter 7 (n 51–52).

financial investors have themselves been modified, shifted, or even eliminated through financial innovation?

## Conclusion

Three important conceptual developments provide the background for the unbundling of key corporate functions made possible by modern financial contracting technology. First, at the most general level, increasing financialization of the large business corporation, and the emergence of 'finance capitalism' encouraged characterization of the relationship of shareholders to publicly held corporations as that of cash flow claimants or passive 'rentiers'[103] rather than as business owners. Secondly, a de-emphasis of the significance of corporate 'personhood' or the concept of the 'corporate entity'[104] beginning in the economic literature and the later widespread embrace by corporate law scholars of the contractarian or 'nexus of contracts'[105] theory of the corporation facilitated a view of the corporation as an instrumental bundle of contractual relationships among transient interest holders rather than a stable, monolithic entity. Thus conceptualized not as a stable rights-bearing, property-owning entity, but as a fluid bundle of contracts and de-personalized relationships, the corporation becomes a somewhat obvious target for financial deconstruction.

However, the link between the impact of financial innovation and the still-evolving, imprecisely defined notion of corporate social responsibility (CSR) (or simply 'corporate responsibility')[106] has not attracted the same degree of scholarly attention. Share price performance can be measured objectively. Corporate social responsibility cannot, although, as discussed in Chapter 7, there has been no shortage of attempts to create meaningful metrics by which to assess corporations' ESG scores.

[103] Paddy Ireland, 'Company Law and the Myth of Shareholder Ownership' (1999) 62 Modern Law Review 32.

[104] Morton Horwitz has written that: 'For almost forty years after 1890, American jurists, like their German, French and English counterparts, were preoccupied with the theory of corporate personality.' See Morton J Horwitz, *The Transformation of American Law, 1870-1960: The Crisis of Legal Orthodoxy* (Oxford University Press 1992) 67. Cheffins, and others, have suggested that the scholarly rumination over the concept of corporate personhood came to end, thanks, in no small part, to John Dewey's influential 1926 article, 'The Historic Background of Corporate Legal Personality' (1926) 35 Yale Law Journal 655. See Brian R Cheffins, 'The Trajectory of (Corporate Law) Scholarship' (2004) 63 Cambridge Law Journal 456, 479.

[105] See Jensen and Meckling (n 9) See also Romano (n 9) 347.

[106] In its June 2013 'Call for Views', the UK Department for Business Innovation & Skills asserted that 'corporate responsibility' is 'the increasingly more acknowledged term for corporate social responsibility'. See Corporate Responsibility: A Call for Views (June 2013) Introduction.

Modern financial theory and the widespread use of innovative financial instruments have encouraged students of corporate law to revisit a number of fundamental principles concerning the relationship between an incorporated entity and its financial investors.[107] Perhaps the deconstruction or unbundling of financial and governance relationships within the modern corporation could be characterized as a further stage in the evolution of the business corporation from a member or shareholder 'owned' structure to a complex interrelationship of claims and interests. This evolutionary change could no doubt prove very disruptive, and it will involve real costs.

It is the awareness of those costs that no doubt accounts for the understandable concern that has been expressed by academics, public policy-makers, and social activists seeking to preserve and rehabilitate the traditional corporation. One notes, for example, that Colin Mayer's thoughtful and carefully reasoned 2013 book, *Firm Commitment*,[108] offers a particular variant on the institutional response to the changing role and function of the publicly traded corporation. Mayer's central thesis, as the book's title suggests, is that 'the corporation [is] a mechanism for providing commitments to others',[109] and that '[t]he moral corporation is an economically efficient corporation'.[110] For Mayer, the suggestion that the central governance problem in the modern corporation is a failure of managerial incentives to align with shareholder interests is profoundly mistaken. Rather, he maintains, problems have arisen because the corporation has allowed shareholders to shelter anonymously behind the corporations in which they invest, and so escape responsibility for the actions of these corporations in which they have invested.[111]

The institutional 'personhood' perspective which animates Professor Mayer's analysis becomes clear in his discussion of the need to rediscover and re-emphasize what he regards as the fundamental fact that the corporation is a separate legal entity, and as a separate legal entity need not be identified with, or beholden to, any particular interest group, including its own shareholders. It is a person that can 'commit to others in a form in which its owners are not able to on their own'.[112]

[107] Hu and Black (n 52); Baird and Rasmussen (n 53).
[108] Colin Mayer, *Firm Commitment: Why the Corporation Is Failing Us and How to Restore Trust in It* (Oxford University Press 2013).
[109] ibid 5.
[110] ibid 11.
[111] ibid 86.
[112] ibid 242. It is noteworthy that, although Mayer puts special emphasis on the need for corporations to have values, he is dismissive of corporate social responsibility. As he notes, 'Corporate social responsibility was rightly dismissed as empty rhetoric and jettisoned when recession forced a return to more traditional shareholder value . . . Without commitment, there is no reason why there should be any trust in the corporation, however much its fine promotional material suggests otherwise' (ibid).

Mayer's call for corporate commitment, and his more recent arguments in favour of placing corporate purpose 'at the heart of corporate law'[113] are insightful attempts to resolve the conflict between the private interests that intersect through and within the corporation. Margaret Blair, likewise, has argued for a renewed emphasis on the corporate persona in place of the contractarian model 'that regards corporations as mere contractual devices, with no truly separate existence, for which it is misleading and even foolish to speak of such things as the goal, reputation, will, or moral duties of the corporation apart from its contracting agents'.[114]

But has the impact of financial economics and the transformative power of financial innovation made it impossible to retreat from a market-based model of the corporation and return to a more entity-focused model, with all that may imply for the framing of corporate purpose or goals that transcend financial performance alone? Do corporate directors, endowed with reason and acting with diligence and good faith, seem doomed to find that their enlightened search for the optimal corporate goal remains forever as elusive as the fruit dangling on the branch above the head of Tantalus?

## Coda

The corporation is a human invention that is superbly well-suited to its function. A well-crafted corporate mission/purpose statement may be a sincere attempt to articulate values. But the measure of any social actor's values is found not in aspirational promises but in faithful performance. The corporation was invented to serve the interests of society, not to debase them. Its role was to generate material prosperity; its powerful and civilizing strategy was to direct and organize human productive activity; its ingenious technique was to harness the human instinct for loyalty. How were corporate directors, the individuals charged with leading the corporation, expected to perform their role whether at the helm of the historically monolithic corporate entity, or in command of the modern deconstructed 'nexus of contracts,' where the rise of institutional investors and the proliferation of innovative financial contracting technology may now obscure or even sever clear connection between corporate activity

[113] Colin Mayer, 'What Is Wrong with Corporate Purpose? The Purpose of Law and the Law of Purpose' (2022) 18 Annual Review of Law and Social Science 283, 284, citing with approval a suggestion to this effect by the British Academy in its 2021 report on the future of the corporation.

[114] Margaret M Blair, 'Corporate Personhood and the Corporate Persona' [2013]University of Illinois Law Review 785, 819.

and the needs, wants, and preferences of individual human shareholders? To serve the shared interest of investors *as investors*, it seems, corporate directors must labour to maximize shareholder value. This is not the indulgence of greed, but the enhancement of social capacity. If investors build wealth, that wealth can then be deployed in an infinite variety of ways, serving an infinite variety of social goals—funding public works through taxation, charitable activities through donations, personal needs and business ventures, large and small, through private spending. Some investor choices will seem trivial and self-indulgent, no doubt. But many more will prove significant and enduring.

The shareholder wealth maximization goal was always subject to important constraints. The constraints included all legal and regulatory boundary conditions, to be sure. But they did not end there. Directors were understood to exercise their duties using their judgment, and human judgment cannot be detached from human wisdom, human empathy, human compassion, and, as Kant said, 'resolve and courage to use [understanding] without guidance from another' and to 'use reason publicly in all matters'.[115] Truly enlightened directors, in short, may be expected not simply to pursue 'enlightened shareholder value',[116] a somewhat narrow rationalization of instrumental nods to non-shareholder interests adapted by some corporate commentators from the old notion of 'enlightened self-interest' or 'self-interest rightly understood'. Instead, as enlightened fiduciaries exercising control over the corporation's resources and with considerable latitude and discretion typically afforded them by the deferential nature of the business judgment rule or similar insulating doctrines, leaders wielding authority over the largest public corporations can be powerful instruments of constructive cooperation in a fractious world. They must act with independence of thought, but with a clear-headed understanding of the unique, indispensable, and paradoxically community-building role that the for-profit business corporation does, and must, play in a free market economy. Too often these corporate leaders have betrayed the trust placed in them, occasionally with disastrous consequences. But the enduring success of the business corporation and the extraordinary advance of human prosperity over the past two centuries are conspicuous reminders that the contemptuous failure of the few should not lead to a reflexive indictment of the many.

[115] Immanuel Kant, 'An Answer to the Question: What is Enlightenment?' (Ted Humphrey tr, Hackett Publishing 1992, originally published in 1784).

[116] See eg UK House of Commons Trade and Industry Committee, *The White Paper on Modernising Company Law*, Sixth Report of Session 2002–2003, 7 https://publications.parliament.uk/pa/cm200203/cmselect/cmtrdind/439/439.pdf; *BTI 2014 LLC v Sequana SA and others* [2022] UKSC 25, paras 372, 380 (per Lady Arden).

# Index

*For the benefit of digital users, indexed terms that span two pages (e.g., 52–53) may, on occasion, appear on only one of those pages.*


Adelphia, 171–72
agency theory, 144, 146, 231
Alchian, Armen A, 43–44, 145
American Law Institute, 190
  Restatement of the Law Corporate Governance, 190–91
anomie, 162
Anthony, Robert N, 133
*AP Smith Mfg Co v Barlow,* 102–4
Arnold, Thurman, 29–32, 50–51
  aggregate vs entity theory of corporation, 30–31
  corporate legal person, 30–31
Arrow, Kenneth, 42–43, 55
  value of specialization, 55
As You Sow, 213
Aspen Institute, 106

B Corp, 156
B Lab, 22–23, 156
Bainbridge, Stephen, 104–5, 159–60
Bank, Steven, 68
Barzuza, Michal, 215
Baumol, William, 132
Bebchuk, Lucian, 173–74
Bénabou, Roland, 79, 179
benefit corporation, 156–57
Bennett, Benjamin, 195–96
Berle, Adolf, 10, 11, 19–20, 28, 58–59, 63–82, 111, 135–36, 169–70, 176, 182–83, 206
"Big Three" asset managers (BlackRock, State Street, & Vanguard), 207
Black, Fischer, 223–24
BlackRock, 7, 207, 214, 215
Black-Scholes (Merton) option pricing model, 226–27, 235
Blackstone, William, 1
Blair, Margaret, 150–51, 242
Blumberg, Phillip, 87
  *The Megacorporation in American Society: The Scope of Corporate Power,* 87
Bratton, William, 30–31, 48
Bretton Woods Agreement, 225
Brookings Institution, 105
  survey of purpose of business in business and law school curricula, 105, 146
Brudney, Victor, 140–41, 230–31
Buffett, Warren, 210
Burnham, James, 136
  *The Managerial Revolution,* 136
*Burwell v Hobby Lobby Stores Inc,* 155–56
Business Roundtable, 85–86, 189–90
  Statement on the Purpose of a Corporation, 85–86, 189–90

capital asset pricing model, 209–10
capital lock-in, 149–52
Case, Anne, 21–22
catallaxy, 29, 116
Chamberlin, Edward, 90–91, 112–13, 123
Chandler, Alfred, 60, 136
  *Visible Hand, The,* 136
Cheffins, Brian, 3–4, 23–24, 68, 87, 138–39, 223–24
Chevron, 213
Chief Executives for Corporate Purpose, 7
Chirelstein, Marvin, 140–41, 146
Clark, Robert, 12–13
  corporate purpose and rôle of government,
    'dualism', 12
    'high idealism', 13
    'monism', 12
    'modest idealism', 12–13
    'pragmatism', 13

Coase, Ronald, 32–33, 35–36, 40–41, 44, 49
boundaries of the firm, 41
intra-firm authority, 42–43
'Nature of the Firm, The', 40–41
transaction costs, 41
Coasean bargains, 174–75
Coates, John, 219
codetermination (Germany), 74
Coffee, John, 220
Collingwood, R.G., 38–39, 55–56, 58
cooperating in competing, 38–39
common agency problem, 239–40
community interest companies (CICs), 157
competition, 37, 38–39
ConocoPhillips, 213
contingent claims analysis, 235–37
implications for shareholder primacy, 235–37
contractarian view of corporation, 144, 147–48
cooperation, 37, 38–39
corporate commitment, 242
corporate personhood, 22–23, 221, 222–23, 240, 241
scholarly 'obsession' with, 30–31
corporate purpose
corporate objects, compared, 5
non-binding statements, 13–17
corporate shares, economically equivalent to call options, 235
corporate social responsibility (CSR), 182, 188, 196, 200, 212–13, 240
corporation as a firm, 48
'black box', 113
*Corporation in Modern Society, The,* 136
corporatism, 30–31

Dana, J, 79
Danone SA, 216
Dasgupta, Amil, 206
Deakin, Simon, 48
Deaton, Angus, 21–22
Debreu, Gérard, 45
Delaware General Corporation Law, 16–17, 111
Demsetz, Harold, 43–44, 145
derivatives, 231
Dewey, John, 23–24
Dewing, Arthur, 124–25
Dodd, David, 65–66, 170
Dodd, Merrick, 69, 136
*Harvard Law Review* exchange with A Berle, 69–70
*Dodge v Ford,* 85–86, 91–97
Drexel Burnham Lambert, 232
Drucker, Peter, 119–20, 123–24
Dyke, Charles, 38–39

Easterbrook, Frank H, 85–86, 145, 146, 148, 153–54
Eccles, Robert, 188
*Economic Structure of Corporate Law, The,* 145
Economics Institute for Federal Judges programme, 146–47
*Economist,* 152–53
Edmans, Alex, 201
Eells, Richard, 136
empty voting, 238
Energy Crisis (1974), 226
Engine No 1, 213
Enke, Stephen, 129–30
Enron Corporation, 13–14, 171–72
ERISA (Employment Retirement Income Security Act of 1974, 223–24
*Escape From Freedom,* 42–43
ESG (environmental, social, governance), 20–21, 23–24, 176, 186–89, 195, 196, 198, 201, 212–13, 214–15, 240
European Corporate Sustainability Reporting Directive (CSRD), 197
ExxonMobil, 213

Faber, Emmanuel, 216
*Fable of the Bees, The* (Bernard Mandeville), 38–39, 54–55
Fidelity, 207
financial innovation, 231–32
Financial Reporting Council (UK), 209
financialization, 222
Fink, Larry, 7, 214, 215
firm-specific investment, 75
Fisch, Jill E, 16–17
Fischel, Daniel, 85–86, 145, 146, 148, 153–54

Fisher, Irving, 79–80
separation theorem, 79–80
Fisher, Jacob, 3–4
Follow This, 213
Freeman, Edward, 19–20
Fried, Jesse, 173–74
Friedman, Milton, 3, 10–11, 52, 85–86, 90, 183, 184, 225, 231
'The Social Responsibility of Business is to Increase its Profits', 3
Fromm, Erich, 42–43
FTX Trading Ltd, 14
Future of the Corporation (British Academy), 7–8

'gadfly' shareholder sctivists, 203–5
Gelter, Martin, 223–24
Gierke, Otto, 57–58
Gilbert, Lewis D, 203–4
Gilson, Ronald J, 206, 211–12, 238–39
Gindis, David, 48
Girard, René, 174
mimetic desires, 174
scapegoats, 174
Glass Lewis, 217–19
Global Compact, 186–87
*Who Cares Wins,* 187–88
Global Financial Crisis, 227–30, 233
Glover, JD, 184–85
Gordon, Jeffrey N, 206, 211–12
Gorton, Gary B, 59
Gower, LCB, 73–74, 122
Graham, Benjamin, 65–66
greenwashing, 189–90
group selection theory, 38
vs individual selection, 38

Hale, Robert Lee, 55–56
Hamman, JR, 79
Hansmann, Henry, 55–56, 74, 85–86, 151–52, 153–54, 178
homogeneous interests of shareholders, 153–54
Hart, Oliver, 32, 134, 215
Hawkins, CJ, 112–13
Hayek, Friedrich, 80–81, 116
hedge fund activism, 211–12
Henderson, M Todd, 134, 178
Hickman, W Braddock, 232
Hirschman, Albert O, 36, 118–19
concept of 'interest', historical development, 118–19
Hodgson, Geoffrey M, 48
Holmstrőm, Bengt, 59–60, 233
Horwitz, Morton, 30–31
Hu, Henry, 238–39
*Hutton v West Cork Railway Co.,* 98–101
'no cakes and ale except as are required for the benefit of the company,' 100

Icahn, Carl, 213
impact activism, 212–14
*Iowa v Securities and Exchange Commission,* 198
ISS (Institutional Shareholder Services), 217–19

Jensen, Michael, 85–86, 128–29, 145, 231
Johnson, Lyman, 87
Joint Stock Companies Act of 1844, 46–47
junk bonds, 147, 231–33

Kant, Immanuel, 243, 243n.115
Kaplan, Steven N, 59–60, 233
Keay, Douglas, 56–57
Keynes, John Maynard, 50–51
Klausner, Michael, 147–48
Knight, Frank, 34–35, 42–43, 67, 116–17, 124
Kraakman, Reinier, 85–86, 151–52, 178
Kronman, Anthony, 147
Krooss, Herman, 136–37

Lazonick, William, 172
Lee, Ivy Ledbetter, 184–85
leveraged buyouts (LBOs), 232–33
Levitt, Theodore, 183–84
dangers of (corporate) social responsibility, 183–84
globalization, 183–84
limited liability, 152–54
List, John A, 196
Livingston, JA, 173–74, 203–4
*The American Stockholder*, 174n.39, 203n.4
Lorsch, Jay, 89–90
Lund, Dorothy, 192–93

Macey, Jonathan R, 232–33
MacIver, Elizabeth, 89–90
Malani, Anup, 134, 178
managerialism, 19–20, 135–38
Mandeville, Bernard, 38–39, 54–55
  *Fable of the Bees, The,* 38–39
Manne, Henry, 104–5, 146–47, 185, 232–33
markets vs corporations, 40–44
Marris, Robin, 27–28, 110, 138, 158–59, 182–83, 232–33
Marshall, Alfred, 67, 159, 180
  *Principles of Economics,* 67, 114–15, 123, 180
Masconale, Saura, 200
Mason, Edward S, 19–20, 136
maximizing utility, 120–21
Mayer, Colin, 6–7, 199–200, 241
McRitchie, James, 205
Means, Gardiner, 10, 11, 28, 63–82, 182–83, 206
Meckling, William, 85–86, 128–29, 145, 231
Merton, Robert C, 237
Merton, Robert K, 161–63
methodological individualism, 56–57
Milken, Michael, 232
Mill, John Stuart, 113–14
Miller, Geoffrey P, 232–33
Miller, Merton, 130–31
Millon, David, 87
Mitnick, Barry M, 77–78
  'fiduciary paradox' 77–79
*Modern Corporation and Private Property, The,* 10, 11, 28, 63–82, 125, 139–40, 170–71
Modigliani, Franco, 130–31
Modigliani-Miller capital structure irrelevance theorem, 130, 140
Momeni, Fatemeh, 196
Morawetz, Victor, 93
Morley, John, 211
Musk, Elon, 172–73
  disputed compensation arrangements, 172–73

National Association of Corporate Directors, 8
negative externalities, 174–75
neoclassical economics, 32, 34
New Deal, 181
nexus of conflicts, 159
nexus of contracts, 144, 145, 163, 240
  linked to capital lock-in, 150
Nixon, Richard, 225

O'Sullivan, Mary, 172
Oakeshott, Michael, 58
  enterprise association, 60–61
OPEC (Organization of Petroleum Exporting Countries), 226

Palia, Darius, 220
*Parke v Daily News Ltd,* 101
Penrose, Edith, 137
performance activism, 212–13
Pigou, AC, 174–75
Pigouvian tax, 174–75
Piketty, Thomas, 21–22
Pirandello, Luigi, 1–3
  *Six Characters in Search of an Author,* 1–3
Poitras, Geoffrey, 133–34
Pollman, Elizabeth, 11
Powell, Lewis, 85–86, 224
  Lewis Powell Memorandum (1971), 85–86, 224
PRI ('Principles for Responsible Investment'), 18–19, 213–14
  increased fund flows for signatories, 213–14
profit maximization, 39–40, 90–91, 104–5, 112–13, 123–24, 127, 130, 131, 133–35, 138
  distinguished from market (share) value maximization, 131
proxy advisory firms, 216–19
public benefit corporation *see* benefit corporation
Purdue Pharma, 171–72

Rajan, Raghuram, 138
Ramella, Pietro, 138
Rand, Ayn, 184–85
Rappaport, Alfred, 138–39
Raymond, Daniel, 63–64
*Revlon Inc v MacAndrews & Forbes Holdings,* 141–42
Ribstein, Larry, 151

Ringe, Wolf-Georg, 208–9
Ripley, William Z, 63–64
  *Main Street and Wall Street,* 63–65
Robé, Jean-Philippe, 47
Robertson, D.H., 40–41
Robinson, Joan, 90–91, 112–13, 123
Romano, Roberta, 140–42, 146, 147, 207–8, 224–25
Roosevelt, Franklin Delano, 30–31
Ross, Stephen, 144
  agency theory, 144
Rostow, Eugene, 138
Ryan, Patrick, 87

satisficing, 33–34, 182–83
Scholes, Myron, 222–23, 238–39
Scitovsky, TS, 125–26, 128, 129–30
  entrepreneur's 'special type of psychology', 128–29
Sealy, L S, 93
*Security Analysis,* 65–66, 124–25
selfishness, 38
separation of ownership and conscience, 60–61
separation of ownership and control, 81–82
Sepe, Simone, 200
shareholder primacy, 73–74, 83–85, 86–90, 134–35, 148–49, 154, 155–56, 160–61, 165–66, 168, 185
shareholder value, 138–39
shareholder wealth maximization, 131–32, 133–34, 139–40
  contrasted with shareholder welfare maximization, 160–61
Sharpe, William, 209–10
Shiller, Robert, 233
*Shlenksy v Wrigley,* 85–86, 97–98
short-termism, 167–68, 234
Simon, Herbert, 33–34, 162, 182–83
  satisficing behaviour, 33–34
Smith, Adam, 9, 27, 50–51, 52, 53, 88, 117, 179
  human propensity to 'truck, barter, and exchange', 27
  invisible hand, 53
  limited use of joint stock companies, 88
Sneirson, Judd F, 88–89
Solomon, Ezra, 133
  *Theory of Financial Management, The,* 133
Solomon, Steven Davidoff, 2
Soss, Wilma, 203–4
Spamann, Holger, 3–4
spontaneous order, 51
Spulber, Daniel, 47
Squire, Richard, 152
Stackelberg, Heinrich von, 90–91
State Street, 207
Stewardship Code (UK), 209
Stout, Lynn, 47–48, 92–93, 151
Strine, Leo E, Jr, 175, 207, 211
Swope, Gerard, 135–36

Tarbell, Ida, 180–81
Thatcher, Margaret, 56–57
Tirole, Jean, 79, 179, 194
Tobin, James, 79–80
  separation theorem, 79–80
Tocqueville, Alexis de, 119
  'self-interest rightly understood', 119
Tolstoy, Leo, 110
transaction costs, 41, 42
triple bottom line, 181
Trump, President Donald, 22
Tyco, 171–72

UK Governance Code, 209
*ultra vires,* 5–6
  corporate objects clause, and, 5
*USA: The Permanent Revolution,* 136
US-European Union framework on trade statement (2025), 199

Vanguard, 207
Veblen, Thorstein, 67, 159
Volkswagen 'Dieselgate', 171–72

Wachter, Michael, 30–31
Wall Street Rule, 210–11
Weber, Max, 57, 118
Wells, Harwell, 19–20
Whitehead, Charles K, 238–39
*Who Cares Wins,* 186–87
Wiles, Peter, 90–91, 112–13

Williamson, Oliver, 42, 44, 52, 70–71, 74, 75–76
  inhospitality tradition, 42
  justification for board representation exclusively for shareholders, 75
Wilson, David Sloan, 38
Wilson, Edward O, 38
Wilson, Woodrow, 221
Winter, Sidney, 183
WorldCom, 171–72
World Economic Forum
  *Davos Manifesto,* purpose of a corporation, 2–3

Young, Owen, 19–20, 135–36, 169–70, 180

Zentefis, Alexander K, 59
Zingales, Luigi, 134, 138, 215